# Criminality and Narrative in
# Eighteenth-Century England

# Criminality and Narrative in Eighteenth-Century England

BEYOND THE LAW

Hal Gladfelder

The Johns Hopkins University Press

BALTIMORE AND LONDON

© 2001 The Johns Hopkins University Press
All rights reserved. Published 2001
Printed in the United States of America on acid-free paper

2   4   6   8   9   7   5   3   1

The Johns Hopkins University Press
2715 North Charles Street
Baltimore, Maryland 21218-4363
www.press.jhu.edu

*Library of Congress Cataloging-in-Publication Data*

Gladfelder, Hal.
Criminality and narrative in eighteenth-century England :
beyond the law / Hal Gladfelder.
p.      cm.
Includes bibliographical references and index.
ISBN 0-8018-6608-1 (acid-free paper)
1. English fiction—18th century—History and criticism.  2. Crime in
literature.  3. Detective and mystery stories, English—History and
criticism.  4. Literature and society—England—History—18th
century.  5. Social classes in literature.  6. Criminals in literature.
7. Narration (Rhetoric)  8. Law in literature.  I. Title.
PR858.C74 G58 2001
823'.509355—dc21            00-010274

A catalog record for this book is available from the British Library.

*For my mother*

*In memory of my father*

# CONTENTS

*Preface*    ix

Introduction    1

## PART I
## Criminal Representations    19

ONE    Constructing the Underworld: Criminal Anatomies    21
TWO    Picaresque and Providential Fictions    33
THREE    Crime Reports and Gallows Writing    45
FOUR    Criminal Trials: Testimony and Narrative Realism    58
FIVE    Criminal Biographies: The Singular and the Exemplary    72

## PART II
## Crime and Identity: Defoe in the 1720s    93

SIX    Colonel Jack's Childhood    102
SEVEN    Moll Flanders and Her Confederates    113
EIGHT    Guilt and the Reader of *Roxana*    131

PART III
## The Judge and the Author:
## Fielding in Midcentury   151

NINE    The Politics and Poetics of Crime and Punishment      159

TEN    Fielding as Magistrate: The Canning and Penlez Cases      174

ELEVEN    *Amelia:* Imprisonment and Transgression      187

Epilogue: English Radicalism and the Literature of Crime      209

*Notes*     225
*Bibliography*     263
*Index*     275

In the nightmare of entrapment and pursuit his life becomes after his accidental discovery of a secret murder, the hero of William Godwin's *Caleb Williams* (1794) tries, after wearying months of flight, to lose himself in London. Disguised by turns as a poor farmer's son, a Jew, and a cripple, shrinking from contact with strangers, he seeks the paradoxical anonymity of hack authorship, taking on the most despised and marginal identities in an attempt to conceal his own origins, only to find the hue and cry raised against him all but inescapable:

I was walking out one evening, after a long visitation of languor, for an hour's exercise and air, when my ears were struck with two or three casual sounds from the mouth of a hawker who was bawling his wares. I stood still to inform myself more exactly, when to my utter astonishment and confusion I heard him deliver himself nearly in these words. "Here you have the most wonderful and surprising history, and miraculous adventures of Caleb Williams; you are informed how he first robbed, and then brought false accusations against his master; as also of his attempting divers times to break out of prison, till at last he effected his escape in the most wonderful and uncredible manner; as also of his travelling the kingdom in various disguises, and the robberies he committed with a most desperate and daring gang of thieves; and of his coming up to London, where it is supposed he now lies concealed.[1]

The shock of hearing misrepresentations of his own story cried in the streets, the panicky sense that a halfpenny paper will turn every passing glance of a stranger into the relentless gaze of the police, pushes Caleb to despairing reflection. The machinery of oppression has been set in motion by his master, Falkland, whose social position and fame as a man of honor enable him to conceal his own crimes while enlisting magistrates, thief takers, and broadsheet printers—all unwitting of his design—to track down and annihilate the servant who chanced to discover his guilt.

Seventy years earlier, in one of the two narratives he wrote on the celebrated house-breaker and escape artist John Sheppard (1724), Daniel Defoe recounts, in Sheppard's voice, a similar episode. After the most spectacular of his escapes from Newgate, Sheppard spends the day in "an Ale-house of little or no Trade, in *Rupert-Street*, near *Piccadilly*," talking with its proprietor about the famous criminal he has become: "The Woman and I discours'd much about *Sheppard*. I assur'd her it was impossible for him to escape out of the Kingdom, and that the Keepers would have him again in a few Days. The Woman wish'd that a Curse might fall on those who should betray him. I continued there till the Evening, when I stept towards the *Hay- market*, and mixt with a Crowd about two Ballad-Singers; the Subject being about *Sheppard*. And I remember the Company was very merry about the Matter."[2] The busking that Caleb dreads is for Sheppard a celebration of virtuosity, freedom, the subversion of solemnity and the law.

Despite the very similar incidents the two episodes describe, their tonal and ideological divergences are considerable. Caleb's encounter with the hawker is filtered through his own constricting experience of dread in isolation, while Sheppard is swept up in the crowd's carnival merriment. The jails from which Sheppard escapes, like the whole system of law he continually evades, are relatively unmonitored: he is able not only to wrench open locks and break away walls in the successive rooms of Newgate his escape leads him through but also to make his way, still fettered, past night watchmen and through diverse quarters of the city without attracting particular notice. But in the world Godwin describes, in which the mechanisms of repression have been articulated through all the domains of private and public life, no real escape is possible. Even when Caleb later reaches a place that seems beyond the range of pursuit, an idyllic retreat in rural Wales, he is run to ground by the same halfpenny pamphlet, a sign of his pursuers' power to control not only legal institutions but also the networks of authorship, publication, and bookselling.

As significant as these divergences, however, are the continuities between the two episodes. Both Defoe and Godwin drew from a popular tradition of criminal narrative—literally incorporating fragments of broadsides, ballads, confessions, and trials within their texts and constructing their own variations on the traditional repertoire of plots. In writing *Caleb Williams*, Godwin looked back to the compilations of his childhood: *God's Revenge against Murder*, the *Newgate Calendar*, and the *Lives of the Pirates*, the same anthologies Defoe in his time had compiled,

berated, and lampooned. Both Caleb and Sheppard inhabit a world caught up in
the lure and threat of the criminal; both feel the discrepancy between their experience and its representations, a discrepancy that ultimately impels them to become
authors of true histories of themselves, claiming the sole right—a right of property over the self and its stories—to the narratives of their own lives.

The more I've thought about these two scenes, the more haunting they've come
to seem to me. Both Sheppard and Caleb are hounded—though Sheppard's ironic
bravado never allows him to seem bothered—by narrative doubles, ghost images
of themselves circulating through publicly hawked broadsheets, which not only
alienate them from what they feel to be the truth of their histories but, more damagingly, function as agents of the law to entrap them. There's no getting away, for
either of them, from these fictions that hunt them down. The doomy apprehension they both feel—again, for all Sheppard's *sprezzatura*—testifies to the virtual
inescapabilty of popular discourses of criminality in eighteenth-century England,
their entanglement in everyday life, work, gossip, and the chance encounters that
structure urban experience.

This study grows out of a curiosity about the reasons for that entanglement,
which strikes me as both unsettling and familiar. In what follows I examine the relations between the genres of eighteenth-century crime narrative and the multiple, conflicting attitudes toward violence and transgression such narratives both
describe and construct. In particular, I seek to explain the connections between
criminality and an emerging narrative congeries—the various extended fictions
that came retrospectively to be seen as making up the early novel—which over the
course of the century moved into a position of cultural centrality despite the frequent marginality and lowness of its subjects. If the criminal's body and voice were
seen as potentially encoding rebellion and political resistance, what was the cultural resonance of a genre of fictions (disturbingly claiming to be true) written in
the assumed voices of the outlaw poor, upstart servants, and rootless adventurers?

My approach to this question has not been through a reopening of the debate
over the origins or rise of the novel nor through an archaeological search for the
early novel's criminal sources—though there are, I think inevitably, points where
my work touches on such concerns. Rather, I have aimed in the first part of this
study to map a complex and heterogeneous network of criminal discourses, diverse
forms of narrative which collectively embodied the range of responses to the transgressive in the late seventeenth and early eighteenth centuries. The definition of
crime is always an assertion of social power and narratives of criminality a locus for

moral and ideological contestation. Whether, in the different texts I have examined here, criminality stands for a common fallen condition or a threatening class
instability or an unregulated sexuality or a mode of political action, representations
of crime implicitly (if not openly) reflect on issues of the most urgent concern to
their authors and audience, and this both explains their popularity and accounts
for the preoccupation with crime in the work of authors whose ambitions extended beyond the generic limitations of the "low" criminal forms. In the second
and third parts of this study I focus on Defoe and Fielding as the two eighteenth-
century authors most directly connected, for professional reasons, to the discourses
of criminality and so the most useful for exploring the connections between those
discourses and emerging novelistic conceptions of character, narrative form, and
readerly response. In choosing to reread Fielding and Defoe, my aim is not to reinscribe an old canon whose disruption and revaluation over (say) the past twenty-
five years have been so productive but, rather, to think through some of the en-
gagements that made their work canonical in the first place. I am interested in the
ways that the materials and representational strategies of criminal discourses are
elaborated in their work into more complex forms according to both their necessarily improvisatory gauging of the literary market and their own (often internally
contradictory) ideological and expressive aims.

Finally, I return to *Caleb Williams* in an epilogue centering on the scenes of criminal trial in three sensational novels of the 1790s: Godwin's Jacobin-anarchist
thriller, Mary Wollstonecraft's *Maria, or The Wrongs of Woman,* and Elizabeth Inchbald's *Nature and Art.* All three works register the degree to which criminal discourses, by the end of the century, had become enmeshed with the novelistic tradition itself, and all three attest to the continued salience of those discourses as
vehicles of contestation and reflection—ultimately permitting a radical critique of
the law itself as an instrument for the enforcement of oppressive gender and class
relations. As hybrids of Radical polemic and Gothic hallucination, these texts embody a struggle to imagine a form of social life which could exist beyond the law,
in which a politically uncorrupted form of truth would sweep away the inequalities of power the law exists to sustain.

I began work on this book in Los Angeles in the last decade of the last century, a
time of police violence, prison building, and the resurgence of capital punishment.
As I continued to work on it in San Francisco and, later, Rochester, New York, the

same social divisions and inequities that run through the eighteenth-century texts I was reading only seemed to be worsening in my own time and nation. I am grateful to the many friends, confederates, and guides who have taught me and enriched my life in dark times. I want to thank first those mentors who were there from the beginning: Max Novak, whose investigations into crime literature prompted my own; Jill Campbell, for friendship and for leading me to some key texts; Carlo Ginzburg, who pushed me to think more complexly about historical evidence and problems of classification; Lucia Re and Anne Mellor, for intellectual (and material!) support; and Ruth Yeazell, whose skeptical, generous, and attentive reading gave me an audience to write for.

The staff of the William Andrews Clark Memorial Library offered help, conversation, and encouragement both during the term of a fellowship I held there and, later, when I became a staff member myself; special thanks to Suzanne Tatian, Carol Sommer, and Michael Halls. John Brewer, as director of the UCLA Center for Seventeenth- and Eighteenth-Century Studies, also provided time, resources, and a favorable climate for research. At Stanford I took heart from the generosity of Linda Paulson, Lynne Vieth, and John Bender. Most recently, my colleagues in the Department of English at the University of Rochester, particularly Bette London, have provided an ideal environment in which to finish writing this book and move on to new projects. A portion of this book first appeared in *Prose Studies*, under the title "Criminal Trials and the Dilemmas of Narrative Realism, 1650–1750" (20, no. 3 [December 1997]: 21-48); I thank the editors for permission to incorporate the revised text here. My thanks also to the anonymous reader for *Prose Studies* and the equally anonymous reader for Johns Hopkins, both of whom provoked me to think harder about, and write more clearly, just what I wanted to say.

The years between the first steps of this work and the last saw the passing of my father, Glenn Gladfelder; my brother-in-law, Robert Morgan; and my dearest friend, Wade Richards. I will miss the pleasure of seeing it in their hands. But I want to remember them here, in the company of other friends who have helped this book to see light: Elena Coda, Marilyn Manners, Randy Rutsky, and Hans Turley; Amy Gustafson, Tina Foster, and Jim Pearson; Henri, Samuel, and the boys; my sister, Anne Morgan; Glenn, Dale, and Kari Gladfelder; Jane Gladfelder, whose faith and good wishes sustained me; and Jeff Geiger, who has shared and inspirited my life through it all.

# Introduction

For mine owne part, I have illustrated and polished these Histories, yet not framed them according to the modell of mine
owne fancies, but of their passions, who have represented and
personated them: and therefore if in some places they seeme
too amorous, or in others too bloody, I must justly retort the
imperfection thereof on them, and not thy selfe on me: sith I
only represent what they have acted, and give that to the publike, which they obscurely perpetrated in private.

JOHN REYNOLDS
*The Triumph of God's Revenge, against the Crying,
and Execrable Sinne of Murther*, 1621

In the fall of 1832 the editor of the *Standard Novels* asked William Godwin for "an
account of the concoction and mode of writing" of *Caleb Williams* (335).[1] Touch-
ing only obliquely on the often bitter ideological divisions between the state and
the radical circles within which he moved during the 1790s, Godwin in his retrospective account drew attention not to the public debates over law, property, and
political authority which shaped the novel's plot—and which at the time of its
writing were provoking more and more violent measures of repression—but to his
private imaginative absorption in certain, as it might seem, crudely moralizing
criminal tales. Among these was a collection from the early seventeenth century:
"I turned over the pages of a tremendous compilation, entitled 'God's Revenge
against Murder,' where the beam of the eye of Omniscience was represented as
perpetually pursuing the guilty, and laying open his most hidden retreats to the
light of day" (340). Reynolds's collection *The Triumph of God's Revenge, against the*

*Crying, and Execrable Sinne of Murther* was thus singled out by Godwin as one of his own work's predecessors, along with the *Newgate Calendar,* the *Lives of the Pirates,* and other similar semihistorical pamphlets of breathless adventure.

By claiming a traceable line of descent from these sensational forebears, Godwin constructs a literary and personal history at the same time he tells how he wants *Caleb Williams,* forty years after its writing, to be read. His preface configures the book as a thriller, not a radical interrogation of "Things as They Are"; his memories authorize a psychological, not a political, reading.[2] To explain what his work has in common with the narratives he was eagerly consuming as it took form, he writes that "we were all of us engaged in exploring the entrails of mind and motive"; and, while he adds to this the project of "tracing the various rencontres and clashes that may occur between man and man in the diversified scene of human life" (340), his example—the story of Bluebeard and his wife—suggests that the rencontres and clashes he means are essentially private, domestic, closeted. His attention is turned not outward, to the institutions he had anatomized in the *Enquiry Concerning Political Justice* (1793), but inward.

As Godwin tells it, his story emerged from feelings of dread, the terror of pursuit, and a guilt reaching back farther than any action that could rationally give rise to it. His account of the stages by which the plot of *Caleb Williams* was conceived, an early illustration of the backward narrative construction characteristic of the crime novel, is important too for its emphasis on the work's psychological origins in an atmosphere of panic so haunted as to verge on paranoia: "I bent myself to the conception of a series of adventures of flight and pursuit; the fugitive in perpetual apprehension of being overwhelmed with the worst calamities, and the pursuer, by his ingenuity and resources, keeping his victim in a state of the most fearful alarm." As he works back from an originary scene of harrying and fear to find what led up to it, Godwin retraces the narrative to a moment of individual transgression, itself rooted in a kind of inner compulsion: the moment when Caleb breaks open a locked trunk to find the clues of "a secret murder, to the investigation of which the innocent victim should be impelled by an unconquerable spirit of curiosity" (337). Having thus been imagined backward from its ending, the text Godwin produces unfolds inexorably, catches its protagonist up in a guilt and a fear that relentlessly overshadow him.

If historical context and ideological controversy are largely absent from Godwin's account, his preface does resonate, at two points, with political tensions. Near the end he includes the "confession of one of the most accomplished readers and excellent critics that any author could have fallen in with (the unfortunate Joseph Gerald)," who "told me that he had received my book late one evening, and had read through the three volumes before he closed his eyes" (341). Godwin fails to explain how he had "fallen in with" Gerald; what linked them in fact were the political beliefs for which Gerald was tried (on charges of sedition) and imprisoned in 1794, the year *Caleb Williams* was published. (Gerald was transported the following year to Botany Bay, where he soon died.) For Godwin to name Gerald as the novel's exemplary reader is, indirectly, to call up the whole complex of political and judicial discourses under the threat of which the text was produced.

The second point at which political tensions surface is in the inventory of *Caleb*'s sensational predecessors. One he mentions in particular is "a little old book, entitled 'The Adventures of Mademoiselle de St. Phale,' a French Protestant in the times of the fiercest persecution of the Huguenots, who fled through France in the utmost terror, in the midst of eternal alarms and hair-breadth escapes, having her quarters perpetually beaten up, and by scarcely any chance finding a moment's interval of security" (340). Here the motivation of the nightmarish "series of adventures of flight and pursuit" is not an inner compulsion, or a private "rencontre," but a state-authored campaign of terror. Mademoiselle de St. Phale's adventures make no sense detached from the historical struggles that led to them; similarly, it is only to the extent that Godwin disengages Caleb's history from the political and social contexts in which it originated that it can seem uncanny or psychotic. The persecution of the Huguenots provides, within the self-imposed silencings of the 1832 preface, a displaced image of the climate of repression, censorship, and harassment which hung over Godwin and the radical subculture of the 1790s.

So, while I began this introduction by opposing Godwin's fascination with the psychology of early sensational narratives to his real but obscured involvement in radical politics, his allusion to *The History of Mademoiselle de St. Phale* disturbs the simplicity of that opposition. Indeed, as Godwin reconstructs a personal and literary history in his account of *Caleb Williams*'s genesis, criminal narratives play a crucial mediating role. For all his reading in literature, history, and political philosophy, Godwin names only this handful of criminal texts as his precursors; and, if in so doing he sought mainly to affirm his own originality—"I and my predecessors travelling in some sense to the same goal, at the same time that I struck out a path of my own, without ultimately heeding the direction they pursued, and disdaining to enquire whether by any chance it for a few steps coincided or did not coincide with mine" (339–40)—it is clear that he mined these ancestral narratives for images, situations, and the energy of their penetration to the sources of violence.

These debts he sometimes acknowledges by notes in the text of the novel; sometimes, more deftly, by allusion and echo. When, for example, Caleb is describing the extreme point of his persecution, the unrelenting and inescapable presence, always just behind him, of Falkland's agent Gines, he writes: "It was like what has been described of the eye of omniscience pursuing the guilty sinner, and darting a ray that awakens him to new sensibility, at the very moment that, otherwise, exhausted nature would lull him into a temporary oblivion of the reproaches of his conscience. Sleep fled from my eyes. No walls could hide me from the discernment of this hated foe" (305). The allusion here, of course, is to *The Triumph of God's Revenge,* "where the beam of the eye of Omniscience," as Godwin writes in the passage quoted here from the 1832 preface, "was represented as perpetually pursuing the guilty, and laying open his most hidden retreats to the light of day" (340). Here the innocent Caleb occupies the place of the guilty sinner, and the eye of omniscience, which in Reynolds is the agency of God's "miraculous detection,"[3] has been disfigured into a creature who serves the most oppressive of ruling-class designs.

The image thus embodies a powerful psychological and dramatic continuity between the two texts, even as it reveals a shift from divine providence to class inequality as the agency of discovery or subjection. The accumulated body of criminal narrative provided Godwin a store of figures, life histories, and dramatic incidents which he could use both to sustain readerly excitement and to formulate a critical analysis of late-eighteenth-century Britain. The stories Reynolds had gathered of murders providentially laid bare and terribly avenged, with the biographies of highwaymen and pirates Godwin read in the *Newgate Calendar,* not only suggested a way to objectify and give narrative shape to the feelings of terror and desire out of which *Caleb Williams* emerged but also constituted a recognizable literary network—however sporadic and ill sorted—to which Godwin saw his own work as belonging.

That network, and its significance for the literary and political cultures of eighteenth-century England, is the subject of this study. Stories of transgression—Gilgamesh, Prometheus, Oedipus, Eve—may be integral to every culture's narrative imagining of its own origins, but such stories assumed different meanings with the burgeoning interest in modern histories of crime and punishment in the later decades of the seventeenth century. At that time such genres as the crime report, anatomy of roguery, providence book, criminal biography, gallows speech, and trial came into a new commercial prominence, which owed something to the development of new printing technologies and mechanisms of book distribution in mid-century and something to an increasingly widespread cultural perception that criminality and the law were lenses that brought into focus much of what was most disturbing, and most exciting, about contemporary experience.[4] Criminal narratives raise in its most aggravated form—at the point of rupture—the problem of the relations between the individual and a community which was coming to define itself more and more through the discourses and institutions of secular law. In foregrounding acts of violence, theft, disruptive sexuality, and rebellion, such narratives test the limits both of individual self-assertion and of communal tolerance as they appeal, often ambiguously, to the threatening possibility of subversive desire in even the most orthodox of their audience.

The whole history of criminal writing in the seventeenth and eighteenth centuries, in fact, is structured by the opposition, implicit in the preceding claims, between religious orthodoxy and what Michael Mascuch has called the "pathology" of individualism, whose political means of regulation is the law.[5] One of my points of departure in thinking about the cultural role of crime narratives in the period is J. A. Sharpe's contention that, by the end of the seventeenth century, law "had come to replace religion as the main ideological cement of society."[6] In a regime held together by law, criminality marks the boundaries of the licit and illicit, the normal and deviant or perverse. And the primary vehicle for instructing a heterogeneous audience in the origins and dangers of crime, for popularizing a newly dominant ideology of legality, was the constellation of narrative forms that are my subject here. Yet, as Sharpe writes elsewhere, "for many inhabitants of seventeenth-century England the distinction between disobedience to royal and divine authority, between crime and sin, was less clear than at present," and the blurring or collapsing of the two categories of sin and crime continued to influence the patterns of criminal narrative through the end of the eighteenth century and beyond.[7]

So, if on a certain level of historical abstraction it can be demonstrated that the law prevailed over religion in the struggle for ideological dominance during the long eighteenth century—a struggle that constituted a key episode in the broader cultural process of secularization—narrative representations of specific criminal lives continue throughout the period to invest matters of legal transgression with the intensities, and the vocabulary, of religious terror and longing. The effect is to bind the reader more indissolubly to the text. For, if, as Cynthia Herrup has written, "crimes were sins, yet sinning was universal," the consequence was that "the threat of criminality was both internal and external; the criminal could not be defined simply as something alien and other."[8] The inescapable inheritance of sin brought the dangers of criminal histories home to the reader's heart.

On the last page of Defoe's *Colonel Jack* the autobiographical narrator, looking back on the whole trajectory of his outlaw life, similarly calls on the reader's identification: "I recommend it to all that read this Story, that when they find their Lives come up in any degree to any Similitude of Cases, they will enquire by me, and ask themselves, Is not this the time to Repent? perhaps the Answer may touch them."[9] The same appeal, according to journalistic reports, was made by criminals at the gallows to those within earshot on execution day and, through the printed texts of their last dying speeches, to an abstract and anonymous readership. Yet, if the bond between criminal subject and reader is presented here in religious terms, evoking a shared bloodline of transgression, the relationship is equally grounded in the problematics of an emerging individualism (which, of course, is itself partly grounded in the forms of religious self-scrutiny of the seventeenth century).[10] The genres of criminal narrative, including the long fictions that would later come to be named as the first (or among the first) novels, suggest that all of us are, like Fielding's Tom Jones, "born to be hanged."[11] That phrase, used conventionally to define a villain whose criminal deviance marks him as outcast and thus unlike us—however the text constructs the "us" it implicitly addresses—turns out, as I mean the readings of specific works in this study to show, to have a more general resonance. The singularity of the individual is transgressive *in itself,* inescapably deviant in its origins and enactment. That is, in choosing to live out a singular, self-authored history, the individual willfully breaks with the sanctioned and self-effacing narratives of identity which were the common cultural inheritance of the period.[12] Lingering over scenes of rupture, alternately celebrating and condemning the violent self-assertion that defines the outlaw, criminal narratives play on a shared anxiety that we only become ourselves at the moment of transgression.

A similar fascination with protagonists shaped by deviant strayings from the path of normality is integral to the contemporaneously emerging genre of the novel. The connection between individualism and the novel, most influentially argued forty years ago by Ian Watt in *The Rise of the Novel*, is unsettled from the outset by the genre's concentration on the experience of a range of socially disruptive figures familiar from the network of criminal narrative: socially climbing servants (as in *Pamela*), illegitimate and outcast children (as in *Tom Jones*), runaway and fortune-hunting adventurers (as in *Robinson Crusoe*). Such figures unmistakably embody "the reversal of the political axis of individualization" which Michel Foucault, in *Discipline and Punish*, describes as taking place a hundred years later, with the emergence of a new, disciplinary regime. "In a system of discipline," Foucault contends, "the child is more individualized than the adult, the patient more than the healthy man, the madman and the delinquent more than the normal and the non-delinquent."[13] I think it is this modern overlapping of the categories of individualism and deviance which gives weight to Lennard Davis's claim that "the whole project of the novel, its very theoretical and structural assumptions, were in some sense criminal in nature."[14] Certainly, the degree of attention they devoted to the lawless made such authors as Richardson, Fielding, and Defoe uneasy about their own work, though they tended to project this fascination as a fault in either their readers or their rivals—as, for instance, in Richardson's disparagement of "the weak, the insipid, the Runaway, the Inn-frequenting Sophia" of *Tom Jones*, deplorably well regarded by his female correspondents despite being "a Fugitive from her Father's House."[15] That his own paragon of orthodoxy, Clarissa, whom he is concerned in the same letters to defend, could be (and had been) characterized in precisely the same terms, only underlines the impossibility of disentangling the lure of the perverse from novelistic attention to even the most virtuous individual.

The focusing, from at least the late seventeenth century, of a "disciplinary" form of narrative attention on the deviant subjects of the various criminal genres responded in part to a desire for social control and the containment of rebellious drives. But this concentration on the malefactor responded equally to a widespread longing to be bad—a longing which took (and takes) the vicarious form of a "seemingly insatiable popular appetite for novel (that is, deviant) experience," in Michael Mascuch's words.[16] Criminal subjects act on impulses—for self-preservation at any cost, for status, property, sex, money, and revenge—which were both fostered by a newly dominant ideology of the individual and held in check by the overlapping agencies of social regulation, religion and law. In the open-endedness of their plots, their violence, multiplicity of voices, obsession with detail, underpinnings of social conflict, and concentration on moral and psychological disturbance, the fictions that Defoe and Fielding constructed from the corpus of criminal narrative articulate a similar ambivalence about the pleasures and dangers of individual desire.

As the terms of this statement suggest, my understanding of the novel, and of the cultural role of criminal narratives in general, is in a way the obverse of the positions argued in two important critical studies of the novel: John Bender's *Imagining the Penitentiary* and D. A. Miller's *The Novel and the Police*. Both Bender, who characterizes "the novel and the penitentiary as fundamentally similar social texts," and Miller, for whom "the novel—as a set of representational techniques—systematically participate[s] in a general economy of policing power," draw attention to the ways in which realist fiction (especially) functions as an apparatus for regulating the heterodox energies both of the self and of social life.[17] This study diverges most fundamentally from theirs in shifting the focus of discussion from the institutions of law (the prison, the police) and the law's strategies of surveillance and control to the experience of the outlaw: the social forces and forms of identity that violate the boundaries of legality. Because of the closeness of their attention to the circumstantial details of criminal experience and to the specific inflections of the criminal's reported voice, crime narratives and the novels that derive from them tend to legitimate, to project as desirable, the very disruptive potentialities they set out to contain.

Writing at the end of the eighteenth century, William Godwin (in *Caleb Williams*) and his Jacobin fellow travelers Mary Wollstonecraft (in *Maria, or The Wrongs of Woman*) and Elizabeth Inchbald (in *Nature and Art*) show, through the use they make of the conventions of criminal literature, how easily reversible the ideological commitments of such literature really are. Even when intended to shore up the authority of the law and the social order it sustains, the various forms of criminal writing always provide, more or less explicitly, the grounds for a challenge to that authority, precisely because they are *structured* by social conflict. In order to present their political and moral warnings efficaciously, the authors of criminal texts needed to make the case of the transgressor compelling, soliciting the reader's identification with the outlaw position—"observing, and seeing herein, as in a Christall mirrour, the variety of the Devills temptations, and the allurements of sinne," as John Reynolds writes in the preface to *The Triumph of God's Revenge*.[18] Only in this way could the real dangers of criminality be revealed. Yet the anxious protestations of innocence later in Reynolds's preface (quoted in the epigraph), like the rather belligerent disavowals of criminal intent in the prefaces to Defoe's fictions, show how tricky it is to write from a position outside or against the law with the aim, in the end, of affirming it. Once readers are drawn into imaginative complicity with deviance, they may not recoil when called on. For not only does the criminal protagonist embody and act on the impulses encouraged by bourgeois individualism itself—that is, by the very ideology underlying the system of property and social relations the law exists to secure—but the audience for criminal writing might share, at least in part, the outlaw's alienation from the centers of economic and ideological power.[19]

That alienation accounts for the politically contestatory messages that can break out from even the most determinedly conservative forms, such as the Ordinary of Newgate's *Accounts* and the last dying speeches of the condemned. While the penitent words of those about to be hanged were meant to affirm the verdicts of the law and to display the values of deference and submission most useful to authority, the condemned frequently used the occasion to protest and even advocate resistance to the institutions of justice and their prefabricated narratives of crime and retribution, and this resistance to the authorized narratives of criminality runs, as a countercurrent, through all the forms of crime literature. It is this countercurrent of opposition, of recalcitrant singularity, which has led me to argue against the emphasis such critics as Lincoln Faller and John Richetti have placed on the "mythic" significance of perhaps the most popular and influential of the genres I discuss in the first part of this study, criminal biography. Against Richetti's claim that "the sensational particular, the violent events of the individual criminal's career, depend for their sensational value and effect upon the moral abstractions which they illustrate so vividly,"[20] I focus on the ways in which the jarringly concrete textures of a closely observed life interfere with and complicate such formulaic narrative patterns as the rebellious apprentice or highwayman's tale. Despite a certain pressure to strip the criminal subject of any features that could not be absorbed into the universalizing patterns of myth, the authors of criminal biographies also aimed at a materially exhaustive registration of the local particulars of speech and action, the less easily assimilable details of an individual career—betraying, in Michael McKeon's words, "a responsiveness to the factuality of individual life so intense that the dominance of over-arching pattern is felt, in varying ways, to be quite problematic."[21] On both the political and the biographical planes, then, the various

forms of popular criminal writing can yield readings that conflict with the sanctioned narratives of deviance and punishment, enlisting the reader's complicity
with the breaking of cultural norms even as they undertake to reinscribe them.

The several strands of criminal narrative which are my subject in the first part
of what follows are not, as I read them, reducible to an unvarying ideological function or myth but make up what the putative editor of Defoe's *Colonel Jack* calls "a
delightful Field for the Reader to wander in"[22]—a ground on which conflicting cultural impulses could, in the form of fearful and compelling stories, be struggled
over, negotiated, variously driven home or cast out. The complexity of the textual
surface unsettles the narratives' often rather obvious underlying design, so that their
explicit moral and political aims, whether authoritarian (in the bulk of cases) or
oppositional, are perplexed by their authors' attention to dissident voices and the
poignancy or glamour of the longings these voices express. Sometimes the longings are spoken openly; sometimes, as from a narrative unconscious, they emerge
by fumbling and indirection, betrayed by articulate silences. It is in their anticipation of the reader's imaginative wandering from terror and disgust to identification
and desire (and then perhaps back again) that crime narratives engage most excit-
ingly with the struggles of individuals to define their place in the suddenly unfamiliar world of modernity.

The argument I make here, tracing a history of the interwoven emergences of
a modern conception of the individual as constructed under the threat of criminality, and of a narrative mode adapted to the representation of such criminally
configured persons, comprises three parts and an epilogue. In the first part I examine the development of the principal forms of criminal publication from the end
of the sixteenth to the beginning of the eighteenth centuries. Criminal texts in the
years before 1720 fall into a half-dozen or so rough genres: criminal anatomies,
picaresque and providential fictions, news reports, execution and gallows literature,
trials, and criminal biographies. If in some cases the generic boundaries were quite
rigid—this is most evident in such species of execution literature as the last dying
speech and Ordinary's *Account,* closely linked to the performance of authoritarian
ritual—there was also a great deal of borrowing from one kind of text to another,
signaled by sometimes jarring shifts in discursive register. So, while I organize my
presentation of these early forms of crime narrative into separate chapters, in which
I reconstruct the history and describe the recurrent traits of each, my larger pur-

pose is to draw the outlines of a heterogeneous but interconnected network of criminal discourse, a cultural assemblage of histories and meditations on deviance.

The category of deviance, of course, is so pliant that a catalogue of its narratives—from histories of religious heresy to autobiographies of cross-dressing actors—could be infinite. My concern here, starting out from the premise that what John Zomchick has called "the juridical subject" was symbolically central to emerging eighteenth-century understandings of political and personal identity, is with published narratives of deviance as defined by law.[23] In them the struggle for preeminence between individual self-assertion and the hegemony of legal authority is set out in the starkest terms, and the reader is led (all the more so to the degree she or he is allowed to feel kinship with the outlaw) to recognize the dangers of acting on the desires the narrative itself elicits.

The primary burden of the texts I collect under the label of criminal anatomies—canting dictionaries, views of Newgate, moral tracts on the causes of delinquency—is to configure the criminal as comfortably, intractably, alien. Whether they adopt a tone of burlesque or of magisterial exhortation, they act as a kind of ethnography, constructing an underworld whose dangers impinge on the world of the reader but whose culture, language, and manner of life are those of a racialized other. In this respect the anatomies seem the opposite of the picaresque and providential narratives, two strains that, for all their obvious differences, are linked by an almost obsessive concentration on the psychological origins and costs of criminality. However divergent their moral ambitions, the picaresque and providential forms draw the reader into a kind of confederacy with characters possessed by violent and uncontainable desires that tear them apart—to the end, of course, of inducing the reader to look inward and reject such destructive passions. Yet, for all their attention to the external marks of difference, the anatomies are equally attentive to the ways in which the underworld they limn is, in John Reynolds's words, "a Christall" (or criminal) "mirrour" of the respectable world.

In subsequent chapters I also address more journalistic or documentary forms. The cheapness and immediacy of newspaper crime reports closed the narrative distance between readers and represented events, bringing the threat of criminality into social spaces that might otherwise be imagined to be secure from such dangers. The proximity of the criminal not only conferred more prominence and authority on the law and its means of quelling disruption but also, as I've suggested in the case of gallows literature, enabled the condemned to call on their likeness to those listening to or reading their words—whether exhorting them to repent or to resist the miscarriage of justice. The same openness to contestation marks the criminal trial reports, which assumed a particular salience in the emergence of realism as the dominant narrative mode of the eighteenth and nineteenth centuries. Changes in the physical format and representational strategies of trial reports from the mid-1670s through the 1720s, particularly their increasing emphasis on verbatim testimony and circumstantial evidence, increasingly situated their readers in the position of judges even as they opened a discursive space for the accused. By incorporating the contested and doubt-charged process of judgment into the structure of narrative itself, trial reports anticipated the openness to discordant meanings and discrepant points of view which I see as characteristic of the fictions Defoe and Fielding created from the struggle between competing stories of innocence and guilt. The first part of this study concludes with an extended discussion of the form of criminal biography, structured, as I've suggested already, on the opposition between the singular and the exemplary, between the obdurate strangeness of the specific case and the mythic or moral rule it is presumed to illustrate. Endeavoring both to describe the whole arc of an individual life and to record its experiential thickness and particularity, such biographies won a massive and heterogeneous readership through their detailed registration of horrors.

It was for this readership, accustomed as much to the antiformulaic as to the formulaic tendencies of criminal narrative, that Defoe wrote much of the work of his last decade: *Moll Flanders, Colonel Jack,* and *Roxana* as well as the biographies of Jack Sheppard and Jonathan Wild and a range of journalistic and sensational texts published in response to widespread disquiet over the highly publicized crime wave of 1720s London. The truth of that crime wave has been called into question, as has the attribution of some of these texts to Defoe.[24] While I touch on both issues, neither is of decisive importance to the development of my argument in the second part of this study, which is concerned, rather, with the ways in which the emerging novelistic practices of the early eighteenth century—in part pioneered by, and linked but not limited to, Defoe—allowed for more nuanced reflections on the causes and cultural meanings of deviance. Making use of the evidential realism of trials and crime reports and of strategies for the representation of the inward experience of criminality familiar from last dying speeches and prison-house confessions, Defoe's narratives concentrate on the contending agencies by which identity is shaped, especially under conditions of outlawry, social dislocation, and urban poverty. So, while his activities as journalist, pamphleteer, political agent, criminal historian, and fictional autobiographer served to fuel the civic mood of apprehension and danger, Defoe also represented criminal careers with a sympathy and complexity that underline their resemblance to the stories readers might tell of their own lives.

In the most conventional of his journalistic performances Defoe did little more than reproduce the genres he inherited. But the more novelistic of Defoe's criminal histories use irony and tonal variation to engage in more complicated and searching ways with the usual criminal subjects. I link three aspects of Defoe's authorial practice to the three texts—*Colonel Jack, Moll Flanders,* and *Roxana*— which throw them into sharpest relief, although I hope the readings are not confined to a purely illustrative or exemplary role. I consider verisimilitude in relation to *Colonel Jack*. Defoe's inventories of stolen goods and his close monitoring of the social and topographical features of the urban landscape through which his characters move have roots in legal deposition and broadsheet crime bills but are also grounded in his attention to the material conditions and practical urgencies of his protagonists' day-to-day lives. The technique is one of accumulation, the exhaustive recording of physical details, yet those details, as in the famous episode of Colonel Jack losing his money in the hollow of a tree where he meant to hide it, are always invested with the first-person narrators' panic and desire, so that their endless cataloguing of the external world is, at the same time, a form of inward accounting.

This sense of inwardness, of access to interior speech, turns on Defoe's skill at the performance of different voices. Although Moll Flanders's voice, like those of Defoe's other criminal heroes, is mediated by the corrective "Dress" of a putative Editor's rewriting, the whole meaning of her story rests on the reader's conviction that it originates in her firsthand (here handwritten) testimony: a set of manuscript memorandums "written in the year 1683."[25] The Editor's uneasy acknowledgment of the coarseness of the original account, its lingering over "the particular Occasions and Circumstances" of wickedness (1), risks calling into question the transformative effect of Moll's penitence in order to foster the illusion that this fabricated text reproduces the grain of a stubbornly real voice. The moral point, as in the confessional genres Defoe in part draws from, is to create so strong a feeling of identification as to compel the reader to confront his or her own likeness in the text; the danger, here magnified by the virtuosity of Defoe's ventriloquism, is that we might take for our own the pleasures of depravity.

The ideological and ethical resonances of Defoe's narratives, ultimately, are grounded in what I describe as a double assumption of guilt: the text is predicated on a residual cultural belief in the universal inheritance of sin, while Defoe's strategies of impersonation encourage the reader to assume the specific guilt of his deviant subjects. The mystery and breakdown of the narrative mechanism in *Roxana* not only evince a sense of panic at the enormity of the crimes both author and reader long to see carried out but also argue for the impossibility of ever freeing oneself of the burden of guilt, whether for past crimes or unacted desires.

Against this drawing out of a problematic complicity with criminal desires, Fielding's criminal texts seem to take as axiomatic a clear-cut opposition between the deviant and the normal. Writing in response to a widely reported crime wave, as Defoe had done a generation earlier, Fielding linked the violence and disorderliness of urban poverty to what he perceived as a broader resistance to the hierarchical authority embodied in law. It was to salvage the law as a mechanism of social control that Fielding, who from 1749 to 1753 combined the careers of author and magistrate for the West End of London, published his diverse studies of transgression and juridical retribution. Yet, if in such texts as the *Enquiry into the Causes of the Late Increase in Robbers* he represents crime as a symptom of alterity, configuring "the Lower Kind of People," as the authors of the old anatomies had done, as members of an alien and disruptive race, Fielding's other writings on criminal themes, culminating in his last novel, *Amelia,* betray a considerable skepticism about the law's powers of ascertaining the truth and a disenchantment with the social order it defends, which together draw his narratives toward an uneasy recognition of the permeability of the border separating the licit from the illicit.[26]

In *Joseph Andrews* and *Tom Jones* (completed just before he assumed his new responsibilities at Bow Street) Fielding had developed a mode of representation in which only so much material detail, so much singularity, was admitted as could be accommodated in a narrative whose meanings were presented as stable, certain, subject to interpretive closure. The ritual of public execution, centered around the last dying speech of the condemned, had been instituted as just such a stable narrative form: an exemplary warning against crime. But Fielding, in his several accounts of hangings, argued that the specificity and force of the representation had dangerously confused the meanings it was meant to convey. The identification between criminal and audience, which was the key to the representation's moral effect, was so powerful and particular that it slipped into sympathy and even support, destabilizing the narrative's predetermined outcome. The solution—analogous to the antirealist model Fielding adopted in his earlier fictions as a means of controlling the promiscuous, anarchic potentialities of Richardsonian realism—was to carry out a judicial "Murder behind the Scenes."[27] In this way the exemplary narrative, in the form here of an official *report* of death by hanging, would mean just what its authors willed. The extraneous, discrepant, ambiguous particulars endemic to more circumstantial modes of representation could be burned off, leaving a purified, depersonalized performance of authority.

Yet, however much Fielding might have aspired to such magisterial control, the conditions of his actual practice as an examining magistrate made these authoritarian postures impossible to sustain. In his two polemical narratives of legal investigation, the *True State of the Case of Bosavern Penlez* and the *Clear State of the Case of Elizabeth Canning*, Fielding was concerned with justifying the law against charges of false conviction, with demonstrating that truth could be discovered through its representatives' careful assembling and weighing of evidence. But the materials of both cases—depositions, affidavits, transcripts of judicial interrogations—were less tractable, more resistant to sorting out, than his prefatory remarks acknowledge. And Fielding's adoption in these texts of a fragmented, discontinuous, open-ended narrative form points to a recognition that the omniscient mode of his first two novels was inadequate to the more contentious and heteroglossic social reality he confronted in the examining rooms at Bow Street. In constructing his evidentiary archive with a view to persuading his audience of the correctness of the court's verdicts, Fielding makes use of the devices of realist narrative familiar from a century of trial reports: the painstaking delineation of times and locales; the cataloguing of documents in evidence, such as inventories of stolen goods; the verbatim transcription of eyewitness testimony, each speaker limited to telling only what he or she had directly seen and heard. Yet the realist strategy (dictated here by the accumulated body of legal practice) of seeming to let the story tell itself through the density of its circumstantial detail fails to lead in either case to certainty or narrative closure. Instead, his texts provide the basis for an endless proliferation of counternarratives, contrary readings of the judicial archive.

The pressures of Fielding's overlapping literary and legal careers, which ultimately destroyed his health, underlie the sense of hopelessness that pervades *Amelia*.

Fielding's portrayal of the criminal and judicial milieu is so disenchanted that what Alexander Welsh describes as a skepticism about witnesses telling their own stories succumbs to despair over the prospects of any search for truth within a regime contaminated by the effects of money, sexual corruption, and class privilege.[28] The institution and image through which that regime is anatomized is the prison. The carceral world is, as in Reynolds's *Triumph of God's Revenge,* a "Christall mirrour" of everyday life in the harrowing, labyrinthine metropolis; Fielding, in fact, calls into question the very distinction between inside and outside, mapping a reversible, shifting topography of imprisonment which author, characters, and audience alike inhabit. Against readings of Amelia herself as the bloodless angel of a sphere of domesticity which needs to be kept safe from the violent incursions of public, political life, I argue that she recognizes from the start that the domestic sphere is a prison too. Happiness, which she equates with sexual passion, depends on her own energy, courage, and resourcefulness in breaking out of the captivity of family life. Like Defoe's fictions, like Richardson's, and seemingly against Fielding's conservative will, *Amelia* evokes the allure of the transgressive acts and desires whose dangers are also its subjects. The more circumstantial and polyphonic the representations—and Fielding moved in this direction not only in response to the novelistic experiments of his rivals but also as an outgrowth of his practice in making narratives from the multiple testimonies of judicial investigations—the more uncontrollable and perverse the possibilities of reading.[29]

The readerly perversion of criminal texts could take many forms: from the "Rancour" with which *Amelia* itself was received, and which led to its being brought to mock trial in the pages of Fielding's own *Covent-Garden Journal,* to the various contestatory readings (including mine) of the evidence Fielding gathered in the Canning and Penlez cases; from an identification with outlaws, founded on a romanticizing of their crimes, to a rejection of the category of crime itself as a ruling-class fiction, a ploy to suppress popular challenges to hegemonic structures of rule. In the epilogue to this study I reflect from the vantage point of the ideologically volatile 1790s on the ways in which criminal narrative had over the course of the eighteenth century become a necessary vehicle for articulating fundamental cultural anxieties and longings. Via Gothic romance, themes of political oppression, prohibited sexuality, and violence had become staples of middle-class entertainment, their ideological dangers largely contained by an aura of exoticism, diseased subjectivity, and the irrational. Wollstonecraft, Inchbald, and Godwin drew out the revolutionary implications of the Gothic plot of labyrinthine entrapment and pursuit and through their furious, mordant evocations of older prison and trial narratives wrote to undermine the very system of social relations those narratives had been written to uphold. For all that was original in their social critiques, their fictions hark back to those "little old book[s]" of transgression and revenge in which the emergence of a modern conception of the individual was prefigured.

## PART I

# Criminal Representations

As the *Polypus* is said to be always of the same Colour with the neighbouring Object, or as the Looking-Glass reflects as many different Faces as are set against its own Superficies; so now a days, a Man here and there (I will not blame all) may be said not to be properly one, but any Body; of the Opinion, and the Humour, and the Fashion of his wicked Companions, as near as his own Weakness will permit him to imitate them.

I know that Evil has very much the Ascendant over the Heart of Man, who is born with a Desire after Liberty, and to do what he pleases; but nevertheless I hope, these Relations, most of 'em impartially penn'd from their own Mouths, will have Efficacy enough to check the Disorders of Mankind, which are almost infinite.

CAPTAIN ALEXANDER SMITH
*History of the Lives of the Most Noted Highway-men*, 1714

# CHAPTER ONE

# Constructing the Underworld

## *Criminal Anatomies*

In the spring and summer of 1726, in the wake of a battery of police raids orches-
trated by the Societies for the Reformation of Manners, the Old Bailey in London was the site of a series of overlapping trials of men accused of what a 1735 text
calls "the heinous and detestable Sin of Sodomy, not to be named among Chris-
tians."[1] This was not the first antisodomite campaign in eighteenth-century London. In 1707 a combination of raids on clubs and entrapments in such cruising
grounds as the Royal Exchange and London Bridge led to the arrests of nearly one
hundred men, several of whom hanged themselves or cut their own throats while
awaiting trial. These suicides were the subject of a moralizing ballad, *The Woman-
Hater's Lamentation,* set, apparently without irony, to the tune of "Ye Pretty Sailors
All." As the author of the *Lamentation* wrote:

> But see the fatal end
> > That does such crimes pursue;
> Unnatural deaths attend
> > Unnatural lusts in you.

> This piece of justice then
> > Has well revenged their cause [that is, the cause of the "hated" women]
> And shows unnatural lust
> > Is cursed without the laws.[2]

But, of course, nothing in the case took place "without the laws," despite the *Lamentation*'s author's effort to represent the suicides (rather incoherently) as a retribution of nature against unnatural desires. It is only because these men were tangled
up *within* the laws that they were discovered and driven to "unnatural deaths" by

the shame of exposure: a punishment that the *Woman-Hater's Lamentation* continues to inflict on them at a distance of 290 years, keeping the three men's names
and their criminal actions persistently in public view.

The 1726 trials, which were collected in the various editions of *Select Trials*
which began to be published in the mid-1730s, offer a much richer, if obviously distorting and fragmentary, representation of a criminally homoerotic underworld.
The primary locus of that underworld was the network of molly houses—private
houses or taverns where mollies, or sodomites, as they were variously named in the
period, could meet. The pogrom of 1726, as Alan Bray has called it, was designed
to scour this network of molly houses from the city, but it had the secondary effect
of producing an archival record of sodomitical practice, which might otherwise
never have come to light or at any rate to so full a textual accounting.[3]

The trial reports, which aimed in part to create a sense of moral panic that would
justify the violence of the police and executioner—three men of the first group of
five brought to trial were hanged a month later, and the campaign of entrapments
and molly house roundups continued for some months—provided also a lexicon
and itinerary to a transgressive underworld, reporting the location and external features of each house, if anything making them, for the curious but uninitiated, easier to find. The most celebrated of the houses was Mother Clap's in Holborn. One
witness, a constable working for the reforming societies, described it in these terms:
"Mother *Clap*'s House was in *Field-Lane,* in *Holbourn.* It was next to the *Bunch of
Grapes* on one side, and join'd to an Arch on the other side. It was notorious for
being a *Molly-house.* I have been there several Times in order to detect those who
frequented it: I have seen 20 or 30 of them together, kissing and hugging, and making Love (as they call'd it) in a very indecent Manner. Then they used to go out by
Couples into another Room, and when they came back they would tell what they
had been doing, which in their Dialect they call'd *Marrying.*"[4] In using what witnesses referred to as the "Female Dialect," a form of cross-gender mimicry or parody of heterosexual institutions and norms, signaled by the radical displacement
of such terms as *marrying, chapel,* and *husbands,* the largely working- and lower-
middle-class mollies articulated their own sense of difference as they marked the
linguistic boundaries of an alien subculture.[5]

In their scrupulous mapping of the topography of deviance and their detailed
recording of strange customs and habits of speech, the 1726 trial reports participate
in that impulse to demarcate a world construed as foreign to the experience of

their intended readers which characterizes the genre of criminal anatomy. Under that term I mean to bring together the several kinds of texts whose principal object is not to narrate a specific criminal act or career but to configure the underworld to which such acts and careers belong.[6] In the language of these reports the fascination and dread of the sodomitical demimonde and its denizens outweigh any juridical interest in sexual crimes themselves. The evidence taken in court lingers over forms of ritual and play which have no real bearing on the criminal charges in question—even though the charges are all that allow such scandalous accounts to be spoken in public and broadcast in saleable texts. Instead, such evidence describes a form of life which the reader is enticed, voyeuristically, to peek in at.

Ultimately, the sodomite is quite visibly marked as ineradicably *other*—portrayed, that is, according to a *racialized* notion of otherness which runs as a persistent undercurrent in many of the forms of criminal anatomy. In a 1752 fulmination from the *Gentleman's Magazine*, for instance, the author explicitly sets the Sodomite in opposition to the Briton: "A love of our species, and the preservation of it; a love of our country, and the preventing of the most dreadful plagues which this sin threatens, should determine all Britons to do their utmost to expose and bring to condign punishment the Sodomite. This is the work of the Lord, *to take away the Sodomites out of the land*."[7] Here the scriptural call inflects the moral offensive against sodomy as a campaign for racial purification.

The name *Sodomite*, insofar as it refers to a faraway city, lends itself to a racializing inflection, but even when the word itself is not written the racial implications are powerfully elicited. When the mollies are not likened to a criminal gang or crew, the name most tellingly applied to them is "tribe," which first appears in a pamphlet written in 1718 by the thief taker and crime boss Jonathan Wild. In his pamphlet Wild reports on a group of men arrested at a molly house and committed to hard labor in a workhouse and notes that, "as a Part of their Punishment, [the Sheriff] order'd them to be publickly conducted thro' the streets in their Female Habits. Pursuant to which Order, the young *Tribe* was carried in Pomp to the Workhouse."[8] The sodomitical tribe is constructed as an alien people in our midst, inciting visitations of plague and somehow, obscurely, threatening to turn us away from our own natures.

The same conflation of criminality and racial difference is inscribed in the most common form of anatomy: the canting dictionary, or glossary to the jargon of deviance. The most frequently reprinted of these texts before the late eighteenth century was the 1725 *New Canting Dictionary*, which enlarged considerably on the glossaries in Richard Head's 1674 *Canting Academy* and Charles Hitchin's 1718 *Regulator*. Head had argued that the cant of London's thieves was descended from the language of the Gypsies, or Egyptians—a group whose manifest and apparently willful estrangement from English normality was taken up later by Defoe as one of the sources of Moll Flanders's overdetermined criminality. The *New Canting Dictionary* elaborates on Head's claim with a history of the Gypsies' progress from Bohemia through Spain to Ireland, "where, joining to their own Villainous Inclinations, the Natural Barbarity and Cruelty of the *Wild Irish*, such was the Influence of the Climate upon them, that, from private Cheats and Thieves, as they had been in other Countries, they threw off all Disguises, and stuck not at the most execrable Villainies, firing of Houses, massacring whole Families, and robbing and plundering in Troops, 'till the Name of *Ægyptians* was wholly lost in that of *Rapparees* or *Tories*."[9] From Ireland the criminal race migrated to Scotland and thence to England.

The topos of the Irish as criminal by nature, owing to both their "Natural" racial characteristics of cruelty and barbarity and their proneness to miscegenation with the Oriental race of *Ægyptians*, persists in much of the criminal discourse of the eighteenth century, even when the author aims for a kind of sociological dispassion, as when Saunders Welch, once Henry Fielding's sheriff at Bow Street, writes that "the unlimited wanderings of the Poor of our own kingdom, and the uncontrouled importation of Irish vagabonds, are two great causes of the supply of rogues to this town."[10] In texts published as popular entertainments, such as Alexander Smith's *Lives of the Highway-men*, the racial denigration is more open, as when, of one malefactor, Smith writes that "he had true *Irish* blood running through all his Veins, for he was stock'd with Impudence and Ignorance to the highest Degree, and was not only skilful in the theorick, but had also the practick Part of the profoundest Villainies which could be acted on this side Hell."[11]

What such passages show, and what the criminal anatomy as a genre argues by its ethnographic mode of presentation, is not that the etiology of crime was necessarily thought to turn on racial difference but that the racializing of deviance was by the early eighteenth century a common discursive practice, whose burden was to deny that the deviant imperiled the moral well-being of the normal, however great a danger it (he, they) might offer from the outside. The anatomies' construction of crime as belonging to a special domain, alien to the social and moral world inhabited by the reader, is integral to their meanings. Even in the cheapest and most lurid of these texts, as Paul Salzman has observed, some effort is made to describe "the thieves' society—its laws, hierarchy, and special language."[12] Their language, of course, is the focus of the canting dictionaries, which provide a lexicon to the specialized and exotic practices of a criminal underclass which, to some degree, they may simply have made up. For it is hard to know how true an image they furnish of the language either of criminals or of the urban poor more generally.[13] Neither the relative absence of thieves' cant from published trials and Ordinary's *Accounts*—and from the autobiographical narratives that Defoe later constructed out of criminal experience—nor its presence in the confessions of such figures as the highwaymen John Poulter (1754) or the corrupt City Marshal Charles Hitchin (1718) is decisive. Yet, even granting a real basis in speech for the terms collected in the canting dictionaries, the lexicons' function was less to offer an aid to translation than to designate the boundaries of a world. They articulate a realm of social experience which is simultaneously laid open to view and glossed as frighteningly, yet also reassuringly, alien.

These vocabularies were often printed as appendices to other texts—criminal "discoveries" and confessions, cony-catching miscellanies, ballads and pantomimes— or as marginal glosses to "canting songs" and comic dialogues that exploited the same vein of linguistic exoticism. In such cases the fiction of sociological value drops away, and the canting lexicons are revealed as compilations of a purely literary language, the accessories of deliberately artificial divertissements. The canting songs that have survived are less the records of a lost popular culture than the highly stylized macaronics of mercenary authors. When, for example, the pantomime devised by John Thurmond in 1724 to commemorate Jack Sheppard's execution concludes with these lines from "A Canting Song, sung by Frisky Moll," there is little reason to suppose, despite the dutiful glosses provided for the canting terms, that this language is grounded in the real speech of any class:

> A Famble, a Tattle, and two Popps,
> > Had my *Boman* when he was ta'en;
> But had he not Bowz'd in the Diddle Shops,
> > He'd still been in *Drury-Lane*.[14]

The canting dictionaries, then, which at first seem transparent, windows to an otherwise hidden milieu, really have a more active, mediating role: they construct,

on the one hand, a picture of criminality and of a distinct criminal class which was
to have important ideological consequences and elaborate, on the other, a highly
artificial literary idiom that could be used to distance and trivialize the social conflicts and pressures from which popular forms of criminality really emerged. Another common form of anatomy, the descriptions of Newgate prison, were less
concerned (to return to Salzman's observation) with the special language of criminality than with the hierarchy and laws of criminal society—or, in some cases,
with its undermining of all hierarchy and law. For the most part these descriptions
aimed less to render the material reality of the prison than to convey a moralized
image of imprisonment in more or less allegorical terms.

The 1705 pamphlet *A Glimpse of Hell: or a Short Description of the Common Side
of Newgate,* a satirical poem in tetrameter couplets, purporting to be written by an
imprisoned debtor, evokes a generalized atmosphere of gross physicality:

> And verily, to speak the Truth,
> 'Tis a fit School to Tutor Youth;
> If Want (the Mother of Invention)
> If noisy Nonsense and Contention,
> If Fraud, Deceit, and Treachery,
> If Whoredom, and if Sodomy,
> And every dreadful Consequence
> Of Drunkenness, that drowns the Sense,
> Can work a happy Reformation,
> *Newgate's* the only School i' th' Nation.[15]

The Newgate the pamphlet imagines, whether or not it originated in a real experience of incarceration, is primarily a locus for the clash of abstract moral qualities
or categories of conduct, a space of license and inversion: "For *Justice* with the
Gaoler's Trade, / In ev'ry point goes retrograde." By representing the prison as a
site of contamination—on the women's side, "well fill'd Chamber Pot[s]" are, "like
Lightning, toss'd from hand to hand" until the whole company is "tyr'd with stink";
among the men, "every single Word they spoke," in their gin- and tobacco-besot-
ted reunions, "Stunk both of Logick and of Smoak"—the author aims to secure
the argument around which his satirical vignettes are organized, that such undif-
ferentiated spaces are schools not of reformation but of vice.

In the 1714 edition of *The History of the Lives of the Most Noted Highway-men*
Alexander Smith inserts a set-piece description of Newgate into the life of the

murderer and housebreaker Tom Sharp which carries even further this tendency toward moral allegory in the prison anatomies. "It is," he writes,

a Place of Calamity, a Dwelling in more than *Cimmerian* Darkness, an Habitation of Misery, a confused *Chaos*, without any Distinction, a bottomless Pit of Violence, and a Tower of *Babel*, where all are Speakers, and no Hearers. There is mingling the Noble with the Ignoble, the Rich with the Poor, the Wise with the Ignorant, and Debtors with the worst of Malefactors . . . There one weeps, whilst another sings; one prays, whilst another swears; one sleeps, whilst another walks; one goes out, another comes in; one is condemn'd, another absolv'd; one demands, another pays; and in fine, one shall hardly find two Persons of one Mind and Exercise.[16]

The place Smith describes is no more "real" than the Slough of Despond in *Pilgrim's Progress* or the Cave of Dulness in the *Dunciad;* that is, Smith has no interest in verisimilitude, in convincing his readers of the literal accuracy of his rendering. His Newgate is a tropological field of paradox and reversal, his description an accumulation of catchphrases for moral irregularity and social disorder. The sentences I have quoted exhibit a notable rhetorical progression: the first stacks up noun phrases in a fever of periphrasis; the second, prepared by the weighing of *Speakers* against *Hearers,* casts over its clutch of antitheses the shadow of promiscuous mingling and the elision of difference; in the third the antithetical pattern continues, but now one action is set in contrary motion to another, and the moral danger is figured as centrifugal (the moral world of the prison is flying apart under the strain of contradictory energies) rather than centripetal (properly opposed social categories are melting into one indistinguishable mass). Each of these figural strategies will recur in later descriptions of Newgate by Defoe, Mandeville, and Fielding, among others.

The 1717 pamphlet *The History of the Press-Yard* adopts a quite different representational strategy, affiliated with contemporaneous work in such journalistic forms as newspaper and trial reports. Here a more literal description of the prison is worked into the autobiographical narrative of an author imprisoned for Jacobite sympathies. Amid its appeals for the king to pardon the rebels captured at Preston are sketches of the condemned hold and, here, of the author's room: "The Bars of the Windows were as thick as my Wrist and very numerous; and the Walls of it, which were entirely Stone and had borne that Hue for above half the last Century, were bedaubed with Texts of Scripture written in Charcoal . . . and with Scraps of Verses, and according to the Dispositions and Circumstances of the several Ten-

ants that had been Inhabitants thereof. As for Beds, there were Steds for three to
be laid upon made of Boards, but neither Flocks nor Feathers enough in all to make
one."[17] In the pamphlet as a whole the governing structure of personal narrative—
from arrest to initiation to release—is overlaid by the structure of the anatomy: a
mapping of the prison's different areas, inhabitants, and customs. This passage
filters visual detail through an intimate, almost tactile memory (the bars "thick as
my Wrist," the poorness of the bedding) and so infuses description with the vividness of a private history. As the author circulates from one part of the prison to
another, he is brought into contact not only with its various locales but also with
the histories of the other prisoners, whom he engages in dialogue; the image he is
thus able to construct of the world of the press-yard has both spatial and temporal, or experiential, coordinates.[18]

The fullest early description of Newgate was published a few years later, in 1724,
as *An Accurate Description of Newgate*, by B.L. of Twickenham.[19] The author draws
the interior of Newgate with minute attention to its spatial configuration; its divisions (often unregulated and so frequently transgressed) along lines of gender, economic condition, and criminal status; its palpable horrors. Describing the Stone
Hold, for example, the first of five wards on the Felons Common side of the prison,
he writes that "it was a terrible, stinking, dark, and dismal place, situate under-
ground, into which no day light can come. It was paved with stone; the prisoners
had no beds and lay on the pavement, whereby they endured great misery and hardship. The unhappy persons imprisoned therein are such as at their unfortunate
entrance cannot pay the customary fees of the gaol."[20] B.L. gives the prices of can-
dles and sheets, the cost of admission to a ward where one could sleep on wooden
rather than stone floors, the kinds of liquor available in the drinking vaults. Of all
the Newgate anatomies his is the most concrete, the most attentive to the ways
that social and architectural structures are mutually constitutive. The world those
structures contain is as complexly articulated, in its gradations of degeneracy and
squalor, as the world outside.

This correspondence, however, between the world inside and the world outside
the walls disturbs the simplicity of the ideologically motivated contrast between
the domains of law and outlawry which is fundamental to the anatomy. Although
it is located near the center of the rapidly outward-spreading agglomeration of
London, Newgate is made to seem in these texts as exotic as Surinam, yet not only
does its arrangement reflect, however darkly, the class hierarchy of the reader's

world, but anyone, it seems, can end up inside: "the Noble with the Ignoble, the Rich with the Poor, the Wise with the Ignorant, and Debtors with the worst of Malefactors," as Alexander Smith asserts. The travelers who come back with these reports of their voyages into the world of the prison most often find themselves there through some misadventure to which those who compose their audience are equally vulnerable: especially debt or the bad luck of being, for the moment, on the down side of the partisan seesaw.[21] To the extent that we as readers are entreated to feel sympathy for these correspondents in Newgate, they need to describe their experience in a way that induces us to identify with them or at least project ourselves imaginatively into their place. So, when the author of *The History of the Press-Yard* unveils the prison's hidden interior, he does this by trying to elicit the sensory assault of the first disorienting moments:

The Condemn'd-Hold, falsly suppos'd to be a noisome Vault under-ground, lies between the Top and Bottom of the Arch under *Newgate,* from whence there darts in some Glimmerings of Light, tho' very imperfect, by which you may know that you are in a dark, Opace, wild Room. By the Help of a Candle, which you must pay through the Nose for, before it will be handed to you over the Hatch, your Eyes will lead you to boarded Places, like those that are raised in Barracks, whereon you may repose yourself if your Nose will suffer you to rest, from the Stench that diffuses its noisome Particles of bad Air from every Corner.[22]

The use of the second-person voice reinforces the appeal for our identification with the author's experience by insinuating us into the moment, inducing us to take as our own the sensations of his criminalized body.

A similar blurring of the boundary between the deviant and the normal is written into the antisodomitical texts. On the one hand, the sodomite is represented as intractably alien, contrary to nature and burning with literally incomprehensible desires; on the other, he's feared as a vehicle of contagion, as when the writer for the *Gentleman's Magazine* warns of "the dreadful plagues which this sin threatens." The threat of contagious desire makes no sense unless the potentiality for deviance is already inscribed in our nature.[23] Certainly, the hint of compulsive voyeurism which runs through the testimony in the sodomy trials betrays a certain ambiguity in the representations. The constables sent to infiltrate one house report that "there was a Door in the great Room, which opened into a little Room, where there was a Bed, and into this little Room several of the Company went; sometimes they shut the Door after them, but sometimes they left it open, and then we could see part of their Actions."[24] That repeated peering into the dark beyond a half-closed door is reproduced in the writing habits of another constable, who testifies that "every Night, when I came from thence, I took Memorandums of what I had observ'd, that I might not be mistaken in the Dates"—the most revealing words being the iterative *every Night*.[25] The spy has to become the sodomites' familiar and to imitate, by the fixedness of his gaze, the raptness of desire.

The same sheriff whom we earlier encountered rounding up the furbelowed "Tribe" to send off to the workhouse—a member in good standing of the very Societies for the Reformation of Manners which sponsored these purificatory campaigns—found himself, ten years later, on trial for the same crime. The witness against him testified that "the Prisoner frequently came to my Master's House with Soldiers, and other scandalous Fellows, and call'd for a private Room, which made me suspect him for a Sodomite. And so when he came with the Prosecutor, I peep'd through the Key-hole, and saw him———and———and———."[26] The textual blanks are a dare, a mirror of the fascination the reader is presumed to feel in common with this spy, unwilling to turn away from the keyhole for fear of missing any evidence.

The prisoner-sheriff whose criminally engaged body was the object of this lingering if textually suppressed gaze was Charles Hitchin, whose 1718 pamphlet *The Regulator*, noted earlier as including a cant glossary, aimed more generally at exposing the workings of the criminal underworld presided over by his former lieutenant, Jonathan Wild. Hitchin was, from 1712 to 1727, Under City-Marshal of London (a position he had bought, as was usual, for seven hundred pounds), and in 1713–14 the soon-to-be notorious Wild worked under him. They fell out; Wild set up on his own as a thief taker, gradually consolidating much of the city's criminal activity into a complicated network of dependence and betrayal; and Hitchin in retaliation published this scathing attack on his former confederate and present competitor.

Described by the editor of the *Select Trials* as "a most stupid Pamphlet," *The Regulator* nevertheless, in the words of the same commentator, "opens an extraordinary Scene of Rogueries, lets some Light into the dark Designs of Villains."[27] Hitchin argues, in what was to become a commonplace of the reformist current (which led over time to the constitution of a standing police at the heart of the social order), that the self-professed thief taker held the law doubly in jeopardy. First, as the state's licensed agent—allowed to operate outside the law, unregulated and unchecked—Wild was able, given the absence of any other agency of detection and arrest, to make himself a necessary intermediary in the processes of capture and prosecution, so that the whole criminal justice system had become increasingly dependent on him: "In short, the Thief, the Gaol, the Justice, and the King's Evidence, all of them seem to be influenced and managed by him, and at this rate none will be brought to the Gallows, but such as he thinks fit."[28] Second, Wild's license to maneuver within an unmonitored space on the verges of legality permitted him to act as the master receiver of stolen goods, orchestrate the whole range of criminal activity, and govern the lawless through his access to the machinery of the law.

The underworld Hitchin draws in *The Regulator* is everywhere pervaded with Wild's presence. Even when he speaks of thief takers and receivers as a class— "Knock but away those Pillars of Debauchery, and the whole Fabrick of Robbing and Thieving, with other disorderly Persons and Practices, will all of them immediately give way and fall of Course"[29]—it is clear that he sees the whole confusedly interconnected structure of criminality as, in essence, an extension of the person of "His Skittish and Baboonish Majesty," Jonathan Wild. As king of the criminal underworld, Wild is a negative image of the figure of the sovereign under the ancien régime, who was, Foucault has suggested, at once source and embodiment of the law.[30] Perhaps as a way of holding the pamphlet's disparate elements together, perhaps out of the passion of Hitchin's animosity, Wild is the sole recurring figure in a succession of disconnected episodes: mock-catechistic dialogues, such as one between Wild and a countryman on flash gaming houses and the different varieties of con artists to be found in them; descriptive sketches of the most common grifts; mock proclamations setting out the practices and prerogatives of the thief taker; a primitive woodcut of a criminal on his hanging day, inscribed with Wild's name in the caption; a plea to the public on behalf of the City Marshal (that is, Hitchin) for money and recognition, so that he can track Wild to his disorderly hiding places.

For all its vindictive and self-serving focus on Wild, *The Regulator* shares with the sodomy trial reports, canting dictionaries, and Newgate descriptions the broader ideological project of mapping deviance. A world is laid open to view, and, if the map is vulnerable to misuse as a guidebook or if the burlesquing style of the pamphlet leads to a greater sense of delight than of danger, the authors or redactors of the anatomies can only blame that on the reader. Like William Brown, who pro-

tested when entrapped by a hustler-turned-informer on the Sodomites' Walk in
Moorfields that "there is no Crime in making what use I please of my own Body,"[31]
readers nowadays are apt to use the claim of lawful freedom in defiance of law. In
the preface to his *Lives of the Most Noted Highway-men* Alexander Smith writes,
"I know that Evil has very much the Ascendant over the Heart of Man, who is
born with a Desire after Liberty, and to do what he pleases."[32] So, while the anatomies demarcate the moral and geographical milieus within which the manifold
forms of criminality thrive, the miseries and horrors of those places can also, perversely, reflect imagined pleasures.

Like the elaborately stylized fictions I address in the following chapter the criminal anatomies are liable to draw the reader into "observing, and seeing herein, as
in a Christall mirrour, the variety of the Devills temptations, and the allurements
of sinne."[33] As maps and lexicons of otherness, they reinforce the distinction between deviant and normal, but, insofar as they aim to provide moral warnings or
immunize their audience against criminal desires, they also, unexpectedly, call that
very distinction into question. It is this hankering after the illicit which links the
anatomies to the more obviously "psychological" fictions I turn to next.

# CHAPTER TWO

# Picaresque and Providential Fictions

The two strains of criminal narrative I consider here are as unlike each other as they are, taken jointly, unlike the quasi-documentary genres I will look at in the chapters that follow. Both exhibit strong continuities with certain strands of the anatomy, yet they reverse the anatomy's basic terms by their concern with the irreducible singularity of criminal acts and lives. In part they are useful to think about together because of the very starkness of their oppositions. Whereas fictions of providential intervention are complexly plotted and highly patterned in their effects—corresponding both to the elaborate machinations of the murderers they portray and to a view of the world as ordered, purposeful, watchfully governed—picaresque stories are episodic and arbitrary in their moral and emotional effects, just as the world they imagine is unstable, disintegrating, catalyzed by chance meetings and clashes. One is tragic, the other comical and satiric: the first occupies a domestic, inwardly focused space; the second, a space that is public and socially striated. In one, events are legible, saturated with meaning; in the other, event follows event randomly, drained of any apparent power to signify.

Yet, however neatly they can be fitted into a structure of binary difference, providential and picaresque narratives are, in a more crucial way, akin, for they are both fundamentally concerned with retracing the origins of criminal rebelliousness, and both forms register with almost obsessive detail the singularity of individual psychic experience, especially in states of emotional extremity or disturbance. Their handling of such states may be rudimentary, as the narrative structures they adopt may be awkward or rigid. But in their nervous, often accusatory posture toward their audience the picaresque and providential strands can elicit a more complex and open-ended response than their plots alone seem to offer. Detailing the turmoil of inward fragmentation and guilt as they solicit the reader to accept such turmoil as his own, these narratives project as universal the currents of violence, disorder, and rupture that animate them.

The basic ingredients of the picaresque are well-known: a protagonist (and first-person narrator) whose social position is marginal and who views events from the perspective of the outsider; an episodic structure, usually organized around a succession of journeys and chance encounters; a satirical presentation of diverse social levels and milieus; a lingering over scenes of brutality, trickery, and humiliation; the exposure of pretense; and a protagonist constantly scrambling to survive. Historically, the form has most convincingly been explained as a response to the collapse of feudalism and the culture it sustained.[1] Originating in sixteenth-century Spain, the genre spread quickly into the rest of Europe, and changed as it met with the diversity of other languages and narrative traditions. The first English translation of the first Spanish picaresque, *Lazarillo de Tormes*, appeared in 1586; James Mabbe's version of Aleman's *Guzman de Alfarache* was published in 1622. Over the course of the seventeenth century excurses and variations on the picaresque continued to be written, and the publication of the first part of *The English Rogue* by Richard Head in 1665 marked the genre's full assimilation into English.

Yet there was another narrative strain, largely native to England, which shaped the picaresque's reception and subsequent history there: that strain of anatomy growing out of the early Elizabethan jest book and including the cony-catching pamphlets that Robert Greene and others took to writing in the 1590s.[2] The most famous of this miscellaneous and impure line, Thomas Nashe's story of *The Unfortunate Traveller, or The Life of Jack Wilton* (1594), though it was written some years after the first translation of *Lazarillo*, is so different in structure and tone as to make influence unlikely. Nashe seems, instead, to have fashioned his text from the situations of jest books and Italian *novelle* (which had begun to appear in English translation in the 1560s),[3] although I would call the work as a whole picaresque in a more general sense.

Jack Wilton, the self-styled "King of Pages"[4]—the phrase points both to his subordinate social position and to his strategy of upending hierarchical distinctions—is first seen following the English court in its wars against France. The year is 1513, although Nashe's use of real historical coordinates is as contradictory as it is insistent. Jack engages in a series of rogueries, some designed to get money, some to get revenge, others for the rough pleasure of practical joking. In his travels between England and the Continent he has dealings with cider men, an "ugly

mechanical Captain," foppish clerks, plague sufferers and physicians, rebel Ana-
baptists, an English earl, women imprisoned, Thomas More and Erasmus, Floren-
tine knights, a Roman merchant with a mechanical garden, an exiled Jew who plots
the wholesale destruction of Rome, and a Bolognese cobbler turned, in a blasphemous act of revenge, "a more desperate murtherer than Cain" (362). The executions of the last two characters are set-pieces of a cruelty so excessive as to be
almost unreadable; they are the culmination of a shift in narrative register from the
loosely strung-together episodes of trickery and offhand humiliation of the first
two-thirds of the work to the complexly interlaced dramas of entrapment, betrayal, and sexual violence of the final third.

If by its finale *The Unfortunate Traveller* seems to have reversed the usual terms
of the picaresque—turning from satire to tragedy, episodic to plotted, public and
exuberant to domestic and grim—I would argue that this hybridity or shifting
between extremes is characteristic of the English incorporation of the genre. Because it was, from the start, grafted onto the older stock of jest books and rogue
anatomies, with their narrative fragmentation and anarchic moral vision, and mixed
with such disparate strains as the Italian *novella* and the traveler's tale, the English
picaresque was never purely itself—or, rather, it fashioned itself out of a com-
pounding of differences. In a passage from the preface to his *History of the Lives of
the Most Noted Highway-men* Alexander Smith writes: "As the *Polypus* is said to be
always of the same Colour with the neighbouring Object, or as the Looking-Glass
reflects as many different Faces as are set against its own Superficies; so now a days,
a Man here and there (I will not blame all) may be said not to be properly one, but
any Body; of the Opinion, and the Humour, and the Fashion of his wicked Companions, as near as his own Weakness will permit him to imitate them" (v). Both
the protagonist and the reader who reflects, and reflects on, him in the slipperily
projective process of reading are not "properly one, but any Body." This awareness
of the insecurity of personal identity, of the permeability and multiplicity of the
self, is given narrative shape in picaresque fictions from the late sixteenth through
early eighteenth centuries.

Nashe's Jack Wilton lacks all consistency; his way of responding to the horrors
among which he moves shifts with little preparation from blithe inhumanity to an
Aristotelian pity and terror that lead him to reformation. His responses and manner of speaking change to suit the tale he is caught up in. Yet he is not, as in some
of the longer jest books, just a name (or a first-person singular pronoun), a pre-

tense for stringing together disjointed anecdotes.[5] If *The Unfortunate Traveller* is not a bildungsroman and does not present what within the norms of a later psychology could be considered a coherent account of individual development, it is nevertheless attentive to Jack Wilton's particular way of seeing, to his voice, and to the tensions within subjectivity. The narrative is ushered in by a call to "every man of you [to] take your places, and hear Jack Wilton tell his own tale" (254), and his claim to speak for himself is vital. As he moves through Europe "like a crow that still follows aloof where there is carrion" (277), for example, he lights on Munster in the year of the Anabaptist uprising, and, though he mocks the rebels as "very devout asses . . . for all they were so dunstically set forth" (284), his description of their defeat exhibits a radically divided sensibility:

> Pitiful and lamentable was their unpitied and well-performed slaughter. To see even a bear, which is the most cruellest of all beasts, too too bloodily overmatched and deformedly rent in pieces by an unconscionable number of curs, it would move compassion against kind, and make those that, beholding him at the stake yet uncoped with, wished him a suitable death to his ugly shape, now to re-call their hard-hearted wishes and moan him suffering as a mild beast, in comparison of the foul-mouthed mastiffs, his butchers. Even such comparison did those overmatched ungracious Munsterians obtain of many indifferent eyes, who now thought them, suffering, to be sheep brought innocent to the shambles, when as before they deemed them as a number of wolves up in arms against the shepherds. (285)

Jack Wilton's contradictory responses are shown rhetorically by the opposition of *pitiful* and *unpitied*, the double superlative of *most cruellest* played off the repetition of *too too bloodily overmatched*, the metamorphoses of wolves into sheep, shepherds into shambles, and by the lie the whole passage gives to his *many indifferent eyes*.

Although he reverts fitfully to the satirical mode of the outset, Jack becomes increasingly the serious "historiographer of [his] own misfortunes" as the story unfolds (326). Nashe's language never loses its writerly thickness and glamour, but the ebullience of the work's opening is gradually replaced by exhaustion and a will to silence—"Conjecture the rest, my words stick fast in the mire and are clean tired" (336)—until Cutwolfe's execution scares Jack Wilton out of narrative altogether. The reader, too, is presumed to take part in this entropic winding down of the narrative: "I'll make short work," Jack promises, "for I am sure I have wearied all my readers" (359). In *The Unfortunate Traveller*, however resistant it might be to the kind of psychological coherence that would become a primary object of the novel after Richardson, Nashe sets out an overall psychological trajectory from exuberance and braggadocio to stunned dismay. The dampening of the language of self-disclosure mirrors Jack Wilton's weakening hold on himself and the world he moves through, his entanglement in a criminality he can no longer master.

The picaresque, for all its sensational unveiling of the circumstantial details of con jobs, murder, rape, burglary, kidnaping, and treason, wastes little time over legalities. The two executions at the end of *The Unfortunate Traveller*, for example, while they serve as exemplary warnings to Jack Wilton to give up his wandering and vagabond life, do not reflect any real interest in the law or in a juridical understanding of crime. Criminality is represented in the two figures of Zadoch and Cutwolfe not as a social fact, a challenge to public authority and order, but as a kind of satanic overreaching, and retribution, although it does come to these two, is in any broader sense capricious. Jack and his mistress endure whippings, imprisonment, and threats of vivisection, but, like Sade's Justine, they suffer for their beauty, not their crimes. For these crimes, including their last—"Against our Countess we conspire, pack up all her jewels, plate, money that was extant, and to the waterside send them. To conclude: courageously rob her and run away" (361)—they are well rewarded. Zadoch's confederate Zacharie escapes capture, and death, brutal and sudden, comes alike to the innocent and the guilty.

Showing how far the narrative has wandered from its lighthearted beginnings, Jack provides a preamble to the scene of Cutwolfe's execution which explicitly recalls the rhetoric of that contrary but blood-related genre, the providential fiction:

Prepare your ears and your tears, for never till this thrust I any tragical matter upon you. Strange and wonderful are God's judgments; here shine they in their glory. Chaste Heraclide, thy blood is laid up in heaven's treasury. Not one drop of it was lost, but lent out to usury. Water poured forth sinks down quietly into the earth, but blood spilt on the ground sprinkles up to the firmament. Murder is wide-mouthed and will not let God rest till he grant revenge . . . Guiltless souls that live every hour subject to violence, and with your despairing fears do much impair God's providence, fasten your eyes on this spectacle that will add to your faith. (363)

In the speech that follows, Cutwolfe tells the story of his revenge killing of Esdras—a ruthless brigand whose crimes included the rape of the gentle Heraclide (which led to her suicide) and the murder of his erstwhile companion Bartolo, who happens to be Cutwolfe's brother. Heraclide was also, coincidentally, Jack Wilton's landlady, and when her body was first discovered Jack was arrested for her murder; he had even prepared a ballad, "Wilton's Wantonness," to be sung at his own execution. It is only because a witness came forward who heard Bartolo's dying words, revealing Esdras's role in the death of Heraclide, that Jack was released.

Plots of this kind, strewn with coincidence and revenge, are inherent to the providential genre and are enlisted as demonstrations of God's power to work through the seemingly random encounters and misprisions of ordinary life to effect his special providences.[6] Nashe, by incorporating this plot into the much looser ethical and narrative framework of the criminal picaresque, calls the providential tale's certainties into question. It is unclear what, if anything, these tragic actions could signify in the morally disjunct world of *The Unfortunate Traveller*. Cutwolfe, in his last dying speech—which is privileged by the terms of Nashe's introduction, his "gloss upon the text," as the authoritative history of the events—undercuts any religious reassurance: "There is no heaven," he declares, "but revenge" (367). By contrast, the thirty stories collected in John Reynolds's 1621 compilation, *The Triumph of God's Revenge, against the Crying, and Execrable Sinne of Murther*, are framed in a way that leaves no doubt about their orthodoxy or moral exemplarity. While bloody revenge is, as much for Reynolds as for Cutwolfe, the necessary and longed-for outcome of every history of murder, it is viewed by Reynolds not as an occasion of personal glory but as a manifest sign of God's presence, as a proof of heaven.

All the tales in Reynolds's collection follow roughly the same pattern. The author writes that he has "indeavoured (as much as in mee lyes) to make my *Reader* a Spectatour, first of these their foule and bloudie Crimes, and then of their condigne and exemplarie Punishments, which (as a dismal Storme and terrible Tempest from Heaven) fell on them on Earth, when they least dreamt or thought thereof."[7] Nashe wrote that the blood of the murdered is "lent out to usury" (363), and Reynolds too, in describing God's "miraculous detection and severe punishment," shows him "revenging blood for blood, and death for death; yea, many times repaying it home with interest, and rewarding one death with many" (iv). This image of retribution has the odd side effect of portraying God as a usurer, metaphorically implicating him in a forbidden economic trade, but the providential genre takes up the image in order to make the stories' warning, their power as a deterrent, more terrible.

Reminders of God's power to detect and punish the most secret transgressions are especially needed, Reynolds believes, in "these last and worst dayes of the world, in which the crying and scarlet sinne of Murther makes so ample, and so bloody a progression" (i). Yet the burden of Reynolds's narratives is not simply to communicate horror at acts of extreme violence or to demonstrate, as Fielding would later undertake in his 1752 pamphlet, *Examples of the Interposition of Providence in the Detection and Punishment of Murder,* that providence will not suffer murders to go undiscovered. They aim, instead, at a more general deterrence, a kind of moral policing: "that the consideration of these bloody and mournfull Tragedies, may by their examples, strike astonishment to our thoughts, and amazement to our senses, that the horrour and terrour thereof may hereafter retaine and keepe us within the lists of Charity towards men, and the bonds of filiall and religious obedience towards God" (iv). The images of deference and constraint which Reynolds evokes in this passage are expressive of a whole system of moral relationships, recurrent in the genre of providential fictions. Virtue is configured as a bounded physical space, vice as any impulse to exceed those bounds. If those limits are overstepped, under the sway of "the treacherous baites of the World, the alluring pleasures of the Flesh, and the dangerous and fatall temptations of the Devill" (iv), we lose the effectual government of our passions and are liable to be drawn by them into every manner of transgression. In this genre of exemplary fictions murder is less a crime than an emblem, the sanguinary image of excessive, unregulated desire.

That is why Reynolds recounts at such length the circumstances of his villains, their histories and dominant passions, the circuitous route by which they arrive at, and justify, their murderous resolutions. By drawing attention to the passional sources of violence, the narratives urge us to locate the same motives and passions in ourselves and to "detest and roote [them] out from amongst us" (i). The circumstantiality and psychological elaboration of Reynolds's approach can be illustrated in his treatment of the following events (printed as a précis to his "History XXVII"): "Father *Iustinian* a Priest, and *Adrian* an Inne keeper, poyson *De Laurier,* who was lodged in his house, and then bury him in his Orchard; where a month after a Wolfe digges him up, and devoures a great part of his body; which father *Iustinian* and *Adrian* understanding, they flie upon the same, but are afterwards both of them apprehended and hanged for it" (369).

When Henry Fielding included a version of this story as one of his thirty-three *Examples of the Interposition of Providence,* he focused, as the summary would lead one to suppose, on the wolf's discovery of the body and reproduced only those points from Reynolds's account which were needed to provide a clear sequence of the principal actions.[8] Reynolds, by contrast, retraces all the twists and turns in Adrian's hatching of the plot against De Laurier, describing him as "of a dissolute

life and carriage, extreamly given to wine and women," a man of "sordid actions
and humors" (370). Adrian's social class and the circumstances of his marriage to a
"well descended" and religious woman provide a context for Reynolds's dissection
of his prodigality, and by that we are prepared for his reaction when De Laurier is
taken ill and forced to stop at his inn: "for hee imagining *De Laurier* to bee rich,
doth therefore verily hope and pray that hee may speedily die in his house, or else
he hath already swapt a bargaine with the Devill, to murther him, thereby to make
up the breaches and ruines of his poore and tottering estate" (371). An unregulated
appetite for pleasure, "the very bane of the heart, and the true poyson and contagion of the soule" (370), has drawn him as if by a kind of moral undertow to the
contemplation of murder.

The same attentiveness to the inward experience of transgression is evident in
Reynolds's handling of the events that follow the wolf's providential discovery of
De Laurier's corpse. Fielding reports the facts briskly:

On hearing the report that De Laurier's body was found, [Adrian and Father Iustinian]
both fled, hoping to escape out of the reach of that jurisdiction; but being fearful of appearing in daylight, they hid themselves in a large wood, about two leagues from Salines, and
lying concealed all day, they only travelled after it was dark. After wandering the whole
night, they constantly, as soon as it was day, found themselves on that side of the wood from
whence they could see the city of Salines; and though they lay for nine days concealed, and
for nine nights travelled with all the speed and care imaginable, yet never could they find
themselves advanced beyond the same side of the wood. (196)

The journalistic detachment of Fielding's style—which reads almost like a dispatch
from *The Covent-Garden Journal*—in its rigorously externalized perspective masks
an atavistic faith in the miraculous: the two villains, making their getaway with
speed and care, seem to be caught in an enchanted forest. Reynolds, although his
language is more archaic, is much closer to a "modern" psychology in his rendering of the disruptive effects of panic and guilt:

Their guilty thoughts and consciences (like so many Ghosts and bloodhounds) so inces-
santly pursued them and stupified their judgements, that . . . they notwithstanding, the
next morning (to their unspeakable fear and vexation) saw themselves againe within a little league [of Salynes] . . . and they could not ascend the least Hill or Hillocke, but they
looking backe behind them, the Towers and Turrets of *Salynes* were still apparent and con-
spicuous to them, as if they pursued and followed them, the which indeed stroke extreame

feare to their guiltie hearts, and infinite terrour and amazement to their foule and trembling consciences. (383)

Reynolds has constructed this admittedly ramshackle sentence in such a way that the inward currents of bewilderment and terror are woven into the outward registration of events, making it impossible to decide if the miraculous entrapment is not just the distorted projection of fractured subjectivities.

In another of the histories, the story of Christina and her inhumane son Maurice, who throws her into a well both for her money and to be free of her reproaches of his profligacy and drunkenness, Reynolds describes the son's eventual imprisonment and madness in an episode that seems likely to have provided Godwin with the model for the first of *Caleb Williams*'s two endings. While in some passages he represents madness as a visitation from God, Reynolds is careful to provide the circumstantial detail to sustain another reading. Maurice is internally, bodily, devoured by the effects of drinking; his debauchery soon makes him "very extreame poore and miserable"; he is "clapt into a stinking Vault or Dungeon" for debt and nearly starved (289); as he returns one evening from the prison yard to his cell, he slips in the darkness and breaks his arm—"and having no Chirurgion to looke to it, it putrifies and rots, so as for the preserving of his life, hee within fifteene dayes is enforced to have it cut off a little below the shoulder" (290). His insanity could be taken as the natural consequence of such bodily suffering.

Reynolds does not oppose naturalistic to providential explanations, for, although he is not above resorting to an occasional well-placed lightning bolt as the instrument of God's justice, he most often shows providence working through what we would think of as plausible channels of circumstance and causation. The wolf in the history of Adrian and De Laurier is acting like a wolf when he digs up and begins to eat De Laurier's corpse; the arm that rots and has to be cut from Maurice's body, however symbolically appropriate its decay may be (since it was the same arm that pushed his mother to her death), rots from no other cause than a lack of medical care. In the same way it is through the convincing portrayal of extreme and distorted psychological states—his "exploring," as Godwin wrote, of "the entrails of mind and motive" (340)—that Reynolds shows providence acting on the souls of his protagonists.

Yet, if the stories thus exhibit a degree of psychological plausibility, they could hardly have been taken for reports of real crimes. It is probably impossible to know whether early readers believed the narratives in *The Triumph of God's Revenge* to be true or, if they did, in what precise sense of *believed*. Certainly, the stories might be true, and the distinction between truth and fiction was very differently conceived in the early modern period than under later epistemological regimes.[9] But the narratives clearly do not aim to convince us of their veracity in the ways that were available to other genres of criminal writing during the same years. No dates, documentary evidence, or sources are given, and, although the volume is full of executions and judicial tortures, there is scant interest in questions of legal procedure. All the stories take place in "forraine parts" (v), in the Italy, France, and Spain of febrile English imaginings. Unlike many of the histories collected in Fielding's *Examples,* which are plain in their presentation of murders (some of them well-known recent cases) revealed and avenged, all the tales in *The Triumph of God's Revenge* are highly wrought and elaborate in their plotting, most involving a number of related murders and a complex overlapping of motives. They are closer to the *novella* than the trial or criminal biography.

Reynolds is ambiguous in what he says of the histories' origins. The *Dictionary of National Biography* states that the stories were translated by him from French originals, a charge also made during Reynolds's lifetime and one that he was at pains to contradict: "for contrariwise I found out the grounds of them in my Travells, and (at mine owne leisure) composed and penned them, according to the rule of my weake Fancie and Capacity, they being so farre from *Translations,* that as I have hitherto refused to imitate any therein, but my selfe, so had I beene so ambitious or vaineglorious to have given way, or consent to it, some Friends of mine in *Paris,* had long since done the three first Bookes into *French,* from my first *Originall* thereof" (i–ii). In contradicting the one charge, however, he opens himself to another, which is equally destabilizing of his position as the true historian of providential interventions: the charge that he made the stories up. By his appeals to "the rule of my weake Fancie," his claim to have "refused to imitate any therein, but my selfe," his plea of originality, Reynolds verges on an admission even more dangerous than that of having been merely a translator—yet the admission is one to which, as an author, he is obviously attracted.

The tension goes deeper, however, than this struggle between the wish to be admired for his invention and the wish to be read as a witness to actual events. If the aim of providential fictions is, as I have suggested, to persuade the reader into a more attentive regulation of passions and desires, they achieve this goal through their concentration on dangerously uncontrolled subjectivities with which the reader is made to feel complicit: "observing," to refer once again to a passage I have cited twice before, "and seeing herein, as in a Christall mirrour, the variety of the Devills temptations, and the allurements of sinne" (iv). In order to produce this intensity of moral identification, Reynolds looks to "the rule of my weake Fancie and Capacity," seeks as an author "to imitate my selfe," that he may effectively capture the subjective allurements of sin. But this mimetic strategy is at odds with an equally compelling psychological need to distance himself from, and objectify, transgressive desire. So, "for mine owne part," he writes, "I have illustrated and polished these Histories, yet not framed them according to the modell of mine owne fancies, but of their passions, who have represented and personated them: and therefore if in some places they seeme too amorous, or in others too bloody, I must justly retort the imperfection thereof on them, and not thy selfe on mee: sith I only represent what they have acted, and give that to the publike, which they obscurely perpetrated in private" (v).

So many of the cross-purposes of the different genres of criminal narrative are visible in this passage that it seems to anticipate much of what I am arguing in this work as to the complicated entanglements of criminality and identity in the seventeenth and eighteenth centuries. The author's disclaimer of responsibility for the sensational *excess* of his writing ("too amorous" or "too bloody") rests on the claims of realistic representation: he is compelled to reproduce what was not original to him but belonged to another, the criminal actor. A strict division is marked between "mine owne fancies" and "their passions," and, if this puts Reynolds's text in the secondary position of an imitation of the real, his last phrase—"and give that to the publike, which they obscurely perpetrated in private"—places the author in the position of providence itself, laying open, in Godwin's phrase, the most hidden retreats of the guilty. And yet the moral and ideological effectiveness of the fictions depends on the author (and reader) assuming the role of neither providence nor scribe but criminal. In exhibiting these divisions within authorship, as within subjectivity more generally, Reynolds in his providential fictions of the 1620s made criminality an especially revealing site for the complex negotiations of identity.

For all their manifest differences picaresque and providential tales enforce a recognition of likeness between reader and criminal, whose violations enact out-

wardly the same internal conflicts and pathologies that constitute our common inheritance. But they assert this likeness in a social context far removed from the
contemporary experience of their audience. It was the task of the documentary
genres I turn to in the following chapters to confront the intrusion of criminality
into the day-to-day reality of their readers.

# CHAPTER THREE

# Crime Reports and Gallows Writing

The reportorial impulse evident in passages of the criminal anatomies—the desire to bring to light areas of the present which would otherwise have been hidden or alien or obscure—also found outlet in a variety of occasional reports of present-day crimes and punishments. In contrast to picaresque and providential stories, which were rooted in the culture and literary language of the sixteenth and early seventeenth centuries, the two documentary genres on which I focus in this chapter grew directly out of the new printing technologies and mechanisms of distribution of the later seventeenth century and articulated a very different sense of being in the world.[1] What the new publishing technologies offered was speed: news of interesting crimes and exemplary deaths could be purchased as broadsheets or pamphlets within a few hours of their occurrence. As Lennard Davis has noted, "with the advent of journalism, the temporal distance between reader and event is bridged by the technology of instantaneous dispersal of news"; what Davis calls "recentness" could thus be embodied in new narrative forms.[2]

The effect of such immediacy was a shift in the temporality of representation. This shift involved more than an increasingly rapid dissemination of striking or unusual reports, important as readers (and those who listened to their reading) must have found that. For what the new technologies of publishing made possible was what Bakhtin, in the context of novelistic discourse, has called "an indeterminacy, a certain semantic openendedness, a living contact with unfinished, still-evolving contemporary reality (the openended present)."[3] Crime and execution reports were linked to the inhabited time of the reader in a way that was, if not new—since, within a more limited geographical range, the oral transmission of rumor and news had always permitted a similar immediacy—then newly available. The actions unfolded within the same temporal horizon as the reader's experience of their printed representations.

While news of recent crimes and dispatches from the scaffold are linked by their concern with contemporaneity, the two genres come at their subjects from opposite ends of a single narrative continuum. One marks the beginning and the other the end of the story. In the first, the crime has just been committed, and the perpetrators are unapprehended (or at least unpunished, untried); in the second, the alleged malefactor has been arrested, convicted, and exhorted to denounce his own guilt and is represented at the moment of passage from this world to the next. Crime reports, then, narrate a story-in-progress; in execution reports (the contrast is almost too stark) the story is very definitely *over*, at least for the condemned. Yet, if the story is resolved in one sense, it might be unresolved in another: neither the condemned nor the crowds gathered to watch them necessarily assented to the law's determination of guilt or the justice of its retribution, and so other narratives of the crime, counternarratives to the story enforced by the law, could proliferate. The increasing accessibility of print meant that narratives were increasingly vulnerable to revision, that cases could be more publicly disputed and reopened, that the story was still, inextinguishably, unfolding.

The inconclusiveness of news reports can be one of their selling points. A pamphlet from the mid-seventeenth century, *Newes from the North*, recounts the robbery, by a group of soldiers, of a rich miser named Tailour, who had refused a request by the king for a loan of one hundred pounds to pay off the troops levied to fight against the Scots. Bursting into Tailour's house one midnight and threatening his life, the soldiers are able to make off with fourteen thousand pounds worth of silver and gold. Every man shifts for himself and escapes, some to France, others to Ireland. Two ploughmen happen on a bag with two hundred pounds in it which one of the robbers had dropped by the wayside; they are seen with the money and arrested. A short time later the soldiers write the king for a pardon, "shewing the cause that they did this deed, because they had not had their Pay, and that iron-bound rogue would not give a Souldier a cup of drinke, if he should come and crave it at his gate."[4] They are pardoned and return to England. But, as for the "two poor plough-men . . . they lie in durance for it at this time, and shall till a Gaol-delivery" (6). The opening to the present of this last sentence—at the very moment you read, the ploughmen are still languishing—marks a significant and in many ways disruptive recasting of the possibilities and boundaries of written representation. The reader is implicated in the process of narration, caught up in the same unfolding of time; histories are acknowledged to be inconclusive and contingent.

The shift I am pointing to is not confined, of course, to criminal reports: the explosion of journalism in all its forms (printed ballads, periodicals, broadsheet proclamations) during the seventeenth and eighteenth centuries meant that every corner of social life was subject to nearly instantaneous rendering in print. But criminality had an especially vivid presence in journalistic literature. Such rituals of justice as (in the countryside) the twice-yearly coming of the assize judges were crucial sites for the display and enforcement of authority; and by locating the extraordinary events of the robbery and its aftermath within an ongoing narrative of such juridical rituals—the ploughmen "lie in durance for it at this time, and shall till a Gaol-delivery"—the author of *Newes from the North* calls on those rituals' glamour to lend drama to his report even as his naming of the ritual of the "Gaol-delivery" in print reinforces its authority by naturalizing it to the reading audience. The immediacy of printed representations helped to secure the ideological centrality of the law, making possible the instantaneous and broadly dispersed publication of its rituals and proceedings.

More important, the sensational and overnight reporting of crimes fueled a pervasive moral climate of panic and danger, which then required the intervention of the law as the political agency of civic order. The 1677 pamphlet *News from Newgate: or, a true Relation of the manner of Taking several persons, very notorious for Highway-men, in the Strand; upon Munday the 13 of this instant November, 1677* is typical in its framing of the events it reports, opening with this sentence: "Notwithstanding the severity of our wholesome Laws, and vigilancy of Magistrates against Robbers and Highway-men, 'tis too notorious that the Roads are almost perpetually infested with them; especially of late, Tidings dayly arriving from several parts of fresh Mischiefs committed in that kind: and having done their wicked Exploits, they commonly retire to, and lurk up and down in this great and populous City, undoubtedly the best Forest for such Beasts of Prey to shelter in."[5] "Dayly tidings" of "fresh mischiefs" were only possible because of the new technologies of publication, which were thus directly involved in the imagining and construction of a specific version of shared social experience. Even though in this instance the robberies and arrests are completed actions—that is, the pamphlet was written after the thieves were taken—the representation is temporally open-ended in its description of a world that author and reader still inhabit. The events of the narrative are located within an unfinished and uncertain history whose real coordinates—*the Strand, Munday the 13, the Friday following, this instant November*—are those of the reader's present experience and memory. By the closing of distance, the world of the reader is permeated with the threat of the criminal. The pamphlet collapses the opposition between wildness and familiarity through images of predation and the oxymoronic rendering of "this great and populous City" as "the best Forest for such Beasts of Prey to shelter in," so that criminality is seen as both monstrous and entangled with the everyday.[6]

If the immediacy of criminal reports implicated the reader in an imaginary unfolding of the present (imaginary because the narrated moment was already, irretrievably, past), this implication led in turn to a new orientation of the narrative toward the discovery of truth. The journalistic sense of time which emerged in the seventeenth century is connected to "a sense of suspense in readers as they watch the world's history unfold."[7] That same hermeneutic suspense, a provisional suspension of knowledge, is carried over into the reading even of narratives whose outcome is known. There is a vivid instance of this openness in one of the trials collected in the 1734 edition of the *Select Trials,* which in its repudiation of the conventional formula (name of accused, charge, summary of evidence and testimony, disposition of case) reveals how the immediacy of news—which, like the novel in Bakhtin's formula, "comes into contact with the spontaneity of the inconclusive present"[8]—made possible a different kind of relationship between reader and narrated event.

The report of the trial of Thomas Billings, Thomas Wood, and Catherine Hays begins:

On *Wednesday March 2,* 1725-6, about Break of Day, one *Robinson,* a Watchman, found a Man's Head (which appear'd to be newly cut from the Body) and a bloody Pail near it, in the Dock before Mr. *Mackreth's* Lime-Wharf, near the *Horse-Ferry, Westminster.* Surprized at this, he call'd several in the Neighbourhood to see it. The Town was soon alarm'd with the News. The Head was carried to *St. Margaret's* Church-yard, and laid upon a Tomb-Stone, but it being much besmear'd with Blood and Dirt, the Church-wardens order'd it to be wash'd, and the Hair to be comb'd, which being done, it was set upon a Post for the publick View, to the End that some Discovery might be made. (*Select Trials,* 2:174)

In the circumstantiality and profusion of its details, the passage reflects a convergence between the mimetic strategies of journalism and criminal deposition. Here the primary direction of influence is from the trial (in which juridical procedures for the taking of evidence were, through the seventeenth and early eighteenth centuries, becoming more formalized)[9] to the news report, although standards of evidence may also have been shaped by conventions of physical description in printed news. In any case both the trial and the news were affected by more general currents of empirical observation and linguistic transparency which asserted their dominance during the same period.[10]

The distinct imprint of news reporting is most evident in the passage's precise attention to what Bakhtin calls "our unpreparedness"[11]—the shock of the present, the bewildering horror and surprise of violent intrusions into the everyday. For that reason the *everydayness* of the scene has to be especially marked, its familiar sites located and named, so that the horrible, original fact—the head and bloody pail on the dock—can be apprehended in all its mystery and enormity. The use of narrative suspense resonates with real uncertainty and is thus essentially unlike the suspense produced by the tactic of starting an epic narrative in medias res, because, however mysterious the epic's beginning, there is never any doubt that the mystery will be resolved, indeed has been resolved already, and only waits to be spun out in the most pleasing way; there is no connection to the real uncertainty of time inhabited by the reader.[12] In this story of murder, by contrast, the mystery of the initial image is genuine. Although its inclusion in the volume of *Select Trials* means that some sort of end has been reached, the trials' outcomes are frequently negative—as when the accused is found not guilty and the question of who committed the crime or, in some cases, whether a crime was committed at all remains unanswered.

Moreover, the brutal, journalistic dispassion of this opening, its simultaneous concreteness and obscurity, bring the reader into contact with an event, a physical object, to which no meaning seems immanent. Unlike the afflicted bodies in providential fictions—saturated, almost articulate, with meanings—the head on the dock is a blank. The world of the news report is full of information but fragmented; if things are to signify, meanings must be *attached* to them. The paragraphs that follow the discovery are devoted to a closely rendered history of the steps by which evidence in the case was solicited and assembled—the head put on display in different settings and eventually identified, a search made for missing survivors, testimony collected from neighbors—and in this way the trial's author retraces the halting, uncertain, discontinuous process by which truth is produced through narrative reconstructions. That truth is never given and never certain; the news is a carrier of mysteries.[13]

. . .

The characteristic forms of execution literature can be viewed as a species, a special kind, of journalistic report. Written for a particular and unrepeatable occasion, "last dying speeches" and Ordinary's *Accounts* had to be printed and sold quickly; their commercial value, like their moral efficacy, was directly tied to their recentness. The ideal was a perfect, and literally impossible, contemporaneity: the sale of printed broadsheets of the criminal's dying words at the site (and moment) of execution itself.[14] Yet in certain respects the literature of the gallows was quite unlike journalistic accounts of crimes. Its main concern was exhortation, not reportage, especially through the end of the seventeenth century. In most of the early examples there is very little description of the actual crimes or their circumstances or causes, and in fact the crime for which the malefactor is to be punished is often presented summarily as just an instance or symptom of a more general pattern of immorality. Further, although they originated in recent events, these confessional and exemplary histories were by their nature retrospective. A sense of closure is crucial to the process by which a criminal's life can yield up its meanings, can be judged, read for signs.

The practice of criminal execution, which the governors of eighteenth-century England inherited as the monitory cornerstone of its Bloody Code, and which they continuously extended to cover more and more types of crime, was structured as a ritual of terror, an enactment of sovereign power. As public drama, its success hinged on its staging of a solemn and implacable violence. Certain stock images and dramatic gestures recur in the descriptive accounts: the prisoner's chains struck off in the Newgate press yard to the tolling of St. Sepulchre's bell; the carts in which the condemned rode, resting against their own coffins and in the company of hangman and priest; bodies of constables and soldiers circling them, opening a path through the crowd. The procession would pause at the church wall for the bellman's exhortation, ending with three repetitions of a plea for God's mercy; for over two hours they would then make their way through the most populous quarters of London, to display the misery of the transgressor and the law's majesty. A dove might be released to signal the arrival at Tyburn; the Ordinary (chaplain of Newgate prison) would speak a sermon, a warning, a blessing; the prisoner's face would be covered with a white handkerchief as a sign to the hangman to roll away the cart from under the victim's feet. Before the technological innovations of the nineteenth century, death came wrenchingly, convulsively, by asphyxiation.[15]

Yet there was more to the ritual than the inscription of state power in the display and rending of the criminal's body. For the criminal also spoke, and his (or, less often but to contemporaries more disquietingly, her) performance of the text of this final scene was a crucial element of the tragic action. These last dying speeches were a central literary-dramatic genre of the seventeenth and early eighteenth centuries. Formulaic and stereotyped, they marked what Mervyn James has called "the internalization of obedience"[16] and were thus, for a society whose police and physical means of enforcing order were comparatively weak, a crucial source of ideological control. In J. A. Sharpe's words, "When felons stood on the gallows and confessed their guilt not only for the offence for which they suffered death, but for a whole catalogue of wrongdoing, and expressed their true repentance for the same, they were helping to assert the legitimacy of the power which had brought them to their sad end."[17] This experience of conversion and acceptance was crucial to the success of the piece. In their penitential speeches the condemned were meant to display the values—of deference and submission—sanctioned by authority. Terror dramatized the malefactor's moral recognition of legal power as legitimate justice.

Or such at least was the hope. One account of the execution of Edmund Allen— "Who was Condemned at the *Sessions-House* in the *Old Baily*, for Abusing his Loving and Tender Wife, by Cruelly Beating her several Times with a *Bull's* Pizzle; and, last of all, most Barbarously and Inhumanely Poysoning of her, by giving her *White Mercury*, which he unhappily mixt with *Rasberry Gelly*"—describes his last moments in the conventionally acceptable terms. "After he was Tyed up in the Cart," the author writes, "he greatly bewailed his former mispent Life; desiring others to be warned, by his unhappy end: He Prayed, and was Prayed with; and according to all outward Appearance, made a very Penitent End; tho' he had lived a Wicked Life."[18] The ending casts a transforming retrospective light over the whole course of his previous life and, by an act of penitential reinscription, gives it a radically new and usefully exemplary meaning. Even the phrase *according to all outward Appearance*, which in a discourse attuned to the disparities between outward and inward truth would be almost inescapably ironic, serves here rather as an affirmation of the spectacular *visibility*, and thus legibility, of the criminal's repentance and warning.

Translations from oral to print versions of the dying speech, however, sometimes blurred the moral. The closeness of observation made possible by the representational resources of print—its immediacy, quickness, attention to the shifting

surfaces of things—encouraged a fullness of scrutiny that could hardly avoid detecting signs of hesitation, hardness, and fear in persons about to be killed. Samuel
Smith, Ordinary of Newgate from 1676 to 1698, reports a number of conversations
from his daily visits to this same Edmund Allen in Newgate, concerning his efforts
to get the convicted murderer to confess. Allen is willing to act the penitent, to
lament the wickedness of his actions, to submit to the force of the laws—but not
to confess this murder: "Urge me no more; do not put me into a Fret, tempt me
not to tell a Lye, but leave me to my self, I will neither confess it, nor deny it. So
that we must leave him [Smith comments] to the Justice of the Omniscient, pity-
ing him in his obstinate Humour and Impenitency."[19] The more detailed a rendering the Ordinary requires—and he was notorious for requiring an even fuller
accounting than the judges who passed sentence of death[20]—the less it accords
with the simple outlines of a popular narrative of fall and redemption. Ambiva-
lences and conflicts emerge: the need to distinguish between real and falsely alleged
crimes, distrust of the Ordinary's motives, terror of dying. The anonymous *Full and
True Account* of Edmund Allen's execution, with its emblematic image of the criminal praying in his cart, presents Allen's death as, in Sharpe's words, "an awful warning,"[21] a plain and morally useful example. Samuel Smith, by contrast, probes more
insistently the inward condition of those he watches over and, in his concern to
trace the precise contours of the criminal's soul, often writes histories less edifying
than unsettling.

What is the effect, for example, of a story like that of Thomas Randal, accused
of murdering "the Quaker," as reported in the Ordinary's *Account* for January 29,
1695/6? Like all the other *Accounts* published by Smith, this follows a conventional
three-part pattern.[22] Smith begins with the text of the sermon he has delivered to
the prisoners awaiting execution. Such sermons usually make up about half the
*Account,* and, unlike the sometimes desultory sketches of the convicts' behavior or
the odd glimpses we are given of the trial and execution, the sermons are recorded
in full, as if they constituted the broadsheet's real center of interest. On this occasion the subject is God's wrath, the text taken from Psalms 90, verse 11: "Who
knows the power of thy Anger?" As preached to the condemned, the sermon aims
to show that they should "fear [God's] Holiness, rather than the penal effects of
Sin . . . Thus you will not be over fond to have your lives spared." Any resistance
to the court's verdict or the prescribed rituals of punishment and expiation is a sign
of rebellion against God's sovereignty and that of his sanctioned authorities in the
City of London.

The second part of the *Account* takes up the crimes of which the prisoners have been found guilty, condensing testimony from the trial and drawing on the Ordinary's interrogations. Here the behavior of the condemned is recorded, the degree of their repentance gauged and (almost always) found wanting. The period of imprisonment is structured as an agon, a struggle between the absolute moral demands of the Ordinary and the prisoners' denials, as in this scene in the struggle between Smith and Thomas Randal:

On *Wednesday* in the Afternoon, I took him aside, and for a considerable time endeavour'd to perswade him, no longer Atheistically to deny the Crime; but he stood out in the denial of it, whereupon I read to him, what was sworn against him at his Tryal, and that the Jury was fully convinced in their Consciences that he was guilty, which they declared, when they gave their Verdict. He reply'd, *That he did not matter that, being clear in his own Conscience.* Then I told him, that he obstructed any Rational Hopes of his Salvation, and that all Persons who read the Book of Tryals, whom I met with, believ'd him to be guilty.

Following Randal's denial of the murder of the Quaker, Smith tells him an anecdote (one he also tells the convicted wife-poisoner Edmund Allen) of another convicted murderer who, after wishing to "be damned thrice successively, if he knew any thing how [his wife] came by her death"—Smith having in his turn "pray'd thrice, that God would perswade him to declare the Truth"—finally relents and admits to the murder before the crowd at Tyburn. The anecdote is pointed but ineffectual: neither Allen nor Randal relents.

This unsatisfying standoff carries over into the third part of the *Account,* a report of the events of execution day. Randal is not taken to Tyburn; instead, the cart carries him past "the Deceased's Door at *White-Chappel,* and from thence to the Place of his Execution at *Stone-bridge* by *Kingsland,* where he is to hang in Irons, on a Gibbet, till his Body be consumed." Smith nowhere explains this deviation from the custom of hanging at Tyburn or the reasons for the court's decision to hang Randal in chains; the omission, I think, reveals a presumption that the case was already familiar from trial or other news reports, so that Smith need only make the barest reference to the testimony of witnesses against Randal for the dramatic situation at the scaffold to be intelligible. Once there Smith writes, "[Randal] did confess that he was at the *Marshalsea* with *Lock* and *Green,* but denied that he never spoke any such Words, that he did kill the *Quaker:* He acknowledged that he did say to the Serjeant when he was Taken, that he was a Dead Man, and that he had been a very wicked Sinner, and had been guilty of all manner of Sins in general; (except that of Murder)." Despite the urgings of "the Worthy Sheriffs" and of the Ordinary himself to confess, Randal keeps to his earlier word, "his Heart being so hardened, he would not discover any thing of the Murder; nor any of the Persons that was with him at that time; but hoped that he had done his work with God-Almighty." Smith presses him one last time to bow to the court's verdict, "but it did avail nothing with him, he still persisting in the same, till the Cart Drew away; He was turned off. *This is all the Account I can give of this Sessions.*" The starkness of the ending leaves exposed Randal's unwillingness to give his story the meaning Smith wants it to bear.

Randal does go partway toward carrying out his role in the spectacle of punishment: he makes that "more general account of past sinfulness and delinquency" which was an essential part of the last dying speech.[23] From Smith's account, in fact, Randal seems to be one of what Sharpe calls "the handful of cases in which condemned criminals professed themselves innocent to the last of the crime for which they had been condemned, but were apparently happy enough to accept their fate as the just deserts of more general wickedness."[24] But, then, Edmund Allen must also be one of this handful; and John Moore, executed on July 12, 1695, for high treason (counterfeiting two coins); and Valentine Knight, executed March 2, 1691/2, for murder; and Richard Buttler, executed July 29, 1695 (after two reprieves), for housebreaking; and the others cited in Sharpe's article—indeed such cases, far from a handful, seem to crop up in almost every *Account* during Smith's tenure and are a particular source of vexation to him. Rather than furnishing, as Sharpe argues, an "impressively successful" demonstration of the power of law and religion to "[bring] people to a true sense of penitence and contrition, and to an acceptance of their fate,"[25] these numerous instances of resistance within submission constitute an embarrassment and a scandal. In one of the passages quoted earlier Smith tells Randal that "all Persons who read the Book of Tryals, whom I met with, believ'd him to be guilty," but in the absence of a confession doubts still play at the margins of belief.[26] Randal's resistance to the Ordinary's pressure clouds the improving spectacle with uncertainty.

Last dying speeches were often published independently of the Ordinary's *Account*—indeed, there were sometimes numerous competing versions of the presumed malefactor's life in circulation—and in these, too, the meanings the execution was meant to convey could be garbled or undermined. Sharpe contends that "the role of penitent might well have been the only one allotted to the condemned by the authorities or the pamphleteer. Defiance at the gallows was unlikely to be permitted and even less likely to be reported,"[27] yet the actual picture that emerges from much of the broadside and pamphlet literature is, to my mind, much more contested. In 1690, for example, Langley Curtiss published *An Account of the Behaviour, Confession, and last Dying Speeche of Sir John Johnson.* Written in what purports to be Johnson's voice as he speaks from the cart to the crowd gathered around him, the text repeatedly and flagrantly contradicts its own protestations of deference to the law. Found guilty as an accessory to the kidnaping of a young woman for a secret forced marriage to a Captain James Campbel, Johnson in his speech claims that he never knew the woman's true identity (she was, it seems, already married under another name) and that in everything he witnessed she appeared to act "with all the freedom that a Woman cou'd, or is possible to be exprest . . . indeed I saw nothing in her Deportment but was frank and free; but for the inward Thoughts of her Heart, what they were I could not tell."[28] He presents himself as a dupe both of the woman and of the men who enlisted him as a witness to the wedding. "I saw nothing," he declares, "but what I thought was justifiable by the Laws of this Kingdom, yet it hath pleased the Laws of this Kingdom to find me Guilty."

There is in this last sentence a mingled bitterness, irony, and protest that would be less obvious were it not for Johnson's continual reversions to the same theme. "I was a stranger to the Laws of *England*," he says, explaining that "I never was bred at Court, neither have I been a Scholar, but a Souldier": only the privileged, his remarks imply, the authors of the law, are learned enough to be safe from it. After he has told his version of the events that led to his arrest, he shifts to describe "the Hardships that I have met with since my Imprisonment; tho' by the way," he adds unconvincingly, "I do not at all reflect upon the good Constitutions of the Laws of this Land, nor upon the King, Judges, nor Jury, but only to some Passages that occurr'd upon my Tryal." Yet these "Passages" are a deadly inventory of obstructions and injustice: witnesses on his behalf arrested upon entering the court, so that their testimony is barred; guilty witnesses against him searched out in exchange for immunity; his own evidence disregarded because of his Scottish origins ("why should a Man meet with that Hardship because he is a Stranger, or an Outlandish-man; and I can't call myself an Outlandish-man, because I am the King's Subject"). Johnson's rights as a subject, he insists, have been violated by the arbitrariness of the judges and the arcana of the law.

As the recent work of legal historians shows, before the introduction of coun-

sel for the defense in the later eighteenth century, the defendant in felony charges
was at the mercy of the court's manipulations of procedure and its constructions
of evidence.[29] Whether in Johnson's specific case the court's rulings were prejudicial, however, matters less to the argument I am making than that he could be reported as saying so from under the gallows. The speech recorded in this *Account*
cannot plausibly be taken for an endorsement of the institutions of political hegemony. If, as Sharpe writes, "the civil and religious authorities designed the execution spectacle to articulate a particular set of values, inculcate a certain behavioural
model and bolster a social order perceived as threatened,"[30] the condemned brought
their own claims and habits of resistance with them to the scaffold, and these claims
found a resonance with at least some sectors of their audience.[31]

In part this was an effect of sympathy. The pamphlet's author writes of Johnson that "in all his whole Deportment from the Prison thither, and in the time of
being there, he behaved himself with great Humility towards God, and very exemplary towards all; which drew great Lamentations, and caused much Concerned-
ness to appear in the Physiognomies of all that beheld him." Such sympathy was
perceived by many of the reformers of the eighteenth century as a principal cause
of the disorders around the procession to Tyburn.[32] But, as Linebaugh, Foucault,
and others have argued, pity and admiration for the individual prisoner often res-
onated with a shared sense of grievance and protest which had much wider and
more threatening implications. Thus, when Johnson circles back a third time to
the theme of the law—"I desire that you would consider of all the Trials that I have
met with, not that I do (as I told you before) find any fault, or any ways arraign the
Constitution of the Laws, or the Justice of the Nation, no, I would not do that by
any means"—his sarcastically overemphatic disavowal of any critical stance, following directly his ticking off of the injustices he has met with, marks his last dying
speech as, precisely, a critique, a politically resistant reading of the narrative of his
own trial and execution. As Sharpe writes, "the ceremonies at public executions,
and, we may add, the popular literature which discussed these ceremonies so avidly,
constituted an important point of contact between official ideas on law and order
and the culture of the masses."[33] But contact, rather than providing the site for a
downward, uncontested diffusion of hegemonic values, also meant struggle.

Johnson's speech shows that this struggle carried over into the domain of printed
representations. In a reference to earlier published versions of his life—which, to
judge from the evidence of the *Account*, libelously accused him of a rape and a rob-

bery committed abroad—he says, "Sirs, in the printed Papers they have wronged me, and have done me a great deal of injury in them." The grounds of Johnson's efforts to gain control over the publication of his own life are clearly personal rather than ideological, yet his pained comments reflect the wider contexts within which this officious but often renegade literature operated. Published lives were coming to be recognized as part of a whole criminal *system,* complicitous with the work of judges and courts both in determining guilt and in defining the nature and extent of criminality but often upending the verdicts and pretensions of the governing orders. The circulation of numerous conflicting texts made for a perplexing and dissonant narrative—or, rather, an uncontrolled dispersal of narratives, each with its own warning, burden, or drift. Clarity of meaning dissolved in a welter of competing commercial and political interests.

In such a climate Swift could publish a fraudulent dying speech in the voice of the Irish horse thief Ebenezor Elliston (1722)—aggressively and very obviously laying bare the genre's hackneyed devices and pieties—and yet have the work taken as genuine.[34] More often, as the examples here have shown, access to print allowed the condemned to publish their own claims, to contest the judgments of courts and other printed accounts, and thus to reclaim some part of themselves from the alienating and distorting spectacle of the law. Unlike such forms of journalism as reports of crimes lately discovered, the literature of execution is connected from the beginning with the rituals and desires of the dominant culture; that is, its meanings are bound up, whether complicitly or oppositionally, with official mechanisms and strategies of social control. But the physical presence of the condemned and, even more powerfully, the prisoner's voice opened the public ritual to the articulation of individual difference. A sense of the self's inviolability might be asserted through a denial, a silence, a gesture of hands, and the condemned knew that the memory of their gesture would be carried in printed texts. Johnson's *Account* ends not with his voice but with a haunting and rather beautiful image, upon which, I think, the reader is tacitly invited to reflect and which seems to be offered as a sign of the disparity between truth and the verdicts of the law: "After he had given the Signal, the Cart drew away, the Prisoner praying to God, and holding up his hands some small time after the Cart was gone away." The inward self is manifest in the visible and in the endlessly reproducible text.

# CHAPTER FOUR

# Criminal Trials

## *Testimony and Narrative Realism*

When Christian and Faithful, in John Bunyan's *Pilgrim's Progress* (1678), are ar-rested for causing a hubbub during their passage through Vanity-Fair, they are straightaway examined, put into a cage as "a Spectacle to all the men of the *fair*," beaten, and led "in Chaines up and down the *fair*, for an example and a terror to others."[1] None of these summary forms of justice sufficing to quiet the civic dis-turbance their presence has aroused, the two pilgrims are, in the end, brought to trial. Arraigned before the presiding judge, Lord Hategood, they are read the indictment against them and allowed to plead—not guilty—to the charge. Three witnesses testify for the king against the prisoners: first Envy, who volunteers, "rather then any thing shall be wanting that will dispatch" the accused, to "enlarge" his testimony as needed (94); next Superstition; and finally Pickthank, who reports that he has heard Faithful speak in leveling contempt of the nobility and gentry. To these testimonies Faithful is permitted to respond in his own defense, but the judge is disposed against him and in his instructions to the jury says that "for the Treason he hath confessed, he deserveth to die the death" (96). The jury retires and, unsurprisingly, brings Faithful in guilty: "Condemned, To be had from the place where he was, to the place from whence he came, and there to be put to the most cruel death that could be invented" (97). As Faithful's executioners carry out the court's will, Christian is remanded to prison to await his own sentencing.

Compounded of allegory, tract, and martyr tale, the episode nevertheless de-pends for its satirical effectiveness on an almost documentary realism of presenta-tion.[2] Each of the events in Bunyan's narrative has its origin and analogue in the real juridical practice of the later seventeenth century in England, and the passage registers, in however symbolic a key, Bunyan's firsthand experience of trial and legal repression. Everything from the ritualized verbal formulas of the indictment and sentence to the witnesses' emphasis on their long acquaintance with the accused, from the judge's vitriolic summation to the jurors' hasty and ill-tempered deliberations, parodically mirrors the customary features of the late-seventeenth-century English courtroom, as described by such legal historians as John Langbein and J. M. Beattie.[3] As Bunyan has rendered it, the miscarriage of justice at Faithful's trial is not a spiritual crisis disseevered from history but is rooted in the specific ideological conflicts and legal struggles in which he and his followers had been caught up since 1660. If he finds, underlying those conflicts, a universal pattern, the representational force of the scene nevertheless derives from its satirical deployment of circumstantial, and thus contingent, evidence to sustain a political critique of a regime whose courtrooms and jails—the very structures of juridical violence the trial scene of *The Pilgrim's Progress* lays bare—had for years been used to silence the dangerous expression of dissent.

Like the last dying speeches the condemned were urged to deliver from the scaffold, criminal trial reports grew directly out of the institutions and rituals of legality. Printed trials reassembled the materials of legal inquiry and judgment into narrative demonstrations of the law's power to locate truth and repair the effects of transgression. Yet, as the courtroom scene from *The Pilgrim's Progress* shows, the judicial reconstruction of truth is not disinterested: the trial, like the crime it seeks to comprehend, takes place in a world riven by social antagonisms and ideological conflict, and the law has a partisan stake in such struggles. Further, the criminal trial and the narratives that derive from it undertook to reconstruct truth, to produce knowledge, at a time when the culture's epistemological confidence had been shaken by skepticism.[4] As a forum for determining the innocence or guilt of an individual accused of crime while affirming the majesty, justice, and mercy of the law itself, the trial was constituted by the tension between an impulse to reinscribe the singular case within a ready-made framework of sin and retribution and a will to discover the truth through empirical methods, chiefly the accumulation and weighing of circumstantial evidence.[5]

Trial proceedings had been published since at least the early seventeenth century, as interest in especially lurid or notorious cases seemed to warrant. It was not until the years around 1675, however, that these began to appear with something like serial regularity and to aim at a greater inclusiveness.[6] The crucial site for this development was the Old Bailey Sessions House in the City of London, where serious criminal cases were tried at sessions held eight times yearly. The first printer who recognized the commercial possibilities of regularly issued sessions papers—pamphlets or broadsheets printed after each session of the court, which aimed to report every case heard—was David Mallet, whose early casting about for a usable form helps to clarify the trial's divergences from, and residual traces of, other criminal genres. Michael Harris has written that Mallet's first penny broadsheets "contained only the briefest abstract of selected cases and still had about them the flavour of the traditional forms. The author at the end of one, for example, 'provided the outcome of the trials in ballad form.'"[7] At the same time, such titles as *The Truest News from Tyburn* and *News from the Sessions House in the Old Bailey* describe an affiliation with the emerging practice of journalism and its attention to the unfolding of the present, the pressing novelty and factuality of the world.[8]

In the wake of Mallet's initial success he and others began tinkering with the trials' form and with the possibilities of criminal inquiry they opened. By 1678 the new pamphlets were already successful enough that city authorities asserted the right to regulate and license their publication, and by the mid-1680s not only had their form become more or less stable, but the enterprise had become an officially protected monopoly, negotiated between would-be printers and the lord mayor.

With such sanctions came an evident pressure to make published trials reflect more closely the actual workings of the law, as a way of disseminating a newly dominant ideology of legality.[9] Balladry and obvious scandal- and gore-hawking began to disappear from the sessions papers, and changes in physical format over the next fifty years reflected a gradual consolidation both of the genre and of the legal culture it affirmed. Harris describes the formal development of the trial report as physical evidence of "the uneasy balance between commercial and official interests . . . the tension between the law and commerce."[10] Yet the changes in form suggest equally a *convergence* between the interests of entrepreneurial booksellers and the purveyors of the majesty and authority of the law. The change after 1712 from a broadsheet to an eight-page pamphlet, for instance, was made partly in response to the introduction of a tax on newspapers by a law that left open a loophole for pamphlets—and was thus a maneuver by publishers to keep costs down—but this dovetailed with the legal community's desire to report trials more fully and to make certain that all cases were at least summarily noted.

The most significant product of the convergence between legal and commercial interests was the gradual change from summary to verbatim reports of testimony and questioning in regular criminal trials.[11] Most of the State Trials published in the seventeenth century had already been printed verbatim, but they were, as Langbein writes, "show trials, closer in function to political pageants than to routine adjudication,"[12] and it was precisely their anomaly and eminence that made them the object of such rapt attention. Since they were concerned primarily with charges of treason, State Trials were often the focus of broader political struggles, and questions of legal procedure could raise more far-reaching issues of the rights of the subject against the power of the state. In 1649, for example, John Lilburne, political agitator and pamphleteer, was charged with treason for having published texts advocating the violent overthrow of the commonwealth and a more democratic constitution than Parliament was ready to adopt. What made his trial compelling, apart from the partisan conflicts it embodied, was Lilburne's open contestation of the juridical procedure itself. Called to the bar by a special commission (that is, the trial was not heard as part of a regular sessions), he spends most of the first day of an extraordinarily long trial—running to three days and 168 closely printed pages in an era when trials of longer than a single day were extremely rare—disputing the court's right to have been convened at all.[13]

Even with that question settled against him, Lilburne resists his judges at every stage of the trial's progress, as when he is asked how he will plead to the indictment:

LILBURN. Give me leave to speak, and I shall not speak 6 lines (which with
     much struggling being granted, Mr. *Lilburn* went on and said to this
     effect.)
     Then Sir, thus, By the laws of *England* I am not to answer to questions
     against, or concerning my selfe.
LORD KEBLE. *You shall not be compeld.*
ANOTHER JUDG. *Mr. Lilburn, is this to answer against your selfe, to say you are
     not guilty, by the lawes of the Land you are to plead to your charge, and it is no
     accusing of your self to say guilty, or not guilty.*
LILB. Sir, by your favour.———
JUDG. KEBLE. *To answer that you are not guilty, is no great matter . . . The law is
     plain, that you are positively to answer, guilty or not guilty, which you please.*
LILB. Sir, By the Petition of Right, I am not to answer to any Questions con-
     cerning my selfe; therefore I humbly entreat you to afford me the priv-

iledges of the laws of *England,* and I will return a positive answer to it, if
you will but please to allow me Counsell, that I may consult with them, for
I am ignorant of the formalities of law in the practick part of it. (26–27)

And so it unfolds, Lilburne in his obduracy compelling an anatomy of the institutions and rituals of criminal justice. It was because of this extraordinary resistance
to the legal machinery that Lilburne's trial became an important source for such
works as Stephen's 1883 *History of the Criminal Law of England* and a rallying point
for more widespread currents of political opposition and discontent during its own
period. Lilburne's contestations had contradictory aims: they seem intended both
to demystify the law and to assert the claims of the subject to the law's protection.
His challenges to the court are thus open to conflicting readings, alternately undermining and endorsing a modern ideology of the legal subject—a complex of
attitudes and ideas whose effect was to naturalize the contentious relationship
between the politically constructed individual and a community defined by its institutions of law.

The trial ends with extended and passionate denunciations of Lilburne by two
of the justices, both for his alleged treason and for his subversion of the authority
by which he is to be judged; despite his appeals to "the laws of *England,*" his resistance testifies to his belief in the illegitimacy of its representatives. The judges' instructions to the jury are coercive, motivated by a combination of personal animus
and fear of the threat the accused poses to the stability of the social order. Yet,
when the jury nevertheless bring in a unanimous verdict of not guilty, they are far
from wishing to undermine the power of the state: instead, their acquittal affirms
the symbolic basis of its legitimacy, its grounding of both individual rights and
political authority in a contractarian system of laws. Certain structural features of
the English jury trial—the division of judicial powers between the presiding judge
and the panel of jurors, the adversarial presentation of testimony, above all the
exposed, spectacular nature of the proceedings, which the publication of trial reports only increased—worked against the formation of a monologic discourse of
criminality and law in English culture. The jurors' defiance of the judges in the
Lilburne case exemplified the provisional, politically conflicted character of the
truth to which the evidence produced under trial could lead.

If Lilburne's trial was long cited for its legal and political meanings, these are
bound up with its representational means. Wordy disputes over the consequences

of pleading to an indictment or the causes for which counsel might be employed were not liable to draw a vast audience, and clearly State Trials were aimed at a different readership than the stark and lurid accounts printed on broadsheets and in chapbooks. But, by publishing all that was said in the courtrooms verbatim, booksellers not only provided the kind of "procedural and doctrinal detail that would have interested lawyers";[14] they also experimented with techniques for the presentation of complex, circumstantially dense narratives. Rather than offer a reconstructed history in chronological order, a summary of the court's final determination of the truth of the case, the publishers of State Trials concentrated on the contentious, discontinuous process of inquiry, forcing the reader to work through the fragmentary, often contradictory evidence in all its multiplicity of voices. The trial takes the form of an agon, a struggle among contending speakers for narrative authority.

This struggle was especially stark in the seventeenth century, as those on trial for their lives had no right to counsel and thus had to conduct all their defense in their own voice—to articulate a persuasive account of their actions, cross-examine the witnesses against them, and challenge the presumption of guilt. The defendant was allowed to call witnesses but had none of the resources of the state for doing so.[15] The accused stood essentially alone at the bar and spoke in a single voice against those ranged on the side of the Crown. The potential for confrontation, revealing the manifest disparities of power, was considerable and was most easily captured in print through the use of a dialogue or play format, as in the excerpts from the Lilburne case. Yet, despite its theatrical qualities, the trial, even when transcribed as dialogue without authorial commentary, is not primarily a dramatic form. While specific passages in a published trial may be configured on the page as drama, testimony is preeminently a kind of narrative, and the project of the criminal trial as an institution is itself narrative: to stitch together a history that explains the signs of transgression.

It was some decades before the standard run of trial reports from the Old Bailey aimed at this degree of narrative and textural thickness. Writing up the 1679 trial of Peter du Val and Thomas Thompson for murder, for example, the reporter made no effort to imitate the form of the trial itself or even to say what evidence was heard or how the sequence of events was reconstructed. The publishers were evidently reaching for an audience they expected would take little pleasure in retracing the tedious process by which testimony was gathered and submitted to proof.[16] What Langbein calls "the bleaching out of legal detail" reflects the publishers' sense of their audience,[17] as does the disproportionate space given to crimes of violence, with their disquieting aura of perversity, threat, and horror.

The case of du Val and Thompson shows the early form of the periodically published criminal trial at its fullest narrative stretch:

the first remarkable Tryal was of *Peter Duval,* formerly keeping a Tobacco and Strong-water-shop neer St. *Giles's in the Fields,* and *Tompson* a Taylor his Companion; who having left, or rather out-run their Trades, were lately turn'd Bullies: and having, according to the fashion of such people, associated themselves with two Baggages of the other sex, going to take a walk, as they pretended, to *Marybone,* about ten or eleven a Clock in the Evening happened in *So-hoe-*fields to come up to a parcel of honest poor men, who after their labour were refreshing themselves with a pot of Drink, and innocently sitting together at the door of an Ale-house: when they came near, *Duval* took upon him to examine them, asking *Who was there?* to which being answered, *Honest men,* he persisted to enquire if they *were the Watch;* and they saying they were not, he replied, then *you are Rogues:* Upon which one *Jenkins,* somewhat scurrilously, return'd a foolish ill-bred Phrase, *Mine Ar—— upon you.* This so heated *Duval,* that he began to swear he had a mind to cut them all to pieces, and that they deserved it for affronting of *Gentlemen;* and to make good his words, drew his Sword, but by the mediation of one of the Company, a lame man, who happened to know him, he put it up again, and delivered it to the woman he led, and went away some small distance; but swearing terribly all the while, and presently in a fury return'd, offering to fight with any of them; and while he was a quarrelling with them, *Tompson, Duval'*s Comrade, drew his Sword, and made at the other men; and the said *Jenkins* seeing him coming, and the lame man to be in danger, caught away his Crutch to keep off the Sword; but *Tompson* following his passes after *Jenkins,* who retreated, and by the unevenness of the ground fell down, he run him into the Belly, whereof he immediately died. So that they both being concern'd in the Quarrel, and *Duval* aiding and abetting the Murther, and no Weapon drawn or blow struck by the other Party, they were both found guilty of the Murther; and their two women who came in as Witnesses to excuse them, being persons of Ill fame, were Committed.[18]

The early trial narratives were rarely even this long and almost never gave any clearer idea of how the trial had actually unfolded. As Langbein has written of a similar case, "so much has been compressed and omitted that we cannot say with any precision what evidence was adduced at the trial, nor how and by whom."[19] It is impossible to know what Thompson and du Val might have given as their version of the fatal encounter, whether there were other witnesses than those caught up in the dispute, whose testimony was given most credit, or how the "lame man, who happened to know him," was connected to du Val.

Despite such silences, the report documents the application of a rough kind of narrative realism to a case that addressed the complex and shifting relationships among criminality, public discourse, and social class. Through the criminal trial and its print renderings the material circumstances, speech habits, and experience of the laboring (and nonlaboring) poor were recorded and conveyed to a more avowedly respectable public.[20] Du Val and Thompson are former small tradesmen turned small-time hoods; though out of work, they pretend to the higher station of gentlemen, using verbal and physical assault against poor workers as a tactic of social leverage. The trial's writer is attentive to details of costume, urban geography, and language: it is the "foolish ill-bred Phrase, *Mine Ar——— upon you*," with its implicit mockery of du Val's gentlemanly pretensions, which triggers the actual violence; the night walk's itinerary is drawn in maplike detail; the fact that du Val and Thompson carry swords places them somewhere in the shadowy area between artificial gentlemen and real brigands. The actions leading up to the stabbing are registered in a series of short phrases whose shifts in focus and rhythmic accumulation elicit the sudden, clumsy unexpectedness of Jenkins's murder. The attention to what can only be called realistic detail in the report was most probably modeled in part on the similar descriptive strategies with which contemporary journalists were experimenting, but is also an index of the courts' increasing reliance on circumstantial evidence beginning in the later seventeenth century. Reliance on testimony unsupported by such evidence presumes the stability of what Raymond Williams called "knowable communities," within which the witness occupies a socially recognized place and has a known character, but, in the increasingly fragmented social environment of the late-seventeenth-century city, knowledge, or conviction, depended more and more on the plotting of material, verifiable coordinates.[21] Reproducing this judicial concern with circumstantial detail, trial reports made available to a large and socially diverse audience a form of narrative realism whose persuasive power and trueness to experience derived from its cataloguing of empirical particulars, which the trial in turn infused with a criminal glamour and dread.

The reporting of legal procedures was still perfunctory, but even these rough notations were beginning to bring the workings of the law to a broader and more dispersed public and to represent the sessions house as a principal site for the negotiation of cultural preoccupations and struggles. Even if the trial reports' ideological aim was largely to affirm the majesty, justice, and mercy of the law, the image they disseminated was never simply affirmative. At the same sessions, for example, Edward Swinney and Henry Harrison were tried for killing a bailiff's assistant, one of six men sent to arrest Harrison for a debt he owed to a tailor. After summarizing the conflicting testimony, the reporter concludes: "The Case seem'd to lye very hard on the Prisoners; the Writ and Warrant were proved; Five Bayliffs swore they did give *Harrison* the words of arrest; and if so, the Killing of *Jones* in execution thereof must needs be Murder. But whether the Jury did not think fit to credit them, so it was, they only found the Prisoners guilty of Man-slaughter; who praying their Clergy, were Burnt in the Hand. And because the Court highly resented their Crime, thought it too much extenuated, they Committed them both back again to *Newgate*, for Eleven Months, without Bail or Mainprize."[22] The explicit division between the court and the jurors is the more striking since throughout the period, as Langbein writes, "the judge exercised so much influence over the jury that it is difficult to characterize the jury as functioning autonomously . . . The jury alone rendered the verdict, but the judge had no hesitation about telling the jury how it ought to decide."[23]

The divergence in judgment between court and jurors in this case is left rather mysterious but was likely a reflection and symptom of other social divisions. Swinney and Harrison were on trial for killing an agent of the police—not the pervasive, disciplined, flexibly articulated police of the nineteenth and twentieth centuries but the much looser and more irregular forces of the seventeenth and eighteenth, who could be called up as a kind of rough posse by anyone able to pay them. How much the jury's feelings may have been swayed by a tradition of resentment against such forces is impossible to reckon—even the trial's author is perplexed—but the jury chose not to credit the testimony of five bailiffs, and their disregard points to a strong current of distrust. Conflicts over the definition of police powers and the rights of the subject against oppression thus figure, if only in a sometimes buried and inarticulate way, in the conduct of trials by jury and in the printed reports that first made them available to a broad public.[24]

If the early sessions papers from the Old Bailey only rarely followed the pattern of State Trials in imitating the verbal textures and narrative complexity of the trial process itself, they often foregrounded cultural antagonisms—conflicts over the role of the police, for example, or over the prerogatives of social rank or the law's encroachment on customary rights—which had no other narrative form of expression. And, because of the criminal law's disproportionate concern with the propertyless, trial reports describe the material conditions and everyday life of the urban poor especially, with a fullness of detail available in no other form of writing until Defoe fabricated the autobiographies of Colonel Jack and Moll Flanders in the 1720s.

On rare occasions a case was sensational enough to warrant verbatim publication even though it lacked the social profile of a State Trial. One such case was the 1702 *Tryal of Richard Hathaway, upon an Information for being a Cheat and Impostor, for endeavouring to take away the Life of Sarah Morduck, for being a Witch.* Both court and publisher brought an extraordinarily close attention to bear on this trial of a poor laborer, servant to a blacksmith, accused on behalf of an old woman, a waterman's wife. For reasons that are never made clear, Hathaway claimed that Sarah Morduck was bewitching him. He won the belief (unless they were already in cahoots) of his master's family and their neighbors in Southwark by acting out a variety of strange afflictions—pretending to be unable to take food for ten weeks, feigning blindness, appearing to vomit chains of strangely shaped pins—and he claimed his enchantment could only be ended by scratching Morduck deep enough to draw blood. He did so and behaved as if the enchantment were lifted, but in time it returned, and again Morduck was accused, hounded by a gang of Hathaway's friends.[25] Even after a skeptical doctor exposed the fraud by substituting the arm of another woman to be scratched in Morduck's stead, to the same disenchanting effect, Hathaway and his mob persisted in harassing Morduck, who was soon imprisoned and brought to trial as a witch. She was acquitted, but Hathaway's fits returned, and a crowd began to form in order to mete out its own justice. Finally, Sarah Morduck's life, and the social peace, seemed to the authorities to be in real danger, and Hathaway was arrested for malicious imposture. He was held at the house of a surgeon, whom the court ordered not only to care for the accused but to keep him under surveillance. The surgeon spied on his prisoner from a secret place, watched him eat and drink when he claimed to be fasting ("sometimes he drank so much that he was perfectly drunk," he notes [26]), and so had enough evidence of fraud to convict him.

The story as it comes out under testimony is so bizarre and unexplained that it may not seem to illuminate the more general characteristics of criminal trials at the beginning of the eighteenth century. Yet its very marginality is exemplary of the way in which trial narratives opened up the cultural field of representation, recounting the histories of those who would otherwise have remained beneath the

threshold of social visibility. Hathaway's trial applies the representational norms of
State Trials—the literal recording of apparently verbatim testimony and an exhaustive inventory of documentary evidence—to a case whose principal actors and
events could become, in Erich Auerbach's words, "the subjects of serious, problematic, and even tragic representation" only at the cost of being criminalized.[26]
Implicit in the decision to record and publish every word said in the hearing of the
court is an almost leveling claim and a commercial gamble: that the malice and
suffering of poor laborers and women might matter as much to the institutions of
law, and to readers hungry for narrative, as the crimes of the great.

Certainly, the legal machinery was singular, for the proceedings already display
the main innovations of the lawyer-driven trials that began to emerge in their modern form during the 1730s.[27] The case against Hathaway was presented by four prosecution counsel—each of whom gave an extended opening argument and questioned witnesses so as to draw out their testimony against the accused—at a time
when such lawyerly interventions were virtually unheard of. Still more unusually,
Hathaway was allowed to have counsel speak for him as well as call and examine
witnesses, a practice Langbein can only trace back to the mid-1730s in his study of
cases at the Old Bailey.[28] Defense counsel objects to much of the evidence against
Hathaway as hearsay—as he tells the jurors, it "is not such Evidence as you are to
take any notice of" (17)—though on Beattie's account the outlines of a hearsay rule
were only drawn in the second quarter of the century.[29] Expert witnesses were called
to testify to the medical issues the case raised: the consequences of prolonged fasting, outward signs of blindness, and the likelihood of Hathaway vomiting pins.
Both in its overall structure—its division into distinct cases for the prosecution and
defense—and in the particulars of its unfolding, the trial foreshadows the later history of the law as it adapts the procedures of State Trials to a much humbler and
stranger dispute.

Why so much legal innovation was admitted, so much trouble taken, over a case
whose social presence seems so marginal is a question that the original lawyers were
at pains to address but which still, centuries later, permits only speculative, unsettled answers. Local discontent with the verdict acquitting Morduck of witchcraft appeared, from the lawyers' statements, to be verging on vigilantism and mass
violence. Whether the popular animus against her was fueled by private enmities
or a genuine fear of sorcerous mischief, its effect was to isolate Morduck from the

community, to mark her as deviant, just as the state, with its very different procedures, marked Hathaway when it brought him to trial. The whole episode embodies the clash between two competing systems of justice and definitions of *deviance*,
and in their effort to construct a narrative of Hathaway's crimes the lawyers have
to negotiate divisive questions of orthodoxy and magic, skepticism and credulity,
legal and religious authority.[30] Through trial the state undertakes to enforce both
the social peace and its own claims to legitimacy, adjudicating among all the contending factions in order to effect a harmonious, and hegemonic, resolution of
motives.[31]

Yet, for all the forces brought to bear on the case, it remains naggingly unresolved in the published report. Hathaway's violent imposture is never explained,
nor does any testimony reveal the reasons for Morduck's status as a pariah. This
opacity or silence at the heart of the trial is its most disturbing—but also, I think,
most typical—trait, suggesting the endlessness as well as the limitations of the new
species of narrative realism. For there is no end to what could count as evidence in
any narrative whose project is to explain a complex series of actions and its causes
by circumstantial methods—as Sterne's *Tristram Shandy* parodically insisted in the
middle of the century. And yet certainty eludes even the most exhaustive accumu-
lations of material or verbal evidence, not only in law but in the natural sciences
and indeed in any narrative of human actions, which is the reason that the activity of recording would, apart from human weariness, be endless, whether in the
form of a legal transcript or a spiritual diary.[32] Despite (and because of) the extraordinary and sometimes numbing detail of the Hathaway *Tryal*, its authors are
finally unable to tell a coherent story. The court finds Hathaway guilty, but all the
meticulously assembled evidence, presented in the order it was introduced into trial,
is ultimately left to the published narrative's readers to sift through as best they can
if they wish to attach any meaning to the circumstances it so scrupulously records.

Cases like Hathaway's, anomalous on its appearance in 1702, prepared the ground
for the gradual enlargement of regular sessions papers to include longer and more
frequent passages of verbatim testimony. Such testimony was increasingly viewed
as a repository of legal practice and a vehicle of popular remembrance and pleasure. Reporters tried to reproduce the precise inflections and wording of witnesses,
often for ludicrous effects—such textual gimmicks as foreign accents and provin-
cial malapropisms—but sometimes in pursuit of a kind of psychological realism,

verbal disorder reflecting moral confusion. In a report of the 1724 trial of John
Alloway on charges of rape and robbery, for example, the following exchange occurs
between the judge and Alloway's accuser, Sarah Muns:

COURT. You must explain yourself. The Law requires it.

MUNS. He had the Car—Car—Carnal Use of my—my—Body.

COURT. Was it without your Consent?

MUNS. Yes—without my Consent—He did it by main Force—whether I would
or no—But not—not against my Will—I did not comply—thro' any
Fear—he forced me to it by great—great—Persuasions—as much as by
any Thing else.

COURT. Did he use no Threats?

MUNS. No, he never threaten'd me—

COURT. He did not?—And yet now, by the Manner in which you give your
Evidence, you seem very willing to pass for a young Woman of extraordinary Modesty.

MUNS. Indeed I can't say whether he had any Thing to—to—do with me or
no—He *mought,* or he *mought* not—But if he did—he never meddled with
me—so as to do me any Harm—for if he had, I should have cry'd out, but
I never made the least Noise in Life.

COURT. Did he take any Money from you?

MUNS. Yes—No—He did not take it from me—against my Will—I think I
gave it him freely—for he was welcome to any Thing I had about me.[33]

Muns's hesitation and struggle to find words were probably read as low comedy
when the *Select Trials* first appeared, but the effect of psychological realism would
always have been of primary importance, for the case at law turns on the assess-
ment of her state of mind at the time of the alleged crimes—on the question, that
is, of consent. The way her sentences turn back against their beginnings, her effort
to master the syllables of unfamiliar words, her unwillingness to finish expressions
against the grain of what she seems bound to reveal of her own perplexed and equivocal feelings, have value not only as traits, comical or poignant, of character but as
signs by which Alloway's innocence or guilt must be judged. (He was acquitted.)

    The more closely printed reports imitated the form of criminal trial, the more
their readers assumed the position of judges. As verbatim transcripts figured increasingly in trial reports, these began to serve as records of legal custom and prece-

dent.[34] And as the evidence came to readers in more inclusive and open-ended forms, presented as literal transcript or exhaustive summary of the facts produced under investigation—not smoothed into a reconstructed history but reported with all its contradictions and gaps in the order the court heard it—those readers needed to sort out conflicting accounts, weigh the speakers' credibility, and fashion a materially and psychologically cogent narrative from suspect and disfigured remains. When the editor of the 1734–35 *Select Trials* noted, concerning the trial of one Matthias Brinden for murder (1722), that "there having been published two Accounts of this Criminal's Life, which disagree with each other, in some Particulars, I shall make Extracts of all that is material in each, that the Reader may the better compare them, and judge which deserves the most Credit" (1:212), he was pointing to the most problematic feature not only of criminal trials but of realist narratives in general: their suspension of resolution or resistance to closure.

The peculiar endlessness of circumstantial realism to which I pointed earlier—its relentless amassing of facts that could count as evidence—endlessly opens the narrative to discordant meanings, contradictory plots. It is this formal resistance to closure which I see as the most *productive* legacy of the criminal trial to the fictions of Defoe and Fielding—and, through them, to what would become the canon of the novel over the later eighteenth and nineteenth centuries. My claim is not that later novelists made literal use of the narrative techniques pioneered by the authors of trial reports but, rather, that trials produced an ideologically resonant and commercially proven model of open-ended narrative construction, staging the conflict between the transgressive individual and a normative community which was also at the heart of the criminal biographies to which I now turn.

# CHAPTER FIVE

# Criminal Biographies
## The Singular and the Exemplary

In February 1685 Thomas Dangerfield was having servant problems. In his memorandum book he records, on February 10, that "*Mark* grew Sawcy, and instead of going to *Enfield* for shirts, he went to *London*." On Monday February 23: "My Dear, my Sister *Judith*, my Friend, and my self rode up to *London* in the Coach from *Enfield*, sending *Mark* up to *London* with the Horses"; two days later Dangerfield writes that "*Mark* having been absent from me from *Munday* Noon, untill then, and not having given me the least account where he was, or when he would return, I took *Robin* in his room." The new servant, however, proved worse than the old, for that Friday Dangerfield writes that "*Robin* let the *Irish* Horse get from him; which had like to have done me much Injury in respect to my bus'ness." On the next day he writes, "I knock'd off; being forc'd so to do by the Idleness of *Robin*," and in fact his accounts show a marked falling off from his usual receipts. Finally, on Tuesday, March 3, "*Mark* came to me laden with Submission; and in the Evening, having sent home the Irish Horse, and dismiss'd *Robin*," Dangerfield takes his old servant back, paying ten shillings to Mark's brother for the privilege.

In *Dangerfield's Memoires,* from which these scenes are drawn,[1] Thomas Dangerfield represents himself as the successful man of business trying to fit himself to the role and habits of a gentleman. He keeps scrupulous account of all his receipts and expenses, makes a note of his New Year's gifts to his servants and to Mr. Cureton the parson, and records his own visits to the surgeon and his horses' to the blacksmith. He drinks French wine and brandy, loses money (but in modest amounts) at hazard and tick-tack, and buys a volume of Lucretius from his friend Wesley at Exeter College, Oxford, for two shillings. There is little description of his business. On March 11, for example, he records receipts of twelve shillings from "a Strong-water man's Wife, at the end of *Sandy-Lane*" and from "a Farmer's Cry-ing Wife" and ten shillings from "a Shopkeeper at the end of *Rusthaw Lane*" and from "a Timorous Farmer" (34). But the exact nature of these transactions is left rather vague. No wonder: Dangerfield was a highwayman.

Dangerfield's *Memoires* are the record of a four-month criminal expedition through the countryside, villages, and towns of southeastern England. His concern for the health of his horses and the quality of their shoes points to his constant state of readiness to make quick getaways, and the *Memoires* record a number of alarms and pursuits, as in this entry from February 3, 1685:

I went from *Middleton* to divers Villages thereabouts, and about 12 a Clock we were over-taken at the End of a Narrow Lane by 7 Horse-men, one of them bid me Stand, and drew forth his Sword; But a fair Heath offering in its Prospect Better Terms, Call'd to me to Whip and Ride for it; and accordingly we did, and by much out-Rode all the Pursuers for the space of an hour Whip and Spur: By this time finding our Horses much Impaired, and perceiving no more than 4 of the 7 in sight that Chased us, we e'en resolved to Turn Back and give 'em Battel; which was accordingly done, and after a Smart dispute as ever I met with, which held about a quarter of an hour, My Self, My Horse, and *Mark,* being wounded, we having put all 4 of 'em to Flight, whipped forwards, afresh, and by the help of several favourable Turnings, we got well off to *Burton* upon *Trent,* 10 Miles from the place of dis-pute: From thence we rode to *Ashby* which is 10 Miles more, and there I was dressed by Mr. *Arme* the Chyrurgion, and Lay all Night. (21)

This is the longest stretch of narrative in the *Memoires,* and it recounts an excit-ing, if breathless, adventure; like the summaries of Dangerfield's business accounts, however, it leaves out crucial facts. Although the diary offers other glimpses of eva-sive maneuvers to avoid arrest, it is impossible to know if the seven horsemen are a posse comitatus or another gang of robbers, and really for Dangerfield it makes little difference. The forces of law, the hired agents of the state, are no different from rival gangs, enemies to keep an eye out for in the ordinary course of predation.

As the title page states, Dangerfield's *Memoires* are "Digested into Adventures, Receits, and Expences." Under the first of these headings he notes each day's trav-els, the comings and goings of his sister and friends, the names of the inns he fre-quents. Few of Dangerfield's "Adventures" are as action-packed as the one quoted here; more often he simply lists the various towns he passed through or notes that he spent the day idly, waiting for a tailor or other tradesman to keep his appoint-ment, or passing his time in company, drinking "very Plentifully of Sherry, untill we all got fox'd" (11). Under *Expences* he lists each day's charges at the inn, his cider-house bills, how much he paid the saddler or ferryman or gunsmith. The only real evidence of criminal activity is found in the list of each day's *Receits*, set down with a dull regularity that bleeds the "Adventures" of any suspense yet has its own drab and laconic allure. "Of Capt. S——," he writes, on a typical day, "10 s.":

| | |
|---|---|
| Of a Parson, | 6 s. 0 |
| Of a Farmer, | 6 s. 0 |
| Of an Ale-house, | 3 s. 0 |
| Of a Wheel-wright, | 6 s. 0 |
| Of a Gentleman, | 6 s. 0 |
| | 37 s. 0 (2) |

The encounters are never described. Once in a great while a detail flickers from the ledgers: *Of a Frank Gentleman, 20 s.*, he notes on March 10 and, on January 31, *Of a Young Powerfull Attorny, 12 s.;* heading the list for December 12 is the entry *Of a Farmer's Wife, So, So, 10s.* Perhaps the frank gentleman bantered with him, the young attorney looked threatening, the farmer's wife tried to put him off by flirting or turned away his advances, but there is no way of knowing, and such details only seem to be of passing interest even to Dangerfield. Occasionally, he records a demand not paid or a refusal—on December 13, for example, he writes, "I refus'd 3, 5 refus'd me," and on January 29 (under *Adventures*): "I went to divers Villages with good Success, meeting only with one *Rebuff,* and that in a Notorious manner from a Parson" (18). The clues are too thin for the scene to be recuperable.

Yet, cumulatively, a certain pattern and texture of life do emerge from these notations. Dangerfield moves restlessly; he pays attention to warnings but never goes into hiding; he seldom risks violence. It is clear (because he remarks that he has lost and had to replace them) that he carries pistols, and he must use them to compel his victims to pay, but he suffers as many as ten refusals in a day, and he rarely takes more than ten or twelve shillings, often much less.[2] He seems virtually immune to what one recent sociologist of delinquency has called the "seductions of crime."[3] Instead, he appears eager to cultivate the postures and accessories of leisure. The *Memoires* record Thomas Dangerfield's attempts to negotiate among the conflicting obligations and anxieties of the gentleman and the hunted criminal.

The *Memoires* were published while Dangerfield was in Newgate, awaiting trial on a charge of libel for one of his many conspiratorial pamphlets.[4] As the opening note "To the Reader" declares, "The Entire Life of This *Hero* is Reserv'd for a Better Pen, and Leisure: The Intent of These Papers being only to Pick up, and to Furnish Fresh Matter toward the Just History of his Adventures." Although in their apparently unconstructed authenticity they exemplify one aspect of the emerging genre of biography, the *Memoires* do not constitute, in any ordinary sense, a life of Dangerfield at all, lacking both the narrative form and the birth-to-death sweep characteristic of the genre. As their editor suggests, they provide, instead, a documentary source from which an "Entire Life" might be written.[5]

The project of biography is double: to create a sense of the whole of a subject's life through narrative and to evoke the singularity and distinctive material texture of that life. To the latter end the biographer accumulates details, registers the momentary experience or sensation, and tries to catch the unfolding of unrepeatable gestures and acts; to the former end he or she draws out the patterns that underlie disparate moments, seeks for origins, and traces the links of cause and effect in the constitution of the self. Because the first-person narrator can claim to express a more authentic inwardness as well as to narrate actions to which no second party was witness, autobiography assumes a certain privilege within the domain of written lives, however vitiated by the reader's suspicion of self-interest. Yet autobiography is haunted by the same doubleness (of subject and/against narrator) as is third-person biography and the same tension between the singular and the exemplary.[6]

Dangerfield's *Memoires* do not aim to reconstruct the whole shape of their author's life, but they render its habitual practices and day-to-day progress with unprecedented immediacy and detail. Perhaps it was the papers' apparently accidental discovery and publication that allowed for their candid delineation of Dangerfield's manipulation of roles—a more calculated or coherent text would have been much less *telling*. A narrative written for publication would likely have left out Dangerfield's problems with servants altogether or else fashioned them into a distinct episode, shaping the unexplained irruptions of *sawciness* and truancy into a fable of conflict between master and man while thinning out the context of daily errands and expenses, risky criminal outings, and the irregularity of wages. In the *Memoires* his servants' moments of rebellion and idleness come on Dangerfield unexpectedly, in the middle of other things, disturbing his performance of the roles of highwayman or householder with unwelcome noise. What makes the *Memoires* interesting as biography is the way in which the passing, sporadic pleasures and vexations of the everyday disrupt the formulaic narrative patterns of the highway-man's adventures or gentleman thief's memoirs.

No other criminal text of the period sets out so exhaustively the material con-ditions of the subject's life. In drawing attention to this side of the biographical project, I mean to diverge from the emphasis that Lincoln Faller and John Richetti have placed on the "mythic" significance of criminal biography.[7] Myth, for Richetti and Faller alike, is a tool for solving problems. In Richetti's argument "the crimi-nal, as a type figure, is a necessary social myth whose triumphs and abasements mirror the ideological tensions between the new secular world of action and free-dom and the old religious values of passivity and submission."[8] Faller parses the whole body of criminal biography into two myths: the life of the highwayman, designed to gloss over the scandal of frequent hangings by progressively dehu-manizing the criminal hero, and the story of domestic murder, in which the pas-sion-fired violation of the most intimate social bonds is repaired by the murderer's ultimate repentance and sacrifice. The function of both myths, he contends, is to limit "the damage that crime—particularly heinous crime—could do not only to people's sense of themselves and their God but to their sense of what it was that held (or might hold) society together."[9] Reading all criminal biographies as mythic narratives, Richetti and Faller accord "myth" a purely ideological function, and that function, as they configure it, is always the same: bolstering the institutions and the logic of authority.

Both critics locate the significance of criminal biographies in their containment of rebellious and disruptive energies, their affirmation of social stability. As Richetti argues: "Highwaymen and whores are heroes, in that their stories are gratifying fantasies of freedom—moral, economic, and erotic. But this freedom is necessar-ily desperate, for the social myth includes the fear that divine surveillance and mys-terious retribution are inescapable. The criminal's end, whether stressed in the nar-rative or not, provides a further gratification and completes the myth, as he suffers for the guilty power and independence which he and his readers have desired and enjoyed."[10] The problem with this formulation, as the phrase "whether stressed in the narrative or not" implicitly concedes, is that it posits a necessary shape and meaning to narratives that often perversely stray from or just ignore the foreor-dained outcomes of myth or authoritarian ideology. What stands out in a text like *Dangerfield's Memoires* is its engagement with irreducible and sometimes arbitrary particulars: unanticipated outbursts of physical violence, weapons and horseshoes that need fixing, chance encounters with strangers, shirts that have to be picked up, inclement weather. The entangling web of petty errands, worries about money, and undependable friends is the constant object of Dangerfield's textual account- ing: his life is just this accumulation of strands of things, becoming more and more complicated but not following any shapely course. The text only ends when he's caught and his notebook is taken from him.

I earlier quoted Richetti's claim that "the sensational particular, the violent events of the individual criminal's career, depend for their sensational value and effect upon the moral abstractions which they illustrate so vividly." Faller, similarly, argues that "crimes in crime-ridden societies are not automatically of interest . . . Dressed in the appropriate myth, however, the bludgeonings, stabbings, and poisonings of the popular literature of crime seem not to have palled but rather to have made occa- sion for special kinds of pleasure."[11] The moral directionlessness of Dangerfield's *Memoires,* however, and their thickness of detail suggest an alternative basis for their appeal to contemporary audiences. The idea that accounts of sensational crime gave pleasure to eighteenth-century readers only when taken for illustrations of "moral abstractions" or when "dressed in the appropriate myth" is belied by the long-running popularity of such morally unpretentious forms as the canting dic- tionary, picaresque tale, and sessions paper. The ideological burden of most crim- inal biographies is, as both Faller and Richetti demonstrate, to reaffirm the legiti- macy of legal authority, but that this constitutes their principal interest, even on the level of ideology, is questionable. The pleasure of such narratives does not derive from their endlessly reiterated endorsement of the prevailing social and political orders, for this is an obligatory gesture, but from their smuggling of vividly con- crete and sometimes problematic material into the traditional patterns and their consequent stirring up of the very subversive possibilities, the threats of disorder, they (presumably) set out to contain.

One of the traditional strains of criminal narrative was affiliated with the Ordi- nary's *Accounts* and was mainly taken up with a detailed recounting of "the crimi- nal's confession, contrition, repentance, and conversion."[12] Such pamphlet or broad- sheet histories, though they made certain gestures toward narrating the whole life, and especially the crimes, of the condemned, took place almost entirely inside the prison cell and under the gallows and often consisted largely of sermon and exhor- tation. Because of their common origins with the forms of execution literature, which had their own carefully prescribed (if not always observed) ritual functions, these lives tended to follow a similar redemptive pattern.

The story of Thomas Savage, for example, which went through at least twelve

editions between 1668 and 1679, was published under the title *A Murderer Punished;
and Pardoned.* Savage was a sixteen-year-old apprentice to a vintner near Lime-
house in the East End of London. As the pamphlet describes him, he was during
the two years of his apprenticeship "a meer Monster in sin: in all that time he never
once knew what it was to hear one whole Sermon; but used to go in at one door,
and out at the other . . . He spent the Sabbath commonly at the Ale-house, or
rather at a base house with that vile Strumpet *Hannah Blay,* which was the cause
of his ruine."[13] He brings her a bottle or two of wine now and then, but she wants
money and urges him to rob his master in secret. To his protest that he cannot do
it because the maid is always at home with him, "Hang her Jade saith this impudent slut, knock her brains out, and I will receive the money; this she many times
said." One Sunday she makes him drunk in the morning with burnt brandy; going
back to his master's house and waiting until the family has gone to church, Savage
then "commeth into the Room where his Fellow-servants were at Dinner: O saith
the Maid to him, Sirrah, you have been now at this Bawdy-House, you will never
leave till you are undone by them; He was much vexed at her; and while he was at
Dinner, the Devil entered so strong into him, that nothing would satisfie him but
he must kill her; and no other way, but with the Hammer" (4). When they are alone
in the kitchen, he beats her to death—"which done, he immediately taketh the
Hammer, and with it strikes at the Cupboard Door in his masters Chamber, which
being but slit-Deal presently flew open, and thence he taketh out a Bag of Money."
At first he feels nothing. He goes back to Hannah Blay and gives her half a crown
but then leaves her. Gradually, remorse comes over him and confusion. He gets as
far as Greenwich, where an innkeeper becomes suspicious of his bag of money, so
he leaves it with her and wanders along the river, seemingly indifferent to whether
he is caught. News of the murder comes to Greenwich, the innkeeper sends men
to find Savage, and he is taken "in an Ale-house, where he had called for a pot of
beer, and was laid down with his head on the Table and fallen asleep" (5). He immediately confesses and is taken to Newgate and visited by a succession of divines,
whose conversations with the prisoner on sin, eternity, and repentance form the
substance of the text. Among these other discourses his trial and sentencing are
reported only in passing, but the authors quote his last speech and prayer at the
place of execution in full, as tokens of the triumph of free grace.[14]

Savage's crimes and exemplary death represent, for Richetti, the pattern of the
"revolted apprentice," whose actions embody "furtive and unnatural longings for

disruptive revolt" which the biographies' readers are supposed to have in some measure shared. Because of that dangerous identification, and the story's "plainly revolutionary character," the apprentice's revolt had to be harshly put down; then, "with his repentance and death, the story of the bad apprentice can end happily, for he has resumed his rightful subordinate place and reaffirmed, in a kind of penitential apotheosis, the existing social and moral order."[15] For Faller, Savage's repentance and willing sacrifice at the gallows dramatized the possibility of being raised from sin through the intercession of providence.[16] Both readings seem plausible but confining, looking through the complexities of the text's surface to a rather obvious underlying design.

Issues of class, hierarchy, and subordination condition our reading of Savage's life. *A Murderer Punished; and Pardoned* begins, in fact, with an address "To the Reader" in which the story's particular applicability to apprentices is set forth. May Savage's crimes and death, the author writes,

> be a means to preserve all young men and Apprentices from being guilty of the like fact. And as a help to you herein, you are advised to be very careful what company you keep. That you addict not your selves to drinking, or gaming, or company-keeping, which is the ruin of many young men, who by getting a habit of keeping company, or other Vices, are too often drawn to purloin from their masters, to maintain them in their extravagancies, by which means they do not only run the hazard of exposing their bodies to publique-shame, if they be discovered, to the great grief, and even heart breaking of their friends, when they hear of their ill courses but the wrath of God and eternal damnation of their poor souls, as you may see in the Narrative of *T. S.* who first began with Company-keeping, from Company-keeping to Whoring, from Whoring to Thieving and Murder. (2)

Yet, if the story is meant to be read in part as a warning to apprentices—if it thus means to carry out a kind of ideological policing—the warning's power is dissipated in the glory of Savage's redemption: the shameful spectacle has been transfigured into an allegory of grace. And in any case Savage hardly seems a figure of revolt; even as a "meer Monster in sin," he is never described as an unwilling or sullen worker, and the text gives no hint of any resentment toward his master or his situation in life. His victim, after all, is another servant. Unlike Dickens's Sim Tappertit, the revolutionary captain of apprentices in *Barnaby Rudge,* Savage exhibits no murderous political ambition nor any desire for revenge against his own condition of dependency and impotence. He follows, instead, the usual trajectory of sin darkening to crime, as formulaic as a catechism: first Sabbath breaking and then, in merciless and inevitable succession, drinking, gambling, company keeping, whoring, robbery, murder, and hanging. As in many, many such tales, the woman's part is the most guilty, and, as a postlude to the narrative of Savage's penitence and death, the author includes "a Relation of what passed in the imprisonment, and at the Execution of *Hannah Blay*," which finds her, predictably, "without the least sign of sorrow or repentance for her abominable whoredoms and wickedness" (36)—drunk, laughing, and rude to the end.[17]

The narrative of Savage's life, then, is variously engaged on the level of ideology: as a warning to apprentices; an affirmation of the power and justice of the law through the spectacular display of the prisoner's shame;[18] a religious admonition, especially to the young, against temptation and the lure of those lesser sins that lead inexorably to greater ones; and a testament to the availability of grace and the sinner's triumph over sin. There are no lasting undercurrents of revolt: religion, social hierarchy, and the law are all affirmed. Yet these various ideological messages, if not contradictory, tend to pull the narrative into different shapes. The story's effectiveness as a warning is diminished by the brightness of Savage's end, the spectacle of redemption; the stern triumph of the law is dampened, at its climax, by sympathy ("Whilst he did thus pathetically express himself to the people, especially to God in prayer, there was a great moving upon the affections of those who stood by, and many tears were drawn from their eyes by his melting speeches" [31]); the pageant of Savage awakening to new life is confused by the sensational details of a minutely rendered violence. None of the story lines fatally eclipses the others, but they tend toward different outcomes, call up different kinds of response, so that, rather than describing a single "myth" of criminality, *A Murderer Punished; and Pardoned* has a certain openness or diffuseness in its moral tenor. The events of the narrative are allowed to evoke a range of conventional meanings that, according to its readers' social and ideological positions, could be variously resisted or embraced.

Whatever the reassuring claims of the pamphlets' authors, the criminals whose lives were told over and over most insistently remained troubling even after the settling of accounts. For, despite a generic pressure to make the criminal protagonist a purely representative figure, stripped of any features that cannot be absorbed into the closed, symbolic patterns of myth, the relationship between the singular and the exemplary in the life-and-crimes pamphlets was more complicated and unresolved. In Savage's case the conventional patterns of sin and redemption, debauchery or rebellion and punishment, represent efforts to come to terms with a crime terrifying partly because of its moral opacity.

The stations of Savage's criminal life are didactically overread so that "the relevance of his career to the life of every man who reads his story" is clear,[19] but the particulars of his actions, rendered in such garish detail, remain unnerving, resistant to any comfortable accommodation on the reader's part. The day of the murder all the dark and ungovernable energies of Savage's life converge: the devils called up by Sabbath breaking, burnt brandy, Hannah Blay's bloody persuasions and greed, and his own anger at the maid's scolding. He has slipped free of God and his master, so that "nothing would satisfie him but he must kill her; and no other way, but with the Hammer." Having laid this groundwork, the pamphlet's author enters into the distended moment:

[Savage] goeth into the Bar, fetcheth the Hammer: and taketh the Bellows in his hand, and sitteth down by the fire, and there knocketh the bellows with the Hammer: the Maid saith to him; *Sure the boy is mad, Sirrah, what do you make this noise for?* He said nothing, but went from the Chair, and lay along in the Kitchin window, and knocked with the Hammer there; and on a sudden threw the Hammer with such force at the maid; that hitting her on the head she fell down presently, screaking out, then he taketh up the Hammer three times, and did not dare to strike her any more, at last the Devil was so great with him, that he taketh the Hammer, and striketh her many blows with all the force he could, and even rejoyced that he had got the victory over her. (4–5)

The passage's accumulation of tension is remarkable, even if its devices are unconscious: the repeated dissolves in verbal tense between present and past, so that the events seem both on the verge of happening and beyond recall; the strange postponement of the action we expect after the words *fetcheth the Hammer,* Savage seeming to have decided just to annoy the maid rather than kill her; the tolling of the word *Hammer* itself, repeated three times between the moment he fixes on it as the weapon for his crime and its sudden, explosive release; Savage's fear-struck hesitation after his first assault, leading him to take up the hammer three times until, swollen with the devil that possesses him, he bursts through the barriers of moral habit and exults in his "victory over her."

A disturbing seam of sexual violence runs through the whole passage and suggests a kind of buried correspondence between the two crimes of murder and robbing his master. For no sooner is the maid struck down than Savage "immediately taketh the Hammer, and with it strikes at the Cupboard Door in his masters Chamber, which being but slit-Deal presently flew open, and thence he taketh out a Bag of Money" (5). The actions are not morally comparable but seem to come out of the same history of humiliations and reminders of powerlessness. Sexual and economic dependency play off each other at every stage of Savage's career. Hannah Blay's murderous promptings—"Hang her Jade saith this impudent slut, knock her brains out, and I will receive the money"—cast her in the conventional role of a Lilith who holds Savage in thrall, but in material terms she survives on the exchange of sexual for financial goods and, economically, is as subservient to Savage as he is to his master. The maid, placed physically between him and the money whose lack bars him from freedom and sexual pleasure, becomes the focus of his rage and the displaced object of revenge for his erotic and economic subjection. The psychology put forward in the text itself, of course, is plainly religious and dualistic: Savage is a sinner and has let the Devil control him. But, along with the religious simplicity it certainly aims at, the text exhibits an impulse toward verisimilitude—that is, toward a registration of the concrete particulars of speech and action, perhaps learned from news reports and printed trials—which allows for less easily assimilable details to emerge, signs of the criminal's singularity, and which leaves room for more complex, psychologically challenging readings.

If Dangerfield's *Memoires* and the pamphlet life of Savage complicate the available structures of myth with naturalistic and contingent details, other texts claiming to narrate criminal lives were parodic offshoots of the anatomy and picaresque. The emergence of the genre was as much a history of unmaking or burlesquing myths as of telling them straight, and the different versions of an outlaw career, patched together from bits of news, trials, last words, and popular tales, were in many cases so brazenly unauthentic as to eliminate any traces of the biographical apart from the criminal's name. The more often a life was told the more it seemed to dissolve into a solution of old stories.

One of the most often told was the life of the highwayman Claude Du Vall, executed in January 1669/70. The earliest account I have found, *A True and Impartial Relation of the Birth and Education of Claudius du Val,* seems to have been published within a few days of his death. "Written," as the title page advertises, "by one that was an Eye-witness, as to the matter of his Tryall; and for his Actions, they were imparted unto him from his own mouth during his Confinement," the eight-page pamphlet recounts Du Vall's life in the serious and monitory language of the Ordinary's *Accounts.* The text begins at the beginning: "Various hath been the Reports concerning the place of his Birth, being strongly averr'd to be in *London* and *Westminster,* and that in severall places, as *Chancery-Lane, Drury-Lane, Covent-Garden, White-Chappell,* and many other places; but he himself owned none of all these, but declared to have drawn his first breath in *Paris* in *France:* his Parents he did not boast of; his Education was there, till a Gentleman of quality liking his Person, in which Nature was bountifull, brought him over for *England* in the nature of a Page."[20] The passage is characteristic of the pamphlet in its concern to establish the grounds of its own authority, setting this author's access to the authentic voice of the condemned in contrast to the "various reports" then in circulation. Du Vall's handsomeness, as it first brought him to England, takes him from one admiring gentleman or noble to another, until a difference arises with one master, who advises him to return to France, "lest bad Company might debauch him" (3). Du Vall passes through London, intending passage home, "but in the interim fell into the acquaintance of some of the Old Gang of Highway-men, who by debauchery corrupted his nature." Thus, he embarks on a criminal career whose details the pamphlet's author is oddly reticent to disclose: "I shall waive Particulars," he writes, leaping ahead to Du Vall's capture "at the Sign of the *Hole in the Wall* in *Shando's*-Street," an alehouse (4).

There follows a report of Du Vall's trial on seven indictments for robbery and burglary, on all of which he is brought in guilty. The crimes are very briefly described, and the witnesses against him, either the victims or confederates turning evidence, are named. Only in one case does the author do more than catalogue the event: "The sixth Indictment was for robbing one *Thomas Harris,* a poor Man of fourteen pounds ten shillings, all that he had, which did so trouble him, that he desired them even to kill him; upon which they sportingly asked him what death would you willingly dye? *Any,* said he. What would you be run through? *What you please,* said he; sayes another, would you be Pistol'd? *What you please,* said he; would you have your Throat cut said another? *What you please,* said he; but God restrain'd them, that they did him no other hurt, leaving him to lament his loss; this was proved also" (6-7). The pamphlet concludes with a page *Concerning His Deportment before and after Tryal,* which reports that during his confinement Du Vall "was very temperate as to drink, and his Actions very modest, and discourse civil" and tells of his bearing at the gallows: "he prayed very earnestly that God would forgive him his world of Sins, and that the World would forgive him; That he dyed in charity with all men, and craved the Prayers of them all, and that they would take Example by him, to amend their lives, lest they fall into the like wayes; for then God's Judgements would overtake them, as it had done him. And so committing his Soul to God Almighty, and often calling upon Christ for mercy, the

Executioner discharged his Office" (8). In his prayerful dying Du Vall satisfies the most conventional longings for sacrifice and admonition.

Yet, if its last sentences could have been lifted from any of a hundred execution broadsheets, the *True and Impartial Relation* has some of the texture of a real biography. The author's explanation of how he came by his knowledge is plausible; the story of Du Vall's start in crime is consistent with his class origins and circumstances, and, rather than spin tales of highwaymen's exploits, the author catalogues the indictments that led to the subject's hanging, grounding the life in verifiable, documentary sources. By the publication, later the same year, of the *Memoires of Monsieur Du Vall*—usually attributed to Walter Pope—these signs of authenticity had been jettisoned, and the descriptive details seem to be drawn more from French *contes* than from legal archives. His parents, of whom all we learn in the earlier text is that "he did not boast of" them, are given respectable families and professions— "His Father was *Pierre Du Vall* a Miller, his Mother *Marguerite de la Roche* a Tailors Daughter"[21]—but these details quickly become little more than props for a series of absurd vignettes supposedly foreshadowing the son's wandering and transgressive life, of which the following is typical: "His Father and Mother had not been long married, when *Marguerite* longed for Pudding and Mince-Pie, which the good Man was fain to beg for her at an *English* Merchants in *Rouen:* which was a certain sign of his inclination to *England*" (2). Like the earlier author, Pope notes the rumor that Du Vall was not French at all. Yet, while his predecessor says simply that "he himself owned none of all these, but declared to have drawn his first breath in *Paris*," Pope's "indignant" response is stagy and arch: "this report is as false as it is defamatory and malicious; and 'tis easie to disprove it several ways: I will only urge one Demonstrative Argument against it. If he had been born there he had been no *Frenchman*, but if he had not been a *Frenchman*, 'tis absolutely impossible he should have been so much beloved in his Life, and lamented at his Death by the *English* Ladies" (1–2). Du Vall's French birth is important not as a fact but as a figural trait of the amorous highwayman.

These changes suggest how readily the real features of a life could be travestied, grafted onto the stock of narrative romance, painted over with the colors of roguery and scandal. Most printed criminal lives did freely sacrifice biographical authenticity in favor of fictional pleasure, but the pleasure they produced was often ironic, playfully anarchic, and morally untroubled, and their incoherence is not straightforwardly translatable into a function of ideology. The cultural responses to criminality were various and conflicted, and even within a single text contradictory strains and motives might jostle for dominance.

This was especially true of a pastiche such as Pope's *Memoires* of Du Vall, and in fact pastiche rather than biography is the characteristic form of the life-and-crimes pamphlet, at least until the mid-eighteenth century. Pope cobbles the *Memoires* together from disconnected, often parodic episodes and a hit-or-miss collection of ironic reflections and asides, mostly directed against the French and against women who are sexually drawn to handsome robbers. The most frequently repeated episode from Pope's account corresponds to none of the indictments in the earlier text but sets a bantering tone that all the later versions of Du Vall's life would copy. The highwayman and his gang have overtaken a coach—said to carry a booty of four hundred pounds—in which a knight, his lady, and a serving maid ride:

The Lady, to shew she was not afraid, takes a Flageolet out of her pocket and plays; *Du Vall* takes the hint, plays also, and excellently well, upon a Flageolet of his own, and in this posture he rides up to the Coach side. Sir, sayes he, to the person in the Coach, your Lady playes excellently, and I doubt not but that she Dances as well; will you please to walk out of the Coach, and let me have the honour to Dance one Corant with her upon the Heath? Sir, said the person in the Coach, I dare not deny any thing to one of your Quality and good *Mine;* you seem a Gentleman, and your request is very reasonable: Which said, the Lacquey opens the Boot, out comes the Knight, *Du Vall* leaps lightly off his Horse, and hands the Lady out of the Coach. They Danc'd, and here it was the *Du Vall* performed marvels; the best Master in *London,* except those that are *French* not being able to shew such *footing* as he did in his great, riding *French* boots. The Dancing being over, he waits on the Lady to her Coach; as the Knight was going in, sayes *Du Vall* to him, Sir, You have forgot to pay the Musick: No, I have not, replies the Knight, and putting his hand under the seat of the Coach, pulls out a hundred pounds in a bag, and delivers it to him: Which *Du Vall* took with a very good grace, and courteously answered, Sir, You are liberal, and shall have no cause to repent your being so; this liberality of yours shall excuse you the other Three Hundred Pounds. (8–9)

The story gives pleasure because it is absurd—which is not to say that no one could believe it, since everything printed is liable to be credited by somebody, but, rather, that it transparently shifts the criterion of belief from rational conviction to desire: this is how we want to meet the real dangers of crime and the road, every brigand a courtier with a flageolet kept next to his pistols. Pope later makes fun of the hero for "being taken Drunk at the Hole in the Wall in *Chandois-street*" (11). Yet, however much he may want to undermine with ridicule the heroic ideal of the highwayman—representing the reader's desire for sexual pleasure, money, and adventure—Pope infuses that archetype with his own delight in good looks and gallantry.

Such delight is manifest in Du Vall's closing "Speech" to the English Ladies. Although this text makes light of what the author regards as women's susceptibility to the sexual fascination of criminality, it calls on that very fascination as a source of narrative pleasure. The brigand whom the *Memoires* invent might have furnished the prototype for the alluring Macheath of John Gay's *Beggar's Opera*, whose outlawry is similarly eroticized. Du Vall's last dying speech, far from penitential, expresses through double entendre the "undercurrents of sexuality" which may have drawn such large crowds to the sites of execution:[22]

> From the Experience of your true *Loves* I speak it; nay I know I speak *your Hearts*, you could be content to die with *me now*, and even *here*, could you be assured of enjoying your beloved *Du Vall* in the other world.
>
> How *mightily* and how *generously* have you rewarded my *little* Services? Shall I ever forget that *universal Consternation* amongst you when I was taken, your *frequent*, your *chargeable Visits* to me at *Newgate*, your *Shreeks*, your *Swoonings* when I was *Condemned*, your *zealous Intercessions* and *Importunity* for my *Pardon?*
>
> You could not have erected fairer Pillars of Honour and respect to me, had I been a *Hercules*, and could have got *fifty Sons* in a Night. (14)

No condemnation can overcome such racy and insinuating discourse.

The authenticity, material particularity, and evidential realism that characterized Dangerfield's *Memoires* in 1685 remained anomalous into the early eighteenth century and only slowly took shape even then as the determining criteria of biographical inquiry. As was true of the criminal trial, the genre of biography took over much of its representational approach from the news report and the emerging novel; it could even be said, without too much exaggeration, that there was no such thing as biography until fiction made it up.[23] But, as early as the 1720s, a number of nonfictional first-person crime narratives that situated individual histories within a virtually sociological account of outlawry and the underworld also began to be printed. It is this impulse to inscribe the narrative of a life (whether invented or real) within a convincingly rendered social (here criminal) milieu which marks such narratives as biographical in a modern sense.

Ralph Wilson's *Full and Impartial Account of all the Robberies Committed by John Hawkins, George Sympson (lately Executed for Robbing the Bristol Mails) and their Companions* was published in 1722, after Wilson turned evidence against his former confederates. Although respectably born and articled as clerk to a lawyer, Wilson had been drawn into the gang by "the Infection of gambling," which brought him into Hawkins's company, and, despite his "Abhorrence of Villainy," by his "pleasure in hearing [Hawkins] speak of his merry Pranks and many Robberies."[24] Criminal stories, though he hopes for better effects from his own, are also sources of moral contagion.

Wilson's fall into criminality is actually presented as a repetition of Hawkins's own history, with which the pamphlet opens. Born of honest but poor farming people in Middlesex, hardly educated, hired on as a tapster's boy, Hawkins got into a gentleman's service, "but being of an unsettled Temper, he seldom tarried long in a Place" (1). Like every servant and apprentice in eighteenth-century crime narrative, "he soon became very assuming, so that he thought it but a small Fault to be out two or three Nights in a Week at the Gaming-Tables . . . These are the Nurseries of Highway-men: here it is that young Fellows being stript of all their Money, are prepared for the most desperate Enterprizes" (2). Gambling led to Hawkins's dismissal from his gentleman's service; unmoored from any stable social position, Hawkins turned to robbery and then to forming his own little outlaw confederacy.

Wilson's pamphlet describes his struggle to get out from under Hawkins's control, narrated as part of a meticulous report of all their robberies and excursions, the arrests and executions of former companions, the parceling out of profits. "There is no Life so gloomy as the Life of a Highwayman," Wilson writes: "he is a Stranger to Peace of Mind and quiet Sleep; he is made a Property of, by every Villain that knows or guesses at his Circumstances: such a Life is a Hell to any Man that has ever had any Relish of a more generous way of living. But I was entered, and must go thorough; for *Jack Hawkins*, who before was all good Humour and Complaisance, was now become my Tyrant: he gave himself a great deal of trouble to let me know, that I was as liable to be hang'd as he, and in all his Actions express'd a Satisfaction that he had me under a hank" (9). After an injury leads him to reflect on his situation, Wilson flies London for his mother's home in Yorkshire, but Hawkins catches up with him after six months and, by trickery and threat, compels him to return to London and to join him and George Sympson in two assaults on the Bristol mail. Those robberies lead to Wilson's arrest. Learning from the police that Sympson plans to inform against him and Hawkins for the forty pounds reward, Wilson decides to impeach Hawkins and Sympson first; they are tried, sentenced, and hanged on his testimony.[25]

Wilson frames his text as an example and "Caution to other young Men" and uses the familiar narrative stages of enticement, corruption, remorse, captivity, and repentance to draw out the moral significance of his violent and disruptive history (25). The moral pattern, however, is articulated through a detailed accounting of specific actions, itineraries, and conversations among thieves; the pamphlet's efficacy as an ethical or legal document depends on the proofs it can offer of its own veracity. Its textures are those of testimony and deposition, its descriptive details taken over from criminal anatomy—but anatomy from which the vestigial traces of canting books and cony-catching miscellanies have been scrubbed clean, leaving what means to pass for a documentary record, a genuine witnessing. His life takes narrative form amid the sentences and discoveries of the law.

A century or so after the publication of Wilson's pamphlet, Thomas De Quincey wrote the first, and still most debonairly subversive, theoretical analysis of criminality and narrative in English, the 1827 essay *On Murder Considered as One of the Fine Arts*. There he noted a growing sophistication on the part of readers: "People begin to see that something more goes to the composition of a fine murder than two blockheads to kill and be killed, a knife, a purse, and a dark lane."[26] But the aesthetic valuation of homicidal violence which De Quincey so suavely undertook was alien to the mentality of eighteenth-century readers, and in any case readers looking for fine art would likely have been discouraged by the perfunctoriness of these early performances. Most of the authors of criminal texts of the seventeenth and early eighteenth centuries are unnamed—and, if they are named, their names are probably fictitious. Lives and last dying speeches may in some cases really have been written or dictated by the condemned, but most were almost certainly ghostwritten by clergymen or hacks or else (but it is impossible to know how often) made up out of whole cloth; like woodcut illustrations, old texts could be attached to a new name and recycled. The Newgate Ordinaries presumably wrote their own *Accounts,* and there are other authors, especially of longer works, whose names can be authenticated. But the great mass of news reports, execution broadsides, trials, and canting books were written by badly paid and anonymous professional authors whose compositions rarely exhibited the qualities—"design, gentlemen, grouping, light and shade, poetry, sentiment"—which De Quincey's murderous amateurs found "indispensable" a century later.[27]

The conditions of authorship during the later seventeenth and eighteenth cen-

turies were marked by a degree of instability which was widely felt to be unprecedented. One consequence of what Goldsmith described as "that fatal revolution
whereby writing is converted to a mechanic trade; and booksellers, instead of the
great, become the patrons and paymasters of men of genius"[28]—a transformation
still being negotiated in the mid-eighteenth century, as Goldsmith's 1761 complaint
makes clear, but strongly in evidence through most of the seventeenth century in
London—was a dramatic enlargement of the social category of authors. Alvin Kernan has written that "the book business, even in its relatively primitive technological stages, was capable, as we have seen, of producing and marketing large numbers of books, and that potential had to be fully exploited to meet the constant need
for working capital and to maximize profits. Full production required a steady
supply of copy for the printer . . . it was the need of print for copy that created writers like Tom Brown, Ned Ward, Oldmixon, [and] Defoe."[29] Bound up with economic motivations for publishable copy were, of course, technological developments in printing and book distribution during the same period, which not only
sped up publication but increased enormously the sheer number of texts that could
find their way into print. Some of these were learned and costly productions designed for an elite audience—folio editions of classical texts, albums of antiquarian engravings, atlases and scientific compendia. But the criminal genres were
easy to write, easy to sell, and easy to find sources for. Those authors who were not
criminals themselves lived in such contagious proximity as to be more a part of
the transgressive underworld than observers from outside it. Newgate, Smithfield,
Moorfields and Bedlam—notorious locales of imprisonment, animal slaughter,
Methodism, carnival, male hustling, burials, and madness—were also sites of authorship and the book trade, especially the trade in broadsheets, cheap pamphlets,
and secondhand books. The forms of popular and sensational literature were thus,
even apart from their content, criminally tainted.[30]

On the day of his execution, November 16, 1724, Jack Sheppard watched from
his cart under the shadow of Tyburn as a man approached: the publisher John
Applebee, according to some reports; "Applebee's man," according to others. Applebee was the leading publisher of criminal lives in the early eighteenth century,
holding the rights to the Ordinary's *Accounts* as well as printing his own *Original
Weekly Journal*, whose principal author, especially on criminal matters, may have
been Defoe.[31] Sheppard gave the man a paper he had carried from Newgate. In
Christopher Hibbert's version of this story Sheppard then "said in a loud clear voice

that this was his authentic confession and that he wished Mr. Applebee to print it for him. It was an effective advertisement. That night thousands of copies of the pamphlet were sold for a shilling each in the streets."[32] The pamphlet—Defoe's *Narrative of all the Robberies, Escapes, &c. of John Sheppard*—was the second life of Sheppard which Defoe had written; the first, *The History of the Remarkable Life of John Sheppard,* was published while Sheppard was still free from the second of his escapes from Newgate. Unlike the earlier text, the *Narrative* was written in what purported to be Sheppard's authentic voice and was apparently worked up by Defoe from a series of meetings with Sheppard during his imprisonment. Sheppard's gesture of handing what was meant to be seen as an authentic paper (though the real manuscript would need to have already been in press to be ready for selling the next day) to the person he had chosen to publish it was a spectacular reenactment of his earlier, private relaying of his life to Defoe the reporter in prison. The worlds of authorship and criminality were contiguous, overlapping; the one spoke in the voice and through the material body of the other.[33]

An author's career also awaits Caleb Williams when he arrives, disguised as a Jew, in London in the last decade of the eighteenth century. Casting about for a kind of work he can practice "with least observation" (257), Caleb settles on writing—at first poems, then essays in the style of Addison. Neither of these really suits him, and he turns to writing tales, especially one particular sort: "By a fatality for which I did not exactly know how to account, my thoughts frequently led me to the histories of celebrated robbers; and I retailed from time to time incidents and anecdotes of Cartouche, Gusman d'Alfarache and other memorable worthies, whose career was terminated upon the gallows or the scaffold" (259). One day Caleb's pursuer, Gines—a thief turned thief taker and the agent of Caleb's wicked former master—happens to visit his brother, who is head workman of a printing office. After listening to Gines's stories of his own adventurous and disreputable career, this brother reciprocates by retelling the very stories of Cartouche and Gusman which Caleb has been selling to the magazines. Gines is piqued and intrigued by these tales. Where did the printer get them? "I will tell you what, said the printer, we none of us know what to make of the writer of these articles." But, as he describes what little he knows of their author, his secretiveness and habit of submitting his manuscripts through the intermediary of an old woman, Gines begins to suspect that the mysterious author may be Caleb himself. And Gines's suspicions are confirmed, Godwin writes in Caleb's voice, "by the subject of my lucubrations, men who died by the hands of the executioner" (264). Drawn to the writing of criminal lives by a fascination born of his own exclusion from the world the law circumscribes, Caleb betrays himself through his texts.

These texts lead in turn to further betrayals. Gines, satisfied that his prey is nearby but unable to catch him, causes to have printed "the most wonderful and surprising history, and miraculous adventures of Caleb Williams," the biography Caleb hears being hawked in the streets (268). This halfpenny paper concludes with an offer of a hundred guineas for Caleb's apprehension, and the offer proves irresistible to Mr. Spurrel, an old watchmaker whom Caleb thought to be his friend and protector. Like the real thief taker Jonathan Wild, Gines is able to disguise criminal manipulations of the law as legality itself and to enlist the world of hack authors and booksellers, the world Caleb furtively inhabits, to bring him to prison and trial. Taking advantage of the overlapping experiences and interests of criminals and authors, publishing and policing developed as mutually predatory, profitably entangled systems of cultural dissemination and authority over the course of the long eighteenth century.

Like Applebee or his agent Defoe symbolically receiving the written text of Sheppard's confessions as he awaits execution at Tyburn, Caleb Williams as outlaw and Grub Street hack embodies the metonymic slippage between authorship and criminality, whose relationship during the seventeenth and eighteenth centuries was intimate, permeable, confused. The cultural space inhabited by writers of criminal texts bordered, even extended into, the sites of a transgressive underworld—prison, liberty, slum—even as those writers offered themselves as spokesmen for the propertied classes and the social order the law sustained. The ostensible practical and moral purposes of their writing could be undermined as much by their (putative or real) criminal associations as by the scandalous contents, the violent and forbidden subjects, they traded in. Wishing to dismiss Fielding's last fiction, *Amelia,* his rival Richardson needed only place him in the wrong part of town: "His brawls, his jarrs, his gaols, his sponging-houses, are all drawn from what he has seen and known," he sniffs in a letter to Ann Donnellan.[34] The fictional Caleb Williams, when he undertakes the composition of a fine murder, yields to the same fatality, mixed of identification, horror, longing, and aversion, which had earlier led Reynolds, Defoe, Fielding, and their audiences to the contested field of criminal representation.

## PART II

# Crime and Identity

## *Defoe in the 1720s*

It was objected, I know, to the former Volumes of this Work, that the *Turk* was brought in too much debasing the Christian Religion, extolling *Mahomet,* and speaking disrespectfully of Jesus Christ, calling him the *Nazaren,* and the Son of *Mary,* and it is certain the Continuation must fall into the same Method; but either *Mahmut* must be a *Turk* or no *Turk,* either he must speak his own Language or other Peoples Language, and how must we represent Words spoken by him in the first Person of invincible *Mahmut* the *Arabian,* if we must not give his own Language; and how can this work be a Translation, if we must not translate the very Stile of the Original?

Let those who think they have Cause for any Observations of this Nature observe, that all Care possible is taken to represent such Passages in Terms that may give no Offence, and with this Caution to the Reader, that when he reads those Parts, he is desired to take them as the Words of the *Arabian,* not the Words of the Translator.

DANIEL DEFOE (attrib.)
*A Continuation of Letters Written by a Turkish Spy at Paris,* 1718

The disreputability and anonymity of the authoring trade plagued Daniel Defoe during his life and continue, almost three centuries later, to bedevil him and his would-be readers. No one is certain just what Defoe wrote. In particular, his connection with the crime publisher John Applebee has been called into question by the revisionist Defoe bibliographers P. N. Furbank and W. R. Owens, who view the evidence for attribution as paltry and the texts in question as dubiously Defoe-like.[1] The problem is not just bibliographical: the protean, chameleonic variability that has come to be thought of as integral to Defoe's authorship threatens to dissipate if the canon is stripped down.

Defoe was the first to protest the attribution of anonymous texts to his name. In the 1715 *Appeal to Honour and Justice* he lamented

that other Oppression which as I said I suffer under, and which, I think, is of a Kind, that no Man ever suffer'd under so much as my self: And this is to have every Libel, every Pamphlet, be it ever so foolish, so malicious, so unmannerly, or so dangerous, be laid at my Door, and be call'd publickly by my Name. It has been in vain for me to struggle with this Injury; It has been in vain for me to protest, to declare solemnly, nay, if I would have sworn that I had no hand in such a Book, or Paper, never saw it, never read it, and the like, it was the same thing.

My name has been hackney'd about the Street by the Hawkers, and about the Coffee-Houses by the Politicians, at such a rate, as no Patience could bear. One Man will swear to the Style; another to this or that Expression; another to the Way of Printing; and all so positive, that it is to no purpose to oppose it.[2]

Yet the protest poses as much of a problem as any scurrilous attribution. For anonymity and disguise are crucial to the effects Defoe actively sought to produce in much of the writing that's known to be his, notably the 1703 satire *The Shortest Way with Dissenters,* whose impersonation of the voice of a High-Church flack was so convincing "that those whom he had mocked, both churchmen and Dissenters, could never forgive him."[3] In that case the discovery of the author's name revealed the text as a hoax, and the reaction of those on both sides who had pronounced on the pamphlet publicly, assuming it to have been written in earnest, was apoplectic. "I fell a Sacrifice for writing against the Rage and Madness of that High Party, and in the Service of the Dissenters," Defoe wrote in the *Appeal*, so that "I lay friend-less and distress'd in the Prison of *Newgate*, my Family ruin'd, and my self, with-out Hope of Deliverance" (11–12).

This was neither the first nor the last time Defoe was thrown into prison. Most of his jail time resulted from arrests for debt (in 1692 twice, 1702, and 1713, as appears from Paula Backscheider's chronicle),[4] and the stays in those cases were brief. But he languished for five months in Newgate for this 1703 crime of writing in an as-sumed voice, a miserable time punctuated by three visits to the pillory, and ten years later he was arrested yet again, evidently for the last time, for another crime of writ-ing. The offending texts in this instance were two recent issues of his periodical *Review*, in which he had published a scathing account of what he took to be a wrongful arrest for having published three *other* texts, these concerning the threat posed by the Jacobites to the Protestant succession. Defoe was eventually pardoned for the anti-Jacobite pamphlets but not before several days' stay in Queen's Bench Prison for the "notorious Contempt" of his protest in the *Review* against the unwar-ranted earlier prosecution.[5] Defoe knew authorship to be a dangerous profession, and, whether he wrote in his own or another voice, the more effectively he carried the performance off, the greater the hazard to himself.

So much of what was published in the eighteenth century was anonymous that it would be misleading to represent Defoe as unusual for so seldom avowing author-ship. Yet the concealment or falsification of the author's name was clearly more to Defoe than a dodge, for an almost pathological fear of being known by one's true name is at the heart of two of the narratives I will discuss at length, *Moll Flanders* and *Roxana*. As a strategy of self-protection, anonymity was obviously of limited usefulness, and for Defoe it clearly backfired: not only was he found out quickly as the author of *The Shortest Way*, but, as the *Appeal to Honour and Justice* complains, from then on he could be attacked as the author of any dangerous or unmannerly text. The custom of anonymity only multiplied the imaginary threat of his writ-ing. And protest was not so much futile as beside the point, for Defoe's very con-ception of authorial success hinged on making the reader uncertain about just who the author was. Attribution attaches the text too bindingly to a single name and so for Defoe would defeat the whole (or the most attractive) purpose of writing, which, as is true of reading too, is the habitation of other identities. That those other identities, in the works on which his long-ranging fame mainly rests—*Robin-son Crusoe* especially, *Moll Flanders*, *Roxana*, and the other fictional autobiographies of the 1720s—belong to characters whom circumstance and impulsive desire draw away from the familiar world, from cultural norms, from normality itself, is at once what defines Defoe's singularity as an author and what accounts for his typicality. The deviant trajectories of his protagonists' lives testify both to Defoe's distinctive ideological and moral concerns and to his awareness of a cultural preparedness to read closely such narratives of transgression.

The criminal discourses that flourished in the first decades of the eighteenth century offered not only a repertoire of saleable plots and character types but a partial adumbration of the scary, disruptive, exalting energies of a new individualist sense of self. Comparing the presentation of identity in these discourses to that which prevailed in the spiritual autobiographies of the seventeenth century, Michael Mascuch writes: "Whereas the pious biographers represented their subjects as static patterns of self-mortification, the criminal lives strongly implied the personal individuality, agency, and authority of their subjects, many of whom embodied a powerful, charismatic ethos in spite of their physical annihilation by the state . . . Both the modern autobiography and its referent, the individualist self, are unthinkable without the development of the tradition of confessional literature in the criminal lives and the scandalous memoirs."[6] The disheveled and perpetually emerging genre of the novel, too, would eventually, retrospectively, come into being around texts that articulated the unease of individualism. It was Defoe's genius or luck to pick up on this undercurrent in popular criminal narrative and then to elaborate in his own long fictions what it might mean to live out the transgressive, improvisatory invention of oneself.

According to the nineteenth-century Defoe bibliographer and biographer William Lee, Defoe went to work for the publisher John Applebee in June of 1720, in the midst of what many of his contemporaries were representing as a crime wave that threatened the very foundations of the social peace. Defoe's connection to Applebee, as I've already noted, has recently been challenged, and, while I think the evidence of thematic and stylistic continuities between certain of the criminal texts published by Applebee and the contemporaneous texts universally attributed to Defoe (*Moll Flanders, Colonel Jack,* and *Roxana*) argues powerfully for Defoe's authorship of the former, my discussion doesn't turn on the disputed attribution. Indeed, were it established that the biographies of Jonathan Wild and Jack Sheppard or the letter to *Applebee's Journal* from Moll King were *not* by Defoe, this would actually reinforce my argument in what follows that, in the works securely ascribed to him, Defoe gave voice to broader cultural apprehensions concerning the universality of outlaw desire. Such de-attributions might also suggest, from the very stylistic and thematic continuities that Lee and others have advanced as evidence for attribution, that Defoe's nuanced, elaborate representations of criminal subjectivities had observable influence on subsequent authors—a claim that seems plausible but nearly impossible to prove. I am satisfied here to let the name Defoe—a name, in any case, that Daniel Foe invented for himself—stand for an indeterminately plural author, a multiply embodied voice. The mystification of textual origins gives the ventriloquist-writer the last laugh.

John Applebee, according to the historian Michael Harris, was "the leading specialist in the field" of crime publishing; from the 1720s through the mid-1740s he was the printer licensed to issue the Ordinary of Newgate's *Account,* and despite litigious conflicts with the Ordinary James Guthrie, Applebee's reputation among the overlapping categories of readers and convicts was such that "numbers of prisoners seem to have granted him exclusive rights to their lives and dying words with or without some form of payment."[7] By the time Defoe's writing began to appear in *Applebee's Journal,* he was the author of hundreds of published works (even granting the Furbank and Owens de-attributions), ranging from leaders in the renegade printer Nathaniel Mist's *Weekly Journal,* which Defoe served in the role of a government double-agent, through controversial pamphlets, conduct manuals, and political satires, to feigned autobiographies (such as *Robinson Crusoe,* published in April 1719). From this almost incredible proliferation of texts, certain motives and habits of writing recur, among them, as we've seen, a concern with questions of legal authority and the threat of social disorder and an impulse to write in the assumed voices of extremist, unsettling personae, such as the virulent flack of *The Shortest Way.* So, when, shortly after Defoe is thought to have started writing for it, Applebee's *Journal* printed a letter purporting to have been written by the pickpocket and shoplifter Moll King, however novel the subject, the broader concerns and stylistic approach were in keeping with those of Defoe's earlier works.

As Gerald Howson's research into the criminal milieu of Jonathan Wild has established,[8] the real Moll King, sentenced to death in 1718 for stealing two watches in the church of St. Anne in Soho, had subsequently been given a reduced sentence of fourteen years' transportation to America. In February 1720, after the birth and nursing of a child, she was put on a ship that arrived two months later at Annapolis, but she returned straight to England, even though the sentence for early return from transportation was death, and on July 2, 1720, an item in Mist's *Weekly Journal* reported that search was being made for her in London. Two weeks later a letter from "Moll" of Rag Fair was published in *Applebee's Journal.* "I am, Sir," its author wrote,

an *Elder,* and well known Sister, of the *File,* but least all the Readers should not understand the Cant of our Profession, you may take it in plain *English,* I was, in the former part of my Life, an eminent *Pick-Pocket,* and you may observe also, that while I kept in the Employment I was bred up to, I did very well, and kept out of Harms way, for I was so Wary, so Dexterous, kept so retir'd to my self, and did my Work so well, that I was never detected, *no never,* was never pump'd, never taken, and I may add I began to lay up Money, and be beforehand in the World; not that I had any Thought of leaving off My Trade neither; no, nor ever should have done it, if I had been as rich as the best of my Trade in *Exchange Alley.*[9]

The mixture of candor and self-promotion, retirement and eminence, thrifty economy and a compulsion to keep accumulating money, is familiar from Defoe's longer autobiographical narratives, and in its general outlines Moll King's career is close to Moll Flanders's. Also familiar, though pressed home less insistently than in Gay's *Beggar's Opera* or Fielding's *Jonathan Wild,* is the equation the writer makes between the crimes of high and low life: the speculators of Exchange Alley are only more nimble adepts of Moll's own trade, and, like them, she sees no reason to leave off her crimes just because they have made her rich.[10]

Moll King exhibits the same qualities of wariness and dexterity Defoe ascribes to the criminal protagonists of his long fictions. Yet, as her letter goes on to observe, no matter how adroitly she manages, the social world she inhabits is a trap, harrowing and sordid:

Now as my being here is a new Trespass, and may bring me back to the Gallows, from whence it may be *truly* said I came; I am not quite so easie as I was before; tho' I am prudently retired to my first Employ, and find I can do pretty well at it; but that which makes me more in Danger is the meeting Yesterday with One of my old Acquaintance; he salutes me publickly in the Street, with a long out-cry; *O brave Moll* says he, *Why what do you do out of your Grave? Was not you Transported?* Hold your Tongue, *Jack,* says I, for God's Sake! What, have you a mind to ruin me? D—— me, says he, *you Jade* give me a Twelver then, *or I'll tell this Minute;* I was forc'd to do it, and so the Rogue has a Milch Cow of me, as long as I live. (180–81)

The networks of complicity, watchfulness, and betrayal organized in the London underworld by Jonathan Wild over the preceding several years mark every human gesture, turning recognition and memory into forms of imprisonment. The mood of uneasiness which pervades the second half of this brief letter is grounded in the real experience of criminality at the time of its publication, the legally approved practices of thief taking and blackmail which were the precursors of the modern police, but it also has affinities to psychological undercurrents in other works by Defoe: a sense of the danger to which all persons are vulnerable, of the sinfulness of desire and the threat of human entanglement.[11] It was, earlier, the *"Curse of ill Company"* which drew Moll away from what she calls her "ordinary and lawful Calling, into the dangerous Business of *Shop-lifting"* (180), but, if criminal confederacies are the immediate danger, the underlying fear, for her as for all Defoe's protagonists, is of the injuries to which intimacy exposes her. Cross-dressing, anonymity, and flight are responses in Defoe to the terrors of vulnerability and discovery, which are only then exchanged for the terrors of isolation and exile. Under the terms of the 1718 Transportation Act, Moll's "old Acquaintance" can get forty pounds for informing on her;[12] the same pressures that drive her as a thief to depend on a network of receivers and false witnesses make her subject to a regime as constricting as the lawful regimes of colonial servitude or respectable urban poverty.

While Moll King and the social world she inhabited were historically real, the letter published in *Applebee's Journal* was a fabrication. As a commodity, its value depended upon its verisimilitude: the convincing texture of its assumed voice, strongly marked by vernacular; the sprinklings of thieves' cant; the brusque energy of Moll and Jack's brief exchange. Even the letter's ineffectual concealments are plausibly motivated by a fear of revealing too much: "How I was sent over, or whether sent over or no, and of what use the little Money I had laid up, *as above,* has been to me in all my Tribulation, is not to the present Purpose, and besides is too long a Story to tell in a Letter; it may suffice to the Case in hand to let you know, *and the World by your Means,* that I am at the present Writing hereof among the Number of Inhabitants of *Old England:* Whether I was Transported, what Adventures I met with abroad, *if I was abroad,* and how I came hither again, I say, are too long for a Letter; *But here I am"* (180).

Defoe's pretense of writing in other voices, though of course not original to him, was felt by some contemporaries to be especially problematic, because his texts pretended also to an authority and a degree of circumstantial truth far in excess of most earlier performances. They exhibited all the signs of authenticity but were not authentic. After the publication of the first two parts of *Robinson Crusoe* in 1719, Charles Gildon issued a withering and quite funny attack, *The Life and Strange Surprizing Adventures of Mr. D—— DeF——*, in which he assails Defoe's uneasy defense of his own invention: "I think we may justly say," Gildon writes, "that the Design of the Publication of this Book was not sufficient to justify and make Truth of what you allow to be Fiction and Fable . . . unless you would have us think, that the Manner of your telling a Lie will make it a Truth."[13] This is probably not how Defoe would have wanted to put it, but his theoretical remarks tend to be equivocal, and in a way it *is* his manner of telling a lie, the experiential verisimilitude of his writing, which matters: the conviction of reality his fiction produces allows him to engage with his material and its "social, religious, economic, political and moral implications" in more complex ways than either strict objectivity or out-and-out romance would permit.[14]

The letter from Moll King is exemplary of Defoe's practice as a criminal author, stirring up real observations, overheard stories, genuine documents, and phantom characters into hybrid texts whose stance toward the real is charged and contradictory. Neither a literal chronicler nor an early Grand Guignol fantasist, Defoe was at once publicist and psychoanalyst of the London crime wave of the 1720s— which was itself situated somewhere between social reality and fearful imagining.[15] His work drew from the inherited genres of criminal narrative, in some cases sticking fast to their conventions, in others extending or disfiguring them so radically as to make a new species.[16] In Defoe's writing the allusive and momentary suggestions of likeness between reader (or author) and outlaw which thread through the established criminal discourses are lingered over and enlarged, so that the narrative escape into exoticism and otherness is overshadowed by the anxiety of kinship.

# CHAPTER SIX

# Colonel Jack's Childhood

Defoe's Colonel Jack begins life as the bastard son of a Gentleman and a Mother who "kept very good Company." Pawned off on a poor nurse who dies before he turns ten, he grows up "a dirty Glass-Bottle House Boy, sleeping in the Ashes, and dealing always in the Street Dirt . . . a *Black your Shoes your Honour*, a Beggar Boy, a Black-Guard Boy, or what you please, despicable, and miserable to the last Degree."[1]

The glass-house district around Rosemary Lane was a well-known site for the recruitment of little criminals. In the 1726 *Lives of the Six Notorious Street Robbers* Defoe (if it was Defoe, and, if it was not, an author very likely familiar with *Colonel Jack*) represented it as a locale "for supplying the places of defunct thieves": "'tis well known that there [are] gangs of poor vagabond boys who having neither father or mother, house or home, to retreat to, creep at night into the ash-holes of the nealing arches of the glass-houses, where they lie for the benefit of the warmth of the place, and in the daytime stroll about the streets pilfering and stealing whatever comes in their way, and begging when sleight of hand will not maintain them."[2] Colonel Jack's brother-orphan, Major Jack, is one day "wheedled a way, by a couple of young Rogues that frequented the Glass-house Appartments, to take a Walk with them, as they were pleased to call it." He goes with them to Bartholomew Fair, and though he knows nothing of their trade of pickpocketing, "as fast as they made any Purchase, they unloaded themselves and gave all to him, that if they had been taken, nothing might be found upon them" (13).

All three return that night to the glass-house, and there they inventory their loot:

I. A white Handkerchief from a Country Wench, as she was staring up at a *Jackpudding* [Clown], there was 3*s. 6d.* and a Row of Pins, tyed up in one End of it.

II. A colour'd Handkerchief, out of a young Country Fellow's Pocket as he
was buying a *China* Orange.

III. A Ribband Purse with 11*s*. 3*d*. and a Silver Thimble in it, out of a young
Woman's Pocket, just as a Fellow offer'd to pick her up.

> *N.B.* She mist her Purse presently, but not seeing the Thief, charg'd
> the Man with it, that would have pick'd her up, and cry'd out a Pick-
> Pocket, and he fell into the Hands of the Mobb, but being known in
> the Street, he got off with great Difficulty.

IV. A Knife and Fork, that a Couple of Boys had just bought, and were going
Home with; the young Rogue that took it, got it within the Minute after
the Boy had put it in his Pocket.

V. A little Silver Box, with seven Shillings in it, all in small Silver, 1*d*. 2*d*. 3*d*.
4*d*. Peices.

> *N.B.* This, it seems a Maid pull'd out of her Pocket, to pay at her going
> into the Booth to see a Show, and the Little Rogue got his Hand in and
> fetch'd it off, just as she put it up again.

VI. Another Silk Handkerchief, out of a Gentleman's Pocket.

VII. Another.

VIII. A Joynted Baby [Doll], and a little Looking-Glass stolen off a Toy Seller's
Stall, in the Fair. (13–14)

Such detailed accounting, derived not from any earlier genres of fiction but copy-
ing the form of criminal deposition and newspaper advertisements of stolen goods,
functions in this passage as a guarantee of authenticity and locates the characters
in the real social space traversed by contemporaries: the glass-house district, Bartholomew Fair, and such commonplace sights as a Jackpudding's performance and
toy seller's stall. The descriptions have an almost clairvoyant lucidity, Colonel Jack
remembering some forty years later not only the exact amount stolen from each
person but the value of each coin and sketching a vividly tactile and kinesthetic
memory of the circumstances of each theft, even though he was not there nor at
the later division of the spoils. The details are recollected in imagination, not directly witnessed, but they are recorded in the format of prosecutorial evidence,
asserting their material exhaustiveness as a marker of truth.

The passage has the thickness of anthropological description as well as a side-
show theatricality: each stolen object summons a tiny but lively, even knockabout,

vignette, and each vignette aims at typicality. The first two objects on the list, for example, are stolen from young country people, drawn perhaps for the first time to London and the dazzling profusion of Bartholomew Fair, their attention too much absorbed in the urban and carnival strangeness of Jackpuddings and China oranges to mind their own goods or the press of bodies around them. Even the "3s. 6d." and row of pins tied up in one end of the countrywoman's handkerchief, especially by its contrast with the next young woman's "Ribband Purse with 11s. 3d. and a Silver Thimble," functions as an illustration of everyday customs and a sign of social class. The episode of the young woman with the ribband purse is the most dramatically exuberant of the vignettes, in quick strokes outlining a plot that hurries from an ambiguous glimpse of a flirtatious overture (the fellow offering to pick her up), through theft and accusation (the fellow's sexual interest perhaps leading her by a kind of figural slippage to suspicion of criminal intent), to a scene of mob violence and narrow escape whose subtext is the persistence of a tradition of popular justice outside the institutions of legality.[3]

Situated somewhere between the first two women on the scales of wealth and urbanity, the maid with a little silver box is shown spending a part of her savings, accumulated in small change, for an entertainment on her day off work; one of the incidental discoveries, in fact, of the whole passage is of the relative freedom of women to circulate unaccompanied in even the more raucous quarters of London around the start of the eighteenth century.[4] The silver box, with its "1d. 2d. 3d. 4d. Peices," has the same synecdochic poignancy as the other stolen things (excepting the two gentlemen's silk handkerchiefs, the actual events of whose theft are passed over): the toy seller's "Joynted Baby" and "little Looking-Glass," the couple of boys' knife and fork, the country girl's white handkerchief with its 3s. 6d. and row of pins, the other young woman's silver thimble and ribband purse. These small and very simple goods not only reveal their owners' straitened material circumstances but also hint at their habits and desires, enumerating along the way some of the typical objects of popular consumption.

This vein of virtually sociological description runs through all the later passages of Colonel Jack's career as a pickpocket—for he is soon inducted into the trade too—and street robber. As in *Moll Flanders,* published earlier the same year, Defoe describes the ruses and techniques of thievery in scrupulous, step-by-step detail, his exposé uncomfortably close to an instruction manual, as he brings the materials of traditional rogue anatomies into a more circumstantially observed present.

The scenes of Colonel Jack's youth, which take up the first third of the work, are structured as a narrative of gradual immersion in, but not hardening to, criminality—for, while "the hardness, and wickedness of the Company I kept" and "the gross Ignorance of my untaught Childhood" have kept Jack in a condition of blindness to good and evil, "yet I had something in me, by what secret Influence I knew not, kept me from the other degrees of Raking and Vice, and in short, from the general Wickedness of the rest of my Companions" (60). Colonel Jack's moral distance from his criminal milieu and companions has been signaled from the editor's preface, where he writes that "though Circumstances form'd him by Necessity to be a Thief, a strange Rectitude of Principles remain'd with him, and made him early abhor the worst Part of his Trade" (1). That abhorrence only becomes articulate following the robbery of an old woman whom Jack's gang meet with on the Kentish Town road. In the wake of that attack Jack feels remorse and then a kind of bitterness against his companion, Will, who has warned Jack that his doubts and fits of conscience will keep him from ever becoming a gentleman:

I came to my self after a little while, and I said to him, pretty Tartly, Why *Will*, do you call this way of Living the Life of a Gentleman?

W H Y, *says Will*, why not?

W H Y, *says I*, was it like a Gentleman for me to take that Two and Twenty Shillings from a poor antient Woman, when she beg'd of me upon her Knees not to take it, and told me it was all she had in the World to buy her Bread for her self and a sick Child which she had at home, do you think I could be so Cruel if you had not stood by, and made me do it? why, I cry'd at doing it, as much as the poor Woman did, tho' I did not let you see me. (67)

Although Will tries to argue him out of his pity—"did you ever see any of them cry when they see Gentlemen go to the Gallows?" (68)—Jack is carried by sympathy to a crisis of self-recognition which leads by slow degrees to his abandonment of crime and his pursuit of the gentleman's life by other means.

Defoe sets this plot of self-discovery and self-fashioning against a catalogue of the varieties of street robbery, whose descriptive and realist pleasures somewhat blur the moral progress.[5] Thus, in one episode Jack and Will, idly strolling through Smithfield Market, catch sight of "an antient Country Gentleman . . . selling some very large Bullocks" (56). As they watch him after the sale, standing by a bulkhead with a bag of money in his hand, he is taken suddenly with a fit of coughing, and Will, seeing an opportunity, "makes an artificial stumble, and falls with his Head just against the old Gentleman in the very Moment, when he was coughing ready to be strangl'd, and quite Spent for want of Breath." Jack grabs the bag and runs off, and Will

in the mean time fell down with the old Gentleman, but soon got up; the old Knight, *for such it seems he was*, was frighted with the fall, and his Breath so stopp'd with his Cough, that he could not recover himself to speak till some time, during which, nimble *Will* was got up again, and walk'd off; nor could he call out stop Thief, or tell any Body he had lost any thing for a good while; but Coughing vehemently, and looking red till he was almost black in the Face, he cry'd the Ro—— *Hegh, Hegh, Hegh,* the Rogues *Hegh,* have got *Hegh, Hegh, Hegh, Hegh, Hegh, Hegh,* then he would get a little Breath, and at it again the Rogue—— *Hegh, Hegh,* and after a great many *Heghs,* and *Rogues* he brought it out, have got away my Bag of Money.

ALL this while the People understood nothing of the matter, and as for the Rogues indeed, they had time enough to get clear away. (56–57)

The comedy of such an anecdote depends on the suspension of sympathy, a kind of materialist detachment. Jack is involved in the action but not morally caught up in it, and so the episode is reported with the outward and uninflected realism of a cony-catching pamphlet or picaresque tale.

As in all the early scenes in *Colonel Jack,* topographical and physical details are well marked. Smithfield Market—located close to Newgate, the Old Bailey, Grub Street, and the houses where Defoe was born and died—was the main livestock market of London, a place where men with a lot of money, unaccustomed to urban life,[6] met and did business, most often in taverns. With the practiced eye of a street robber, Jack keeps close watch on the positions of bodies and objects: "having some of [the money] in a Bag, and the Bag in his Hand, [the Country Gentleman] was taken with a sudden fit of Coughing, and stands to Cough, resting his Hand with the Bag of Money in it, upon a Bulk-head of a Shop, just by the *Cloyster-Gate* in *Smithfield, that is to say,* within three or four Doors of it; we were both just behind him." (56). This close observation—like the otherwise meaningless listing of all an escape route's twists and turns—is justified by Jack's trade, whose prosecution depends on a practiced eye and an intuitive grasp of the city's endlessly expansive, rhizomic, configuration. The narrator's circumstantial and plain-spoken realism is grounded in practical necessity, in the specific requirements of criminal activity. But it derives also from that strain of blunt, rather unfeeling laughter which runs through canting books and the picaresque, two of the genres Defoe worked into his own polysemous fictions.

If many episodes in *Colonel Jack* adopt the circumstantial realism of crime reports, the plot of self-fashioning, with its retrospective structure, steers Defoe at the same time toward a more inwardly directed, psychological verisimilitude. Certain passages have the wobbly irresolution of real memory. When Captain Jack, another of Colonel Jack's foster brothers, falls in with a gang of kidnappers, our Jack writes: "There was it seems some Villainous thing done by this Gang about that time, whether a Child was murther'd among them, or a Child otherwise abus'd; but it seems it was a Child of an eminent Citizen, and the Parent some how or other got a Scent of the thing, so that they recover'd their Child, tho' in a sad Condition, and almost kill'd; I was too young, and it was too long ago for me to remember the whole Story, but they were all taken up, and sent to *Newgate,* and Capt. *Jack* among the rest." (11). The haze of uncertainty evaporates in the immediately succeeding paragraphs, describing Jack's visit to the Captain in Bridewell, where the latter has been committed to be whipped. Defoe's rendering of the scene of the Captain's whipping—the alderman soberly "preaching to him about how young he was, and what pitty it was such a Youth should come to be hang'd, and a great deal more . . . all this while the Man with a blue Badge on, lash'd him most unmercifully," so that all through the sermon "the poor Captain stamp'd, and danc'd, and roar'd out like a mad Boy" (12)—contrasts so obviously, in its concreteness and immediacy, with the vague recollection leading into it, that he seems very pointedly to be demonstrating the ways in which memory can be clarified or muddled by intense feeling. The narrator's fuzziness of memory about the "Villainous thing" done, underlined by the repetition of "it seems" and stated outright in the phrase "I was too young, and it was too long ago for me to remember the whole story," is clearly the *object* of Defoe's representation, not the accidental residue of authorial carelessness. Perhaps Jack never did know what his friends had done or wished very much not to know, not to have it in mind. By contrast, the "sensible Impression" that the sight of the Captain's punishment makes upon Colonel Jack—opening his eyes to the connection between criminality and the violence of retribution—is still apparent, forty years later, in the painful clarity of his remembrance.

Defoe's distinctive brand of realism is most evident in passages in which intensity of emotion infuses physical description with a sharpened, distended lucidity. On his own first criminal expedition, led by the "exquisite Diver and Pick-pocket" Will, Jack is given orders to keep Will in sight from across the Long Room at the Custom-house: "I observ'd my Orders to a tittle, while he peer'd into every Corner, and had his Eye upon every Body; I kept my Eye directly upon him, but went always at a Distance, and on the other Side of the Long Room, looking as it were for Pins, and picking them up on the Dust as I cou'd find them, and then sticking them on my Sleeve, where I had at last gotten 40 or 50 good Pins; but still my Eye was upon my Comrade." (19–20). The scene gradually accumulates tension by cutting between close and distant perspectives, as Jack's gaze shifts from the forty or fifty little pins stuck on his sleeve to his comrade across the Long Room, marking the contrast between Will, who has "his Eye upon every Body," and himself, as he keeps "my Eye directly upon him." The tiny and utterly insignificant action of picking up pins blocks the principal action—Will's pickpocketing—from view until, at the end, the trivial action slips into the dangerous one: "at length he comes over to me, and stooping as if he would take up a Pin close to me, he put something into my Hand and said, put that up, and follow me down Stairs quickly" (20). The whole episode, in fact, works by a kind of substitution, since Defoe never shows the actual crime, and Jack never sees it, yet all the small events at the scene's periphery become charged with the aura of criminality.

This first expedition's success leaves little Jack more anxious than exultant,[7] for he is at a loss about what to do with his money. In what are arguably the most impassioned and acutely observed passages in any of Defoe's fictions, Jack confronts all the psychic terrors of loss and abandonment in his search for a secure hiding place. The whole sequence's close attention to the particular, its piling up of material evidence, extends inward as well, to register the confusions of Jack's innocent guilt, his mixture of worry, desire, and fearful investment.

It is Jack's raggedness that sets the whole sequence in motion. When he takes the share Will has given him of the money from one of the stolen goldsmith's bills—four gold guineas and fourteen shillings—he is perplexed:

what shall I do with this now, *says I,* for I have no where to put it? why have you no Pockets? *says he,* yes *says I,* but they are full of Holes; I have often thought since that, and with some Mirth too, how I had really more Wealth than I knew what to do with, for Lodging I had none, nor any Box or Drawer to hide my Money in, nor had I any Pocket, but such, *as I say,* was full of Holes; I knew no Body in the World, that I cou'd go and desire them to lay it up for me; for being a poor, nak'd, ragg'd Boy, they would presently say, I had robb'd some Body, and perhaps lay hold of me, and my Money would be my Crime. (22)

Jack's negative inventory of his possessions lays bare a poverty so absolute that money itself, were anyone to learn he had it, would necessarily be read as a sign of criminality. He is defined by lack. Only people who already have money—or, as in a later passage, decent clothing—are permitted by law openly to desire it.

Although he is quite innocent of any knowledge of money or property, and thus of any notion of crime, Jack has both a primitive sense of honesty ("if a Goldsmith had left me in his Shop with heaps of Money, strew'd all around me, and bad me look after it, I should not have touch'd it, I was so honest" [19]) and an alertness to the frightening and violent desire money awakens in others: he knows enough, that is, to keep what he has secret. But, having no pocket or lodging or little box, he can only hide the coins in his hand. He tries putting them in his shoe—"but after I had gone a while, my Shoe hurt me so, I could not go, so I was fain to sit down again, and take it out of my Shoe, and carry it in my Hand, then I found a dirty Linnen Rag in the Street, and I took that up." The rag lets him clutch the money more closely but no more securely, and the need for concealment and silence only results in a more fearful isolation: "if I had let any of the black Crew I was with, know of it, I should have been smother'd in the Ashes for it, or robb'd of it, or some Trick or other put upon me for it; so I knew not what to do, but lay with it in my Hand, and my Hand in my Bosom, but then Sleep went from Eyes: O! the Weight of Human Care!" (23). The moral distance Jack feels from his companions and the world he inhabits becomes more pronounced, more unbridgeable, the more his actions come to resemble theirs; his friends were never a "black Crew" before, unless from their having to sleep in ashes. Yet his response, though tending to mitigate his own guilt, is not really hypocritical, since, for one thing, he has only tagged along blindly while his companion stole the gentleman's letter case and, for another, he really has no desire for money but a purely imitative one, a mirroring of the fury of possession he sees all around him. Violence he always dreads. Yet the knowledge that others would commit it for what Will has given him attaches him to it all the more tenaciously and poisons his dreams.

On his rambles the next day Jack hits on the idea of hiding the money in a tree. He is so possessed by his wealth that every human presence is a threat: "the Fields were so full of People, that they would see if I went to hide anything there, and I thought the People Eyed me as it was, and that two Men in particular follow'd me, to see what I intended to do." The city's labyrinth of passageways and closes offers numberless possibilities of escape, disappearance, concealment, but also enables the paralyzing watchfulness of strangers, creating an atmosphere of suspicion and danger. "This drove me further off," Jack writes, until he comes to Bethnal Green, then at the northeastern outskirts of London. There he finds his hiding place:

at last one Tree had a little Hole in it, pritty high out of my Reach, and I climb'd up the Tree to get to it, and when I came there, I put my Hand in, and found, (as I thought) a Place very fit, so I placed my Treasure there, and was mighty well satisfy'd with it; but behold, putting my Hand in again to lay it more commodiously, as I thought, of a Suddain it slipp'd away from me, and I found the Tree was hollow, and my little Parcel was fallen in quite out of my Reach, and how far it might go in, I knew not; so, that in a Word, my Money was quite gone, irrecoverably lost, there could be no Room, so much as to Hope ever to see it again for it was a vast great Tree. (24–25)

The breathless, disordered surface of Defoe's writing is perfectly calculated to catch the rush of Colonel Jack's sensations, the horrible rapidity of loss. Occurring somewhat past the midpoint in a series of loosely conjoined clauses, involving many separate actions, the sudden fall of his treasure arrives with the shock of accident, and the three phrases rapidly falling away after the catastrophe—"and I found the Tree was hollow, and my little Parcel was fallen in quite out of my Reach, and how far it might go in, I knew not"—imitate the bombardment of impressions by which he takes in the truth of his money's disappearance. Defoe's style tends toward plainness, and his sentences are often long and bumpy. But, in its piece-by-piece accumulation (or aggregation, in Ian Watt's phrase) of physical details and his narrators' fleeting apprehensions of the world, his style registers the momentary, contingent qualities of experience with a distinctive flexibility and directness.

　　When he realizes his loss, Jack becomes frantic. The atomizing particularity of Defoe's rendering is counterbalanced by the paragraph's boundaries, so that the string of little phrases works itself out as a single, strongly and confusedly experienced, representation:

well, I thrust my Hand quite up to my Elbow, but no Bottom was to be found, or any End of the Hole or Cavity; I got a Stick off of the Tree and thrust it in a great Way, but all was one; then I cry'd, nay, I roar'd out, I was in such a Passion, then I got down the Tree again, then up again, and thrust in my Hand again till I scratch'd my arm and made it bleed, and cry'd all the while most violently: Then I began to think I had not so much as a half Penny of it left for a half Penny Roll, and I was a hungry, and then I cry'd again: Then I came away in dispair, crying, and roaring like a little Boy that had been whip'd, then I went back again to the Tree, and up the Tree again, and thus I did several Times. (25)

The overwhelming force of Colonel Jack's feeling of loss is caught in the retelling through an obsessive closeness of registration, an unwillingness to disregard the slightest action, even if it only repeats an action that has already proved futile, such as his hopeless circling back to the place and (metonymically) the moment of loss: "then I got down the Tree again, then up again, and thrust in my Hand again." Defoe refuses to condescend to what might seem childish expressions or gestures of despair: the "Passion" he represents is articulated in the words and physical movements appropriate to a child but is not made to seem any less serious or intense than the passions of later life—if anything, it is purer, more authentically felt.[8] The passage's meticulous verisimilitude brings the reader into an almost bodily complicity with Colonel Jack's frenzy and roaring for what he has lost.

Soon he finds that his linen-wrapped bundle has simply fallen through the tree to an opening lower down on its opposite side, and "a Flood of Joy" overwhelms him. Jack's joy is expressed through the same concreteness of detail as his despair: "then I run to it, and snatch'd it up, hug'd and kiss'd the dirty Ragg a hundred Times; then danc'd and jump'd about, run from one End of the Field to the other" (26). As he makes his way back to familiar haunts, he stops off first for the halfpenny roll that came into his mind as he raged at the tree, then at a second-hand clothes shop. He is made much of by two women there as "a pretty Boy . . . a very well-looking Child, if he was clean and well dress'd, and may be as good a Gentleman's Son for any thing we know, as any of those that are well dress'd." If the appearance of poverty has, to this point, limited Jack's freedom of movement and confined him to a specific social narrative of identity—so that a man standing at the clothes shop door tries to shoo him away as a member of "the ragged Regiment" (27)—his prettiness points to another way of reading who he is, another set of narrative possibilities, which his happily rediscovered bundle of money will permit him to realize.

The pattern of the moral progress, with its correlative history of struggle to attain the status of a gentleman, comes back into focus here, as Jack, like any foundling hero in Fielding or Dickens, is recognized by strangers as superior—in beauty, manners, and sensibility—to his low station. His lifelong effort to reach the position of gentleman, in fact, is colored from the beginning by an intimation that this position is his real one. Jack never learns the actual circumstances of his birth, but he has a story for it: "all I know of it, is by oral Tradition thus; my Nurse told me my Mother was a Gentlewoman, that my Father was a Man of Quality, and she (my Nurse) had a good peice of Money given her to take me off his Hands . . . she should always take care to bid me *remember, that I was a Gentleman* . . . for [my Father] did not doubt, he said, but that sometime or other the very hint would inspire me with Thoughts suitable to my Birth, and that I would certainly act like a Gentleman, if I believed myself to be so" (3). The plot of *Colonel Jack*—the hero's movement from "a dirty Glass-Bottle House Boy, sleeping in the Ashes," through pickpocketing and street robbery, soldiering and indentured servitude, to slave overseer, colonial planter, unhappy husband, and, in the end, rich penitent—unfolds from this germ of family romance, which Defoe realizes in insistently concrete terms as a drama of class hierarchy, cash reserves, and social imposture.

In the second-hand clothes shop Jack takes his second step toward gentility (if the first was assisting, even innocently, at a robbery and thus beginning to assemble his fortune): he buys "a good warm Pair of Breeches." As the shopkeeper tells him, "they are very tite, and good; and, *says she,* if you should ever come to have so much Money, that you don't know what to do with it, here are excellent good Pockets, *says she,* and a little Fob to put your Gold in, or your Watch in, when you get it." There is obvious dramatic irony here, both in that pockets are exactly what Jack learns to breach as a pickpocket and in that he already has the money the shopkeeper only supposes he might one day acquire. But in another sense the passage is not ironic, since for all his present appearance of poverty she recognizes Jack as a person who could use "a little Fob" to put his gold in. As for him, "it struck me with a strange kind of Joy, that I should have a Place to put my Money in, and need not go to hide it again in a Hollow-Tree" (27). And so the sequence of Jack's search for a hiding place ends where it began, but happily, with pockets. Clothes, as in all Defoe's fictions, are both a disguise and a kind of currency, a means for negotiating identity and social position. "I was but a Boy 'tis true, but I thought my self a Man now I had got a Pocket to put my Money in," he ends by saying (28), in an observation that shows how closely material objects and moral states are linked in the fine mesh of Defoe's narration.

# CHAPTER SEVEN

# Moll Flanders and Her Confederates

The effect of inward verisimilitude in Defoe's narratives turns, as certain passages from *Colonel Jack* have already suggested, on his skill at ventriloquism. Defoe allows his garrulous criminals to speak in their own voices, to spin out their tales in tones of apology, mockery, and self-elevation. A sense of the psychologically telling detail, of the plural and uneven textures of memory, an openness to the idiosyncratic rhythms of speech and the awkward refractions of writing, all are strategies of habitation, devices to link printed texts to their fictional origins in the voices of real persons. The realistic effect of Defoe's writing comes in part from his willingness to follow out the implications of the voice he has called up, to disregard conventions of stylistic decorum or even, in any but the most nominal ways, moral improvement, in his pursuit of a necessarily feigned authenticity of witness.

The claim of authenticity is advanced most intently in the prefaces to *Moll Flanders*, *Colonel Jack*, and *Roxana*, all of which are more elaborately set out than the very brief preface to *Robinson Crusoe*. There, after a quick enumeration of the tale's moral wonders, Defoe had written, "The editor believes the thing to be a just history of fact; neither is there any appearance of fiction in it: and however thinks, because all such things are disputed, that the improvement of it, as well to the diversion as to the instruction of the reader, will be the same."[1] Perhaps stung by Gildon's attack on *Robinson Crusoe*'s historical veracity or perhaps, given the many charges of lying made against the Ordinary of Newgate and other criminal authors, to assert the legitimacy of his own impersonation, Defoe constructed a more complicated history of authorship for *Moll Flanders*.

The enabling pretense of that history is that the woman who presents her memoirs under the alias of Moll Flanders left behind her a manuscript "written in the Year 1683."[2] This original text, however, was too coarse in its language, and had for decency's sake to be overhauled by its nameless and apologetic editor; how the original came into his hands or came to be written at all, we are not told. So, while, as the editor writes, "the Author is here suppos'd to be writing her own History," nevertheless, "it is true, that the original of this Story is put into new Words, and the Stile of the famous Lady we here speak of is a little alter'd, particularly she is made to tell her own Tale in modester Words than she told it at first; the Copy which came first to Hand, having been written in Language, more like one still in *Newgate,* than one grown Penitent and Humble, as she afterwards pretends to be." This displacement of the original text, along with the editor's unwillingness, even after forty years, to disclose the Author's true name, catches the work up in that more general climate of suspicion which has come to surround all such publications, doubts of the genuineness of purported histories: "The World is so taken up of late with Novels and Romances, that it will be hard for a private History to be taken for Genuine, where the Names and other Circumstances of the Person are concealed, and on this Account we must be content to leave the Reader to pass his own Opinion upon the ensuing Sheets, and take it just as he pleases" (1). It was both to disarm and to circumvent the skepticism of readers like Charles Gildon that Defoe constructed a fiction of authorship and revision, explaining not only his own practice but also the moral lessons Moll's hard and criminal life affords once "the whole Relation is carefully garbl'd [cleansed] of all the Levity, and Looseness that was in it" (3).

Yet, if Defoe argues, as in all his fictions' prefaces, that whether the story is taken for true or not, it is so lively and edifying that the reader should purchase it anyway, the persuasion of authenticity is obviously crucial to the effects he wants to produce. Defoe's struggle to reconcile verisimilitude and propriety is nowhere clearer than in the attention he pays here to language as a sign both of moral and of social condition. "The Pen employ'd in finishing her Story, and making it what you now see it to be," he writes, "has had no little difficulty to put it into a Dress fit to be seen, and to make it speak Language fit to be read: When a Woman debauch'd from her Youth, nay, even being the Off-spring of Debauchery and Vice, comes to give an Account of all her vicious Practises, and even to descend to the particular Occasions and Circumstances, by which she first became wicked, and of all the progression of Crime which she run through in threescore Year, an Author must be hard put to it to wrap it up so clean, as not to give room, especially for vitious Readers to turn it to his Disadvantage" (1). The editor's disavowal here is double and on one level is obviously strategic, self-protective. Any viciousness a reader may find in the book originates either in the woman's language or the reader's imagination; for the editor the purpose of writing has been to dress her story in "Language fit to be read," to wrap up "all the progression of Crime which she run through" in a narrative of penitential design. Yet her original language has a troubling persistence, which presses the whole text toward less orthodox meanings. If the editor offers the narrative as, starkly, "the History of a wicked Life repented of" (2), the words of Moll's handwritten text, underlying the text ultimately published like a palimpsest, reveal that the experience of transgression is more intractable and more tenaciously rooted in material conditions than his moral tag allows him to know.

The roughness and immodesty of Moll's language, which calls on Defoe as editor to "put into new Words"—to *alter, finish, garble, wrap*—the ancient, Newgate-debauched original, vouches for the truth of her narrative (in the version withheld from us) while casting doubt on the truth of her repentance. Her words, more fitting for "one still in Newgate, than one grown Penitent and Humble, as she afterwards pretends to be"—this telling last phrase, with its undecidably ambiguous *pretends*, invests all her moral claims with an ironic suspicion—are symptomatic less of a life shaken and transfigured by penitence than of a life marked from the outset by the social inheritance of criminality and imprisonment. Moll is born to crime—born in Newgate, like the narrator of *Street-Robberies Consider'd*, to a woman sentenced to death for shoplifting[3]—so that, when, at the abrupt end of her own career as a thief, she is brought to Newgate herself, the moment has a kind of inevitability: "the Place, where so many of my Comrades had been lock'd up, and from whence they went to the fatal Tree; the Place where my Mother suffer'd so deeply, where I was brought into the World, and from whence I expected no Redemption, but by an infamous Death: To conclude, the Place that had so long expected me, and which with so much Art and Success I had so long avoided" (273).

Moll carries Newgate with her as an inheritance and a contagion. Yet, if that contagion exceeds a purely sociological explanation—there is a kind of blood fatality in Moll's repetition of her mother's history—Defoe avoids mystifying her fall into transgression. Like her mother, who "had fallen into very ill Company in *London* in her young Days, occasion'd by *her* Mother [my emph.] sending her frequently to carry Victuals and other Relief to a Kinswoman of hers who was a Prisoner in *Newgate*" (87), Moll is led along her own moral itinerary by social and material pressures: above all by poverty and the absence of institutional supports.[4] Her mother's crime, itself the effect of material desperation and a corrupting environment, is passed on to Moll in the form of social dislocation and dependency: she wanders as a child from one home, one social class, one repertoire of possibilities, to another, a wandering symbolized most neatly by her possibly imaginary sojourn "among a Crew of those People they call Gypsies, or Egyptians." Moll's lack of any stable position in what Raymond Williams would call a knowable community is the source of both her vulnerability to seduction (not only sexual) and her freedom, the contradictory but twin aspects of her married and criminal life.[5]

What John Bender has called the "discordant profusion" of Defoe's tales[6]—their narrative bagginess, vivid excess, and moral disharmony—works against the schematic plainness of their allegorical plots, such as the "History of a wicked Life repented of" of *Moll Flanders*. And his writing's profusion and discord both stem from the intensity of his identification with the voices he invokes at the outset of each narrative. Moll's voice is expressly mediated in the text Defoe published, for its persistent Newgate immodesty threatens the value of her memoirs as an allegory of penitence. But Defoe's presentation of character, and the story's edgy, comic excitement, both hinge on the reader's conviction of a vocal (and psychological) *presence* spun out in the words of the text, a stubbornly real person talking. When her words are at odds with the editor's, hers are the more persuasive.

In the preface, for example, Defoe in his persona of editor, still uneasy over the story's wickedness, writes: "It is suggested there cannot be the same Life, the same Brightness and Beauty, in relating the penitent Part, as is in the criminal Part: If there is any Truth in that Suggestion, I must be allow'd to say, 'tis because there is not the same taste and relish in the Reading, and indeed it is too true that the difference lyes not in the real worth of the Subject so much as in the Gust and Palate of the Reader" (2). But Moll, less squeamish an author though equally sold on repentance, near the end of her narrative writes of her one truly loved husband that "I believe he was as sincere a Penitent, and as thoroughly a reform'd Man, as ever God's goodness brought back from a Profligate, a Highway-Man, and a Robber. I could fill a larger History than this, with the Evidences of this Truth, and but that I doubt that part of the Story will not be equally diverting as the wicked Part, I have had thoughts of making a Volume of it by itself" (339). As readers, we are implicated in Moll's judgment of what will divert us, and, given that something over four-fifths of the text he produced is spent on "the wicked Part," so is Defoe. Her remark leaves open the possibility of a sequel to Moll's history, either a volume of reflections on criminality and penitence like the *Serious Reflections of Robinson Crusoe* or one of the two "beautiful Parts" proposed by the editor in his preface: the life of Mother Midnight, Moll's criminal governess and protector, or "the Life of [Moll's] Transported Husband, a Highway-man." But, however drawn Defoe may have been to serious reflections, Moll, whose own memorandums drift so violently toward "Levity" and "Looseness," would make an unlikely author of them. As a very old, very rich woman, Defoe writes, she "was not so extraordinary a Penitent, as she was at first" (5)—an insight that the coolness, self-exculpation, and delight in physicality of Moll's narration of her life's story betray from the moment she begins speaking.

Counterfeit gestures of attribution and disavowal trigger all Defoe's histories of transgression. The frame of the editor's preface is preserved in *Colonel Jack,* although Defoe's handling of the device here is closer to the offhand disclaimers of *Robinson Crusoe* than to the more elaborate textual biography of *Moll Flanders.* After running through a few of the many readerly "Improvements," or moral lessons, of which the narrative is capable, our "Humble Servant, the Editor" writes, "neither is it of the least Moment to enquire whether the Colonel hath told his own story true or not; If he has made it a *History* or a *Parable,* it will be equally useful" (2). While the editor figure leaves open the question of Colonel Jack's veracity, however, he implicitly guarantees the authenticity of his voice: true or not, the text is a genuine replica—this paradox, verging on oxymoron, stands as the trademark of Defoe's realism—of speech claiming to be true.

The preface to *Roxana* returns to treating questions of authorship in the uneasy mode of *Moll Flanders,* as a problem, a complexly mediated transaction. Apologizing for any shortcomings in his "Performance" of the text, the story's "Relator" employs the same metaphor as Moll's editor, that of dressing a flawed text with new language, but the image coils back on itself doubtfully: "if all the most diverting Parts of [the history] are not adapted to the Instruction and Improvement of the Reader, the *Relator* says, it must be from the Defect of his Performance; dressing up the Story in worse Cloaths than the *Lady,* whose Words he speaks, prepar'd it for the World."[7] It is strange that the editor's *performance* might interfere with the reader's "Instruction and Improvement"; absent any suggestion of rough habits of speech, it is unclear why her narrative should be dressed up at all. More disconcertingly, in describing Roxana as "the Lady, whose Words he speaks," the Relator confuses the usual terms of mimesis, calling attention to his textual appropriation of her voice (he is putting words into her mouth) even as his authorship is drained of real meaning (she is putting words into his). The categories of original and simulacrum spin into perplexity: which one of them is the ventriloquist and which the dummy?

Yet, for all the editor's emphasis on mediation and the elusiveness of textual origins, by drawing attention to his *impersonation* of Roxana's speech and claiming "that it was necessary to conceal Names and Persons; lest what cannot be yet entirely forgot in that Part of the Town, shou'd be remember'd, and the Facts trac'd back too plainly" (1), he underlines even more powerfully Roxana's textual and bodily presence, her dangerous authenticity. His anxious readiness to speak for her, to suppress the details of her revelations, makes her more damagingly and vulnerably real: her voice, even muffled, is suffused with threat and remorse.

Finally, Defoe uses a still plainer device to vouch for the truth of the account: he claims to know the persons involved. His role as witness and familiar gives him a more secure purchase on the questions of truth Roxana's flamboyantly scandalous narrative raises. His testimony vouches for what can only be known on her word: "The *Writer* says, He was particularly acquainted with this Lady's First Husband, the *Brewer,* and with his Father; and also, with his Bad Circumstances; and knows that first Part of the Story to be Truth . . . This may, he hopes, be a Pledge for the Credit of the rest, tho' the Latter Part of her History lay Abroad, and cou'd not so well be vouch'd as the First; yet, as she has told it herself, we have the less Reason to question the Truth of that Part also" (1–2). Once he has vouched for the authenticity of Roxana's narrative, however, the Relator withdraws, passing on the history unaltered. Even this passage, in which he testifies on behalf of her story's truth, ends oddly, with the remark that "yet, as she has told it herself, we have the less Reason to question the Truth" of the later, foreign parts of her history as well— suggesting that our conviction should depend not on the external evidences of corroborating testimony but, rather, on the persuasion of Roxana's voice. And the rest of the preface turns away from an account of the editor's role to reflect on what "is evident" from "the Manner she has told the Story" (2): her way of speaking, again, is the key to an unraveling of her story's meaning. Detailing the most notable features of Roxana's manner of narrating her life—her frequent "excursions" away from the main line of the story to linger over her present condition of terror and guilt;

her plain renderings of all the "Scenes of Crime"; her supple registrations of both "the Pleasure of her Wickedness" and the "secret Hell within, even all the while, when our Joy was at the highest" (260)—Defoe gradually dissolves the textual intermediary of the Relator, so that the text comes to us as an extension of Roxana's voice, her speaking of self and memory.

All of Defoe's criminal texts raise problematic questions concerning the relationship between the voices he projects and his own ideological and authorial stance. The *Great Law of Subordination Consider'd,* for instance, published in 1724 under the pseudonym of Andrew Moreton and described in a subtitle as "ten Familiar Letters" on "the Insolence and Unsufferable Behaviour of Servants in England," contains this observation on criminality in London during the heyday of Jonathan Wild: "our famous Thief-taker (as they call him) has a List of 7000 *Newgate*-Birds, now in Services in this City, and Parts adjacent, all with Intent to rob the Houses they are in; and the Reason of this I hinted at in one of my last, namely, that it is certainly encreas'd by the Pride and Insolence, which Servants in general now are arriv'd to; for that (as I said then) when once Servants are brought to contemn the Persons and Authority of their Masters, or Mistresses, or Employers, they soon come to despise their Interests; and at last to break into their Property; and thus they become Thieves, in a manner insensible."[8] For "Moreton" the insolence of serving maids is a synecdoche for the greater unruliness of the poor, the "world turn'd upside down." "'Tis apparent," he writes in another letter, "that the many Ways which the Poor find to make themselves uneasie to the Rich, are such, and the Advantages which they have in this Country, by the Privileges they enjoy, are also such, that they bid fair for inverting the Order of things; *in a Word,* it is already true, in a great measure, that in *England* the Poor govern, and the Rich submit" (105).

Read against the pages narrating Colonel Jack's boyhood or Roxana's terrified slipping into poverty after her first husband abandons her with five children, these passages from *The Great Law of Subordination Consider'd* are so grotesquely patrician as to seem almost Swiftian: bitter mockeries of ruling-class fear and contempt, derisive underminings of self-satisfied notions of hierarchy. But Defoe meant every word of them literally—at least when he inhabited the role of the gentleman who speaks them, as he also meant the carnivalesque, violent memoirs of the narrator of *Street-Robberies Consider'd,* four years later. There are moments, in thinking about Defoe, when one feels a kind of dizziness: he seems to contain and articulate all the contradictory strains of his culture. An eighteenth-century Zelig, he takes on, uncannily, the characteristics of those personae whose words he speaks yet never loses his sense of estrangement from them nor (in Defoe's case, not Zelig's) a corrosive, distancing irony. While he identified most strongly with the interests and social values of tradespeople, dissenters, and the emerging middle classes—the accumulation of wealth through patient, thrifty labor; contractual as opposed to station-bound deference on the part of servants and apprentices; the tranquillity of private property—Defoe, through his surrogate and alien voices, wrote of criminality not just as an object of warning or horror but from inside the act, and the thought, of transgression itself.

The freedom that Defoe allows the textual masks he puts on, to speak from marginal or dangerous experience in their own vernacular, signifies more than a propensity to trick up his discourse in a variety of colors. Defoe's writing in voices argues, implicitly, for forms of cultural emancipation tied to the emergence, in the early eighteenth century, of a new public sphere. As outlined by Jürgen Habermas, this was a social and discursive domain combining aspects of private, domestic life with a more inclusive, commercially mediated form of public interaction—mediated, above all, through the institutions of publishing and literary performance.[9] As these institutions became more accessible, through the commerce-fueled enlargement of the reading public as well as the increasing attention paid, especially in the genres of criminal writing, to the poor and socially marginal, those who in a more restricted literary culture had been below the threshold of visibility, or of audibility, found increasing opportunities to take part in a shared culture of letters.

The public sphere was not, of course, really open: while it idealized "a kind of social intercourse," in Habermas's words, which "disregarded status altogether,"[10] such institutions as coffeehouses and the periodicals that grew out of them were in practice bound to the interests and cultural habits of a quite specific, if somewhat permeable, social grouping. Women had access, though hard won, to certain forms and sites of representation—domestic and scandalous fictions, private letters, conduct books, playhouses—but were largely barred from speaking parts in other discourses: science, religion, trade, government, law. The vagabond or laboring poor, women and men alike, had next to no means for engaging in this newly powerful cultural domain, although there was no need to marshal explicit notions of class or hierarchy to exclude them: property and education, and the version of rationality these posited as *natural,* were barrier enough.[11]

And yet I think there is no question that this construction of a public sphere could be genuinely emancipatory. As the trade in low and criminal genres, in particular, grew during the late seventeenth and early eighteenth centuries, the voices and experience of the poor became available to a more socially diverse audience and were made the objects of a complex textual sanctioning: as I have argued, the poor could become, in Erich Auerbach's words, "the subjects of serious, problematic, and even tragic representation" but only at the cost of being criminalized.[12] Read through the filter of trials, canting books, rogue stories, and last dying speeches, the customs and discourse of poverty could hardly avoid being linked, metonymically, to threats of violence, social upheaval, and sexual disorder, but, to the extent that the poor in their roles of accused, victim, and witness were able to speak for themselves, they became subjects as well as objects of representation and could give their own reasons and meanings to events. If not the beginnings of equality, such speech stood at least for the possibilities of advocacy and contestation.[13]

Defoe's criminal narratives, like the last dying speeches they sometimes resemble in their exhortatory fervor, aim at two kinds of truth: outward (the circumstantially accurate narration of events) and, more challengingly, inward (the elucidation of subjectivity). The two aims are interconnected through the fiction of self-disclosure—that is, by the claim that the text originates in the speech of the criminal subject. For the putative speakers the motivation for such disclosure is in essence proprietary. Jack Sheppard, claiming for himself in the first sentence of his ghostwritten autobiography (Defoe's *Narrative of all the Robberies, Escapes, &c. of John Sheppard* [1724]) "the Liberty of publishing his Case," betrays a desire not so much to justify or gloss over his actions as to assert a right of property to the representation of his own experience: "As my unhappy Life and Actions have afforded Matter of much Amusement to the World; and various Pamphlets, Papers, and Pictures relating thereunto are gone abroad, most or all of them misrepresenting my Affairs; 'tis necessary that I should say something for my self, and set certain intricate Matters in a true Light; every Subject, how unfortunate or unworthy soever, having the Liberty of publishing his Case" (209). Sheppard holds out for a kind of moral copyright, against an unregulated public domain in which his "unhappy Life and Actions have afforded Matter of much Amusement" through the selling of "various Pamphlets, Papers, and Pictures." Yet the same lack of regulation in the pamphlet and book trade which leads to misrepresentations of his history lets Sheppard narrate his life in his own terms. Public consumption is the condition of private authenticity.

Certain of Defoe's criminal narratives, such as the earlier *History of the Remark-*

*able Life of John Sheppard*, are written in the third person, but they too are authenticated by their claim to originate in their subject's voice. The path of vocal or textual transmission is always visible. In this text the different episodes of Sheppard's career are reported, Defoe alleges, "from the most authentick Accounts, as the Informations of divers Justices of the Peace, the several Shop-Keepers abovemention'd, the principal Officers of *Newgate* and *New Prison*," and, crucially for the episodes of housebreaking and prison escape which lay at the source of Sheppard's transgressive glamour, "from the Confession of *Sheppard* made to the Rev. Mr. *Wagstaff*, who officiated for the Ordinary of Newgate."[14] This reported confession not only sets confused points in the criminal record straight and furnishes the key to certain mysteries (notably, how did he manage to break out of the condemned hold in Newgate under his keepers' very noses?) but evokes the bantering, recriminatory, impenitent glee of Sheppard's habitation of the role of criminal prodigy. "Neither his sad Circumstances," Defoe writes, "nor the solemn Exhortations of the several Divines who visited him, were able to divert him from this ludicrous way of Expression; he said, *They were all Ginger-Bread Fellows*, and came rather out of Curiosity, than charity; and to form *Papers* and *Ballads* out of his Behaviour" (201). This last charge suggests both the extent of the penetration of the literary trades into the world of crime and the prison and Sheppard's clear-sightedness concerning his own celebrity—which, as the sheer number of pantomimes, ballads, trials, romances, and biographies published in the wake of his hanging reveals, was extraordinary.[15]

Defoe's *History*, published after Sheppard's second escape from Newgate, while he was still at large, ends with several pages of anecdotes exhibiting the escape artist's cynical and materialist wit, a lowlife precursor to the table talk of Dr. Johnson and Coleridge. His most famous line, spoken "passionately, and with a Motion of striking," comes at the end of one of the Reverend Mr. Wagstaff's spiritual visits, as Sheppard dismisses his calls to repent: "one *File*'s worth all the *Bibles* in the World" (202). Sheppard's estrangement from religion, the laws of property, and the jail itself—from the dominant institutions of his culture—is so complete it amounts to a form of subversion: by burrowing out from under them, he repudiates their legitimacy. And once he is out he scarcely bothers to hide; rambling through the streets and public houses of London, he acts as if he had become invisible. In the *History* Sheppard's mocking and disruptive voice comes more and more to the center, finally taking over the narrative from its ostensible third-person author.

In the narratives that grew up around him Jack Sheppard was as much an imaginary as a real creature. But Sheppard was also subject to a whole series of concrete and well-documented interventions of law—arrest, deposition, trial, imprisonment, notice of escape, interrogation, and hanging—and so, however fancifully portrayed, was obstinately caught up in the real. The authenticity of Defoe's biographical account is bolstered by the authoritative deployment of external, corroborating evidence: trial records, sworn testimonies, papers handed over in full view of the Tyburn crowd. But, when he wrote in the voices of such invented personae as Moll Flanders, the effect of authenticity depended more on the convincing evocation of the inward disturbances and inconsistencies of subjectivity.

Moll's words are so often at odds with her actions, or with words she has written before, that her history can seem wilfully secretive, duplicitous, suspect—or merely incoherent, as Ian Watt argues, "blind and almost purposeless" in its concentration on the fleeting minutiae of action and memory.[16] For Watt the work's most damaging incoherences stem from Defoe's unconsciousness of the contradictions Moll's voice, and his own plot, betray. The intensity of Defoe's identification with the subjectivity Moll speaks as her own blinded him to all the narrative's discrepant and incongruous postures. Thus, the moral claim of the preface—that "there is not a wicked Action in any Part of [this Book], but is first or last rendered Unhappy and Unfortunate" (3)—is brazenly contradicted by Moll's most fortunate history of wicked appropriation and thrifty investment, which ends with the arrival at her Virginia plantation of a fine cargo purchased in London out of just a part of her criminal hoard. "From the sentence and the incident to the fundamental ethical structure of the whole book," Watt writes, Defoe's "moral attitude to his creation is as shallow and devious and easily deflected as his heroine's": like Moll, he is almost instinctively fraudulent, caught up unwitting in the psychic and ideological tensions within Puritanism.[17]

Defoe's failure to imagine Moll as other than a surrogate for his own "unconscious and unreflective" perceptions of the world accounts also for what Watt represents as a kind of blankness in her, despite the excessive clarity of her recollection. "She seems fundamentally untouched," he writes, "by her criminal background"; in fact, her character "is not noticeably affected either by her sex, by her criminal pursuits, or indeed by any of the objective factors which might have been expected to set her apart from her author." The autobiography she spins out never jostles her materialist and self-interested equilibrium. Neither the long history of crime she relates nor the repentance she asserts seems to change her, except that crime makes her rich, and penitence allows her to consolidate and enjoy her riches. Moll's Newgate conversion is thus, for Watt, a point on which nothing turns, a moment of negligible crisis—one of "a series of somewhat inexplicable religious breakdowns in the psychic mechanism, breakdowns, however, which do not permanently impair her healthy amorality."[18]

Conversion is at the center of Homer Brown's essay on the displaced self in Defoe's fictions but in a rather specific sense: a death of the self which is at the same time a return to self but experienced now as "perfectly chang'd," as, in Moll's words, "another Body" (281).[19] Yet the kind of conversion Moll undergoes in Newgate is always, necessarily, insecure: "conversion is a recurrent need, a revelation followed each time by another lapse, a forgetting that is like an absence, requiring a new dialectical struggle."[20] Augustine's *Confessions* were the crucial model for Defoe's account of conversion, according to Brown, but Defoe has lost Augustine's confidence in the endurance of conversion and the stability of the recovered self.

Brown's attention to the erosions and instability of self acknowledges a complexity that Watt sees without seeing. For, as Watt complains, even after the painful rehearsals of guilt during Moll's familiarization to Hell in Newgate prison and the hard accession of repentance, she still seems much the same person she has always been: scared off from criminality but not from the self-interested calculation of goods and hazards nor from the social pretensions that lead her to tell the captain of the ship on which she is soon to be transported that she and her unlawful highwayman husband "had been Persons of a differing Character from the wretched Crew that we came with" (313). But these incongruities in her character are not authorial lapses. Moll herself worries over the faults and irresolutions her memorandums reveal, and, for all his seeming dissolution of authorship in the grain of Moll's voice, Defoe constructs her confessions so that they always betray the strains of unconsciousness and misprision which thread through subjectivity.

Through the long Newgate episode Moll tracks the desperate turnings of her own unrepentant intelligence, blocked by her custom of inward scrutiny from changing or even from making what she knows to be counterfeit gestures of change. In one passage, for example, she describes her feelings shortly after arrest: "Then I repented heartily of all my Life past, but that Repentance yielded me no Satisfaction, no Peace, no not in the least, because, *as I said to myself,* it was repenting after the Power of farther Sinning was taken away: I seem'd not to Mourn that I had committed such Crimes, and for the Fact, as it was an Offence against God and my Neighbour; but I mourn'd that I was to be punish'd for it; I was a Penitent as I thought, not that I had sinn'd, but that I was to suffer, and this took away all the Comfort, and even the hope of my Repentance in my own Thoughts" (274). Her words here stand directly against Watt's claim that "the central confusion in Moll Flanders's moral consciousness [is] her tendency to confuse penitence for her sins with chagrin at the punishment of her crimes."[21] Yet Watt's observation is also true, for Defoe clearly registers, at the same time that Moll torments herself over the confusion of motives, the ways in which her own reformation turns on this very confusion.

The further she travels from Newgate and the threat of hanging, the more pallid her sense of her own trespasses, as Defoe's offhand remark in the preface ("she liv'd it seems, to be very old; but was not so extraordinary a Penitent, as she was at first") foreshadows. For all her exacting spiritual accounting and her grief over her own part in the criminal career of her imprisoned husband, it is only after she has been sentenced to death "that for the first time I felt any real signs of Repentance" (287). And, although she advances in penitence under the watch of a minister sent by her old governess, the appearance of her name on the "Dead Warrant" for the next hanging day at Tyburn throws her back into dejection, from which only the joy of a reprieve, and the eventual commutation of her sentence to transportation, can spring her.

The "good Minister," in fact, who solicited her reprieve only that she might have time to make a more heartfelt contrition before dying, "mourn[s] sincerely" the news of her commuted sentence, and, if at first Moll has "a melancholly Reflection upon it in my own Mind . . . that the good Minister's fears were not without cause," her thoughts speedily turn to more practical concerns when her governess—herself "a very great Penitent" during the almost fatal course of an illness—comes to visit. To Moll's fears of suffering a spiritual relapse among the "dreadful Gang" of transported convicts, "Well, well, *says she*, but I hope you will not be tempted with such a horrid Example as that, and as soon as the Minister was gone, she told me, she would not have me discourag'd, for perhaps ways and means might be found out to dispose of me in a particular way, by my self, of which she would talk farther to me afterward . . . I look'd earnestly at her, and I thought she look'd more chearful than she usually had done, and I entertain'd immediately a Thousand Notions of being deliver'd, but could not for my Life imagine the Methods" (294). Her

governess responds to Moll's fears of spiritual contamination with a plan for secur-
ing her a private cabin by means of a bribe to the boatswain—as if the contamination she feared, that is, were not spiritual but social. And she has read her
confederate rightly, for Moll never again speaks of her spiritual fears, during all the
fifteen weeks she is kept waiting in Newgate nor during the complex negotiations
for a cabin and a seat at the Captain's table. What is most telling in their exchange
is not the governess's pragmatic concern for Moll's material comfort but, rather,
Moll's unspoken and immediate acquiescence in her friend's dismissal of the good
minister's anxious, sacrificial religiosity. Deliverance is a fact of this world and needs
to be bargained for.

By the eve of her departure for America, Moll is more frank, at least inwardly.
The good Minister, she writes, "was sensibly griev'd at my going, because, *as he
said,* he fear'd I should lose the good impressions, which a prospect of Death had
at first made on me, and which were since encreas'd by his Instructions, and the
pious Gentleman was exceedingly concern'd about me on that Account . . . On the
other Hand, I really was not so sollicitous about it, as I was before, but I industri-
ously conceal'd my Reasons for it from the Minister, and to the last he did not
know, but that I went with the utmost reluctance and affliction" (306). There is no
reason, I think, to question the authenticity of Moll's Newgate conversion: she
traces all its stages and backslidings with a scrupulous hand, and it acts as the point
at which all the text's accumulated dangers and warnings converge. Her abandonment of criminal labor lets Defoe shape his fiction to lawful and morally orthodox
ends, at least in appearance and frees her from the psychological burden of a long
history of guilty desire. Yet, if Moll is repentant, she is not cripplingly repentant.
She and her husband have cash to pay off their indentures, to lay in "a Stock of
Tools and Materials for the Business of Planting" (317–18) and to order an "abun-
dance of good things for our Comfort in the Voyage, as Brandy, Sugar, Lemons,
&c. to make Punch" (316); their colonial prospects are bright, and she is dead to her
criminal past. Despite the good minister's pietistic scruples, there is no need to
belabor a reformation she is happy to undergo.

For, as the "pious Gentleman" is right to lament, transportation offers not penitence but forgetting: a new life, as Moll persuades her husband, "where no Body
could upbraid us with what was past, or we be in any dread of a Prison; and without the Agonies of a condemn'd Hole to drive us to it, where we should look back
on all our past Disasters with infinite Satisfaction, when we should consider that

our Enemies should entirely forget us, and that we should live as new People in a new World, no Body having any thing to say to us, or we to them" (304). All through Moll's narrative of her history and misfortunes runs a tension between confessional and evasive desire. If, on the one hand, she is drawn to disburden herself of guilt and to brag of her outlaw dexterity, on the other, she struggles to conceal as much as she can of her life, to dissociate herself from the outward traces of her activities in the world. Even during the scene of reunion with her husband in Newgate, in the thick of her remorse and tortuous self-examination and with both their lives forfeit to the law, Moll gives Jemy an account of her life since their parting which is, in its lies and disavowals, pure fiction. "Representing myself," Moll writes, "as fallen into some Company that led me to relieve my Distresses by a way that I had been utterly unacquainted with . . . I told him I far'd the worse for being taken in the Prison for one *Moll Flanders,* who was a famous successful Thief, that all of them had heard of, but none of them had ever seen, but that *as he knew well* was none of my Name" (298). Her falsification comes as a surprise in the wake of her seeming conversion into "another Body," her flood of confession to the minister (who "unlock'd all the Sluces of my Passions: He broke into my very Soul . . . I hid nothing from him" [288]), and her passionate, even supernatural, fondness for Jemy,[22] but the compulsion to secrecy is stronger than love or religion, and the moment is fully in keeping with her whole history of disguise.

Moll never appears except under cover of an alias, least of all to the reader, who is warned from trying to learn too much by her memorandums' very first words: "My True Name is so well known in the Records, or Registers at *Newgate,* and in the *Old-Baily,* and there are some things of such Consequence still depending there, relating to my particular Conduct, that it is not to be expected I should set my Name, or the Account of my Family to this Work" (7). The project of anonymity is carried on by Defoe in his role of editor even at a distance of forty years from the time of Moll's writing and, it must be, at least thirty years after her death would seem to have effaced the urgency of concealment. For both the text's authors, however, secrecy is not only a practical need but also a source of glamour and pleasure. The disguises Moll assumes on her criminal expeditions—she takes the parts of a gentlewoman, a beggar, and a porter's wife and for three weeks wears the "Dress so contrary to Nature" of a man, acting as partner to an unsuspecting male shop-lift—help her to thrive in her practice and evade capture, but she carries the impulse further, into the heart of private life. Even with her governess and Jemy, as in the story she tells at their Newgate reunion, Moll misleads by omission, glosses over her own most criminal actions, shifts guilt onto her victims or confederates, and guards her money, her origins, and her name as dangerous mysteries. The name, in fact, or the name's multiplicity and absence—the very problem posed by Defoe's anonymous and pseudonymous authorship—is *Moll Flanders*'s most vivid figure for identity itself.

Moll's "True Name," never pronounced, haunts her autobiography. If the first three words of her text prefigure a truth the narrative never delivers, her evasion of that truth reflects the imperatives of a world in which identity is mercurial, suspect, uncertain. True names embody a solidity and fullness that sort ill with the waywardness of Moll's life, which unfolds from the very start—her stories of traveling with Gypsies, her maneuverings to be adopted into a rich family—as a series of shifts and improvisations of identity. The weakness of the social and political apparatus of identification before the later eighteenth century meant that it was possible, especially in the labyrinthine and unregulated spaces of London, to cut oneself free from the name's burden of memory or kinship.[23] Moll's unspoken true name would, if known, bind her to her mother, biological origins, her birth in the condemned ward, and a criminal genealogy—and, even more punishingly, to a fixed class position, a future of housework.

If the plot of *Moll Flanders* describes her struggle to elude the captivation of a stable, socially recognized and constrained, identity—an identity whose sign is the name others know her by—criminal names plague her like revenants and nearly destroy her. On her first trip to America with her third husband, at what seems the furthest possible distance from her Newgate origins, "I thought my self," she writes, "the happiest Creature alive" (85). In order to marry she has deftly concealed her lineage and scant fortune, and the fact that she has a second husband still living, and she seems truly shed of her past. But then her mother-in-law begins to tell her own story—that she was herself a criminal, burned in the hand and transported from Newgate—and at last, Moll writes, "she went on with her own Story so long, and in so particular a manner, that I began to be very uneasy, but coming to one Particular that requir'd telling her Name, I thought I should have sunk down in the place . . . [for] this was certainly no more or less *than my own Mother,* and I had now two Children, and was big with another by my own Brother, and lay with him still every Night" (88).

However dextrously she covers the traces of her own history and origins, her success in concealing the "True Name" that would identify her leads, paradoxically, to a loss of control, an upsetting return. It is the suppression of her birth name which permits her incestuous marriage, as its utterance leads to a recognition of guilt. Later, in Newgate, it is the very success of her self-concealment—the masking of her true name under the estranging alias of Moll Flanders—which leads to her close brush with the gallows: for, as soon as she is arrested for one case of shoplifting, the "harden'd Wretches" of Newgate connect her (275), through all the false names she has assumed, to the long history of criminality associated with the name of Moll Flanders, and so, as by rumor "an old Offender" (282), she is found guilty and sentenced.

Moll protests, accurately under the law if also a bit absurdly under the circumstances of her autobiography, that, by acting under the sway of "the fatal Report of being an old Offender," the law's agents "did not do me strict Justice, for I was not in the Sense of the Law an old Offender, whatever I was in the Eye of the Judge; for I had never been before them in a judicial way before, so the Judges could not Charge me with being an old Offender, but the Recorder was pleas'd to represent my Case as he thought fit" (295). It is never clear under what name Moll is tried, the one inherited from her mother or one of her own making or one of those— "Mrs. *Mary*, Mrs. *Molly*, and after that plain *Moll Flanders*" (275)—with which her criminal fellows burden and mock her, and thus it remains uncertain what the True Name is by which she is "known in the Records, or Registers at *Newgate*, and in the *Old-Baily*" (7) or why, since she has "perform'd much more than the limited Terms of my Transportation" (342), the revelation of her legal identity should constitute a threat.

But, if, as Defoe intimates in this text, identity consists precisely in the endless shuffling and displacement of names and the conflicting histories they embody, the closure and inescapability of a True Name represent a deadening constriction of identity, and so Moll's aversion may be less pragmatic than symbolic. Even the choice of *Moll Flanders* as the alias to cover her autobiography is a kind of perverse dismantling of the name, since its origins are so resistant to meaning: some envious fellow criminals gave her the name, she writes, though "it was no more of Affinity with my real Name, or with any of the Names I had ever gone by, than black is of Kin to white . . . nor could I ever learn how they came to give me the Name, or what the Occasion of it was" (214). Whether the true name of criminal genealogy or the unaccountable false name her criminal confederates know her by, any single, immutable name exposes Moll to discovery, arrest, and imprisonment—the diverse forms of social regulation and control. The name is an agent of the police.

The writing of autobiography thus becomes, for Defoe, as it is for Moll, a strategy of evasion, a way of assaying and multiplying identities. Moll's history originates in a condition of transgressive rootlessness, a wandering and dislocation marked as criminal from the beginning—indeed, from *before* the beginning, since in its progress toward Newgate her history turns out to be, inexorably, a repetition of her mother's and of her kinswoman's before her. Through all her narration of the vivid and disruptive experience of sexual adventurism and urban criminality, Moll articulates, in the vocal mimicry of her unflagging *écriture*, a troubled, extravagant, and violent subjectivity: one with which the reader is invited to feel complicity by Defoe's textual impersonation of her imagined voice.

# CHAPTER EIGHT

# Guilt and the Reader of *Roxana*

The reader's complicity with criminal voices is implicit in the form of Defoe's mock-autobiographical texts, but that form's effectiveness depends upon a culture of guilt and uncertainty. The resonances of Defoe's histories, in fact, are bound up with a double assumption of guilt:[1] not only does the author (real or imagined) rely on a persistent cultural belief in the universal inheritance of guilt to furnish the context for moral exhortation, but the reader, in the course of reading, is urged to assume the specific guilt of the criminal protagonist. Both through direct cues and through the energy and nervous gregariousness of his textual voices, Defoe solicits our identification with the experience of transgression and the guilty pleasure or fear that grows out of it and then, by a conversion worked out in the transaction of reading, with the protagonist's reform and eventual, if precarious, happiness.

This aim is clearest in those passages clustered at the stories' beginnings and endings, in which various uses of the narrative are sanctioned. Colonel Jack brings his history to a close, for example, with the recommendation "to all that read this Story, that when they find their Lives come up in any Degree to any Similitude of Cases, they will enquire by me, and ask themselves, Is not this the Time to Repent? Perhaps the Answer may touch them" (309). If a certain inward scrutiny on the reader's part is thus textually enforced, any suspected pleasure in wickedness is reproved, as in the preface to *Roxana:* "Scenes of Crime can scarce be represented in such a Manner, but some may make a Criminal Use of them; but when Vice is painted in its Low-priz'd Colours, 'tis not to make People in love with it, but to expose it; and if the Reader makes a wrong Use of the Figures, the Wickedness is his own." Yet, as a similar passage from the preface to *Moll Flanders* allows, the tracking of crime to its mixed origins in poverty and a sinful heart and the urging of readers to find their own experience reflected in the autobiography of a transgressor—with whose voice they come to identify over the course of a long narrative—produce ambiguous, uncontrollable effects: "It is suggested that there cannot be the same Life, the same Brightness and Beauty, in relating the penitent Part, as is in the criminal Part: If there is any Truth in that Suggestion, I must be allow'd to say, 'tis because there is not the same taste and relish in the Reading, and indeed it is too true that the difference lyes not in the real worth of the Subject so much as in the Gust and Palate of the Reader" (2). If, by bringing us closer to the private experience of criminal breakdown and repentance, the inward concentration of Defoe's first-person writing means to provide an efficacious model for an inner moral accounting and conversion, it can also lead, as he seems nervously aware, to a dissolution of moral patterns, a spellbound lingering over scenes of disruption and excess. Defoe throws the responsibility back onto his readers for their wicked absorption in crime, but with mixed success, and a bad grace.

At the time Defoe wrote, the cultural reserves of guilt from which he could draw in constructing his criminal protagonists and their audience were mainly religious. Even the most novel of his texts are shot through with traces of Puritanism, and their governing narrative structures are taken over from such forms as spiritual autobiography and penitent last dying speech.[2] Yet, while the specific religious tradition Defoe was shaped by was Dissenting, the conflation of criminality with sin was universal at the start of the eighteenth century. The emergence of law and the material practices of policing, criminal trial, and secular punishment as the crucial underpinnings of a new bourgeois social order took up the whole of the eighteenth century in England and was never uncontested. But, if this emergence forms part of a larger cultural history of secularization, it drew, especially near the beginning, from religious customs and structures of feeling for its force. Guilt, in particular, was marked by the contradictory bloodlines of sin as an inescapable inheritance and crime as a startling rupture.[3]

Defoe's most driven and conflicted representation of guilt is contained in *Roxana*—or, rather, is not contained, since it is the psychological *excess* of guilt which pulls the narrative framework apart and leads to the collapse of the expected plot of trespass and redemption. Roxana's horror at the heart of her own darkness is a stray thread that, once pulled, unravels the whole moral fabric of her account. "Psychological guilt," Alexander Welsh has written of the novel after Walter Scott, "is this loose end to the plot of realism,"[4] but equally in Defoe there is no acquittal, no final clearing of the books. What Welsh describes in the context of a social contract and a developing ideology of historical and collective responsibility—whose terms are always impossible to satisfy and whose residue is thus a burden-some, guilty sense of failure—is already, eerily visible in *Roxana* as an instance of the gradual criminalization of subjectivity, a process that called for a more and more attentive policing of the inward and concealed shifts of desire.

At the climax of her history of sexuality and profit, at the highest point of her social trajectory, the Lady Roxana—yet another false name—is weighed down by a sense of moral cost, by "a Heart loaded with Crime" (265). After the "chearful Work" of watching her final husband, a Dutch merchant, open his boxes of account books and goldsmith's bills to reveal his wealth to her and after displaying her own high-yield mortgages and securities to him, Roxana grows less and less easy with her prosperous condition (259). "Let no-body conclude," she writes, "from the strange Success I met with in all my wicked Doings, and the vast Estate which I had rais'd by it, that therefore I either was happy or easie: No, no, there was a Dart stuck into the Liver; there was a secret Hell within, even all the while, when our Joy was at the highest; but more especially *now*, after it was all over, and when according to all appearance, I was one of the happiest Women upon Earth; all this while, *I say*, I had such a constant Terror upon my Mind, as gave me every now and then very terrible Shocks" (260). The stage is set, of course, for conversion.

With her investment portfolio secure and her sexual waywardness regularized by marriage (which also affords her the longed-for title of ladyship), Roxana has attained the position from which all Defoe's protagonists begin the work of repen-tance and exculpation, their self-reproaching reconciliation to the rich, happy end-ings of their lives. Like Moll Flanders in Newgate, she is at first cast down by the afflicting memory of "all the gay and wicked Course which I had gone throrow before," but soon she begins "to look back upon it with that Horror, and that De-testation, which is the certain Companion, if not the Forerunner, of Repentance." (261). If at first her remorse is "of another and lower kind of Repentance," so that she is "rather moved by my Fears of Vengeance, than from a sense of being spar'd from being punish'd, and landed safe after a Storm," she is acutely conscious of the difference, and she begins, in very concrete ways, to make reparation (261). On the poor Quaker woman with whom she has lived Roxana settles, with her husband's kind offices, a good income for life. Her own estate she is at pains to keep separate from her husband's, so "that I should not bring my Husband under the Blast of a just Providence, for mingling my cursed ill-gotten Wealth with his honest Estate"

(260), even as she allows the income from her holdings to be used for both their maintenance and so to be washed clean by her generous devotion. Her two sons and two daughters she provides for well, if in secret. Everything seems ready for the heart's scouring and reformation, the swift end to a troubled but exemplary life.

Yet this outcome is just what her history abjures. *Roxana*'s deviation from the expected narrative pattern of crime, remorse, and reward involves the reader in unaccountable breakdowns of authorship, obscurities of plotting, and sudden blanks that make it impossible to know even what exactly is going on in the text's final pages. The chronicler's mystifications and half-suppressed clues disturb the normal workings of narrative representation.

Roxana's history of her life is knocked off course by the fear that her daughter will recognize her. Roxana has all along provided for her children under cover of anonymity, afraid for their sake and her own to acknowledge them. Until she can sever her present identity from a history of crimes, recognition poses a threat to well-being, both morally ("I cou'd by no means think of ever letting the Children know what a kind of Creature they ow'd their Being to, or giving them an Occasion to upbraid their Mother with her scandalous Life, much less to justifie the like Practice from my Example" [205]) and socially ("I wou'd not have been seen, so as to be known by the Name of *Roxana*, no, not for ten Thousand Pounds; it wou'd have been enough to have ruin'd me to all Intents and Purposes with my Husband, and everybody else too; I might as well have been the *German Princess*" [271]). Roxana's allusion here to the notorious Mary Carleton—a con artist whose impersonation of a German princess was but one of numerous masks tried on in a career of social climbing, false marriages, and lawsuits—is obviously, self-laceratingly, ironic: she has just been made a Dutch countess herself, her merchant husband having bought her an aristocratic title, and her likeness to the "Counterfeit Lady" of Francis Kirkman's 1673 narrative of the Carleton case suggests Defoe's indebtedness to such earlier criminal histories and scandalous memoirs.[5] Roxana is at least as vulnerable to unmasking as the false princess and as chained to the past. Mary Carleton had been exposed by a letter from Dover as a polygamist and former prisoner; Roxana, even as she tries to annul all trace of her past as a whore and the king's mistress, is linked by "broken Fragments of Stories" and a discharged servant's memory of seeing her dance in a Turkish dress, to the very history she means to escape (269). Unhappily, as this servant's confused feelings of betrayal and abandonment eventually lead her to suspect, she is the Lady Roxana's younger daughter, her orphaned and avenging namesake.

Roxana, unlike Moll Flanders, lets her "True Name" slip as she recounts the uneasy negotiations between her daughter and her lifelong servant and companion, Amy, whom she employs to mediate all contact with her children. This child perplexes her conscience, for Amy chances to learn that, having for a time lost track of the two surviving girls from her mistress's first marriage, she has unknowingly hired the younger as a maidservant in Roxana's own household. Fearful that the girl might discover her mistress's identity, Amy "took Occasion some time after, without letting me know any-thing of it, to find some Fault with the Maid, and turn her away." Roxana, however, "too tender a Mother still, notwithstanding what I had done, to let this poor Girl go about the World drudging, as it were, for Bread," sets her up, like Dickens's surrogate self Pip, with great expectations, leaving her to wait for her mysterious good fortune to be realized (197).[6] During this period of waiting the girl comes to tell Amy of her luck: "*Amy* pretended to be much surpriz'd at the Alteration, and overjoy'd for her sake, and began to treat her very well, entertain'd her handsomely, and when she wou'd have gone away, pretended to ask my Leave, and sent my Coach home with her; and in short, learning from her where she lodg'd, which was in the City, *Amy* promis'd to return her Visit, and did so; and in a Word, *Amy* and s u s a n (for she was my own Name) began an intimate Acquaintance together" (205). But the intimacy that grows up between them is infected with thwarted longings and dangerous, unstable doublings of identity. Susan, bearing her mother's name and shaped by her abandonment, acts out her mother's suppressed hope to be known to her, but the daughter's very violence of desire leads Roxana to more and more desperate concealments.

The nearer Susan comes to knowledge of her own history, the more she encroaches on the secret parts of Roxana's: even the class differences that seem to confine them to separate spheres give Susan a threatening degree of access to her mistress, for as a lower servant she is invisible to the woman whom she watches with such intensity.[7] Although Susan at first tells Amy that she has only seen Roxana once and then only as a masked, spectacular presence—"*'twas very strange:* Madam, *says she to* Amy, but tho' I liv'd near two Years in the House, I never saw my Mistress in my Life, except it was that publick Night when she danc'd in the fine *Turkish* Habit, and then she was so disguis'd, that I knew nothing of her afterwards" (206)—she remembers things differently to Roxana herself:

when she talk'd how handsome and how fine a Lady this *Roxana* was, I cou'd not help being
pleas'd and tickl'd with it; and put in Questions two or three times, of how handsome she
was? and was she really so fine a Woman as they talk'd of? *and the like* . . .

Indeed, *says she at last,* she was a most beautiful Creature, as ever I saw in my Life: But
then, *said I,* you never had the Opportunity to see her, but when she was set-out to the best
Advantage.

Yes, yes, Madam, *says she,* I have seen her several times in her *Dishabille,* and I can assure
you, she was a very fine Woman; and that which was more still, every-body said she did not
paint. (287)

The conflict between these two stories only draws attention to the ways in which
Susan's social insignificance, her invisibility as a servant, gives her a keen if slippery edge over the lady Roxana. Her power to see without being seen threatens to
undermine Roxana's fictive remaking of her own identity.

Ironically, and then (it seems) tragically, Susan's search for a mother is undermined by her very success in penetrating her mistress's various masks. Drawing
inferences from the scant and garbled evidence she has in the case, the "broken
Fragments of Stories" picked up here and there in her unsettled life (269), she concludes at first that her mother is Amy, not the fine lady but her agent and serving
woman. And Amy's vehement denials, intended to thwart the girl's poor efforts at
investigation, only serve to divert her suspicions onto Roxana herself. Once Susan
has been unwillingly cornered into that surmise, the problems she has had in making sense of the evidence begin to dissolve, and the crime of her abandonment
comes to seem more terrible as the romance of her origins becomes more alluring.
If Susan seeks her mother at first from a confused sense of love and betrayal, she
swiftly becomes, in the face of Amy's cruel repulses, a kind of implacable demon
and reflection, a hellhound running Roxana to ground.

"I was continually perplex'd with this Hussy," Roxana records bitterly, after
learning of Susan's plan to pursue her through all the towns of England and Holland, "and thought she haunted me like an Evil Spirit" (310). *Roxana* itself becomes, in its final pages, the most haunted and broken of all Defoe's fictions. After
the ground has been prepared for the heroine's repentance and conversion to a new
life, Susan's inquisitorial harrying pulls Roxana back to the very "Complication of
Crime" from which she thought to have twisted herself free (301). It is the discovery that Susan has been living in her house in Pall Mall as a lower servant which
first leads Roxana to resolve "to put myself into some Figure of Life, in which I

might not be scandalous to my own Family, and be afraid to make myself known to my own Children" (206). And so with Amy's connivance she slips out of her identity as the Lady Roxana and becomes, in the Quaker's apartments, a respectable unmarried woman and then the Dutch merchant's wife. But the pressure of Susan's inquiries keeps entangling her in the past. The scraps of testimony and evidence her daughter collects bind the willfully disjunct stages of Roxana's career into a connected history and thus betray how far she is subject to the past she keeps struggling, through concealment, flight, and penitent autobiography, to escape.

It is not so easy to live, as Moll Flanders held out as a hope to her Lancashire husband, "where no Body could upbraid us with what was past, or we be in any dread of a prison . . . [to] live as new People in a new World" (304). Susan bursts into the trite confines of spiritual autobiography—whose formal sameness and unvarying roles of sinner and penitent force a kind of blankness on the identity of the person writing—as a violent figure of negation. Roxana cannot shed the burden of guilt by speaking of it or by renaming herself: her history has a material and painful residue, a living, desperate *presence.*

The only solution to this haunting by the past in the form of her daughter is murder. Amy proposes it first, as she has proposed all of Roxana's most felonious deeds, and, as always, Roxana immediately reacts in anger and moral revulsion: "all my Blood ran chill in my Veins, and a Fit of trembling seiz'd me, that I cou'd not speak a good-while; at last, What is the Devil in you, *Amy, said I?* Nay, nay, *says she,* let it be the Devil, or not the Devil, if I thought she knew one tittle of your History, I wou'd dispatch her if she were my own Daughter a thousand times; and I, *says I in a Rage,* as well as I love you, wou'd be the first that shou'd put the Halter about your Neck, and see you hang'd, with more Satisfaction than ever I saw you in my Life; nay, *says I,* you wou'd not live to be hang'd, *I believe,* I shou'd cut your Throat with my own Hand" (270–71). Her language here has a penny broadsheet bloodiness that picks up on a rather odd strain of primitivism in the text. Throughout *Roxana* flit ensanguined apparitions, providential discoveries, death's-head portents, all in curious juxtaposition with the modernity of Defoe's representations of psychological extremes and with certain of his attitudes toward women, social class, and sexuality (about which more later). The bloodline of *God's Revenge against Murther,* like those of spiritual autobiography, confession, and trial, is most apparent at the extremities of Defoe's fiction, when he suddenly shifts to a new narrative register. But, if such moments reveal his borrowings (or thefts) from one or another traditional form, they are perhaps less archaic than premonitory of the early Victorian Newgate horrors of *Oliver Twist* and *Barnaby Rudge*. Dickens's ghosts and visions can seem old-fashioned as well, but he uses such sensational throwbacks to give accessible form to a complex, and complexly tormented, modern psychology. So, in a more scattershot way, does Defoe in *Roxana*.

The murderous extravagance of Roxana's response to Amy's provocation is a tactic of overcompensation, as suspicious readers might guess, for her own inclination to agree to her daughter's killing, and the relish with which she pictures herself with a hangman's rope or bloody knife in her hand, murdering her most beloved confederate in transgression, testifies to the attraction she obscurely feels for Amy's illicit design. Her horror is no less real for that attraction, but as in an earlier sequence, in which Amy insists that her poverty and her first husband's abandonment give clear grounds for Roxana to lie with the jeweler, should he ask her, Roxana calls on her servant to argue for what she inadmissibly desires herself.

"The Jade prompted the Crime," she writes of those earlier scenes, "which I had but too much Inclination to commit"; yet even after this glint of candor, she hastens to obscure the guilt of her wicked inclination, alleging that she was inclined to what she calls *the Business* "not as a Crime, for I had nothing of the Vice in my Constitution; my Spirits were far from being high; my Blood had no Fire in it, to kindle the Flame of Desire; but the Kindness and good Humour of the Man, and the Dread of my own Circumstances concurr'd to bring me to the Point, and I even resolv'd, before he ask'd, to give up my Virtue to him, whenever he should put it to the Question" (40–41). Her extreme obligingness somewhat undercuts her denial of desire, but she has already given contradictory evidence of her feelings. On the same afternoon that she argues with Amy about the sinfulness of yielding to the jeweler's advances (which he has not yet made, after all), it is Roxana who presses him, contrary to his plans, to stay the night in the lodgings he has provided her: "in short, I courted him so, that he said, he cou'd not deny me" (35). After he has spoken to her, in vague terms, of his wish that they might live together as pretended husband and wife, she writes that "this kind of Discourse had fir'd my Blood, I confess," and, just after, she tells Amy, "I am all in a Sweat at him" (36). The "Spirits" and "Fire" she claims never to feel in herself are thus sensibly woven into the confessional text, and such warmth undermines the clear moral contrast she wants to draw between herself and Amy, charged with coaxing her into the crimes she has already, inwardly, committed.

Amy acts in every part of the narrative as Roxana's surrogate, the agent of her guilt and self-interest. She is so wholly devoted to her mistress that she becomes a monster of selflessness. In their running argument over the jeweler's sexual intentions, Amy offers several times to lie with him herself rather than have Roxana lose him from squeamishness, just as, in the passage quoted earlier, she says she would murder her own daughter a thousand times "if I thought she knew one tittle of your History." Such professions of criminal willingness may be largely tactical, ploys to diminish the moral gravity of the transgressions she urges on Roxana. Yet in her actions, too, Amy balks at no sacrifice of herself, nor any excess of guilt, where Roxana's well-being is at stake. And for Roxana well-being turns on an almost nihilistic attraction to ruin.

No sooner has Roxana let Amy put her to bed with the jeweler than she skips ahead in her chronicle to the devising of what she calls "Amy's Disaster," as if this were something that befell her by accident. One morning it occurs to Amy to wonder why Roxana has not become pregnant by the jeweler: "*Law*, Madam, *says Amy*, what have you been doing? why you have been Marry'd a Year and a half, I warrant you, Master wou'd have got me with-Child twice in that time" (45). In rather vitriolic response Roxana determines to try the experiment. That night she tells her faux-husband he is to lie with Amy, notwithstanding that Amy says no each time the question is raised, to try if he might get her with child, as she says. He yields to the thought, Roxana writes,

but *Amy* did not go: Go, you Fool, *says I*, can't you, I freely give you both Leave; but *Amy* wou'd not go: Nay, you Whore, *says I*, you said, if I wou'd put you to-Bed, you wou'd with all your Heart: and with that, I sat her down, pull'd off her Stockings and Shooes, and all her Cloaths, Piece by Piece, and led her to the Bed to him: *Here*, says I, *try what you can do with your Maid* Amy: She pull'd back a little, would not let me pull off her Cloaths at first, but it was hot Weather, and she had not many Cloaths on, and particularly, no Stays on; and at last, when she sees I was in earnest, she let me do what I wou'd; so I fairly stript her, and then I threw open the Bed, and thrust her in. (46)

The scene is structured and paced as pornography, torn between breathlessness and deferral, the action distended by a visual and tactile lingering over details of dress and undressing but soon recalled to the violence of compulsion. Roxana insistently foregrounds her own role in the rape of her servant, counterposing her coldly registered stripping of Amy to her husband's rather languorous sexual acquiescence and to Amy's frightened and constrained gestures—constrained by both trust and economic dependence—of unwillingness.

If Roxana starts out as the only real actor in the scene, she soon becomes its fascinated observer, first as Amy tries to get out of bed—"but [my husband] said to her, Nay, *Amy*, you see your Mistress has put you to-Bed, 'tis all her doing, you must blame her; so he held her fast, and the Wench being naked in the Bed with him, 'twas too late to look back, so she lay still, and let him do what he wou'd with her"— and then as the jeweler rapes her: "before my Face," as Roxana writes, "for I stood-by all the while" (46–47). Her chilling account of the rape is, in itself and in the context of Defoe's other writing, upsetting and perverse, especially for its voyeuristic estrangement from every trace of erotic desire. The scene is perverse, that is, not because Roxana is there, watching the sexual surfaces and movements of other bodies, but because her involvement comes out of a desire for the power to compel degradation rather than, simply or complicatedly, for pleasure. Her substitution of Amy for herself means to cancel Amy's difference from her as it displaces her own sexuality and remorse onto a suspect and criminally tainted double.

Roxana seems driven to damn anyone unlucky enough to be devoted to her, first blaming her transgressions on them and then catching them up in crimes whose guilt exceeds what she feels for her own. Of her forcing Amy to lie with the jeweler, she writes that, "as I thought myself a Whore, I cannot say but that it was something design'd in my Thoughts, that my Maid should be a Whore too, and should not reproach me with it" (47). Yet, as her lingering to watch the sexual act suggests, there is more to her authorship of this scenario of violation than an intent to cut Amy down to her own level. As she watches—and then, on later nights, forces them to repeat an act that disgusts both of them—she exhibits a will to master the disruptive currents of sexuality which figure so violently in her own life, to turn them against others as instruments of subjection. Roxana is Juliette without the Sadeian delirium of holocaust.

Once she has led Amy and the jeweler to suffer with the guilt she feels for her own trespasses, Roxana quickly regains her equanimity, her almost psychopathic conventionality: "We liv'd as merrily, and as happily, after this, as cou'd be expected, considering our Circumstances," she writes, Amy having brought to term the child she was forced into conceiving and given it away again, in order to return "to live with her old Mistress," apart from whom she seems to have no being (48). Roxana's crimes, in fact, are always being shifted onto her servant, either by literal rep-

etition—as when Amy is forced to lie with the jeweler—or by a kind of displacement of dark impulses, so that Amy gives outward shape to compulsions and longings that gnaw inwardly at her mistress.

The workings of this psychic doubling (or division) are murky but most vivid
at certain moments of extremity, as when Amy and Roxana are caught by a storm
on their return voyage to England. "If I am drown'd, I am damn'd!" Amy cries out,
*"Don't you know what a wicked Creature I have been?"* (125). Roxana hears these cries
as "so many Stabs into the very Soul of one in my own Case," reflecting, *"Poor* Amy!
*what art thou, that I am not?* what hast thou been, that I have not been? Nay, I am
guilty of my own Sin, and thine too . . . It is true, this Difference was between us,
that I said all these things within myself, and sigh'd, and mourn'd inwardly; but
*Amy,* as her Temper was more violent, spoke aloud, and cry'd, and call'd out aloud,
like one in an Agony" (126). Amy's violence is most starkly displayed, and most terrifying to Roxana, in the history's tortured last scenes, yet it is there, too, that she
acts most unrestrainedly as the agent of Roxana's inadmissible drives. The heroine's outward passivity and silence seem to fuel her servant's murderous agitation,
and the more harshly Roxana denounces her the more fixed Amy becomes in her
purpose. Roxana produces, through her own (discursive and moralistic) violence,
the violence (gestural and sanguinary) of Amy's reaction; she also, in small, tacit
admissions, signals her violent designs in the text.

Immediately after Amy's first outburst of passion against Susan—surely not
meant earnestly as a call to murder—and her own tellingly vengeful and gory reply,
Roxana takes a moment to brood on her peril, and then, she writes, "I set *Amy* to-
work." The specific job she gives her is investigative: "to find out which way this
Girl had her Knowledge; but more particularly, how much Knowledge she had"
(271). But in the wake of Amy's desperate language it is hard not to read Roxana's
words as setting a more fatal "work" in motion. By her strenuous bids to threaten
and mock Susan out of her suspicions, Amy only adds to them, twists them into
more bewildering shapes, so that Susan, scenting real fear, redoubles her own
inquiries. Amy keeps coming back to her mistress with new alarms. Susan has
found out the name of Roxana's husband and is making inquiries to discover where
they lodge, Amy reports after one interview with the girl. Then, in a passage that
evokes in miniature much of the vexed complementarity of their relationship, Roxana writes, "I thought I shou'd have sunk down at the very Words; in the middle
of all my Amazement, *Amy* starts up, and runs about the Room like a distracted

body; I'll put an End to it, that I will; I can't bear it; I must murther her; I'll kill her B———, *and swears by her Maker*" (272). Roxana sinks into tormented wonder; Amy bursts into frenetic activity: an inward darkness issues in uncontrollable violence.

Although she tries to contain Amy's fury and blasphemous tongue, Roxana's argument is usefully ambiguous: "you shan't, *says I*, you shan't hurt a Hair of her Head; why you ought to be hang'd for what you have done already; for having resolv'd on it, is doing it, as to the Guilt of the Fact; you are a Murtherer already, as much as if you had done it already" (273). The severity of such a view of criminal guilt makes innocence impossible and smooths Amy's path to the act itself: if guilt inheres in the thought, there is no extra moral cost to the deed. But, equally, there is no escape, even in innocence, from the guilt of commission.

The modernity of *Roxana*—if I may use such an overburdened term to point to the emergence in Defoe's writing of a new form of psychological realism at the same moment that he calls on traditional, even archaic, notions of portent and augury to embody it—consists in its apprehension of identity as multiple, disjunct, compounded of memory and forgetting, rattled by estranging desires. If Defoe is, in terms of plotting and psychology, more in control of *Roxana* than of his earlier fictions, Roxana herself is the least in control of all Defoe's narrators, disordered and self-incriminating. The nearer Susan approaches a discovery of her mother, the more fractured Roxana becomes, split into inward and outward speech and veering in a page from pious reflection to frenzy to a detached contemplation of murder.

When all seems on the point of a disastrous revelation—the captain who is to take them on his ship to Holland has given Roxana's husband a garbled report of her long-lost daughter—Roxana collapses in tears of despair, but then, she writes, "I cannot help saying, that some very good Reflections offer'd themselves upon this Head; it presently occurr'd, What a glorious Testimony it is to the Justice of Providence, and to the Concern Providence has in guiding all the Affairs of Men . . . that the most secret Crimes are, by the most unforeseen Accidents, brought to light, and discover'd" (297). Further good reflections, however, leave her in much the same state as before, frantic and exhausted, until she tells Amy what has happened. "This put *Amy* into such a Hurry," Roxana observes, "that she cry'd; she rav'd; she swore and curs'd like a Mad-thing; then she upbraided me, that I wou'd not let her kill the Girl when she wou'd have done it; and that it was all my own doing, *and the like.*" Having wound up her shadow-avenger to a pitch of murderous extravagance, Roxana can then relax into prim disavowal: "Well however, I was not for killing the Girl yet," she demurs, "I cou'd not bear the Thoughts of that neither" (298). Defoe dangles the tiny *yet* of that last sentence as a peep under the mask, a slip of self-betrayal: not *yet,* not until she is out of London and so exempt from criminal blame. But Roxana's slip is only partly an accident, and her complication of impulses to confess and to disguise her role in plotting Susan's death drives the mystery and breakdown of the story's end.

In Roxana's wracked and tortured narration guilt comes before the crime it springs from; the mystery's hints and foreshadowings are never finally satisfied. No one can come to the end of the story in much doubt that Amy has somehow done away with Susan, but Roxana fills our minds with gruesome thoughts while never making good on the accusation. Just after her marriage she expresses a "fear the wicked Jade shou'd make [Susan] away, which my very Soul abhorr'd the Thoughts of; which however, *Amy* found Means to bring to pass afterwards; *as I may in time,*" but she never does, "*relate more particularly*" (302). She makes the same charge and the same retreat—"But this Tragedy requires a longer Story than I have room for here"—in the next paragraph, and a half-dozen more times over the text's final pages.[8] Her confessions disintegrate into bleak, accusatory sputterings before going out.

The most powerful impression *Roxana*'s last pages convey is of a history spinning out of control, a narrative voice riven by guilt into frenzy and a paralysis of meaning. In her autobiography's final sentence Roxana pulls out of nowhere a legion of untold disasters: "Here [in Holland], after some few Years of flourishing, and outwardly happy Circumstances, I fell into a dreadful Course of Calamities, and *Amy* also; the very Reverse of our former Good Days; the Blast of Heaven seem'd to follow the Injury done the poor Girl, by us both; and I was brought so low again, that my Repentance seem'd to be only the Consequence of my Misery, as my Misery was of my Crime" (329–30). A mood of desperation and entropy pervades these last words, as if it were impossible either to speak coherently of the truth or to abandon speech. The breakdown of Roxana's, and Defoe's, authorship into shadowy and allusive fragments of testimony signals the exhaustion of both the traditional plot of conversion and the strategy of displacing guilt onto a double, whether the guilt of remembered crime, embodied in Roxana's daughter, or the guilt of unruly desire, embodied in her wicked and loving servant Amy. Neither the past nor her own transgressive impulses can be evaded or murderously put down: "to have fall'n upon *Amy*, had been to have murder'd myself," Roxana writes, recognizing the blurring of their two bodies (302). As for Susan, "she was ever before my Eyes; I saw her by-Night, and by-Day; she haunted my Imagination, if she did not haunt the House . . . sleeping or waking, she was with me" (325). Criminality burns inwardly, however strenuously Roxana tries to shift its actions and effects onto the figures of her poor dependents.

If Roxana calls upon conventional notions of crime as the special domain of servants, unattached women, and the wandering poor in her efforts to elide her own complicity in the acts that come back to shatter her luxurious calm, her displacement of legal guilt onto such a standard criminal type as the evil servant collapses under the weight of unwanted self-consciousness. Far from being confined to a distinct social class, Defoe suggests through his shadowing of Roxana, the most damaging crimes emerge from the repressed inward violence of the respectable self. The hierarchies of social difference, however closely monitored, are permeable to currents of desire—for freedom, pleasure, power—which threaten, and more than threaten, to undermine them.

In his criminal histories Defoe looked on these currents with a mixture of attraction and horror, much as he regarded the lives of his protagonists in crime. Outwardly a spokesman for middle-class respectability, the model of a modern "social reformer," to quote Michael Shinagel, "anxious to discover ways of curtailing the crime rate and alerting the citizens of London on how to protect themselves and their property,"[9] Defoe nevertheless registers, in his fiction, the strains of an unresolved political ambivalence, which led him to portray sympathetically the striving and perpetual discontent of his outcast heroes. The temptations of wandering are a constant in all his fictions from *Robinson Crusoe* on, but the theme assumes more specific material coordinates in the criminal lives, whose marginal subjects act out disruptive claims to a freedom their social position forbids.

Sometimes, as in the lives of Jonathan Wild and John Sheppard, the hated constraint is an apprenticeship, a form of contractual bondage and dependency. The eldest son of a carpenter, Jonathan Wild is "taught in the Free-School of *Wolverhampton*, to read and write, and then his Father put him Apprentice to a *Birmingham* Man, or as they call them there, a Hardware Man, and particularly a *Buckle Maker*."[10] Despite his suitable education, a kind of wanderlust, or aspiring temper, edges Jonathan toward the criminal freedoms of urban life: "his Thoughts, *as he said*, being above his Trade, tho' at that time he had no Tast of the Life he afterwards led, yet he grew uneasie in the Country, was sick of his Work, and in short, after a few Years came away to *London,* to see if he could get into any Business there" (237). The combination of low wages and discontent with his tedious employment leads him first into debt and then into criminal relations with Mary Milliner, who sets him on the path to fencing stolen goods and juggling the roles of thief taker and crime boss. Yet, if Defoe (if it was Defoe), in the earlier of his two lives of Wild, condemned the apprentice's *greatness* with disdainful irony, seeing it as emblematic of a more widespread crisis of subordination,[11] in the *True and Genuine Account* he treats Jonathan's striving sympathetically, for all the ideological dangers it embodies. Even if Jonathan's bridling at restraint conjures a threatening current of rebellion and mischief, his *uneasiness* mirrors the vague, irresistible longing that circulates among all Defoe's surrogate voices. In time Wild becomes an almost comic figure, a parody of cruel masters and a monster of exploitation, but in its early stages his criminality reflects a thwarted, grasping form of unpropertied-class consciousness.

If Wild resists the obligatory postures of deference and self-control in class terms, Roxana, most extravagantly of Defoe's unruly female protagonists, resists them in the fields of sexuality and gender. Against the arguments of her eminent (and historically real) financial advisor Sir Robert Clayton—that the best way to keep her "vast Fortune" intact would be to marry a rich merchant who, not being himself "in Want or Scarcity of Money, but having a flourishing Business, and a flowing Cash, wou'd at the first word, settle all my Fortune on myself and my Children, and maintain me like a Queen" (170)—Roxana offers a critique of marriage and the legal construction of woman as abject:

I told him, I knew no State of Matrimony, but what was, at best, a State of Inferiority, if not of Bondage; that I had no Notion of it; that I liv'd a Life of absolute Liberty now; was free as I was born, and having a plentiful Fortune, I did not understand what Coherence the Words *Honour* and *Obey* had with the Liberty of a *Free Woman;* that I knew no Reason the Men had to engross the whole Liberty of the Race, and make the Woman, notwithstanding any desparity of Fortune, be subject to the Laws of Marriage, of their own making; that it was my Misfortune to be a Woman, but I was resolv'd it shou'd not be made worse by the Sex; and seeing Liberty seem'd to be the Men's Property, I wou'd be a *Man-Woman;* for as I was born free, I wou'd die so. (171)

Sir Robert responds to her argument by "laughing heartily at" her, but, exactly as the Dutch merchant had done in an earlier scene, in which Roxana outlined even more vehemently her reasons for shunning marriage, he "gave over offering any more Arguments," only appealing, rather lamely, to custom.

As she does in rejecting Sir Robert's advice, Roxana rejects the Dutch merchant's first offer of marriage primarily on economic grounds, arguing that for women of property the marriage contract is a form of enslavement, a yielding of all independence of fortune and power of estate to their husbands. "All he cou'd say," Roxana notes pleasantly, "cou'd not answer the Force of this, as to Argument," but he tries to shift the conversation onto another ground, calling on notions of mutual love and an emerging ideology of companionate marriage to overcome her resistance: "he had Reason to expect I shou'd be content with that which all the World was contented with . . . that a sincere Affection between a Man and his Wife, answer'd all the Objections that I had made about being a Slave, a Servant, *and the like;* and where there was a mutual Love, there cou'd be no Bondage; but that there was but one Interest; one Aim; one Design; and all conspir'd to make both very happy" (149). Although Roxana never doubts the sincerity of the merchant's affection or his assurances concerning her property and estate, she recognizes this argument as a mystification of the actual, material conditions of women's lives within the sanctions of English law. *"Ay,"* she answers back to this talk of mutual love, *"that is the Thing I complain of;* the Pretence of Affection, takes from a Woman every thing that can be call'd *herself;* she is to have no Interest; no Aim; no View; but all is the Interest, Aim, and View, of the Husband" (149). As she notes later, the calamity of her first marriage resonates in her words, but there is more in them than an aversion to dependency on fools and tyrants: her words, as Sir Robert observes, threaten sexual mayhem.

Once Roxana has given her reasons for choosing not to accept any offers of marriage, "Sir *Robert* smil'd," she writes, "and told me, I talk'd a kind of *Amazonian* Language" (171)—which echoes her earlier statement that, rather than be confined by sex, "she wou'd be a Man-Woman." Her refusal of marriage, that is, entails not just an intention to live single but a will to live not as a woman at all. "Woman" is constructed under a system of laws and cultural imagining which women have no part in making. To imagine "the Liberty of a Free Woman" is, for Roxana, to imagine herself into the position of men's power, into a repertoire of possibilities at odds with the values of the governing heterosexual economy.[12] Sir Robert's patronizing gloss on her argument as *"Amazonian* Language" uses an image of monstrosity to mock her into a more tractable temper but also suggests how bound up Roxana's assertion of freedom is with threats of sexual blurring and excess.

When she puts Amy to bed with the jeweler, for example, she assumes the rapist's part in everything but penetration, stripping Amy, throwing open the bed, thrusting her in; even her watching of what follows is an enforcement of power over sexuality which is symbolically figured, in a patriarchal economy, as male. In her full-fledged debate with the merchant over the rights and dangers of a married state, Roxana responds to his picture of a conjugal Land of Cockaigne—"the Woman had nothing to do, but to eat the Fat, and drink the Sweet; to sit still, and look round her; be waited on, and made much of; be serv'd, and lov'd, and made easie"—with a return to the actual fallen world of gendered liberties: "I return'd, that while a Woman was single, she was a Masculine in her politick Capacity; that she had then the full Command of what she had, and the full Direction of what she did; that she was a Man in her separated Capacity, to all Intents and Purposes that a Man cou'd be so to himself" (148). Most scandalously, Roxana claims for herself a masculine prerogative in the field of sexual pleasure: the power to say no to the social compulsion of heterosexual pairing—"it was my Opinion, a Woman was as fit to govern and enjoy her own Estate, without a Man, as a Man was, without a Woman"—and to do what she pleases for sexual partners: "if she had a-mind to gratifie herself as to Sexes, she might entertain a Man, as a Man does a Mistress" (149). This last is not a freedom she ever takes—she always acts the mistress's part to a powerful man—and she brings it into her argument as much for rhetorical triumph as out of conviction or desire. But the point is crucial as a sign of her recognition that for women, subject to a masculine enforcement of cultural and legal sanctions, the road to an imaginable freedom has to pass through sexual transgression.

Even if Defoe's other writings, and Roxana's own later history of terror and remorse, argue against the claims she makes here to an independence of the rule of gendered hierarchy, she gives voice to those claims with a passion of intelligence he cannot annul. Defoe was led over and over to dramatize the conflict between the tranquillity of a dominant social order and the disruptive wanderlust of colonial adventurers, poverty-stricken apprentices, unmarried women, and artists of prison breaking and, more important, to write that conflict from the position marked as criminal.[13] If Defoe's crime prevention tracts *Augusta Triumphans* and *Second Thoughts Are Best* and the moral tags to his criminal lives seek to control the damage bred by such transgressive dreams and to reassert a stable, hierarchical system of property relations and deference to authority, his most influential criminal histories disrupt hierarchy by their identification with dangerous and outcast subjectivities. Under the pressures of urbanization, colonial expansion, the explosion of cheap print, dissenting religion, and shifting configurations of gender, Defoe's garrulous criminals patch together a way of life and a way of articulating the warring, half-understood drives that lead them in and out of transgression. As readers we are solicited to condemn the actions that our reading impels us to desire, even to take as our own.

In their concentration on the projected voices of outlaws, lost children, rebellious women, and apprentices, Defoe's histories already imagine "the reversal of the political axis of individualization" which Foucault, in a passage I cited earlier, describes as belonging to a "system of discipline." There "the child is more individualized than the adult, the patient more than the healthy man, the madman and the delinquent more than the normal and the non-delinquent."[14] But such has also always been, following Defoe, the "system" of novelistic representation. Even when the author's attention is focused on the outwardly respectable or socially well-adjusted (which is not so often, after all), that attention characteristically exposes some hidden delinquent strain, whether in the form of a buried past or impulses at odds with the dominant cultural codes. Defoe is often thought to be *undisciplined* in his writing, but his most complex interrogations of subjectivity are carried out, too, in the voices of wayward and marginal personae, and the effect is to unsettle sanctioned forms of identity, to write selfhood as always, inwardly, verging on crime.

As he brought the experiences of poverty, petty crime, prostitution, and imprisonment to the center of complex histories of self-fashioning and inward conversion or decay, Defoe broke quite intently with conventions of what Erich Auerbach has called "the several levels of literary representation." In the epilogue to *Mimesis* Auerbach writes, "When Stendhal and Balzac took random individuals from daily life in their dependence upon current historical circumstances and made them the subjects of serious, problematic, and even tragic representation, they broke with the classical rule of distinct levels of style, for according to this rule, everyday practical reality could find a place in literature only within the frame of a low or intermediate kind of style, that is to say, as either grotesquely comic or pleasant, light, colorful, and elegant entertainment."[15] Defoe's criminal histories initiate, a century earlier, the same opening in the social field of representation. There is certainly a grotesque dimension to some of Defoe's narratives, as indeed there can be to Stendhal's or Balzac's, but in *Colonel Jack, Moll Flanders,* and *Roxana* the rough comedy of violence is worked into more searching and tormented forms than was the case even for such a brilliant earlier work as Nashe's *Unfortunate Traveller,* and Defoe's texts are far more "embedded"—again appropriating Auerbach on Stendhal—"in a total reality, political, social, and economic, which is concrete and constantly evolving" than anything in the earlier criminal or picaresque line.[16] A contentious, classicist hierarchy of literary genres, which was still (and for the rest of the eighteenth century) asserted as a principle of social division and order, was at the time Defoe wrote being variously undermined but perhaps most effectively (as measured, in the long run, by the eventual canonical status of his narratives) by the sort of realism he was experimenting with in the criminal lives.[17]

Defoe's reworking of the conventional materials of criminal writing also involved a knotting and unraveling of inherited plots, a complication of simple patterns. If the histories' prefaces and asides tend to affirm their most formulaic elements—mythic structures of wickedness or repentance—the texts are strained past recognition by contingency, ambiguous shifts in tone, reckless and conflicted details. In his radical recasting of the criminal life, Defoe drew from an emphasis on singularity common, as Michael McKeon has argued, to much late-seventeenth-century writing, from Puritan spiritual autobiography to the picaresque: a novel "responsiveness to the factuality of individual life so intense that the dominance of overarching pattern is felt, in various ways, to be quite problematic."[18] Factuality, however, is not everything, for facts admit of innumerable constructions. What governs the unfolding of Defoe's criminal histories is, rather, a responsiveness to the conflicted recollection and texture of a specific individual career, "the long Series of Changes, and Turns," in Colonel Jack's words, "which have appear'd in the narrow Compass of one private mean Person's Life" (307). Defoe locates his inwardly focused histories of transgression and guilt within precise representations of the material conditions of London life in the 1720s. By disfiguring the inherited genres of criminal writing with an exhaustive, evidential realism and a harrowing concentration on the grain of an imagined voice, he articulated a new sense of estrangement, complicity, and risk, of identity eroded and shaped by transgressive desire.

## PART III

# The Judge and the Author
### *Fielding in Midcentury*

But, gentle Readers, must it not be pleasant enough to hear this *Mite of Magistracy* haranguing his gaping Brethren upon the *Licentiousness of the Press,* which he himself had so many Years polluted; and thundering out his *harmless Vengeance,* against the honest Exercise of that *Liberty,* which he had so shamefully *abused?*

No sooner had this *new Convert to the Gospel and the Ministry,* by a most flagrant Prostitution of his Tongue and Pen, wriggled himself into a *little dirty Authority;* but he at once commences Zealot in the Work of Reformation.

*An Apology for the Conduct*
*of Mrs. Teresia Constantia Phillips,* 1748–49

When the ghost author of *An Apology for the Conduct of Mrs. Teresia Constantia Phillips* (1748–49) attacked Henry Fielding as a "Mite of Magistracy," he was pointing to what Fielding's numerous enemies saw as the egregious hypocrisy of the newly appointed Westminster magistrate's moral and juridical pronouncements.[1] The one-time playwright Fielding, whose politically contentious burlesques were often blamed for the censorial clampdown of the 1737 Licensing Act, had become a "Zealot in the Work of Reformation," inveighing against the publication of libels and scandalous memoirs (like the first two volumes of Phillips's text) and calling, in his *Charge Delivered to the Grand Jury*, for the prosecution of their authors. Phillips's *Apology* likens the reformed Mite of Magistracy to his own tiny hero Tom Thumb, "thundering out his harmless Vengeance," in order to mock his political posturing, and turns the charge of prostitution (Phillips herself was "a notorious courtesan")[2] against Fielding as a way of undercutting his "little dirty Authority." In doing so, the *Apology*'s author challenges Fielding's right to pass judgment but does not call into question the absolute moral distinction between respectability and deviance which Fielding as judge seemed to take as axiomatic. If anything, he reaffirms that distinction by disputing Fielding's authority to speak for the former.

The cultural battle lines at midcentury were drawn according to an oppositional rhetoric that seems remote from Defoe's intimation of a problematic complicity or slippage between licit and illicit forms of experience. Yet the very extremism of that rhetoric can itself be read—as indeed is also the case of those passages in which Roxana or Defoe's alter ego, Andrew Moreton, unleash their most virulent language—as a sign of profound anxiety. Fielding, for all his apparent confidence in both his magisterial authority (embodied in such texts as the *Charge to the Grand Jury*) and his authorial mastery (acted out by the narratorial personae of his fictions), betrays increasingly obvious signs of unease the further he becomes embroiled in the actual workings of legal investigation and judgment. Setting out to control both the disruptive energies of "the Lower Kind of People" and the aesthetic unruliness, the openness to misreading, of narrative realism, Fielding comes to question the very ground of his own authority in both domains.[3] In the mock trial that I discuss below he represents himself as at the same time enforcer and victim of censorial severity, but the outcome of the trial marks his ultimate identification with the latter role and signals his abandonment of, or release from, the burden of authorship itself. The trial thus reproduces in miniature a broader trajectory of disenchantment.

Fielding's career as an author of fictions ended, as it had begun, with a woman on trial for crimes against art. In the *Covent-Garden Journal* for January 25, 1752, he placed his own recently published *Amelia* in the dock of the "Court of *Censorial Enquiry*," on charges "that the whole Book is a Heap of *sad Stuff, Dulness, and Nonsense;* that it contains no Wit, Humour, Knowledge of human Nature, or of the World; indeed, that the Fable, moral Characters, Manners, Sentiments, and Diction, are all alike bad and contemptible."[4] Fielding assumed a double role in the proceedings, imaginatively projecting himself into the positions of both criminally accused and judge, though in both roles he is represented by fictional personae: in the dock, by Amelia herself, who takes the heat for the authorial crimes really perpetrated by Fielding as "the Father of this poor Girl the Prisoner at the Bar" (65); and on the bench, by the putative author of the *Covent-Garden Journal*—Sir Alexander Drawcansir, Knight Censor of Great Britain.

Drawcansir, despite the rather absurd circumstances of this trial, embodies Fielding's genuine convictions on the need for a cultural office of censor to counteract the modern corruption of morality. In the *Charge to the Grand Jury* of 1749 Fielding had written that "Grand Juries, Gentlemen, are in Reality the only Censors of this Nation. As such, the Manners of the People are in your Hands, and in yours only."[5] But, if the office of censor belonged to grand juries as the official overseers of public manners, the moral responsibility of censorship belonged even more properly to authors as the guardians of public taste. In a contribution to his sister Sarah's *Familiar Letters,* Henry had written that "what the Ministry are to the State, the Bishops to the Church, the Chancellor and Judges to the Law, the Generals to the Army, and the Admirals to the Fleet; that is the great and good Writer over the Morals of his Countrymen."[6] Four years later, in a passage from *Amelia* linking aesthetic judgment to moral action, he contended that "true Virtue is, indeed, nothing else but true Taste."[7] To the end of correcting public morality, then, Drawcansir charges himself with the task of endeavoring "to restore," in the pages of the *Covent-Garden Journal,* "that true and manly Taste, which hath, within these few

Years, degenerated in these Kingdoms." And, as this degeneracy flows from "those base and scandalous Writings, which the Press hath lately poured in such a Torrent upon us, that the Name of an Author is, in the Ears of all good Men, become almost an infamous Appellation," Drawcansir is forced to work long hours in his Court of Censorial Enquiry, where *Amelia* stands on trial (43).

The book she represents has been charged in accordance with the court's obligation "to examine, try, recommend, or condemn, all Books, and Pamphlets, of whatever Size, or on whatever Subject." Any text "judged worthy of Condemnation" is then subject to one of the following sentences, whose language parodies the conventional juridical formulae for imprisonment, transportation, and (for first offenses) being burnt in the hand and released: "1. To be imprisoned on the Shelf, or in the Warehouse of the Bookseller. 2. To be immediately converted into waste Paper. 3. To be burnt by the Hands of the common Hangman, or by those of some common Publisher of Scandal, which are, perhaps, much the more infamous" (45). Once sentence has been passed, no one is permitted to buy or read the condemned text, under penalty of contempt.

Fielding's use of criminal sanctions as a figure for the act of literary judgment is ironic in the *Covent-Garden Journal,* but he was serious in arguing for the necessity of moral policing in the literary domain. The role of censor reflected what Fielding viewed as an urgent social need for authoritarian control over cultural productions and their interpretations and responded to his sense of the ideological dangers posed by current popular but degenerate forms of representation. His fictional elaboration of that role in the *Covent-Garden Journal* is thus linked to his assault a decade earlier on Richardson's novel *Pamela* for its meretricious posturing of moral piety.

The problem with Richardson's unmonitored, first-person registrations of experience in *Pamela* was twofold, from Fielding's perspective. The desire to trace the littlest, most fleeting details of thought and expression led Richardson into absurdity, a fixation on the trivialities realism is prone to accumulate endlessly. His concern with the momentary and circumstantial—including, of course, the circumstances of the act of writing itself—yielded, unchecked, what Fielding saw as the tawdry mimetic excess of *Pamela.* But more unsettling than this were the moral implications of Richardson's narrative mode. *Pamela*'s story unfolded through the journal and letters of a servant girl, addressed to her parents—and so not only the story's events but also their interpretation are in her hands. The reader is immersed in her view of things and can gain no authoritative or ironic purchase on her descriptions. Thus, her accounts of her own motivations have (implicitly) to be taken without question, despite what Fielding and many other readers have seen as her hypocritical and mercenary calculations of profit.[8]

A few months after *Pamela*'s publication Fielding issued his parodic corrective in the form of the "authentic" letters of the *real* Shamela Andrews, who blasts through *Pamela*'s pretenses: "I thought once," Shamela writes halfway through her adventures, "of making a little Fortune by my Person. I now intend to make a great one by my Vartue."[9] The two aspects of Fielding's critique of *Pamela*—for its representational literal-mindedness and its moral shallowness—famously converge in such passages as this, from Shamela's sixth letter (it is late on a Thursday night, and her confidante, Mrs. Jervis, has urged her to yield to her master's sexual advances):

No, Mrs. *Jervis*, nothing under a regular taking into Keeping, a settled Settlement, for me, and all my Heirs, all my whole Life-time, shall do the Business——or else cross-legged, is the Word, faith, with *Sham*; and then I snapt my Fingers.

*Thursday Night, Twelve o'Clock*

Mrs. *Jervis* and I are just in Bed, and the Door unlocked; if my Master should come—— Odsbobs! I hear him just coming in at the Door. You see I write in the present Tense, as Parson *Williams* says. Well, he is in Bed between us . . . (330)

Fielding turns the devices of Richardsonian realism inside out to show how its obsessional registration of each moment as it passes through the consciousness of the narrator leaves the resulting text open to misreading and confusions of moral intent.[10]

To the disorder, ambiguity, and circumstantial immediacy of Richardson's (and, earlier, Defoe's) renderings of their protagonist-narrators' experience, Fielding opposed a narrative model founded on the classicist principles of decorum, lucidity, and generalization—principles essential to the control of narrative meaning and the governance of interpretation. Clarity of underlying design enabled Fielding to indulge his inclination to raucous and knockabout humor without risking anarchy of meaning. It was from within the ideological role of censor that Fielding, in the famous introductory chapter to book 3 of *Joseph Andrews*, articulated the theoretical basis of his fiction: "I declare here once for all, I describe not Men, but Manners; not an Individual, but a Species." The aim of such description, whatever other kinds of pleasure it might provide to the reader in private, was ultimately corrective and public: "to hold the Glass to thousands in their Closets, that they may contemplate their Deformity, and endeavour to reduce it, and thus by suffering private Mortification may avoid public Shame."[11] The insistent visibility of Fielding's rhetoric, and of his management of the plots he so obviously sets in motion, is critical to his purpose. "Raw facts are not allowed," in Claude Rawson's words, "to take their own course, unframed by authorial arrangement."[12] An excessive emphasis on physical details and an uncritical identification with the protagonist's perspective and voice bred politically dangerous sympathies.

*Shamela*, then, was an act of censorial defamation, a counter-reading of *Pamela*'s plot of imperiled virtue and social climbing. In Fielding's trial by parodic revision Richardson's working-class heroine is found guilty of moral fraud and publicly exposed as a sham, her deep-dyed hypocrisy inscribed in her true name. She is sentenced without mercy or delay. Eleven years later, however, at *Amelia*'s trial for dullness, his magisterial confidence seems considerably shaken. After transcribing all the charges and testimony against his textual *Creature* Amelia, he short-circuits her defense with a wounded, sentimental apology for her faults. Adopting the persona of "a grave Man" in the court's audience, he addresses the judge:

"If you, Mr. Censor, are yourself a Parent, you will view me with Compassion when I declare I am the Father of this poor Girl the Prisoner at the Bar; nay, when I go farther, and avow, that of all my Offspring she is my favourite Child . . . I do not think my Child is entirely free from Faults. I know nothing human that is so; but surely she doth not deserve the Rancour with which she hath been treated by the Public. However . . . I will trouble the World no more with any Children of mine by the same Muse."

. . . Then Amelia was delivered to her Parent, and a Scene of great Tenderness passed between them. (65–66)

In keeping with what J. Paul Hunter has characterized as the "flight into the interior" of *Amelia* as compared to the aggressively public and social energies of Fielding's earlier fictions,[13] this allegorical scene of judgment substitutes private, domestic affections for an ideological defense (or critique) of the text on trial. And, as with the earlier trial of *Pamela*, it substitutes the fictional body of a transgressive woman for the male author, who is the real focus of indignation and envy.

Fielding could blame the bad example of Richardson's story on the all too easily compromised sexuality of Pamela herself, as Fielding's critics denounced the sordidness of his subject through mockery of the heroine's disfigured (though later repaired) face. In a youthful accident, we are told, "her lovely Nose was beat all to pieces";[14] the extravagant phrasing led some readers to link Amelia to the syphilitically noseless Blear-Eyed Moll in the novel's Newgate scenes and, by extension, to a whole iconography of sexual excess and pathology.[15] By using figures of female immodesty and promiscuity to stand in for the defects of male authorship, both Fielding and his critics could gain rhetorical advantage over their opponents, yet, in representing the attacks on himself as attacks against Amelia, Fielding also suggests a somewhat unexpected reciprocity, a tentative identification with the woman in the dock.

The censorial function Fielding lodged in the persona of Sir Alexander Drawcansir appears ineffectual, ultimately, in the face of the age's corrupted tastes. Rather than weighing the various testimony presented, in order to form a judgment conducive to "restoring that true and manly Taste, which hath, within these few Years, degenerated in these Kingdoms," the judge rests virtually mute through the proceedings, only acceding at last to the popular "Huzza!" at Fielding's retirement from writing (43). The prospect of literary and moral correction seems vestigial; the dim remains of an old confidence.

*Amelia*'s entanglement with questions of criminality and power binds it in complex ways to the other works Fielding wrote from 1749 to 1753, the years of his tenure as magistrate to the West End of London. The texts I want to read against and in the light of *Amelia* include his most significant juridical tract, the *Enquiry into the Causes of the Late Increase of Robbers* (1751), and two polemical narratives of legal investigation, the *True State of the Case of Bosavern Penlez* (1749) and the *Clear State of the Case of Elizabeth Canning* (1753), the last publication Fielding saw through the press. In all of them, as in the other journalistic and autobiographical work he produced before his death at age forty-seven, in 1754, Fielding engaged with the social realities of poverty and dislocation, urban violence, popular uprising, and legal malfeasance, acting as both an apologist for the repressive force of the law and a mordant chronicler of its corruptions. If in his juridical writings Fielding adheres to the role of reactionary ideologue, upholding an almost terroristic conception of authority, his registering of dissonant voices and fascination with the energies of the outcast and rebel expose a certain disenchantment with the authoritarian positions he was called on so often to justify and an affiliation with the very disruptive agents he furiously, anxiously condemned.

# CHAPTER NINE

# The Politics and Poetics
# of Crime and Punishment

When Fielding, in the winter of 1748–49, was appointed justice of the peace, first for the city of Westminster and then for the county of Middlesex, the jobs were universally regarded as mercenary and corrupting, and the "trading justices" who took them were seen as "the scum of the earth," as Edmund Burke was to call them thirty years later: "carpenters, brickmakers, and shoemakers; some of whom were notoriously men of such infamous characters that they were unworthy of any employ whatever, and others so ignorant that they could scarcely write their own names."[1] Through his anti-Jacobite journalism of the later 1740s Fielding had earned a certain claim to the attention of such patrons as the dukes of Bedford and Newcastle, though the reward seems, by the evidence of his abject pleas for favor and his later, bitter reflections in the *Journal of a Voyage to Lisbon,* to have been grudging. But, if the offices were disappointing, Fielding threw himself into the work with a passionate intensity that fatigued, sickened, and ultimately killed him. In the crucible of London all the disruptive and degenerative forces he saw endangering the social peace were magnified: the city was slipping into anarchy, and there seemed to be no vehicle through which authority could become articulate. It was to recuperate the law as an instrument of hierarchical stability and social power that Fielding, in the years of his magistracy, undertook to write narratives that could both explain and repair the disorder he felt closing in on him.

That disorder was most visible in the increasing violence of social antagonisms. If "London proletarians, excluded from its hegemony, held the law in contempt," as Peter Linebaugh has written,[2] such contempt, and the terror it partially masked, were reciprocal. Especially in the years just after the peace of Aix-la-Chapelle in 1748, reports of assault, shoplifting, street violence, river thefts, and burglary multiplied through newspapers and handbills, and the crime wave such reports helped to configure was always seen as originating in the culture of urban poverty. The rate of migration to London both from the countryside and from abroad had been increasing almost uncontrollably from the mid-seventeenth century, and such urbanization—a word that tends to neutralize the processes of rural expropriation and colonialism which compelled so many to resettle in London[3]—put enormous pressure on labor, as so much of the work available in London was seasonal or dependent on trade.

Military demobilization after the wars of the later seventeenth and eighteenth centuries made the pressures of urban dislocation still grimmer. J. M. Beattie has shown that for the urban parishes of Surrey levels of prosecution for property crimes were lowest during wartime in the eighteenth century (1739–48, 1756–63, 1776–82, and 1793–1815) and highest after the wars ended. For those who noted this at the time the reason was obvious: "The peace brought back to England large numbers of disreputable men who had spent several years being further brutalized by service in the armed forces, without any provision being made for their re-entry into the work force."[4] As this characterization suggests, the consequences of demobilization could be described in either moralizing or economic terms or by a combination of discourses permitting both a rational comprehension of the causes of crime and an extreme severity of judicial response. Thus, Smollett, for example, could write that "all the gaols in England were filled with the refuse of the army and navy, which having been dismissed at the peace [of 1748], and either averse to labour, or excluded from employment, had naturally preyed upon the commonwealth."[5] Such thinking had been commonplace for decades: in 1701 the author of *Hanging, Not Punishment Enough, for Murtherers, High-way Men, and House-Breakers* wrote of an earlier crime wave (following the demobilization of 1697): "we need not go far for Reasons of the great numbers and increase of these Vermin: for tho' no times have been without them, yet we may now reasonably believe, that after so many Thousands of Soldiers disbanded, and Mariners discharged, many of them are driven upon necessity, and having been used to an idle way of living, care not to work, and many (I fear) cannot, if they would."[6] Demobilized soldiers and sailors, already assumed to have been brutalized by war, were especially prone to form themselves into gangs, parodying the solidarities and rigid hierarchy of military culture and adapting the skills of battle to the largely unpoliced field of urban illegality.

The city came to be figured as a war zone, as in Horace Walpole's letter from the winter of 1749–50 (he had not long before been mugged in Hyde Park) to Horace Mann: "you will hear little news from England, but of robberies," he wrote; "the numbers of disbanded soldiers and sailors have all taken to the road, or rather to the street." As a consequence, "one is forced to travel, even at noon, as if one were going to battle."[7] In the end, as Beattie writes, "it is the problem of structural unemployment and underemployment that demobilization exposed so clearly and devastatingly."[8] However tenaciously authors such as Fielding (and, some forty years later, Martin Madan) persisted in describing crime as a function of sin and moral depravity, its origins in the material conditions of labor and the fluctuating political requirements of the state were commonly recognized by midcentury.

When Fielding came into the office of magistrate in the winter of 1748–49, then, London was wracked by a crime wave that was broadly understood to be only the most visible symptom of a more general crisis in social relations. Even when he presents his account of the causes of crime in terms of moral denunciation, the burden of explanation rests on the material conditions of the poor and the ideological tensions fracturing the stable hierarchy of class relations. But there are also, woven irregularly into this protosociological discourse, flashes of racializing language which reach back to the rhetoric of the criminal anatomies, by which Fielding could allusively call on deep-rooted notions of the criminalized poor as intractably, essentially, other.

In the 1749 *Charge Delivered to the Grand Jury,* the first of Fielding's publications as magistrate, he concluded that "if those Immoralities of the People, which will sprout up in the best Constitution, be not from Time to Time corrected by the Hand of Justice, they will at length grow up to the most enormous Vices, will overspread the whole Nation, and in the End must produce a downright State of wild and savage Barbarism."[9] Here the criminality of the poor is represented as a kind of vegetative pathology, an innate tendency to revert to a primitive state of savagery which can only, and barely, be held in check by the law.

This foregrounding of the law's function as a censor of immorality was carried over to the more ambitious *Enquiry into the Causes of the Late Increase of Robbers,* published two years later, in which Fielding aimed to develop both an etiology of crime and a set of practical recommendations for its containment. He traces the origins of the present social crisis to a shift in the constitution, as he calls it, of England,[10] brought on by the demise of feudal relationships of tenancy and property rights and, even more instrumentally, by the burgeoning of trade. "Nothing," he writes, "hath wrought such an Alteration in this Order of People [those whom he calls the *Commonalty*], as the Introduction of Trade. This hath indeed given a new Face to the whole Nation, hath in a great measure subverted the former State of Affairs, and hath almost totally changed the Manners, Customs, and Habits of the People, more especially of the lower Sort. The Narrowness of their Fortune is changed into Wealth; the Simplicity of their Manners into Craft; their Frugality into Luxury; their Humility into Pride, and their Subjection into Equality" (69–70). By this alteration in the material circumstances of the "lower Sort," their old subservience to the civil power embodied in the law is overthrown, so that "as to the Magistrate of a less Fortune, and more Knowledge, every riotous independent Butcher or Baker, with two or three thousand Pounds in his Pocket, laughs at his Power" (72). The picture Fielding draws is a caricature, but, in his undisguised nostalgia for a lost and in any case largely imaginary economy of political subjection and humility, he implicitly recognizes that private immorality is grounded in history, in economic and ideological process.

Trade brings in its wake luxury, and luxury is a kind of contagion that breeds social upheaval and crime promiscuously. The principal luxuries with which Fielding is concerned are those not of ostentatious display but of idle pleasure: public entertainments, masquerades, and "Scenes of Rendezvous" such as Vauxhall and Ranelagh (82). On a practical level the problem with these "too frequent and expensive Diversions among the Lower Kind of People" is that, whether vicious or merely silly, they lead to a dangerous extravagance and an addictive hunger for money. Social life is fueled by a fury of emulation:

Vices no more than Diseases will stop with [the Great]; for bad Habits are as infectious by Example, as the Plague itself by Contact. In free Countries, at least, it is a Branch of Liberty claimed by the People to be as wicked and as profligate as their Superiors. Thus while the Nobleman will emulate the Grandeur of a Prince; and the Gentleman will aspire to the proper State of the Nobleman; the Tradesman steps from behind his Counter into the vacant Place of the Gentleman. Nor doth the Confusion end here: It reaches the very Dregs of the People, who aspiring still to a Degree beyond that which belongs to them . . . they disdain the Wages to which their Industry would intitle them; and abandoning themselves to Idleness, the more simple and poor-spirited betake themselves to a State of Starving and Beggary, while those of more Art and Courage become Thieves, Sharpers, and Robbers.

The patrician contemptuousness of Fielding's language disguises rather crudely what was, in fact, a much more complicated and ambivalent relationship on his part toward received ideas of social class. For all his deference and dependency Fielding scorned the moral stupidity of high life,[11] yet he begins his diatribe against the contagion of pleasure by announcing, "I aim not here to satirize the Great, among whom Luxury is probably rather a moral than a political Evil" (77). Immorality is an object of the law's attention only as it constitutes a demonstrably *political* threat, even though this threat is to a property-owning class whose moral character Fielding contemned.

Excess of luxury, when it involves the rich in massive debts, leads only to "the Misery, Distress, and sometimes utter Ruin of a private Family," he contends, in illustrating the difference between moral and political evils, while a similar wreck of fortune involves "the Tradesman, the Mechanic, and the Labourer" in "many political Mischiefs, and among the rest is most evidently the Parent of Theft and Robbery" (78). The distinction is spurious, resting as it does on a denial of all the crimes—trade in political influence, forgery, fraudulent speculations, bribery, and administrative corruption—by which the great could seek a restoration of their fortunes and a deflection of creditors. But, while Fielding was bitterly aware of the "political Mischiefs" committed by the great—these are the subject, after all, of his *Jonathan Wild*—he passed over them in the *Enquiry* for three reasons. He was, first of all, serving at the commission of the great, however little reason he had to be thankful for their patronage, and was charged with the responsibility of upholding a stable (albeit uneasy) political regime. In the second place great political and financial crimes do not excite the same fear as those on a smaller scale, with their threat of bodily violence and palpable, intimate loss. Third, and most critically, the crimes of the "lower Sort" arise, in Fielding's view, from a subversive claim of liberty. "In free Countries," he writes in the passage quoted earlier, "it is a Branch of Liberty claimed by the People to be as wicked and as profligate as their Superiors"—and such a false idea of liberty leads, as the same passage further suggests, to a collapse of industry and a confusion of social positions, a masquerade of inherited hierarchical roles. "In Diversion, as in many other Particulars, the upper Part of Life is distinguished from the Lower," he advises. "Pleasure always hath been, and always will be, the principal Business of Persons of Fashion and Fortune" (83). The reckless and leveling pursuit of pleasure is dangerous not just because it leads the poor into robbery and theft when they run out of money; rather, pleasure for the "lower Orders" is already criminal in itself.[12]

In succeeding chapters Fielding addresses the indulgence of the poor in the luxuries of gin drinking and gambling: two forms of pleasure which, taken in conjunction with the first chapter's masquerades and entertainments, form, in Malvin Zirker's phrase, a somewhat "incongruous ensemble."[13] The logic of Fielding's denunciation lies in his attention to the ways in which a hunger for pleasure draws the "Commonalty" into criminal calculations as it draws them away from labor and a dependency on scant wages. Once the floodgate of pleasure is open there is no controlling the aspiring of the lower sort, by which the customary relations of deference are undermined. Fielding in fact argues, in the *Enquiry*'s central chapter—"Of the Laws that relate to the Provision for the Poor"—that wages need to be kept low, in order both to promote a favorable balance of trade and to compel workers to keep at their work;[14] without the legal compulsion to labor for low wages, those whom Fielding calls "the Incorrigible in Idleness" soon fall into beggary or crime (120). The liberty, and Fielding seldom invokes this word except in warning, insisted on by "the lowest Artificers, Husbandmen, and Labourers [to] exact what Price they please for their Labour" (117) verges on a liberty of refusing labor altogether, and this in turn leads to a threatening *mobility* on the part of the poor.

The rigidly stratified social order that the law upheld was endangered as much by what Fielding called "the Wandering of the Poor" as by their idleness and luxury. As he writes in the chapter "Of Laws relating to Vagabonds," the criminal's success turns on the hope of eluding discovery, and this hope was great in the labyrinthine city and suburbs of London. "Had they been intended for the very Purpose of Concealment," Fielding writes, "they could scarce have been better contrived. Upon such a View, the whole appears as a vast Wood or Forest, in which a Thief may harbour with as great Security, as wild Beasts do in the Desarts of *Africa* or *Arabia*. For by *wandering* from one Part to another, and often shifting his quarters, he may almost avoid the Possibility of being discovered" (131). In this passage Fielding uses the same imagery of a wilderness as the author of *Hanging, Not Punishment Enough* fifty years earlier, who had warned that "we shall shortly not dare to Travel in *England*, unless, as in the Desarts of Arabia, it be in large Companies, and Arm'd."[15] But Fielding follows out the implications of the image a step farther, likening the poor thief to the "wild Beasts" at home in such a savage landscape.

Throughout the *Enquiry* the explosive and largely unregulated growth of the city, whose very configuration is an encouragement of crime, is connected to a corrosive social fragmentation and uprootedness. Vagabondage and crime were unknown in King Alfred's time, when "a Traveller might have openly left a Sum of Money safely in the Fields and Highways, and have found it safe and untouched a Month afterwards": under the ancient constitution "every Subject in the Kingdom was registered in some Tithing . . . nor were they at Liberty [to depart from their Dwelling or] to leave the Country, without the Licence of the Sheriff or Governor of the Same." Without testimonials of respectability and good conduct from their original tithing, none of "the meaner Sort of People" could shift their habitation (132–34).

In this discourse of an ancient, prelapsarian constitution of England, Fielding turns antiquarian legal history—a digest of old laws and legal commentaries by Rapin, Nathaniel Bacon, and others—to harsh ideological ends. Since "most of the Rogues who infest the Public Roads and Streets, indeed almost all the Thieves in general, are Vagabonds in the true Sense of the Word, being Wanderers from their lawful Place of Abode," the only cure to such a criminal infestation is a prohibition of mobility (142–43). "Where then is the Redress?" Fielding asks, after summarizing the report of his constable, Saunders Welch, on the proliferation in Shoreditch and Bloomsbury of houses for Irish and other vagabond rogues: "Is it not *to hinder the Poor from wandering,* and this by compelling the Parish and Peace Officers to apprehend such Wanderers or Vagabonds, and by empowering the Magistrate effectually to punish and send them to their Habitations? Thus if we cannot discover, or will not encourage any Cure for Idleness, we shall at least compel the Poor to starve or beg at home; for there it will be impossible for them to steal or rob, without being presently hanged or transported out of the way" (144). The violence of Fielding's rhetoric barely masks a sense of ideological panic at the disorderliness of urban poverty.[16]

This panic rested on a conviction that the uncontrolled migration of the poor from all over Britain and Ireland had not only swelled the criminal ranks of London but had given an almost insurrectionary power to the mob. In issue 49 of the *Covent-Garden Journal,* dated June 20, 1752—whose motto is translated from Horace: "I hate the Mob"—Fielding anatomizes the populist economy of the London crowd, exploring its resistance to legality and customary subservience. Characterizing the crowd as a "fourth Estate" that has usurped the accustomed power of the nobility, gentry, and commons, Fielding writes that "tho' this Estate have not AS YET claimed that Right which was insisted on by the People or Mob in old Rome, of giving a negative Voice in the enacting Laws, they have clearly exercised this

Power in controlling their Execution."[17] The 1749 riots in the Strand of sailors against bawdy-houses, which form the background to Fielding's *True State of the Case of Bosavern Penlez*, and the violence surrounding the same year's Westminster elections, had convinced Fielding that the civil peace and the authority of the law were in jeopardy; his own magistracy had come under bitter attack for his defense of Penlez's hanging.

Calling for, and exercising, its own forms of rule, the fourth estate obstructed the law's work as it enforced its own system of deterrence and retribution. "They well know," Fielding continues in the *Covent-Garden Journal*, "that the Courts of Justice cannot proceed without Informations; if they can stifle these, the Law of Course becomes dead and useless. The Informers therefore in such Cases, they declare to be infamous, and guilty of the Crime LAESAE MOBILITATIS. Of this whoever is *suspected* (which is with them a synonymous Term with *convicted*) is immediately punished by Buffeting, Kicking, Stoning, Ducking, Bemudding, &c. in short, by all those Means of putting, (sometimes quite, sometimes almost) to Death, which are called by that general Phrase of *Mobbing*" (269). The play on *laesa majestas*, crime against sovereign power, embodies the essay's picture of a political world upside down, in which the fourth estate enjoys an "exorbitant Degree of Power . . . which seems to threaten to shake the Balance of our Constitution" (272). The crowd's resistance to the machinery of the law—its apparatus of informers, thief takers, watchmen, a nascent police—was just one aspect of its broader resistance to hierarchy and regulation, visible at its most threatening in the demonstrations on hanging day.

Public executions marked the limit of state violence and dramatized the law's power to enforce the social peace. Yet Fielding argues in his several accounts that the institution had gone awry—that, rather than instilling dread through "the Terror of the Example," the Tyburn progress and the hangings themselves were producing contradictory, anarchic effects. This subversion of the ritual's sanctioned meanings had two principal sources. The first was the crowd's sympathetic identification with the condemned, described here in a passage from the *Enquiry*'s last chapter:

The Day appointed by Law for the Thief's Shame is the Day of his Glory in his own Opinion. His procession to *Tyburn*, and his last Moments there, are all triumphant; attended with the Compassion of the meek and tender-hearted, and with the Applause, Admiration, and Envy of all the bold and hardened. His behaviour in his present Condition, not the Crimes, how atrocious soever, which brought him to it, are the Subject of Contemplation. And if he hath Sense enough to temper his Boldness with any Degree of Decency, his Death is spoke of by many with Honour, by most with Pity, and by all with Approbation. (167)

The second source of the corruption of meaning attending the rite of execution was what Fielding represents as the mob's carnivalesque love of misrule. In a Tyburn dispatch published in the *Covent-Garden Journal* he complained that "the Day of Execution is a Holyday to the greatest Part of the Mob about Town. On every such Occasion they are sure to assemble in great Numbers and as sure to behave themselves with all kinds of Disorder. All the Avenues to Tyburn appear like those to a Wake or Festival, where Idleness, Wantonness, Drunkenness, and every other Species of Debauchery are gratified" (447).

To keep up the spirits of the condemned, Fielding wrote in another hanging report, "all Manner of Sports and Pastime" are practiced by "their Friends and Successors in Shame, who are destined to be the Heroes of a future Holiday . . . For this Purpose great Numbers of Cats and Dogs were sacrificed, and converted into missile Weapons, with which together with Dirt, Brickbats, and suchlike Ammunition, a sham Fight was maintained, the whole Way from Newgate to Tyburn." Fielding's purpose in evoking such scenes of disruption was not "to raise my good Reader's Mirth, but his Indignation," for the burlesque of legal authority had become in his view both a practical problem for the police and a danger to the whole system of deference and terror on which law, and the social order, depended. "The real Fact at present," he wrote at the close of one execution report, is "that instead of making the Gallows an Object of Terror, our Executions contribute to make it an Object of Contempt in the Eye of a Malefactor; and we sacrifice the Lives of Men, not for *the Reformation, but for the Diversion of the Populace*" (*Covent-Garden Journal*, 416).[18]

Fielding was not the first author to recognize that the crowds who came out for executions were neither awed nor terrorized by these manifestations of state power. In his 1725 *Enquiry into the Causes of the Frequent Executions at Tyburn* Mandeville characterized the "Torrent of Mob" in terms of violent class loathing:

Amongst the lower Rank, and working People, the idlest, and such as are most fond of making Holidays, with Prentices and Journeymen to the meanest Trades, are the most honourable Part of these floating Multitudes. All the rest are worse. The Days being known before-hand, they are a Summons to all Thieves and Pickpockets, of both Sexes, to meet. Great Mobs are a Safeguard to one another, which makes these Days Jubilees, on which old Offenders, and all who dare not shew their Heads on any other, venture out of their Holes; and they resemble Free Marts, where there is an Amnesty for all Outlaws. All the Way, from *Newgate* to *Tyburn*, is one continued Fair, for Whores and Rogues of the meaner Sort. Here the most abandon'd Rakehells may light on Women as shameless.[19]

The overheated rhetoric in Mandeville's account takes to an infuriated extreme that criminalization of the poor which ran as an undercurrent in the anatomies. Distinctions between labor and criminality are dissolved in the free-floating, sexualized mob of execution day.[20]

Mandeville's fear and contempt for the crowd notwithstanding, his description is valuable for pointing to precisely those elements in the ceremonial of punishment which worried Fielding and became fixtures in the debate over public execution during the second half of the eighteenth century. The progress to Tyburn was far from the solemn ritual of intimidation London's magistrates must have originally envisioned. The tumbril might stop at a half-dozen public houses along the way for the prisoner to be plied with beer; gifts of nosegays and cakes, in conjunction with the typical white nuptial clothes of the condemned, evoked a common comparison—celebratory or sarcastic—of hangings to weddings and drew out what Linebaugh has called the "undercurrents of sexuality among the crowd at Tyburn."[21] Attacks on the constables guarding the condemned, threats of rescue, the victim's friends' struggle to keep his corpse out of the hands of body snatchers and anatomists, the hangman pelted with fruit and dead animals: all these forms of opposition, mockery, violence, and celebration revealed deep conflicts between the culture of the mob and the didactic, authoritarian project of the law's representatives. Divergent, even mutually incomprehensible attitudes toward death, sexuality, religion, money, and the relative claims of private property and bodily survival were acted out in the theater and counter-theater of criminal execution.[22]

Mandeville's description of the scene of execution remains by far the most vivid, as it was the most influential, eighteenth-century account. Almost all the points of later ideological contention are addressed in his analysis, and he usefully articulates one version of what might be called a reformist or modern position were it not so vitriolic in its contempt for popular custom and belief. He argues, for example, for the necessity of dissection to the advancement of anatomical and medical science, deploring the superstitious attachment of the poor to the malefactor's body and dismissing their feelings of bereavement: "What if it was a Disgrace to the surviving Relations of those who had Lectures read upon their Bodies, and were made use of for Anatomical Preparations? The Dishonour would seldom reach beyond the Scum of the People; and to be dissected, can never be a greater Scandal than being hanged" (27). If Mandeville's lexical brutality was somewhat softened in later accounts, his scenic renderings were often followed quite closely: Richardson's description of a hanging in the 1741 *Familiar Letters* is basically a more muted and seemly repetition of what Mandeville had written sixteen years earlier. Whether or not Richardson was consciously drawing from Mandeville's work in preparing his epistolary guidebook, the earlier text functioned as a repository of figures by which the scene of punishment could be represented.

Similarly, Mandeville's pamphlet anticipated both Fielding's ideological perspective and his practical arguments concerning the principle of exemplary terror. "For it is not the Death of these poor Souls that is chiefly aim'd at in Executions," Mandeville writes,

but the Terror we would have it strike in others of the same loose Principles: And, for the same Reason, these Executions are little better than Barbarity, and sporting away the Lives of the indigent Vulgar, if those valuable Sacrifices we are obliged to make to the publick Safety, are render'd insignificant. If no Remedy can be found for these Evils, it would be better that Malefactors should be put to Death in private; for our publick Executions are become Decoys, that draw in the Necessitous, and [are], in effect, as cruel as frequent Pardons; instead of giving Warning, they are exemplary the wrong Way, and encourage where they should deter. (36–37)

Fielding was similarly discomfited by the ways in which exemplary meaning had been drained from the spectacle of punishment, for this represented not only a defeat for the institutions of social control but also an intimation of a terrible, gratuitous violence at the heart of the law. Like Mandeville, Fielding saw an unsettling affinity between too-frequent pardons and too-frequent hangings: in both cases the forms of the law were hollowed of meaning. "If therefore the Terror of [the] Example is removed," Fielding wrote, "(as it certainly is by frequent Pardons), the Design of the Law is rendered totally ineffectual; The Lives of the Persons executed are thrown away, and sacrificed rather to the Vengeance than to the Good of the Public" (*Enquiry*, 166). Mandeville even anticipates Fielding's (and Bentham's) proposal of solitary confinement for the production of a more compliant subject.[23]

Yet, if Fielding closely followed Mandeville in his description and juridical critique of the state of executions in midcentury London, he introduced a new ingredient into the debate through his characterization of the criminal's death as a tragic representation. Inasmuch as the aim of the death sentence is to terrorize the poor into a lawful subservience, he argues, "the Design of those who first appointed Executions to be public, was to add the Punishment of Shame to that of Death; in order to make the Example an Object of greater Terror" (*Enquiry,* 168). Yet the very representational devices intended to produce aversion had, in practice, wicked and unpredictable effects. For, if the ritual's exemplary warnings against crime were to be effective, they needed to induce an identification between criminal and audience, a recognition of common impulses, temptations, and opportunities to transgress. The highly formulaic plotting of last dying speeches, for instance, meant to generalize the experience of criminality in such a way that listeners would respond to that experience as recognizably like their own and would cling to the shame and horror the spectacle evoked as their only defense against the same lapse into crime.

But the event failed to correspond to the conception. "I will appeal to any Man who hath seen an Execution," Fielding wrote, "or a Procession to an Execution; let him tell me when he hath beheld a poor Wretch, bound in a Cart, just on the Verge of Eternity, all pale and trembling with his approaching Fate, whether the Idea of Shame hath ever intruded on his Mind?" (168). Instead, identification slipped into either admiration or pity—which, as Fielding cites Aristotle to observe, "are very apt to attend whatever is an Object of Terror in the human Mind" (169). In consequence, for the crowd the focus of aversion tended to shift from the invisible offense to the hangman's visible infliction of suffering. Further, the frequency of executions and their openness to either heroic resistance or disruptive burlesque led to the coarsening of tragedy into vaudeville: "As the Looks and Behaviour of the Spectators so well bespeak them to be assembled to see some Shew or Farce, those who are to exhibit the Spectacle seem brought thither only as the Performers of such ridiculous Drama. Some, indeed, as in the Case of all Players, perform their Parts beyond others, have much more Mirth in their Countenances, and of Jest in their Mouths, and do consequently entertain the good Company better than their Companions; but . . . tho' not all can force a Laugh, there is scarce one who doth not refrain from Tears, and from every other Mark of Fear or Contrition" (*Covent-Garden Journal,* 447). Instead of a terrifying sacrifice to the law, the criminal becomes a figure of hilarity, a Punchinello of the scaffold.

As the principal source of these subversions of authoritarian ritual was the dramatic force of the representation itself, whether comical or lachrymose, the solution, Fielding argued, was to carry out the execution in private. It is telling that, to present his case for the elimination of public or spectacular execution, Fielding appeals to the authority of "the Poets" to explain its dangers—"for the good Poet and the good Politician do not differ so much as some who know nothing of either Art affirm" (*Enquiry,* 168). What connects them is an acute sense of how all the varied forms of representation—rituals, hangings, puppet shows, trials, and processions—act on the souls of their audience. Echoing such earlier critics of the excessive violence of the English stage as Dryden and Voltaire, Fielding writes that "a Murder behind the Scenes, if the Poet knows how to manage it, will affect the Audience with greater Terror than if it was acted before their Eyes" (169). His immediate model for this was David Garrick's production of *Macbeth,* in which the offstage murder of the king had the power to make "the Hair of the Audience stand an End. Terror hath, I believe, been carried higher by this single Instance, than by all the Blood which hath been spilt on the Stage" (169–70). Garrick's staging had its theoretical roots in Aristotle's *Poetics,* in which the effects of spectacle are condemned as, at best, redundant: in the words of an English translation published in 1705, "the Fable must be composed in such a manner; that he who understands the things which happen, altho' he see them not, yet tremble at the Recitation of them, and feel the same Compassion, and the same Terror . . . Now *to endeavour* to excite these *two Passions* by the sight . . . is what the Poet has no concern with."[24] Indeed, Fielding carries the argument against spectacular display a step further, writing that "the Mind of Man is so much more capable of magnifying than his Eye, that I question whether every Object is not lessened by being looked upon" (170).

The antirealist implications of this passage are considerable. The aim of the tragic representation Fielding takes for his model is not an accurate likeness of the outward appearance of things but, rather, an exemplary mystification, an icon. The poets he invokes prey on the imagination's susceptibility to hidden terrors and thus provide the "good Politician" with a strategy for manipulating the crowd's responses to theatrical enactments of lawful power. In a striking turn from the authority of poets to that of priests—"whose Politics," Fielding approvingly notes, "have never been doubted"—he asserts that "those of *Egypt* in particular, where the sacred Mysteries were first devised, well knew the Use of hiding from the Eyes of the Vulgar, what they intended should inspire them with the greatest Awe and Dread" (170). There is a whiff of smoke-and-mirrors hucksterism in Fielding's solemn advice to England's rulers, a sense that these sacred mysteries are not so distant from the vulgarian dazzle of a puppet show. Only the stakes are different. Power is most feared, least questioned, when invisible. Public executions, with all their openness to misreading and misrule, only undermine the effects they were instituted to produce: they should be replaced with judicial murders offstage.

"If Executions therefore were so contrived," Fielding writes, "that few could be present at them, they would be much more shocking and terrible to the Crowd without Doors than at present, as well much more dreadful to the Criminals themselves, who would thus die in the Presence only of their Enemies" (170).[25] The strategy of visibly keeping the execution from view magnifies its terrors, as an item, possibly fabricated, from the *Covent-Garden Journal* means to show. In a sort of advertisement for the recently published *Enquiry* Fielding writes: "I cannot help adding, as an Instance of the greater Efficacy of such Executions as are recommended in the Book I have hinted at, what I myself observed on Saturday last, when a Report prevailed, that three of the Felons were executed in Newgate. The Horror which this Report spread among the lower People is astonishing" (416). Fielding never takes his argument to the logical extreme of simply making up scary execution reports to substitute for actual executions, but the combination of severity in enforcement and secrecy in execution aims to do away with popular forms of representation—public, contentious rituals—in favor of a more depersonalized, authoritarian regime. Characterizing the dramatic enactment of justice as a kind of mystery play, Fielding imagines a poetics of execution which rests on obscurity, concealment, and rumor.

It was not until 1783 that the site of hangings was removed from Tyburn to Newgate, and eighty-five more years passed before the construction of a windowless execution shed inside Newgate yard marked the end of public hanging in England. Although such later advocates of public execution as Boswell, Reynolds, and Burke adopted the same imagery of scenic representation and the staging of tragedy which Fielding put at the center of his analysis, the conclusions they draw from that imagery are remote from his. Criminal deaths, as in this 1785 letter from Reynolds to Boswell, are judged according to their aesthetic qualities, their intensity of arousal:

I am obliged to you for carrying me yesterday to see the execution at Newgate of the five malefactors. I am convinced it is a vulgar error, the opinion that it is so terrible a spectacle, or that it any way implies a hardness of heart or cruelty of disposition, any more than such a disposition is implied in seeking delight from the representation of a tragedy. Such an execution as we saw, where there was no torture of the body or expression of agony of the mind . . . I consider it is natural to desire to see such sights, and, if I may venture, to take delight in them, in order to stir and interest the mind, to give it some emotion, as moderate exercise is necessary for the body.[26]

The terms that Reynolds, Boswell, and Burke adopt in framing their arguments— *delight, sensibility, affecting, curiosity, sublime*—reveal a moral detachment from the experience of suffering that Fielding would have found incredible. Tragedy and carnival are just modes of aesthetic pleasure and stimulation for the jaded. For Fielding, instead, the parallels between executions and tragic performances were problematic in both aesthetic and moral terms, and his discussion of them in the *Enquiry* suggests a crisis in his thinking about the consequences of visual and verbal representations, whose power to instruct can be undermined by their awakening of unconscious and disruptive sympathies.

# CHAPTER TEN

# Fielding as Magistrate

## The Canning and Penlez Cases

Fielding should not really have been involved with the Elizabeth Canning mystery at all; if he had gone into the country a day earlier, he would have had no part in it. Instead, "upon the *6th* of *February,* as I was sitting in my Room," he writes in *A Clear State of the Case of Elizabeth Canning* (1753), "Counsellor *Madan* being then with me, my Clerk delivered me a Case, which was thus, as I remember, indorsed at the Top, *The Case of* Elizabeth Canning *for Mr.* Fielding's *Opinion,* and at the Bottom, *Salt,* Solr. Upon the Receipt of this Case, with my Fee, I bid my Clerk give my Service to Mr. *Salt* and tell him, that I would take the Case with me into the Country, whither I intended to go the next Day, and desired he would call for it on the *Friday* Morning afterwards; after which, without looking into it, I delivered it to my Wife, who was then drinking Tea with us, and who laid it by."[1] Canning's Solicitor Salt begs Fielding, however, to read over the case then and there: "it was a Matter of some Haste, being of a criminal Nature, and he feared the Parties would make their Escape" (298). So Fielding finishes his tea, orders his wife to "fetch [him] back the Case," and sets to reading. Mr. Salt at first seems only to want advice on what course to follow in the case, which Fielding gives, but soon Salt is asking him to take Canning's affidavit and to arrest and examine another witness, Virtue Hall, a young woman Canning had named in passing in her narrative. "And a very extraordinary Narrative it is," Fielding was to write later in his own text, "consisting of many strange Particulars, resembling rather a wild Dream than a real Fact" (288).

Nevertheless, at first Fielding turned down Salt's request: the events had taken place far away from Bow Street, and witnesses had already been questioned by another justice. Most of all, Fielding's work was, quite literally, killing him: "I had been almost fatigued to Death, with several tedious Examinations at that Time, and had intended to refresh myself with a Day or two's Interval in the Country" (298). But Salt persists, and Fielding finally yields, pulled, as he acknowledges, by his own curiosity to know more of the strange history.[2]

On New Year's Day 1753 Elizabeth Canning had gone to visit her aunt and uncle near Rosemary Lane in London. Around nine in the evening she started back for the house where she worked as a servant; since it was late, her aunt and uncle walked partway home with her. Soon after they parted, opposite the gate to Bedlam hospital in Moorfields, two men—"who both had brown Bob-wigs on, and drab-coloured Great-coats," as she remembered in her affidavit (299)—assaulted her, first robbing her of her hat, stuff gown, and linen apron, and half a guinea in gold and three shillings in silver, then dragging her along a gravel path, where one of the men, who had "threatened to do" for her, "gave her a violent Blow with his Fist on the right Temple, that threw her into a Fit, and intirely deprived her of her Senses," as Fielding writes in his own summary of the case. "These Fits," he adds, "she says she hath been accustomed to; that they were first occasioned by the Fall of a Cieling on her Head; that they are apt to return upon her whenever she is frightened, and that they sometimes continue for six or seven Hours" (287).

When she came to, she was being carried along a broad road, and though she was soon able to walk by herself, the men continued to drag her along for another half-hour, until they came to a house. Taken into the kitchen, Canning met a grotesque Gypsy woman, who "took hold of her by the Hand, and promised *to give her fine Cloaths if she would go their Way.*" When Canning refused, the woman took a knife from a drawer, cut the lace of her stays, took them and her cap away from her, and pushed her upstairs "into a Back-room like a Hay-loft, without any Furniture whatsoever," containing only "a large black Jug, with the Neck much broken, filled with Water, and several Pieces of Bread, amounting to about the Quantity of a Quartern Loaf scattered on the Floor, where was likewise a small Parcel of Hay." There, after warning her "that if she made the least Noise or Disturbance, the old Gipsy Woman would come up and cut her Throat," the three miscreants left Elizabeth Canning utterly alone for twenty-seven days, with no other food than the bread scattered on the floor and a little mince pie she had in her pocket for her younger brother (287–88). Four weeks later, "almost famished with Hunger, and starved with Cold," she broke out through a window and found her way back to her friends in London, after a six hours' walk (300).

Such is the essence of the narrative that Fielding elaborates from the piecemeal and disorderly accumulation of testimony. Fully reconstructing Canning's experience or even a coherent sequence of her different versions of events from Fielding's text is impossible. What the *Clear State of the Case* makes available, instead, is a documentary narrative of legal inquiry, a designedly fragmentary presentation of Fielding's methods of assembling and weighing evidence. Even that documentary narrative has, in a sense, to be reconstructed, since Fielding has structured his text rather as a polemical justification of the system of English criminal justice than as a plain autobiographical testimony of his involvement in the case. But in order to justify the law—the verdicts found against the old Gypsy woman, Mary Squires, for the felony of stealing Canning's stays (which earned her a sentence of death) and against the house's owner, Susannah Wells, for abetting the felony—Fielding has to justify his own role in the investigation against charges of partiality or coercion of testimony. So he needs to make clear his neutrality and initial reluctance even to hear the evidence in the case, in order for that evidence to assume its full authority. The efficacy of his defense (of himself, Canning, and the law) depends on the circumstantiality of his narrative of juridical reconstruction.

The day after Fielding agrees to hear the evidence, Elizabeth Canning is brought to his court in Bow Street, where her affidavit—presumably written out by Solicitor Salt—is read to the court, sworn, and signed. Some of this affidavit I have quoted here; it offers a similar chronicle of events to the composite account I have provided, but it also includes two parenthetical remarks that raise certain questions about the purity of Canning's testimony. When the story gets to the house where Canning was taken, the affidavit reads that this "House, as she, this Informant, hath since heard and believes, is situate at *Enfield-wash* in the County of *Middlesex,* and is reputed to be a very bad and disorderly Bawdy-house, and occupied by one ——— *Wells,* Widow" (299). In the kitchen there, along with the Gypsy, are two younger women, the affidavit continues, and "the Name of one of them, this Informant hath since heard, and believes is *Virtue Hall*" (300).

Both remarks derive from information acquired after Canning's return home, after an investigation had gotten under way but before Fielding had become involved. Canning had told her story first, of course, to her friends, one of whom, "a hartshorn rasper named Robert Scarrat, who had been a patron of Mother Wells's 'hedge bawdy-house,' was probably largely responsible for fixing on Wells's house as the scene of Elizabeth's trial."[3] Canning had then spoken to an alderman,

Thomas Chitty, who issued a warrant for "the Body of a Person *that goes by the Name of Mother Wells, and lives at Enfield-Wash,*"[4] so, by the time, next day, that she was taken to Wells's house, her story had gained a certain geographical and even sociological specificity: she had been kidnaped to be forced into prostitution at a known bawdy-house. Once at the house Canning "fixed on the Gipsy Woman," Fielding writes, "whom she had very particularly described before, and who is, perhaps, the most remarkable Person in the whole World" (296). But the Gypsy woman was not named in the warrant, nor in fact had Canning described her, either during her interview with the alderman or in the published announcement, a kind of Wanted poster, placed in the *London Daily Advertiser* by Canning's friends. So the question of what Canning actually said immediately after her reappearance is troublingly murky.

Little of this background, or the questions it raises about the status of Canning's testimony, is visible in Fielding's text, apart from the two remarks attaching identities to her otherwise almost dreamlike oppressors. But what I wish to emphasize in pointing out these problematic details is the already-constructed character of the evidence Fielding heard as magistrate. The originating documents in the case— the warrant for Wells's arrest, the Wanted advertisement, Canning's affidavit—had already been worked over, collaborated on, pieced together out of memory, inference, and secondhand speculation. If Fielding's *Clear State of the Case,* by its gathering of documentary fragments, reproduces the history of his own witnessing and judgment, the fissures and discrepancies it enables the reader to see reveal equally the difficulty of disentangling what he calls *evidentia rei* from narrative *elaborations* of the evidence of things.[5]

After witnessing Canning's affidavit, Fielding issued a warrant against everyone at Wells's house (the Gypsy and Wells herself having already been arrested), and Virtue Hall and Judith Natus were accordingly brought to the office in Bow Street. Hall's testimony was to prove crucial. "When she came before me," Fielding writes, "she appeared in Tears, and seemed all over in a trembling Condition," but he reassures her, and "after some Minutes [I] began to examine her; which I continued doing, in the softest Language and kindest Manner I was able, for a considerable Time, till she had been guilty of so many Prevarications and Contradictions, that I told her I would examine her no longer, but would commit her to Prison, and leave her to stand or fall by the Evidence against her, and at the same Time advised Mr. *Salt* to prosecute her as a Felon, together with the Gipsy Woman"

(301). The threat of imprisonment proves wonderfully effective: Hall answers Fielding's next questions "with more Appearance of Truth than she had done before; after which, I recommended to Mr. *Salt,* to go with her and take her Information in Writing; and at her parting from me, I bid her be a good Girl" (302).

This terse passage represents both the turning point of Fielding's inquiry and the point at which the arguments of Canning's defenders were later to break down. Fielding gives no example of Hall's initial "prevarications" or "contradictions" nor what "appearances of truth" she gave after his threat to have her prosecuted as a felon.[6] It seems likely that the most compelling "appearance" was that of agreement with the story he had previously heard from Canning: after six hours of skeptical interrogation in front of Fielding and "ten or a dozen [other] Persons of Credit" at Bow Street, and having also been present at Enfield for the arrests of Mary Squires and Susannah Wells, Hall must have known the gist of Canning's allegations. In any case, her appearances of truth satisfied Fielding that a usable affidavit could now be taken and sworn. But, disastrously, instead of taking her statement himself, he allowed Salt—Canning's solicitor, after all—to take Hall's testimony in private. "*Virtue Hall* then went from me, and returned in about two Hours," he notes, with an affidavit "which was, as she said, taken from her Mouth," though in Salt's hand and, strangely like Canning's, in Salt's lawyerly voice (302).

To Fielding, and to the jurors at the trial a fortnight later of Mary Squires and Susannah Wells, Hall's evidence—the congruence of her testimony with Canning's own story—was decisive. Fielding sets the groundwork early in his text by announcing, "And now I come to a Piece of Evidence which hath been the principal Foundation of that Credit which I have given to this extraordinary Story" (295), but then he defers telling us what that "Piece of Evidence" is until he has returned to the beginning of the case, to recount all the events "down to the Time when *Virtue Hall* appeared first before me." In this narrative of investigation Fielding becomes an actor caught up in an ongoing history of strange allegations and crimes, a detective. Only when he has concluded his account of gathering evidence for a prosecution of the two women (the men who allegedly kidnaped Canning, Squires's son George and a friend, had disappeared) does Fielding return to the evidence that, to him, clinches the case, "a Point indeed on which any Cause whatever might be safely rested: This is the Agreement, in so many particular Circumstances between the Evidence of *Elizabeth Canning* and *Virtue Hall*" (307). For so long postponed a *coup de texte,* the revelation would be disappointing even if Fielding had not made the fatal misstep of allowing Canning's lawyer to take Hall's affidavit in private. After encouraging us to expect one concrete, irrefutable proof—a secret witness, an inadvertent material trace of the crime—all Fielding has to show us is two witnesses telling the same story. And no coincidence admits of more doubt or qualification.[7]

In his discussion of Fielding's strategies of narrative and judgment in *Tom Jones*, Alexander Welsh writes that "as novelist [Fielding] was far more skeptical than Defoe or Richardson about witnesses telling their own stories." If Richardson and Defoe often treated their characters' testimony with just as much suspicion and irony, Fielding's skepticism extended not just to the veracity of individual narrators but to the *form* of first-person narration itself. The narrator in Fielding, so unlike the chatty, harrowing voices of Defoe's autobiographers, "is not an eyewitness but a manager of the evidence, analogous to a prosecutor or a judge and to later defense attorneys in a trial."[8] As a magistrate, too, Fielding was skeptical and exacting. Near the end of the *Clear State of the Case* he writes that "I have never spared any Pains in endeavouring to detect Falsehood and Perjury" (310), and his conduct of the Canning case bears this out. Not only did he question Virtue Hall for nearly six hours when she was first brought to him, but he had her swear to her evidence a week later in the presence of Mary Squires and Susannah Wells; confronted with a number of credible affidavits placing Squires halfway across England on the day she allegedly robbed and imprisoned Elizabeth Canning, Fielding "sent for [Canning] once more; and endeavoured by all Means in my Power to sift the Truth out of her, and to bring her to a Confession if she was guilty; but she persisted in the Truth of the Evidence she had given, and with such an Appearance of Innocence, as persuaded all present of the Justice of her Cause" (306–7).

Yet, as scrupulous as he was in this case in attending to the conflicting claims of evidence and in weighing probabilities, Fielding ultimately had to rely on the forcefulness of "witnesses telling their own stories," in Welsh's phrase. As a judge he was closer, because of his vulnerability to misrepresentation, to Squire Allworthy or *Amelia*'s Dr. Harrison than to the fictions' magisterial narrators. In *A Clear State of the Case of Elizabeth Canning* Fielding exhibits the constraints under which juridical descriptions of truth are made: in the absence of material proofs, circumstances can only be known by the stories people tell of them. The problems inherent in human testimony and witness cannot be overcome by the rules of evidence at law.

In his two roles of author and magistrate Fielding considered questions of evidence and interpretation from distinct but reciprocal perspectives: if in *Tom Jones,* for example, he structures fictional narrative according to the model of a (benign) prosecutorial argument, as Welsh argues, in his Elizabeth Canning pamphlet he articulates the fragmentary and contradictory material of criminal inquiry into a detective fiction, a narrative of suspense. As sure as he is of Canning's story, Fielding is still aware, even in his most positive declaration, of the impossibility of his ever coming to certain knowledge: "I am at this very Time," he writes, near the end of the pamphlet, "on this 15th Day of *March* 1753, as firmly persuaded as I am of any Fact in this World, the Truth of which depends solely on the Evidence of others, that *Mary Squires* the Gipsy Woman, IS GUILTY of the Robbery and Cruelty of which she stands convicted; that the *alibi* Defence is not only a false one, but a Falsehood very easy to be practiced on all Occasions, where there are Gangs of People, as Gipsies, *&c.* . . . and that *Elizabeth Canning* is a poor, honest, innocent, simple Girl, and the most unhappy and most injured of all human Beings" (310–11). Conviction, he acknowledges here, "depends solely on the Evidence of others." And, if the alibi defense—the testimony of witnesses (suggestively constructed here as "Gangs of People, as Gipsies, *&c*") who located Mary Squires in Dorset on the day of Canning's disappearance—is "a Falsehood very easy to be practiced," the same is true of any testimony concerted among friends or taken in private by lawyers or heard by a justice drawn to a certain image of female innocence.

As a writer on the law, Fielding became embroiled in a number of cases of contention and doubt, in which the evidence was so hybrid and contradictory as to make all presumptions of truth suspect. If one way of trying to address such uncertainty was, as in *Tom Jones,* to construct a narrative form in which knowledge was articulated through authorial mastery and penetration of evidence, by the time of *Amelia,* two years later, Fielding's trials as an agent of social control seem to have led him to wonder if authors had such a secure hold even over the outcomes of fiction. Besides narrative the most prominent cultural mechanism for allaying doubt was the law, whose rules of evidence, arrest, and appeal, as Fielding outlines them in the opening pages of the *Clear State of the Case,* had been established to protect the rights of the subject and to provide for certainty of judgment. Fielding's polemical intention in writing on the Canning affair was in fact to justify the institutions of criminal law against charges of false conviction, to draw attention to the law's scrupulous procedures for arriving at truth.[9] The enveloping irony of

Fielding's text, however, is that the law finally betrayed his defense. The year after he wrote his justification of the verdicts against Squires and Wells, Elizabeth Canning was found guilty of willful and corrupt perjury. It was typical of the whole muddled history of the case that two jurors tried to withdraw their guilty votes, but the verdicts were upheld, and Canning was transported to America on the same day that Fielding, close to dying, arrived in Lisbon. In the end the law proved his case by overturning his verdict.

Fielding wrote the *True State of the Case of Bosavern Penlez* to justify the state's execution of Penlez for stealing a bundle of linen in the midst of three days of rioting against bawdy-houses in the Strand.[10] Although several hundred sailors and their supporters seem to have been involved in the disturbances, which at their worst led to the burning of one house and the looting of at least two others, only seven persons were arrested and committed by Fielding to Newgate, and of these only the hapless Penlez was sentenced to death. The invidious singling out of a local resident with no stake in the bawdy-house protest to suffer the full violence of the law seemed to many contemporaries a symptom of a more general pattern of legalized oppression. To justify the sentence of death Fielding had to reconstruct the threat the rioting posed to the social peace, and reconstruction took the form of a legal archive.

Fielding was out of London when the troubles that came to be known as the Penlez riots began. On Saturday, July 1, 1749, three sailors were robbed at a bawdy-house in the Strand and were driven off when they raised a protest. That night they came back with their shipmates, invaded the house, and burned its featherbeds in a huge bonfire in front. According to one account they "turn'd the women naked into the street"; according to another, they "suffer'd no Injury to be done to the poor Damsels."[11] But in any event the rioters, who had moved on to another house, the Bunch of Grapes, were soon dispersed by two detachments of soldiers stationed nearby. The next morning the owner of the Bunch of Grapes went to Fielding's right-hand man, Saunders Welch, for help in case the rioters should return, but Welch told him that, since Fielding was still in the country, he needed to apply for a warrant from another magistrate.

That night the sailors burned the Bunch of Grapes down. On his way home from a friend's house in the City, Welch, as he later testified, "perceived a great Fire in the *Strand*, upon which he proceeded on till he came to the House of one *Peter*

*Wood,* who told this Informant that the Mob had demolished the House of *Stan-hope* [the Bunch of Grapes], and were burning his Goods, and that they had threat-ened, as soon as they had finished their Business there, that they would come and demolish his House likewise." Welch managed "with much Difficulty" to get hold of a troop of forty soldiers, and, as they advanced on Wood's house, the Star, they beat drums to disperse the crowd before the house's furnishings, piled up in the street, could be fired. According to Welch, "had the Goods of the said House been set on Fire, it must infallibly have set on Fire the Houses on both Sides, the Street being there extremely narrow" (51). One person was arrested inside Wood's house as a rioter, and several others milling around in front were also taken to jail.

Fielding returned to London around noon on Monday, the third day. When he called for those arrested to be brought to Bow Street for questioning, he also "sent an Order for a Party of the Guards to conduct the aforesaid Prisoners to his House, the Streets being at that Time full of Mob, assembled in a riotous and tumultuous Manner, and Danger of a Rescue being apprehended" (52); during the examina-tion crowds threatened to break into the Bow Street office. Afterward the consta-ble who attended the prisoners back to Newgate testified that "it was not without the utmost Difficulty that the said Prisoners were conveyed in Coaches through the Street, the Mob frequently endeavouring to break in upon the Soldiers, and crowding towards the Coach Doors" (50). The previous night, two watch-houses had been forced open by crowds rescuing prisoners; on Monday a crowd gathered at the Old Bailey had broken the windows of an adjacent house. To Fielding the attack on bawdy-houses had clearly metastasized into an assault on authority itself. Welch later deposed that he was with Fielding "when several Informations were given, that a Body of Sailors, to the Number of four Thousand, were assembling themselves at *Tower-hill,* and had declared a Resolution of marching to *Temple-Bar* in the Evening" (53); Fielding may also have believed that some of them wanted "to raid the armoury in preparation to launching an insurrection."[12] Bawdy-house riot seemed to be verging on civil war.

As it turned out, the rioting had largely run its course, and the threats of insur-rection were unrealized. For those, starting with the author of *The Case of the Unfor-tunate Penlez*—an oppositional pamphlet published eleven days before Fielding's— who have written against Fielding and the administration he served, these threats were never more than self-justifying phantoms. The bonfires, according to the *Un-fortunate Penlez's* author, were carried out "with so much Decency and Order, so little Confusion, that, notwithstanding the Crowd gather'd together on this Occasion, a Child of five Years old might have crossed the Street in the thickest of them, without the least Danger."[13] Apart from this good order it was clear to the onlookers that the attacks were focused on redressing a social evil: "As to the Neighbours, who were at their Doors and Windows, seeing the Whole without the least Concern or Alarm, there was not probably one of them who, though as good and as loyal Subjects as any his Majesty has, and as well affected to the Peace and Quiet of his Government, imagin'd or dream'd there was any Spirit of Sedition or riotous Designs, in all these Proceedings, beyond the open and expressed Intention of destroying these obnoxious Houses."[14] Fielding's archive, of course, means to tell another story—and to explain the necessity of one subject's death.

Fielding gathers the documents in the case without smoothing them into a comprehensive, chronological narrative; instead, he presents a series of affidavits in roughly the order of the witnesses' first observations of the uprising. All of Fielding's witnesses are agents of the police: beadles, constables, watchmen. The pamphlet does not give voice to the rioters, nor, except in terms of contemptuous dismissal, does it inquire into their motives. The archive Fielding assembles has an unconstructed appearance, the better to display the disinterested procedures by which the representatives of the law uncover the hidden truth of a case. Beginning with a digest of legal commentaries to explain the history and origins of the Riot Act (the formula by which magistrates could compel unlawful or tumultuous mobs to disperse), Fielding then shifts to the collection of testimony. A beadle recounts his view of the first hours of the riots: his attempt "to seize one of the Ringleaders" (47), the crowd's violent resistance, their attack on the "Night-Prison" beneath his house to free two prisoners on the following night. The beadle having left the scene before the lighting of a bonfire to burn the featherbeds and other contents of one of the houses, a constable testifies to what he saw of the fire and tells how he requested a detachment of soldiers to help restore order. As the affidavits accumulate, a plural, discontinuous text of the uprisings begins to emerge. The accounts do not conflict—indeed, any contesting voices are suppressed—but the narrative is pocked with gaps, jumps from one time or location to another. Meanwhile, Bosavern Penlez has become something of a mystery: three-quarters of the way through the text his name has not even been mentioned.

It is not until after the statement of Fielding's lieutenant, Saunders Welch, which ends with police patrolling the streets and "the public Peace . . . again re-

stored" (53), that Fielding presents the testimony of the watchmen involved in Penlez's arrest a few streets away from the disorders. A little after one in the morning
on the second night of the troubles, one of these watchmen got word of "a Man
above who had a great Bundle of Linnen," and, following his informant into Bell
Yard, he saw a man stuff something under his clothes (54). When he called out, the
man fled. A second watchman caught up with the suspect and held him against a
railing while they questioned him. "'So, Brother, what is all this you have got here?'"
one of them asked (55). The suspect said it "belonged to the Bitch his Wife, who
had pawned all his Cloaths; and that he had taken away these that she might not
pawn them likewise" (54). The watchmen, however, did not believe him, so Bosavern Penlez, a local peruke maker and son of a clergyman, was put under arrest.

Penlez "was then a little in Liquor," as the witnesses later testified (54). In the
watch-house he changed his story, now claiming "that the Woman to whom the
Linnen belonged was not his Wife; for that he was an unfortunate young Fellow,
and had kept Company with bad Women, and that he had been robbed by one of
them of fifteen Shillings, and had taken away her Linnen out of Revenge" (55).
Later that night, however, he told a constable he had found the linen in the street.
Penlez was taken the next day to Fielding's house in Bow Street and examined.
Even after the linen—"*To wit*, Ten lac'd Caps, four lac'd Handkerchiefs, three Pair
of lac'd Ruffles, two lac'd Clouts, five plain Handkerchiefs, five plain Aprons, and
one lac'd Apron"—had been sworn to by Jane Wood as her property, Penlez stuck
to his story, saying he had found the bundle in the street, denying he had been in
or near Peter Wood's house the night of the disorders (56). Nevertheless, he was
committed to Newgate to await trial on charges of riot.

The watchmen's testimony, coming as an afterword to the main arc of the riot
narrative, is clear in itself but rather incongruous as the linchpin of Fielding's argument, which proves revealingly disconnected. Despite all the meticulous registering of detail—the time and place of Penlez's discovery, his exact and contradictory
words, the inventory of stolen linens—no witness locates Penlez among the riots
Fielding was investigating. The last bit of evidence, in fact, is a sworn statement
from one of the watchmen "that when *Penlez* was examined before the Justice, he
solemnly denied that he was in the House of *Peter Wood,* or near it" (56). Nothing
in the evidence Fielding collected or in Penlez's subsequent trial provides any reason for doubting the truth of that denial.[15]

Instead of being connected by proofs or compelling inference, Penlez is linked metonymically to the disorders. The rioters were not, Fielding argues, acting out of legitimate "Zeal against lewd and disorderly Houses"; instead, they were "Thieves under the Pretence of Reformation," whose violence posed a political threat to a regime founded on the fundamental value of private property (58). The conflation of thievery and riot at once trivializes the reasons for popular uprising and turns each theft into an assault on the public order. If the rioters, whose crimes call for "Censure and Example," were no different from thieves, the thief who was taken, however far from the scene of violence, was no different from a seditionary (57). His execution will serve to censure that other crime.[16]

The particulars of Penlez's innocence or guilt, in fact, have no place in Fielding's account: "As to the Case of the Sufferer," he writes, rather incredibly, given the pamphlet's title and the severity of his punishment, "I shall make no Remarks" (59). This lacuna at what one would expect to be the heart of Fielding's prosecutorial narrative—the lack of any real case against Penlez, the absence of compelling evidence connecting him to the riots he was hanged for embodying—lays bare the limitations of the circumstantial realism Fielding experiments with in the *True State of the Case*. In assembling his evidentiary archive with a view to persuading his audience of the correctness of the court's verdict, Fielding makes use of the devices of realist narrative familiar from a century of trial reports: the careful delineation of times and locales; the cataloguing of circumstantial details, such as inventories of stolen goods; the verbatim transcription of eyewitness testimony, each speaker limited to reporting only what he or she had directly seen and heard. As far as it goes, the evidence he incorporates fits with Fielding's, and the court's, view of Penlez's guilt, but where the evidence stops, on the crucial question of Penlez's actual presence at the scene of the disorders, Fielding's documentary text has to fall silent. The realist strategy of seeming to let the story tell itself through the density of its circumstantial detail only reveals, in the end, the limits of the law's knowledge. Fielding's commitment here to the procedures of circumstantial realism forces him to reveal the obviously *constructed* character of the narrative the representatives of the law have to fabricate to justify Penlez's suffering.

And it is, finally, Penlez's suffering that matters. His effectual silencing within Fielding's text betrays an anxious unwillingness to let us see him too closely. At the scaffold Penlez is both expiatory symbol and (masked) tragic actor, assuming the role of Rioter, even of Riot itself. His death thus becomes, within the dramaturgy of the law, a spectacular demonstration and warning of the consequences of popular disorder. As Fielding was to write two years later in the *Enquiry*, "the Terror of the Example is the only Thing proposed, and one Man is sacrificed to the Preservation of Thousands" (166): Penlez's death is excessive and disconnected from any intimate or complex apprehension of his humanity by political design.

Yet, in reporting just enough of Penlez's drunken, guilty, contradictory gestures and speech to account for the watchmen's arrest, Fielding has already brought him too close for us to dismiss what we have seen from memory; he is no longer simply a body on whom the narratives and exhortations of the law can be spectacularly, impersonally inscribed. His innocent incompetence at making up a plausible story, his panicky inconsistency, flicker disruptively through the deliberately anonymous testimony of the watchmen. Trying to come up with a story that will get him out of trouble, he could be Fielding's next hero, Billy Booth, telling self-exculpating lies to his wife, Amelia, and, even though Booth's sins are darker than Penlez's, Fielding allows himself and his readers to pardon him. Penlez makes the same appeal through the circumstantial report of his arrest. Setting out to dissever Penlez from his humanity, to make him an abstraction of riotous anarchy in order to justify his punishment, Fielding fails in his project, precisely because his representation brings Penlez too stubbornly and sympathetically before us. In his pamphlet written to justify the law's severity, Fielding betrays the law as a cruel and exemplary fiction.

# CHAPTER ELEVEN

# *Amelia*

## *Imprisonment and Transgression*

*Amelia* is, with *Jonathan Wild* and *Bosavern Penlez*, Fielding's most urban story, and the London it portrays is what Roland Barthes, in his work on Racine, has called a "panic milieu" (98).[1] The heroine's husband, Billy Booth, is committed to Newgate in the opening scene of the story and lives out the rest of the narrative inside or in the shadow of the full range of eighteenth-century carceral institutions: from Newgate to the country house where Amelia's mother keeps her confined, from Mr. Bondum's sponging-house (a kind of halfway house for debtors on their way to prison) to the locked box in which Booth's servant has secreted a stolen portrait of Amelia. But, if spaces of captivity and enthralment are everywhere in *Amelia*, there is a special bond between prisons and everyday life in the nightmarish, labyrinthine metropolis. Newgate stands at the threshold of the fiction as it stood historically at the threshold of London.

Prisons, marking the boundary separating the licit from the illicit, were traditionally built at the gates that led in and out of the city, and the symbolic weight of this location is evoked by Fielding's use of Newgate as the scene of the first third of his story. Introducing himself to Booth in the text's opening pages, the petty criminal and con man Mr. Robinson says, "I perceive, Sir, you are but just arrived in this dismal Place, which is, indeed, rendered more detestable by the Wretches who inhabit it, than by any other Circumstances" (29). The "dismal Place" he leaves carefully unnamed could be either Newgate or London itself, for Booth is freshly arrived from the country. As the site of passage into the scary and chaotic urban landscape *Amelia* describes, Newgate conditions our apprehension of London as just a more extensive and uncanny space of imprisonment. Over and over we are made to see that the world inside is a grotesque double of the world outside the walls; Fielding, in fact, calls into question the very distinction between inside and outside, drawing a reversible, shifting topography of imprisonment which all the characters—along with the narrator and, by extension, his audience—inhabit.

The inescapability of the prison image in *Amelia* has led to two dominant ways of reading the text: as an allegory of human enslavement (to passion or error) and eventual freedom, in which prisons are the symbol of a moral state; or as a realist study of a system of criminal justice and the social order it supports, in which the prison is a real historical site, rendered in all its material particularity. Most commonly, Fielding has been held to be wavering, ruinously, between the two kinds of writing.[2] This fluctuation, in turn, is most often read as a symptom of creative exhaustion, brought on by Fielding's strain at trying, for once as a novelist, to be good. ("Poor Fielding, I believe, designed to be good," Ann Donnellan wrote to Samuel Richardson, "but did not know how, and in the attempt lost his genius, low humour.")[3] So, just as often as Fielding has been set in dialectical opposition to Richardson, *Amelia* has been taken as Fielding's attempt to write more in the arch-rival's manner, in which he adopts the vocabulary of sentimentalism, portrays the depredations of aristocratic rakes upon middle-class virtue, confines the action to enclosed domestic interiors, and aims at both a greater psychological realism and a loosening of authorial control.[4]

The stakes of the contest between allegorical and naturalist readings of *Amelia*, or between a moral and juridical construction of its meanings, are most exposed in Fielding's narrative treatments of carceral space.[5] These representations show him to be at once more nostalgic, in his appeal to a lost constitutional order, and more radically skeptical, in his interrogation of epistemological and political authority, than his equivocal, defensive posture as an authoritarian reformer seems at first to warrant. Like Richardson's *Pamela* and *Clarissa*, *Amelia* evokes the allure of the transgressive acts and desires whose dangers it wishes to show us; the more inward and complex the representations, the more slippery and contaminated our response. The moral theme and the stability of the social and ideological frameworks within which that theme can be articulated are both potentially undermined by the emotional force of the representation itself, which involves the reader in unsuspected sympathies.

Richardson had confronted this problem during all the years of writing, publishing, and revising *Clarissa:* his correspondence with the book's readers, responding to drafts and alterations of the work in progress as well as to its successive editions, reveals his struggle for control over the work's meanings and its readers' interpretive options. Readings that ran contrary to the moral signification he meant the narrative to embody—from correspondents who blamed Clarissa for crossing the threshold of her father's property into Lovelace's grasp to those who found Lovelace spellbinding and hoped for his full, lawful possession of his object of desire—angered and upset Richardson and led him to add the moralizing table of contents, the clarifying italics and footnotes, the flood of new letters and little shifts of emphasis which swelled the work's third and fourth editions and outlawed the most dangerous forms of misreading. But laws exist to be broken, and *Clarissa* has proven resistant to any unitary imposition of meaning, even with the author's intentions so heavily signaled. Fielding's use of a strongly inflected irony, along with direct narratorial intervention, is more obviously controlling than Richardson's illusion of mimetic transparency, but his constant intrusions and frettings at the text only underscore the dangers of misconstruction. And, as the story of *Amelia* unfolds, or comes unraveled, even the narratorial puppet master seems to lose his hold of the tangled narrative threads.

Fielding's fullest visual description of a prison comes with Mr. Booth's arrest by bailiff's men working for his ex-benefactor, Dr. Harrison. Lured from the debtor's sanctuary of the Verge of the Court by a false report that Amelia has been taken violently ill in a toyshop, Booth is served with a warrant and driven by coach to the sponging-house. "At length," Fielding writes, Booth "arrived at the Bailiff's Mansion, and was ushered into a Room; in which were several Persons. *Booth* desired to be alone, upon which the Bailiff waited upon him up Stairs, into an Apartment, the Windows of which were well fortified with Iron Bars; but the Walls had not the least Outwork raised before them; they were, indeed, what is generally called naked, the Bricks having been only covered with a thin Plaister, which in many Places was mouldered away" (310). Bondum's sponging-house marks a crisis in Booth's fortunes: the point of his greatest estrangement both from the friends he has almost passively betrayed—and who, misconstruing false semblances of guilt, betray him in turn—and from a social order riddled with legal snares and miscarriages. But it is also, later in the fiction, the site of his moral awakening and an unraveling of the plots and conspiracies in which he and Amelia have been caught since before their arrival in London. The ethical and sociological strands of the text converge in Fielding's circumstantial rendering, through an accumulation of visual signs—the iron-barred windows, thin plaster, and patches of brick—of the oppressive apartment where Booth is confined.

The naturalistic textures of Fielding's description instance what Roland Barthes named the "reality effect," a representational desire growing out of an "incessant need to authenticate the real."[6] *Amelia* thus participates, if only tentatively, in that emerging practice of realism that aimed to register fully the concrete particularity of experience. Condemned by Barthes as a kind of mystification of a specific ideological construction of reality, which uses the superfluous and irrelevant detail as a sign of the *naturalness* of that construction, realist description is in practice more troubled and hybrid than he allows. The specific details of the sponging-house scene convey more than material guarantees of authenticity. The iron bars, for example, are both a synecdoche for the prison and an emblem of Booth's captivity to philosophical error (his belief in the determination of human actions by dominant passions), while the mouldering patches of plaster metonymically evoke a history of poverty and neglect and metaphorically represent the weakness of Booth's resolve as well as, more generally, the tawdry thinness of surfaces—linking this scene to the theme of masquerade and false appearances which, as Terry Castle has demonstrated, threads through the novel. Fielding's details share as much in the polysemous textures of allegory as in the thin, exhaustive factuality of naturalism; they are neither "structurally superfluous" nor simply the "irreducible residue" of an endless recording.[7]

Fielding's use of historically specific sites is comparable to Hogarth's in such narrative series as the Harlot's and Rake's *Progresses:* their settings are both literal and emblematic of the social forces that have shaped them. The peeling walls of the apartments where Moll dies in *A Harlot's Progress* are like those of Bondum's sponging-house in their mixture of protosociological observation and allegorical emblem, and the Bridewells and Bedlams in Hogarth, like Newgate in *Amelia,* are at the same time literal places of incarceration and symbolically permeated spaces of enthrallment, degeneration, and injustice. Hogarth likened the human figures in his progresses to "players in a dumb show," and each narrative scene has the character of an exemplary staging.[8]

The interior of Newgate in *Amelia* is similarly presented as a sequence of pictorial tableaux. Fielding's two early chapters, "Containing the Inside of a Prison" and "Disclosing further Secrets of the Prison-House," offer no sense of what Newgate actually looks like: at one point Booth is described as "standing near the Gate of the Prison," but the space is otherwise indeterminate (38). Instead, the prison is represented by a series of vignettes of its inmates, punctuated or moralized by dialogues between Booth and his fellow prisoner Robinson. Each paragraph exhibits a distinct individual or dramatic ensemble, each is characterized by a symbolic posture or bit of business, and each stands for a specific criminal or moral condition. In virtually every case Fielding indicts not the inmate but the oppressive power of the laws and the system of social and economic relations they enforce. The following is typical: "Mr. *Booth* took Notice of a young Woman in Rags sitting on the Ground, and supporting the Head of an old Man in her Lap, who appeared to be giving up the Ghost. These, Mr. *Robinson* informed him, were Father and Daughter; that the latter was committed for stealing a Loaf, in order to support the former, and the former for receiving it knowing it to be stolen" (33–34).

Figures of legal authority are inscribed in most of these emblematic pictures, to distinctly mixed effect. If in one scene an otherwise unspecified *Authority* rescues a sodomite from the hideous Blear-Eyed Moll and her confederates, who "were giving him various Kinds of Discipline, and would probably have put an End to him, had he not been rescued out of their Hands" (33), in a prior scene a fellow "condemned by the Court of Quarter Sessions" to be whipped for larceny gets out of his punishment by "having advanced another Sixpence" to a jailer, and this follows a paragraph in which a "little Creature" is committed by Judge Thrasher at the bidding of her burly father-in-law, as posing a physical threat to him. Although Bender has described these scenes as composing "a Newgate of substantial factuality,"[9] the vivid and abbreviated ironies of each little episode are anything but naturalistic. Each scene illustrates its species of wickedness or folly, and the stage is cleared for the next tableau.[10]

By opening *Amelia*'s narrative in Newgate, Fielding overshadows the whole of his represented world with the terrors of imprisonment. A sense of oppressive confinement strangles the exuberance found in Fielding's earlier tales and disfigures every human intimacy. Although the narrative unfolds in a quite diverse array of urban settings—the Booths' small rented apartments in Spring Garden, Bondum's sponging-house in Gray's Inn Lane, St. James's Park, a masquerade in the Haymarket, the gardens at Vauxhall, and Brown's coffeehouse, for a few—the governing narrative mood is close to the feverish claustrophobia of *Clarissa* and arises from a similar concentration on the experiences of violation and enclosure.

The tiniest enclosed spaces of *Amelia* are three locked boxes that Peter LePage has described as "minor analogues of the prison":[11] the little casket Amelia gives Booth on his departure for the wars, as a keepsake; an iron snuff box stolen from Booth inside Newgate, worthless in itself "but that he had a capricious Value for it, for the Sake of the Person who gave it to him" (40); and Booth's servant Atkinson's "little Box, of which he always kept the Key himself" (481), enclosing Amelia's picture "set in Gold, with three little Diamonds" (482). The last of these is crucial to *Amelia*'s plot, for it not only leads Amelia to a recognition of Atkinson's secret love for her—and her own confused feelings of tenderness for him—but its later discovery in a pawnshop by the guilt-wracked and incorrigibly criminal Mr. Robinson leads him to confess the long-hidden conspiracy to rob Amelia of her inheritance. The three boxes are enclosures of hidden feeling, unspoken intimacy—spaces of refuge from the encroachments of political history and the social determinants of permissible desire. Even so, they are subject to the same material pressures as every other represented space in the text, sold to a pawnbroker to pay for food or pilfered for the value of a few shillings. In *Amelia* a private sphere of seclusion and domesticity is repeatedly shaken by the violent intrusions of a public sphere of poverty, fraud, and authoritarian conflict.[12]

The characteristic space of interiority and domesticity in *Amelia* is the parlor or private room, from Miss Matthews's secluded apartment in Newgate to the furnished rooms in Spring Garden where the Booths live with their two small children. Yet, if the idealized values of the domestic parlor, as of the "eulogized space" of the house in Bachelard's *Poetics of Space,* are conjugality, shelter, and friendship, these are undermined by what Castle calls "the moral pathology associated with the little world of the prison," so that each private room comes to be felt as a space of entrapment.[13] Such spaces disfigure the stories told inside them as they poison close relationships with plotting. In Miss Matthews's room, for example, the romance of marital devotion Booth tells her—the story of his love for Amelia—provides the impetus for an acerbically noted drift into adultery, as the eroticism and tenderness Booth evokes in the telling are turned through her interruptions and asides into the occasion of a week-long criminal conversation.[14]

Booth's infidelity in Newgate taints his return home with remorse and introduces secrecy and deception into the family's private heart. His illicit sexual adventures inside the prison, the "sweet Lethargy of Pleasure" he guiltily savors seven nights running (154), blasts not only his happiness but the physical excitement he should feel at Amelia's touch, so that "poor *Amelia*, instead of a fond warm Husband, bestowed her Caresses on a dull lifeless Lump of Clay" (161). On his first night back with her, "her Spirits were at length over-powered by discerning the Oppression on his," Fielding writes, leading to this laconic report of sexual disappointment: "they retired to Rest, or rather to Misery, which need not be described" (163). Amelia's disappointment is especially marked in the context of her earlier expression of desire when she comes to her Billy in prison: it was not "without great Difficulty, that poor *Amelia* put some Restraint on her Fondness, in a Place so improper for a tender Interview" (159). Given the ongoing adulterous conversation between Billy and Miss Matthews, which they seemed on the verge of taking up again when Amelia burst into the room, this "impropriety" of the "Place" for "tender Interviews" needs to be read ironically, or ironically and straight at the same moment—for, even as the passage opposes the propriety and tenderness of Amelia's desires to the impropriety and violence of Miss Matthews's and sets the world of domesticity in opposition to the world of the prison, it points to underlying resemblances between them.

Amelia's desire is lawful and prone to self-sacrifice but not so distant from the carnality of Miss Matthews's. Even her entrance in the prison scene—"and presently a female Spectre, all pale and breathless, rushed into the Room" (159)—which has been read by John Zomchick as exemplary of the absolute difference Fielding wants to construct between Amelia's disembodied, domesticated virtue and Miss Matthews's insistently *embodied* sexuality, betrays the intensity of her desire as much as its sublimation, as, even etherealized, she bursts physically into the sphere of captivity from the world outside.[15] There is a wantonness in Amelia's entrance and her almost unrestrainable "Fondness" that belies Terry Castle's references to her "unambiguously pure status" in these early scenes of the narrative.[16] Castle argues that the later episode of masquerade compromises, for the first time, Amelia's "erotic invulnerability" and thus calls into question her "paragon status."[17] But this scene of reunion inside Newgate, particularly as it follows Booth's narrative of Amelia's youthful defiance and ardor, points to a powerful and domestically transgressive sexuality from the very beginning and an emotional volatility at odds with the expected maidenly, or wifely, restraint. Fielding seems almost to be alluding to the erotic undercurrent of this early scene in a passage near the end of the novel, in which Amelia embraces Billy in another prison, the bailiff's house, with such "violent Fondness" that the bailiff's wife begins to suspect she is not Mrs. Booth but one of the "Town Ladies" (497).

One of the most remarkable things about *Amelia*, in fact, is its heroine, whose desires are a complication of domestic inwardness and transgressive, romantic adventure.[18] This is apparent not just in the beautifully unresolved moment, late in the story, when Atkinson's ardent confession of the theft of her picture elicits an intense, involuntary recognition of her own susceptibility to illicit desire—after she recovers from breathlessness and tears at his kiss, she exits "with a Confusion on her Mind that she had never felt before" (482–83)—but is evident from the beginning of Booth's narrative. Like Richardson's Clarissa, Amelia is kept by her family "a close Prisoner" in her chamber (78), from fear of the strength and unruliness of her sexual impulses—the fear that her longings will upset her family's crudely laid plans for gaining property through the daughter's marriage. Both daughters are intransigent, both families driven by possessiveness and revenge. But, unlike Clarissa, Amelia intrepidly breaks out of her confinement, even after a rather absurd scheme of Dr. Harrison's, to smuggle Booth into her house in a wine hamper, has come a cropper. When Booth is sent away, abject, by her mother, Amelia flies from the house, finds him near the verge of their property, throws herself into his arms, and shows him how to dodge their pursuers. Like the heroine of a fairy tale, Amelia has to cross three barriers to escape her enchanted castle, scrambling over gate, hedge, and ditch, "performing the Part of a Heroine all the Way," until she and Booth arrive at a "green Lane, where stood a vast spreading Oak, under which we sheltered ourselves from a violent Storm" (84). The protoromantic oak and storm emphasize the couple's estrangement from ordinary social constraints: still unmarried, no longer subject to birth family or home, not yet connected to property or resident in London, they are, momentarily, outside the law.

Far from being the bloodless angel of a private sphere of domesticity which she tries to preserve from the violent incursions of public, political, or criminal life, Amelia recognizes from the beginning that the domestic sphere is a prison, too, and that happiness—which is equated with sexual fondness in Fielding's narrative—depends on her own energy, courage, and resourcefulness in breaking out of the captivity of family life. Amelia's weird, parodic resemblance to Blear-Eyed Moll—the grotesque, merry, noseless, sexually monstrous prisoner of Newgate who accosts Booth in the text's opening pages—is not purely antithetical: they have crucial impulses in common. Like Moll, although more chastely, Amelia "was taken in the Fact with a very pretty young Fellow" (28), and the whole of *Amelia*'s narrative is set in motion by that first disobedience.

As her family's house is turned into a prison by greed, sexual jealousy, and physical constraint, so the Booths' lodgings in Spring Garden become, by force of law and custom, a somewhat permeable space of incarceration for Booth. When Mrs. Ellison, Booth's landlady, learns that he has been pursued to the door of their house by "two or three very ugly suspicious Fellows" (205), his creditors' goons, she warns Booth "to keep yourself close confined till the Lawyer hath been with you. I am sure he will get you your Liberty, at least of walking around within the Verge . . . However, in the mean time you must be a close Prisoner with your Lady" (205). The "Liberty, at least of walking about within the Verge" to which she refers is a masked form of confinement, a phantom of liberty within a zone of incarceration. Here, as throughout *Amelia,* the word *Liberty* points to a space of free movement within captivity, or of real captivation within an (ideologically) imaginary freedom. The Liberties of *Amelia* thus embody what Bakhtin called the chronotope of the threshold, a liminal space governed by the contradictory energies of freedom and arrest.[19]

Fielding introduces the word *Liberty* in the very first sentence of the history proper, setting the scene of Booth's arrest and appearance before Judge Thrasher within "the Liberty of *Westminster*" (17). As Martin Battestin has observed, this inaugurates a line of bitter and upsetting invocations of the word.[20] After Booth arrives in Newgate, for example, and is stripped of his coat by the other prisoners, he is set "at Liberty, and declared free of the Place" (27), meaning only that he can go where he likes inside the prison walls. But even such circumscribed liberty is administered unequally and has to be paid for—which leads to Booth's dependence on Miss Matthews. After his second arrest, at the characteristically misguided hand of his oppressive benefactor Dr. Harrison, Booth is told by Mr. Bondum, the bailiff, "that he was welcome to the Liberty of the House with the other Gentlemen" (312), but, again, the liberty he is offered is little more than a freedom to pace the cage. All the accused brought before Thrasher by the Watchmen of the Liberty are innocent; all are robbed of their liberties as ostensibly free subjects under an administration of justice whose *injustice* Fielding shows to be systematic. Booth is committed to Newgate for coming to the aid of an assault victim and for not having money to pay off the constable as the real assailants, "Men of Fortune" (24), have found means to do. *Liberty* stands for the zone of contact between private experience and the increasingly pervasive apparatus of the law, the threshold between private life and the police.[21]

The most tangible of *Amelia*'s narrative thresholds are literal prisons. Booth is confined to three: Bondum's sponging-house, a way-station or place of transition to Newgate; the Verge of the Court, a zone of sanctuary for debtors; and Newgate itself, marking the threshold of London. Of these the Verge is the most problematic because it designates a space that is neither outside nor inside, neither subject to civil authority nor free from its repressive power; it marks the overlapping of two historically disjunct economies of legal rule. As John Stephens has written, the name of the Verge had come, by the eighteenth century, "to be applied to a neighborhood of some extent near Whitehall and St. James's in which offenders were free from arrest by the ordinary officers of the law. It was in particular a haven for debtors"[22]—who, unless they were pursued by their creditors through the offices of the king's steward and the Palace Court, a path seldom taken, were safe as long as they never crossed over the imaginary but perilous line. Booth is immune from arrest within this protected zone. But even this haven is a form of exile, a space of quarantine and constraint.

At one point, to explain why Booth cannot accompany Amelia to the Oratorio in the Haymarket, Fielding jokes that the theater is not "within *hallowed Ground*, that is to say, in the Verge of the Court" (187; emph. mine). His acid, offhand remark, which seems only flippant, actually connects the Verge to what Angus Fletcher calls the cosmic center of allegory, "a place free of contamination, a safe place": under an archaic symbolic regime "the fugitive was theoretically untouchable if he stood on sacred ground."[23] In fact, the historical origins of the Verge as a sanctuary for debtors lie in precisely such a conception of sacred space. The "King's Peace," as Stephens reports, was originally "an area extending for twelve miles around the seat of the king's court, wherever that might be at any particular time": it was a kind of sacred extension of the king's body. "Within this area," he continues, "the ordinary civil authorities had no power, and any offenses committed within its bounds were construed as having been committed against the person of the king himself."[24] By Fielding's time the original notion of topographical space as, sacrally, part of the king's body had narrowed to a legalistic mechanism allowing for a certain flexibility in the enforcement of civil law—crucial to the normal functioning of the urban economy, which could hardly afford to lock everyone who owed money in jail.

The withering irony of Fielding's use of the words *hallowed Ground* to refer to the sordid criminal sanctuary of the Verge looks at first like a repudiation of allegory, a token of the demise of the sacred. Far from providing freedom from contamination, the Verge seems continually to set traps in Booth's way, temptations to repeat his falls into sin and insolvency: wine, high-stakes gambling, libertine friends, blackmailing ex-lovers. *Amelia* offers a vision of urban life shaped by distrust and an anxiety bordering on panic. "We come soon enough to scrutinize the fictional landscape with cynicism, even paranoia," Terry Castle writes, as plots to deceive and entrap multiply within the transgressively charged confines of the Verge; Booth and Amelia "are close prisoners in a metropolis of evil."[25] While it offers a degree of security from arrest, the Verge is, from the same historical causes, a largely unregulated area, immune to censorial control or to considerations of the sacred. Yet, if he skews traditional conceptions of sacred space with ironic ambivalence, Fielding still presents the Verge within an allegorical structure of meaning, as an unstable, transitional space of criminality and surveillance, contagion and safety—the exemplary space of modern urban life, given the embattled conditions of legal authority in eighteenth-century London. Negative sanctuaries, the threshold prisons of *Amelia* carry a traditional economy of the licit, in which transgression and law are the agents of sacred conflict, into the era of penal reform and the policing of everyday life.

The most symbolically potent of the text's liminal prisons, Newgate, is not, I have argued, naturalistically represented in *Amelia*'s opening chapters, although examples of such reporting were certainly available to Fielding, and there are similarities of verbal texture between his descriptions and some of the earlier Newgate anatomies, especially Smith's 1714 *Lives of the Highwaymen* and the 1717 *History of the Press Yard*.[26] It is not important to my argument to establish that Fielding actually drew from either of these or from any specific earlier text, although I think it likely; what matters is that by midcentury there was an established, popular, and very widely circulated body of texts in which the interior of Newgate was represented, and that Fielding followed this tradition in some of his rhetorical strategies (the allegorical, world-upside-down figurations) but not others (the naturalistic reporting of concrete details). Although Bender contends that Fielding "etches life in the old prisons with an exactness unprecedented by any fictional work I know,"[27] there is none of those earlier writings' vivid use of circumstantial detail in Fielding's text, whose rendering of Newgate consists, rather, of a series of emblematic miniatures in an indeterminate, theatrical space of representation. It is integral to Fielding's very conception of fiction that the exhaustive inventory and accounting of factual details of the 1724 *Accurate Description of Newgate* formed no part of it. What *Amelia* offers instead is an image of Newgate as a space of license and permeability to transgression and breakdown. Even more than the Verge, it is a sacred space of negative valence, a site of contagion.

As Fielding's sentimental defense of *Amelia* in the "Court of Censorial Enquiry" acknowledges, the moral charges against his narrative—"that the Book now at the Bar, is *very sad Stuff;* that Amelia herself is a *low* character, a *Fool,* and a *Milksop;* that she is very apt to faint, and apt to *drink Water,* to prevent it . . . That the Scene of the Goal [gaol] is *low and unmeaning,* and brought in by Head and Shoulders, without any Reason, or Design" (*Covent-Garden Journal* [58–59])—had too many "appearances of truth" to be dismissed or proved false. The "lowness" of both setting and character was seized on by Richardson as evidence of Fielding's poverty of imagination: in a letter to Ann Donnellan on February 22, 1752, he wrote that "Booth, in his last piece, [is] again himself; Amelia, even to her noselessness, is again his first wife. His brawls, his jarrs, his gaols, his spunging-houses, are all drawn from what he has seen and known. As I said . . . he has little or no invention."[28]

Richardson's comments are rancorous and trivial but useful in showing both that *Amelia*'s presentation of the urban milieu of poverty and criminality was accepted even by its detractors as largely authentic and that the use of such a milieu as a setting for serious fiction was still aesthetically and ideologically problematic. Fielding's endless repetitions of the word *low* in his own mock trial underline the most remarkable quality of the text: its harrowing, oppressive concentration on the lives and quarters of those whom the political machinery of his society forced into an underworld of criminal contagion and squalor. The scene of the prison—the constant scene of the narrative—is indeed *"low and unmeaning"*; it can neither be reduced to a stable symbolic code of meaning nor transcended. The represented world of *Amelia* is pervaded with a sense of entrapment, moral recklessness, disguised and upsetting desires: such a world, to recall what Fielding wrote in the preface to the *Miscellanies,* is only "Newgate with the Mask on."[29]

Even the charges against Amelia herself—that "she is very apt to faint, and apt to *drink Water*, to prevent it"—ridiculous as they appear, point to a problematic feature of Fielding's representation. Fainting, in *Amelia* as in much later-eighteenth- and nineteenth-century writing, operates as an image of sexual abandon or, rather, as a morally acceptable substitute for such abandon, a displacement of the (female) body's response to the presence of sexual danger. Amelia faints twice in the earlier books, when faced simultaneously with Billy's physical presence and the threat of a physical separation from him in the shape of war or prison. She drinks water to keep from fainting a number of times, notably during the course of Mrs. Bennet's narrative—when Amelia realizes, by the similarity of her friend's story to her own, that the noble Lord's invitation to the masquerade conceals a plot of rape—and again after Sergeant Atkinson's confession of his romantic crime and the gentle kiss he gives her hand: "she then hastened down Stairs and called for a great Glass of Water, which having drank off, she threw herself into a Chair, and the Tears ran plentifully from her Eyes" (482). Fainting and water drinking are figures of the fear and allure of sexual passion in *Amelia,* so their inclusion in the indictment against the book and its heroine is not purely (though it is partly) absurd.

All the principal characters in *Amelia* are similarly marked by ambiguous mo- tives, unarticulated desires, shifting and contradictory behavior. Terry Castle has argued that following the masquerade there is an "outbreak of ambiguity" which extends even to the seemingly straightforward villains and paragons of Fielding's moral drama;[30] I depart from her reading in locating such ambiguity back at the story's beginning, so that the allegorical pattern is complicated from the outset by moral, and epistemological, opacity. The difficulty and insecurity of judgment— both for the characters in their relationships with one another and for the reader in his or her relationship to the text—are at the heart of the narrative's meanings.

This is nowhere more evident than in the often perplexing figure of Dr. Harri- son. The considerable authority the Doctor wields in the world of the text shows the force of his charisma, such that his mere physical entrance into her room is enough to act on Amelia as a "Cordial" in her time of greatest anguish (346). In an earlier scene Fielding explains how Harrison bullies Amelia's mother into keeping her promise to permit her daughter's marriage: "The Doctor's Voice, his Look, and his Behaviour," Fielding writes, "all which are sufficiently calculated to inspire Awe, and even Terror, when he pleases, frightened poor Mrs. *Harris,* and wrought a more sensible Effect than it was in his Power to produce by all his Arguments and En- treaties" (90). But beyond his physical glamour and intimidation Harrison wields the authority of reason and sympathetic insight, as Booth declares to Miss Matthews in Newgate: "Of all Mankind the Doctor is the best of Comforters. As his excessive Good-nature makes him take vast Delight in the Office; so his great Penetration into the human Mind, joined to his great Experience, renders him the most wonderful Proficient in it; and he so knows when to sooth, when to reason, and when to ridicule, that he never applies any of those Arts improperly" (104).

Moreover, again according to Booth's evidence, the Doctor's moral supervision has those good effects on the larger community which Fielding saw as following from the proper exercise of the censorial function: "All his Parishioners, whom he treats as his Children, regard him as their common Father. Once in a Week he constantly visits every House in the Parish, examines, commends, and rebukes, as he finds Occasion. This is practised likewise by his Curate in his Absence; and so good an Effect is produced by this their Care, that no Quarrels ever proceed either to Blows or Law-suits; no Beggar is to be found in the whole Parish; nor did I ever hear a very profane Oath all the Time I lived in it" (145). With such testimony as this, and Amelia's declaration to the Doctor that "your Opinion is to me always Instruction, and your Word a Law" (504), it is no wonder that John Bender describes Harrison as "Fielding's fantasy-ideal of himself as juridical moralist."[31]

Yet from the very start of the narrative Fielding complicates this idealized portrait with dissonant elements. Even before he meets Booth, Dr. Harrison misjudges him as a fortune hunter; and, while the judgment is not unreasonable and reflects Harrison's care for Amelia, it also exposes a habit of basing judgments on prejudice (in this case against soldiers) and gossip (Booth is "a young Fellow of whom I had heard no good Character" [78]). He is, however, ready to revisit his judgments in the light of new evidence, and in this way Harrison embodies in his own manner of proceeding the narrative logic of *Amelia* itself, which is built on a pattern of initial misjudgment and later reconsideration. But, if the Doctor's effect on the unfolding of events is ultimately benevolent, his misjudgments and misreadings of the people around him are so numerous and so often potentially tragic in their consequences that he becomes almost an allegorical figure of susceptibility to unreason and false appearance.

Among those who line up to pay tribute to the Doctor's penetration is an unnamed old country gentleman, who, after one of Harrison's impromptu sermons, bursts out, "Indeed, my good Friend, no one retires from you without carrying away some good Instructions with him" (403). As the reader quickly learns, Harrison's "old Friend" is a mere hypocrite who has contrived through years of massaging the Doctor's vanity to advance his family's interests (387). Long friendship has not enabled Harrison to see into the character of the gentleman at all, any more than he picks up on any of the clues that should tell him of Colonel James's adulterous designs on Amelia. Harrison's old friend confides to his son, "I never told you he was a wise Man, nor did I ever think him so . . . [but] would you lose such a Milch-cow as this for Want of a few Compliments?" (404), and, while Fielding very clearly shows that this friend's criteria of judgment are debased, even the narrator acknowledges that the Doctor has been "too easy a Dupe to the gross Flattery of the old Gentleman" (429).

Harrison's good opinion of Colonel James and the flattering gentleman is predicated on nothing more than class prejudice and old-school masculinist loyalty, while the same uninterrogated biases lead him to denigrate the understanding of both the principal female characters. He is pompous and condescending toward Mrs. Bennet, whose modest but real classical learning he never misses a chance of disparaging, so that—against Booth's claim that "he so knows when to sooth, when to reason, and when to ridicule, that he never applies any of those Arts improperly"—the Doctor finally exasperates her into lashing out at her innocent and well-loved husband.[32] And in his many conversations with Amelia he consistently disregards her far more clear-sighted apprehensions of the motives and moral qualities of other characters. In order to justify what the Doctor has mocked as her "unreasonable" objections to being left in the care of Colonel James during Booth's absence, Amelia has to lay all the evidence against the colonel before him, yet, while he does allow the evidence to convince him, Fielding's account of his reaction is telling: "The good Man seemed greatly shocked at the Relation, and remained in a silent Astonishment.—Upon which, *Amelia* said, 'Is Villainy so rare a Thing, Sir, that it should so much surprize you?' 'No, Child,' cries he; 'but I am shocked at seeing it so artfully disguised under the Appearance of so much Virtue. And to confess the Truth, I believe my own Vanity is a little hurt in having been so grossly imposed upon'" (374). Harrison seems never to have learned to recognize the epistemological dangers of outward appearances, and his judgments are often most harsh and precipitous against those whom he should know the best.

Harrison's arrest of Booth just past the novel's halfway point marks a crisis in Fielding's representation of authority. Amelia, learning of it, says, "Well then, there is an end of all Goodness in the World. I will never have a good Opinion of any human Being more" (307), and, indeed, she holds true to that disenchanted vision of the world she inhabits, a disenchantment that makes her perceptions much more reliable than the Doctor's. Although the narrator assures us that Harrison's conduct, "however inconsistent it may have hitherto appeared, when examined to the Bottom, will be found, I apprehend, to be truly congruous with all the Rules of the most perfect Prudence, as well as the most consummate Goodness," his judgment against Booth demonstrates Fielding's awareness of how vulnerable to false constructions even the most seemingly transparent evidence can be (357).

Booth is in debt to the Doctor for the rent of some lands and has been guilty of extravagance and mismanagement, as the Doctor learns by letter while abroad. "Nevertheless," Fielding writes, "he resolved to suspend his final Judgment till his Return; and tho' he censured him, would not absolutely condemn him without ocular Demonstration." So far, so good. But when he returns home the Doctor uncritically absorbs all his parishioners' testimony, not only "several gross and scandalous Lies, which were merely the Inventions of [Booth's] Enemies" but also the gossip of the obviously malicious curate's wife, who "still preserved," Fielding tellingly notes, "the outward Appearance of Friendship" to Amelia: "She introduced all with *I am sorry to say it*; and *it is Friendship which bids me speak*; and *it is for their Good it should be told you*; after which Beginnings, she never concluded a single Speech without some horrid Slander and bitter Invective" (357).

"Poisoned with all this Malice," Harrison comes to London, ransacks the Booths' apartment without waiting for them to return, and sees "the little gold Watch, and all those fine Trinkets with which the noble Lord," plotting to seduce Amelia, "had presented the Children." The servant, in her confusion, seems to confirm his presuppositions concerning Amelia's extravagance, and thus he reaches his conclusions: "This Account tallied so well with the Ideas he had imbibed of *Booth's* Extravagance in the Country, that he firmly believed both the Husband and Wife to be the vainest, silliest, and most unjust People alive. It was, indeed, almost incredible, that two rational Beings should be guilty of such Absurdity; but monstrous and absurd as it was, ocular Demonstration appeared to be the Evidence against them" (358). Not only testimony but circumstantial evidence, too, lies, at least to a mind "poisoned with all this Malice." Evidence is usable only as it can be fit into a narrative, and narratives start to take shape, as the Canning and Penlez cases also showed, before evidence can even be thought of *as* evidence. Harrison sees, as he has earlier heard, only what confirms the poisonous tales told against the Booths, even though this requires him to disregard all of his prior knowledge and love of them. His lack of faith in persons he should know well and his inexplicable confidence in the word of obvious rogues links the Doctor to Allworthy in *Tom Jones*, who reaches a similarly false verdict in the case against Tom.[33]

Dr. Harrison begins to suspect he has judged too harshly and too soon; he is troubled with uncertainty and remorse. As the narrator observes after granting that the Doctor was "too easy a Dupe to the gross Flattery of the old Gentleman," if readers are disturbed by this, "we are heartily sorry as well for them as for the Doctor; but it is our Business to discharge the Part of a faithful Historian; and to describe Human Nature as it is, not as we would wish it to be" (429). Dr. Harrison is flawed not just in peripheral ways but, like the other characters in *Amelia*, through the very heart; he is deeply implicated in the unfolding of the different levels of the novel's plot but is only fleetingly and accidentally in control of the scenes he inhabits. As the figure within the story who is closest to a representative of political and moral authority, Harrison reflects most intimately Fielding's own sense of uncertainty in the face of cultural instability and contestation over the control of narrative meanings. This embodiment of sober, censorial regulation is even for a moment transfigured, in the suggestible imagination of the Booths' maid, into *Amelia*'s most vivid figure of criminal violence: "he was a great swinging Man with a Pistol in each hand," the girl tells them, "and if I had dared to call out, to be sure he would have killed me" (242). The roles of outlaw and judge seem suddenly to be reversible, and any sequence of actions to be liable to multiple, even contradictory, narrative constructions.[34]

Justice is done in the end: Booth is released from captivity; Amelia's fortune is restored; secret conspiracies are sorted out. Such an ending could suggest, as John Bender writes, that "both providence and plot in *Amelia* are representations of reason in human affairs."[35] Providence does step in, at the close of *Amelia*, to salvage concord from discord, but the intrusion feels more strained than in Fielding's earlier fictions—not, as J. Paul Hunter has shown,[36] because the plot is really any more contrived but because the narrator pretends to so much less control over the profusion of plots *within* the text. The comparative suspension of narratorial authority in *Amelia*, culminating in the scene of masquerade—in which we are told, for example, the thoughts of a character we presume to be Amelia but not that she is, in fact, someone else entirely—suggests, in a way that still seems experimental for Fielding, that, like the bewildered reader or the easily misled Dr. Harrison, the narrator himself is unable to guide the plot's unfolding, gain access to the complex inward speech of another person, or make secure judgments from fragmentary and disputed evidence.[37] Fielding's difficult and often contentious practice as examining magistrate seems to have led him to doubt the possibility of ever fully ascertaining the truth, as the narrator of *Tom Jones* had, in fictional terms, done effortlessly: the problems of evidence, and all the material and imaginary forces that condition it, were too intractable to allow for confidence in narrative reconstructions. *Amelia*'s plot is, if anything, a representation of unreason in human affairs— our inescapable vulnerability to unrecognized biases, unacknowledged desires, and the duplicity of outward appearances.

When the first edition of *Amelia* was published, in December 1751, critics were quick to locate and mock one tawdry, anachronistic bit of self-promotion: while the main body of the story can be dated by internal evidence to 1733, there are a half-dozen references in the text to Fielding's own fledgling business enterprise, the Universal Register Office, which he had founded in February 1750 along with his half-brother John and a vague "Society of Gentlemen." Thus, when Booth, after a spat with Mrs. Bennet, goes out to find new lodgings or when Amelia needs the name of an ethical moneylender, they take advantage of the Register Office in the Strand, "a Place where all the Necessities of Life were provided for" (572). "The Design" of the Universal Register Office, Fielding wrote in the advertisement he issued a year after its opening, "is to bring the World as it were together into one Place. Here the Buyer and the Seller, the Master and the Scholar, the Master and the Apprentice, and the Master and Servant are sure to meet: Here ingenious Persons of all Kinds will meet with those who are ready to employ them, and the Curious will be supplied with every thing which it is in the Power of Art to produce."[38] For an initial fee of sixpence—and a further threepence for a successful outcome—workers of any kind seeking positions, employers looking for workers, those who wanted to buy or sell land or let rooms, travelers needing company, midwives, artisans, moneylenders, and auctioneers could register themselves, their names, offers, and references with the Fieldings' register office and expect to find there what they sought.

　　If the Universal Register Office was thus in one sense comparable to the classified section of a modern newspaper, it also had, as one might expect in Fielding's case, a police function. This side of the business is brought out in an advertisement headed "To the Public" that Fielding placed at the end of the 1751 *Enquiry into the Late Increase in Robbers*. There he writes that "the rude Behaviour and insolence of Servants of all Kinds is become a general Complaint," one instance of that more general inversion of a stable social hierarchy which the *Enquiry* seeks to anatomize and contain. The law as it stands gives no authority for punishing insolent and rebellious servants, but the Register Office can, in effect, neutralize their subversion by holding the threat of unemployment over them: for "no Servant shall ever be register'd, who cannot produce a real good Character from the last Place in which he or she actually lived" (173). Information—not only on servants but on apprentices, farm laborers, stolen goods, and suspected criminals—comes to the Universal Register Office from every part of the kingdom to be catalogued, scrutinized, and rebroadcast in such periodicals as the *Covent-Garden Journal* and *Public Advertiser:* both, as Bertrand Goldgar writes, "under the proprietorship of the Universal Register Office and thus of the Fieldings themselves."[39] The criminal dangers of everyday life will one day be regulated through written instruments.[40]

Three years after opening the Universal Register Office, two years after writing *Amelia*, a half-year following his involvement in the Elizabeth Canning case, Fielding was charged with another, more urgent job of policing. "In the beginning of August, 1753," as Fielding writes in the introduction to his *Journal of a Voyage to Lisbon*, "when I was almost fatigued to death with several long examinations, relating to five different murders, all committed within the space of a week, by different gangs of street robbers," he was sent for by the duke of Newcastle "to discourse . . . on the best plan which could be invented for putting an immediate end to those murders and robberies which were every day committed in the streets."[41] As the intertwining of medical and criminal history in the *Journal*'s introduction makes plain, Fielding's use of the words "almost fatigued to death" was not empty: his exemplary dedication, or abject dependency, first in drawing up a plan for the duke to read then in carrying out the task of "demolish[ing] the then reigning gangs" (188) led to a rapid physical deterioration. From "a lingering imperfect gout" (187), his condition had degenerated to include "no fewer or less diseases than a jaundice, a dropsy, and an asthma, altogether uniting their forces in the destruction of a body so emaciated, that it had lost all its muscular flesh" (189).

Meanwhile, as Fielding's single, physical body was destroyed, the social body was purged and cured of disease by his labors: through the mercenary betrayals of an informer and the "intrepidity" of his own set of thief takers, he writes, "I had the satisfaction to find my endeavours had been attended with such success, that this hellish society were almost utterly extirpated, and that, instead of reading of murders and street-robberies in the news, almost every morning, there was, in the remaining part of the month of November, and in all of December, not only no such thing as a murder, but not even a street-robbery committed." The symmetry between his own physical degeneration and the restoration of a long-lost state of social health lends narrative force to Fielding's (partly ironic) characterization of himself as a "voluntary sacrifice to the good of the public," while, more generally, it configures criminality as disease, a form of moral and political contagion (188–89). This figural likeness is underlined in a passage praising Fielding's clerk at Bow Street, Joshua Brogden, whom he describes as being "but ill paid for sitting almost sixteen hours in the twenty-four, in the most unwholesome, as well as nauseous air in the universe, and which hath in his case corrupted a good constitution without contaminating his morals" (190).[42] If crime is parallel to disease in its means of transmission, the strategies Fielding adopts to put it down are analogous to the techniques of a somewhat primitive surgery: first to cut out the diseased member, then to keep the body in a kind of preventive quarantine, monitoring it for symptoms of relapse.

Fielding's significance to a history of the police, then, is twofold: as the *Voyage to Lisbon* shows, he was instrumental in organizing the first standing police force in Britain, the Bow Street Runners, a professionalized body of constables paid by subscription and thus in theory immune from the corruption of the old system of rewards, and, as his *Plan for the Universal Register Office* and the periodicals connected to it attest, he played a crucial part in the development of modern systems for the centralization and dispersal of information about the laboring and criminal class (for the purposes of social control they were the same). The term *police* comprehends more than a constabulary or detective force: it refers, especially in the work of Fielding's brother John and their followers, to a whole system of social regulation and the exercise of authority.[43]

Fielding's dual career seems almost too literal an instance of the possibility raised by D. A. Miller in *The Novel and the Police*—"the possibility," that is, "of a radical *entanglement* between the nature of the novel and the practice of the police."[44] Fielding's important role in the virtually simultaneous origins of the novel as a new species of writing and the police as a new technology of social control makes him seem, again, the literal embodiment of what Miller's way of framing the following question takes for granted: "how does the novel—as a set of representational techniques—systematically participate in a general economy of policing power?"[45] Both Miller and Bender, echoing Foucault, invoke Bentham's *Panopticon: or, The Inspection-House*—in which, with a kind of hallucinatory lucidity, "a simple idea in Architecture" is extended into a principle for the organization of society, "a new mode of obtaining power, power of mind over mind, in a quantity hitherto without example," as Bentham writes in his preface.[46] The architecture of surveillance—Bentham's *Inspection-House* is constructed so that every person who works or lives in a collective institution, whether penitentiary, factory, hospital, or school, imagines him- or herself at every moment to be visible to an unseen, omniscient inspector—encodes a new, disciplinary regime of power, in which authority is abstracted, diffused, and inescapable. The nineteenth-century novel, Miller suggests, is effectively in cahoots with this disciplinary form of police, and a crucial part of Bender's project in *Imagining the Penitentiary* is to anatomize Fielding's role in the emergence of that complicity.[47]

The perspectives of novelist and judge were entangled in Fielding's late work—but not, I think, in the rigorously supervised, almost technocratic mode envisioned in Bender's and Miller's bleak arguments. Like Bentham's Panopticon, the Fieldings' Universal Register Office was less an effectual technology of regulation and containment than an emblem of a kind of dream (or, maybe, nightmare) of social order. The very extremism of the rhetoric both authors employ—"the Design" of the Register Office "is to bring the World as it were together into one Place"; the Panopticon will offer "a new mode of obtaining power, power of mind over mind, in a quantity hitherto without example"—signals the imaginary character of both projects: the longing for a simple, totalizing cure to the myriad, endlessly mutating disorders of social life. Not that either invention was without consequences: prisons and factories built on the model of the Panopticon, networks for gathering information on the criminal and unruly. But the real police, the assorted institutions of political and social control, were never the impersonal, rationally ordered, ideologically self-consistent apparatus projected by Fielding's and Bentham's texts. At the most basic, material level real power continued to depend on real violence, which is precisely what both projects were intended to obviate.

In Fielding's case the effective exercise of authority, as in his breaking of the street gangs, depended less on impersonal surveillance than on a highly personal, insistently physical form of intervention—which is why he places so much empha-

sis on the toll his police work took on his already suffering body, not to mention
the physical "intrepidity" of his own force of thief takers. He got the evidence he
needed not through any newfangled information technology but the old, grubby
way, by paying an informer. The work of policing, as Fielding presents it in the
*Journal*, hinges on circumstance, opportunistic alliances between enemies, physical intimidation, and a charismatic authority rooted in (his own) blood sacrifice.
Any order it restores is precarious.

Fielding's late fiction, too, enacts the struggle to make sense of the fragmented,
heteroglossic uproar of life in midcentury London. In *Amelia* Fielding casts doubt
on the judgments both of the representatives of authority within the text and, more
strangely, of his own narratorial persona, in order to dramatize a skeptical, troubled
epistemology. Unlike the magisterial narrator of *Tom Jones,* who manages the evidence accumulated through testimony and circumstantial detail to reveal the truth
that prior, more partial accounts have obscured,[48] the narrator of *Amelia* demonstrates little confidence in his power to shape or even comprehend the opaque, discrepant narratives the characters tell one another. The restoration of order, the plot's
happy ending, is emphatically, even aggressively, make-believe. But the losses of
epistemological certainty and institutional confidence seem—if the intimate, acid
entries in the *Journal of a Voyage to Lisbon* can be read as clues to the trajectory of
Fielding's late thinking—not so much to have depressed as to have released Fielding from the anxiety of his authoritarian postures, as *Amelia's* proleptic imagining
of a Gothic topography of imprisonment released in his fiction a more supple, inward expression of subjectivity shaken by the alternating currents of criminal desire
and repression.

# Epilogue
## English Radicalism and the Literature of Crime

> You certainly ought not to employ against people that you
> hate, supposing your hatred to be reasonable, the instrumental-
> ity of that law which in your practice you defy. Be consistent.
> Either be the friend of law, or its adversary. Depend upon it
> that, wherever there are laws at all, there will be laws against
> such people as you and me. Either therefore we all of us
> deserve the vengeance of the law, or law is not the proper
> instrument of correcting the misdeeds of mankind.
>
> WILLIAM GODWIN
> *Things as They Are; or, The Adventures of Caleb Williams* (1794)

Newly escaped from the prison where Falkland's agents have confined him, Caleb
Williams is set upon and beaten nearly to death by several of a gang of thieves.
Soon after, a compassionate stranger chances to discover Caleb and helps him to
a squalid habitation hidden in the passages of a ruined castle: a thieves' den, it turns
out, for this samaritan is no other than the captain of the gang whose most brutal
renegade had earlier led the assault against Caleb. Outraged by the attack, Captain Raymond holds a kind of people's trial of the murderous Gines, Caleb's
assailant. "Comrades," he addresses his men, "it is for you to decide upon the conduct of this man as you think proper. You know how repeated his offences have
been; you know what pains I have taken to mend him. Our profession is the profession of justice."[1] Caleb as narrator is skeptical of this last claim, observing, "It is
thus that the prejudices of men universally teach them to colour the most desper-

ate cause, to which they have determined to adhere" (216). Yet, as Godwin develops this episode of Caleb among the robbers, he gives expression to an oppositional critique of the law and of the system of social relationships it supports which, despite the outlaws' occasional malevolence, echoes the critique he had offered in his own voice in the *Enquiry Concerning Political Justice,* published the year before.

With Gines's expulsion Caleb is able to reflect on the political stakes of criminality in terms that anticipate Eric Hobsbawm's category of the social bandit.[2] These robbers, Caleb writes, "did not impose upon themselves the task, as is too often the case in human society, of seeming tacitly to approve that from which they suffered most; or, which is worse, of persuading themselves that all the wrongs they suffered were right; but were at open war with their oppressors" (218). But, as he goes on to discover, all, except for Raymond, have been degraded by the brutality and meanness of their occupation, which sets them irreconcilably at odds with their community. The implicitly communitarian and local basis of the robbers' struggle against the oppressions of property and law, in other words, is vitiated by the tendency of criminal actions to drive the one who commits them further and further apart from other persons, who become simply victims, or threats to survival. The outlaws' "good qualities and their virtues," in Caleb's eyes, "were thrown away upon purposes diametrically at war with the first interests of human society" (226).

Yet if, driven to crime by a "perception of [the law's] iniquity" (227), in Raymond's words, the robbers are then, through their crimes, only further alienated and brutalized, that original perception of iniquity is allowed to stand, is even endorsed, in the unfolding of Godwin's fiction. When a reward of a hundred guineas is offered for Caleb's arrest, Captain Raymond, through a sincere appeal to his confederates' sense of justice, secures their promise to harbor the outcast Caleb and to repudiate both the reward and the verdict pronounced against him: "If no other person have the courage to set limits to the tyranny of courts of justice, shall not we? Shall we, against whom the whole species is in arms, refuse our protection to an individual, more exposed to, but still less deserving of their persecution than ourselves?" (224). Rough and bad as they are, the robbers never betray Caleb, and by the role they assume in Godwin's plot they embody, however darkly, Raymond's political challenge to the ruling institutions of late-eighteenth-century English society: "Since by the partial administration of our laws innocence, when power was armed against it, had nothing better to hope for than guilt, what man of true courage would fail to set these laws at defiance, and, if he must suffer by their injustice, at least take care that he had first shown his contempt of their yoke?" (220). When, at narrative's end, Caleb uses the mechanisms of the law to vindicate his character against Falkland's trumped-up accusations and to bring his secret crimes to light, Caleb sees, too late, that his recourse to the institutions of justice is a betrayal of all he holds true, subjecting his trust in reason and openness of heart to the coercions of legal power.

The use of criminal narrative for the purposes of political critique did not originate with Godwin, as I have tried to show throughout this study: the recognition of criminality as a shifting term of class warfare is often explicit in the writings of Defoe and his contemporaries—in the *General History of the Pyrates,* for example, or, from a contrasting position, in *The Great Law of Subordination Consider'd*—as it also is in the picaresque fictions, last dying speeches, and criminal biographies from which both Godwin and Defoe drew much of their material. Certainly, Fielding, from an explicitly conservative position, viewed crime as inescapably political in its origins and implications. But the 1790s saw the publication of a number of sensational fictions in which the radical potentialities of criminal narrative were brought out more insistently than ever before—including, in addition to *Caleb Williams,* Mary Wollstonecraft's *Maria, or The Wrongs of Woman* (left unfinished in 1797; published in 1798), and Elizabeth Inchbald's *Nature and Art* (1796). In each of these narratives there is both tension and complicity between the political message—rationalist, progressive—and the traditional genres in which it is inscribed.

The first words of Wollstonecraft's novel capture the mingled strains of political protest and Gothic romance that run through the text: "Abodes of horror have frequently been described, and castles, filled with spectres and chimeras, conjured up by the magic spell of genius to harrow the soul, and absorb the wondering mind. But, formed of such stuff as dreams are made of, what were they to the mansion of despair, in one corner of which Maria sat, endeavouring to recall her scattered thoughts!"[3] If in this opening scene Wollstonecraft sets the two strains in opposition to each other, contrasting Maria's legally engineered imprisonment in a lunatic asylum to the unreal, labyrinthine confinements of the Gothic, the rest of the narrative mixes them so extravagantly that a certain ideological confusion results: Wollstonecraft's protest against a culturally enforced irrationality for women is conducted in the most antirational of fictional languages.[4] So, when, for example, at the end of Maria's memoir-letter to her stolen (perhaps murdered) child she describes her incarceration in the prison where the story is set, she adopts the very "abodes of horror" imagery Wollstonecraft seemed to want to hold at a distance: "The gates opened heavily, and the sullen sound of many locks and bolts drawn back, grated on my very soul, before I was appalled by the creeking of the dismal hinges, as they closed after me. The gloomy pile was before me, half in ruins . . . and as we approached some mouldering steps, a monstrous dog darted forwards to the length of his chain, and barked and growled infernally" (134).

Wollstonecraft's use of such Gothic trappings in a narrative whose motives are openly radical brings to light what was only a shadowy subtext in the novels of Walpole and Radcliffe, in which a vague dread of the repressive horrors of the ancien régime seems to persist even after the restoration of orthodoxy, in the obsessive detailing of scenes of political terrorism and inescapable violence. "A fear haunted the latter half of the eighteenth century," Foucault observed with his characteristic melodramatic panache in an interview on the subject of Bentham's Panopticon: "the fear of darkened spaces, of the pall of gloom which prevents the full visibility of things, men and truths."[5] Such darkened spaces are the architectural embodiments of institutional power—"chateaux, lazarets, bastilles and convents"— and in the wake of the French Revolution, as Ronald Paulson also observes, these sites of Gothic fantasy are inflected with intense, if often ambiguous, political meanings.[6] Wollstonecraft and Godwin brought the darkened spaces of the Gothic back to England and the present moment of partisan crisis, making the case for a radical breaking and remaking of the social order by drawing out its likeness to the tyranny of the French old regime.[7]

Like *Caleb Williams* and *Maria,* Inchbald's *Nature and Art* gathers much of its narrative and political force from its incorporation of old criminal plots and milieus. Inchbald's astringency emphasizes the social ironies rather than the sentimental calamities of her history of the seduction and abandonment of Hannah Primrose, a cottager's daughter, by William Norwynne, a ruthless social climber. His ascent from dean's son to judge of the assizes is matched by her fall from rural health to urban contagion, "till at last she became a midnight wanderer through the streets of London, soliciting, or rudely demanding money of the passing stranger."[8] She has a degree further to descend, however, as the familiar stages of transgression found in last dying speeches and lives of the condemned should lead us to expect: she falls into larceny. Inchbald's choice of crime is somewhat unusual—Hannah, she writes, "became an accomplice in negotiating bills forged on a country banker"—

and the reasoning that leads her to join with a gang of "practised sharpers and robbers," although it is rejected by Inchbald as founded on "false, yet seducing opinions," betrays a sympathetic comprehension of the material bases of crime which is far removed from the traditional genres' reliance on the categories of sin and depravity. Hunted by the watch, Hannah finds herself one night in front of the mansion where William now lives, and despair hardens into outlawry: "Taught by the conversation of the dissolute poor, with whom she now associated, or by her own observation on the worldly reward of elevated villainy, she began to suspect 'that dishonesty was only held a sin, to secure the property of the rich; and that, to take from those who did not want, by the art of stealing, was less guilt, than to take from those who did want, by the power of the law'" (113). Hannah is not really persuaded by her own rhetoric of class warfare, and so her criminal career is cut short by bungling and arrest, but it is remarkable how closely the matrix of poverty, sexual exploitation, and ruling-class brutality Inchbald draws in this story corresponds to Wollstonecraft's analysis of the conditions of criminality in *Maria*.

There in the embedded autobiography of Maria's prison guard, Jemima, Wollstonecraft consolidates into one history all the horrors to which women born into poverty and scenes of sexual and domestic violence were subject. Jemima is branded before her birth with the label of illegitimacy. Her mother having died from the withholding of care during childbirth, Jemima is forced to endure a cruel stepmother and her father's beatings, only to be traded into virtual slavery in a slop-shop in Wapping, where she is starved and repeatedly raped. Made pregnant, she is thrown out of the shop and forced to take a draught to induce abortion, which nearly kills her. Slipping from beggary into prostitution and thieving, she chances to come to the notice of an old libertine, who encourages her efforts to educate herself at the same time that he draws her into loathsome, unspeakable practices. His death, from an apparent overdose of aphrodisiacs, throws her back on the world, and, after a dehumanizing spell as a washerwoman and a tawdry liaison during which Jemima, to secure her own position, drives a pregnant girl to suicide, she becomes the inmate of a grim sequence of carceral institutions: hospital, prison, house of correction, workhouse, and finally, shifting from prisoner to guard, private asylum.

If the piling up of all these miseries on one character runs counter to the (still developing) canons of fictional realism, Wollstonecraft's excess of sociological determinants situates *Maria* well outside the by now customary boundaries of the novel as an essentially naturalistic genre. Jemima's story is a distillation of the whole tradition of ordinaries' accounts and halfpenny criminal lives with, as in Inchbald, the difference that her crimes are traced not to a sinful nature but to the corrupting power of institutions—especially the institutionalized power of men over women. Jemima's fall into crime, like Hannah's, is prompted by a consciousness of oppression—"I began to consider the rich and poor as natural enemies, and became a thief from principle" (68)—but Jemima is better able to sustain the anger of her political analysis, and, even when she becomes an agent of the police, in the form of an asylum-keeper, she never renounces her criminal revolt against the institutions that made her an outcast.

Like Godwin, Wollstonecraft and Inchbald signal their indebtedness to an ongoing tradition of criminal writing by incorporating fragments and pastiches of the popular genres in their own texts. Hannah's story in *Nature and Art* culminates in "a printed sheet of paper accidentally thrown in [William's] way a few days after he [presiding as judge at her trial for forgery, although he fails even to recognize her] had left the town in which he had condemned her to die." Inchbald quotes the document verbatim, perfectly capturing the formulas of the genre she reproduces, starting from the title—"The last dying words, speech, and confession; birth, parentage, and education; life, character, and behaviour, of Hannah Primrose, who was executed this morning between the hours of ten and twelve"—and continuing with the ready-made moral: "being led astray by the arts and flattery of seducing man, she fell from the paths of virtue, and took to bad company, which instilled into her young heart all their evil practices, and at length brought her to this untimely end.—So she hopes her death will be a warning to all young persons of her own sex" (118).

As with the somewhat overstated Gothic atmosphere of *Maria* or the false texts of himself that Caleb Williams overhears in taverns and sees being peddled in the streets of every town in Britain, Inchbald presents the text of Hannah's last dying speech ironically, at least in part. The inadequacy of these repetitive and essentially static forms for representing the complex, conflicted truth of their cases is shown by means of both dramatic irony (what the ignorant reader of Caleb's biography never suspects, for example, is that the text has been deliberately falsified by the real criminal, Caleb's avenging master Falkland, in order to keep Caleb perpetually on the run and estranged from humanity) and rhetorical irony (Wollstonecraft

uses Maria's lapses into a language of Gothic extravagance to signal her susceptibility to the very romantic and sentimental delusions that have already robbed her
of her freedom). Inchbald, like Godwin, puts a kind of frame around the familiar
genre she incorporates and mixes the two kinds of irony for the purposes of political satire. The crucial dramatic irony of the whole plot is the meeting of William
and Hannah in the roles of judge and accused and his failure to know who she is;
because of this, all the catchphrases of her last dying speech—"seducing man,"
"bad company," and "the young man who first won her heart"—as hackneyed and
inexpressive as they are, take on a mordant note of protest by their reference to the
very person of "the judge who condemned her to death" for crimes far less corrupting than his own (118).

But, if these scraps of traditional forms are presented ironically, as if to set off
the contrasting ideological clear-sightedness and modernity of the fictions that contain them, there is another sense in which their incorporation is not ironic at all.
Although none of the three works of the 1790s should be taken as an attempt at
realism, their attention to the cultural roles and ideological stakes of what we might
call popular forms of representation—from gallows speeches to Gothic and sentimental tales—shows an acute consciousness of the extent to which private experience is regulated by contact with written and oral texts.

Maria's "romantic peculiarities," for example, are shown by Wollstonecraft to
have originated in the melancholy but impassioned speech of her uncle, who "drew
such animated pictures of his own feelings," she later records, "as imprinted the
sentiments strongly on my heart, and animated my imagination"—an imprinting
deepened by the giving of books, "for which I had a passion, and [which] conspired
with his conversation, to make me form an ideal picture of life" (78). So, when she
meets the scion of a local family at a dance, she overlooks even her real observations of him ("his manners did not entirely please me," she notes) and constructs
him according to the lineaments of romantic desire: "when he left us, the colour-
ing of my picture became more vivid—Whither did not my imagination lead me?
In short, I fancied myself in love—in love with the disinterestedness, fortitude,
generosity, dignity, and humanity, with which I had invested the hero I dubbed"
(80). Caught up in the narrative expectations by which her experience of the world
is governed, Maria is drawn into a disastrous marriage, the wreck of her fortune,
and a perpetual imprisonment. And yet, as Mary Poovey notes, Maria's continued

reliance on the language of Gothic and sentimental fiction to express her feelings for her fellow prisoner Darnford suggests that she is on the brink of falling a second time into a fatal dependence on a stranger she invests with heroic qualities.[9]

The character of Falkland, in *Caleb Williams,* is similarly constituted and undone by the internalization of fictional paradigms—as Caleb laments, "thou imbibedst the poison of chivalry with thy earliest youth" (326)—so that his jarring contact with the local oppressions and brutalities of country life leads to a kind of madness, the pursuit of a "phantom of departed honour" even at the cost of repeating, but now on a broader, juridically sanctioned scale, the same violence by which he has suffered. Both in *Caleb Williams* and *Nature and Art* the incorporated genres of last dying speech and criminal biography function as more than inadequate, ironically rendered distortions of a complex reality: they are involved in the *making* of the social reality they represent. Preserving, as Bakhtin writes of such incorporated genres in the novel, "their own structural integrity and independence, as well as their own linguistic and stylistic peculiarities" (321), the criminal forms used by Godwin, Inchbald, and Wollstonecraft reveal how thoroughly the social world has been penetrated by the rituals and discourses of legality. The psychological and political horizons of the world that characters, authors, and readers alike inhabit are in equal parts reflected and reshaped by the narrative forms in which their experience is configured. At the end of the eighteenth century in England the crime and sensational genres that had begun to assume distinct form a hundred years earlier served to epitomize both the hegemony of the law and the struggle to resist its incursions into the spheres of intimacy and desire.

The two sides of this struggle between an increasingly pervasive police authority and the scattered sites of progressive or traditional resistance are shown most clearly in the trial scenes central to all three of these fictions. In the fragmentary second part of *Maria* the heroine's husband brings a legal action for seduction and adultery against Darnford, Maria's fellow prisoner and now lover—whom, outside the law, she has taken as her true husband. "The dogs of law were let loose on her," Wollstonecraft writes (145), for Maria takes the responsibility on herself to answer her husband's, Venables's, charges in court, determining "to plead guilty to the charge of adultery; but to deny that of seduction." The basis of Maria's plea is her insistence on what she calls "the privilege of her nature" (146): her resistance to the "false morality" of "chastity, submission, and the forgiveness of injuries" imposed on women by the laws governing marriage and property (147). She repudiates the charge of seduction by asserting her claim to the responsibilities of moral agency: "I was six-and-twenty when I left Mr. Venables' roof; if ever I am to be supposed to arrive at an age to direct my own actions, I must by that time have arrived at it.—I acted with deliberation" (148). Maria has no wish to assume the position of an outcast, but she rejects the subordination of her private moral sense to the abstraction of legal authority—and, in doing so, invokes an important historical feature of English juries, their discretionary power to tailor verdicts and sentences in accordance with circumstances, social dangers, and the character of the accused. "I wish my country to approve of my conduct," she acknowledges, "but, if laws exist, made by the strong to oppress the weak, I appeal to my own sense of justice" to counteract them and to "the justice and humanity of the jury—a body of men, whose private judgment must be allowed to modify laws, that must be unjust, because definite rules can never apply to indefinite circumstances" (148–49).

Maria's, and her author's, position mixes customary and progressive claims: for if she appeals to a long native tradition of what J. M. Beattie calls "a personal and particularistic administration of the criminal law" (421)—often defended by conservatives against the rationalist and strictly egalitarian, even mechanistic, administration favored by liberal admirers of Beccaria and partisans of the Enlightenment and French Revolution[10]—she also denounces the law as a medium of social oppression and injustice, because it elides all material differences of circumstance or motive in its pursuit of an abstract, totalizing system of rules.

And yet women, by an especially glaring contradiction at the heart of the laws regulating marriage, family, and rights of property, are indeed held to be different from men and perpetually subject to their governance. Summing up the evidence to the jury after Maria has read her justification of her own, and Darnford's, conduct, the judge expresses his objection to "the fallacy of letting women plead their feelings, as an excuse for the violation of the marriage vow . . . What virtuous woman thought of her feelings?" By the law's construction of female virtue the possibility is almost unthinkable. Yet, as another of his arguments implicitly recognizes, contesting ideologies of the rights of women under the law, and of the rights of subjects of either sex to act according to conscience even in defiance of law, were now taken seriously enough to demand at least a dismissive response: "For his part, he had always determined to oppose all innovation, and the new-fangled notions which incroached on the good old rules of conduct. We did not want French principles in public or private life" (149). The judge's position likely prevails in the case

at hand—the "scattered heads" Wollstonecraft left on the story's continuation suggest that Maria is not granted the "divorce, and the liberty of enjoying, free from
molestation, the fortune left me" (149) that she claims. But, as we saw with John
Lilburne and the other political defendants of the *State Trials,* the form of the
criminal trial itself permits the airing of oppositional and often dangerously popular ideologies whose articulation is otherwise suppressed, and so Wollstonecraft's
heroine is enabled, by the legal mechanisms set in motion to restrain her, to call
for a radical overturning of the laws to which women and the poor are peculiarly
subject.

Neither *Nature and Art* nor *Caleb Williams* confronts actual provisions of the
law with the furious programmatic clarity of *Maria;* instead, both works represent
the criminal trial as a symbolic enactment of deeper, ineradicable structures of social
inequality and an instance of the destructive effects of a newly dominant ideology
of the law—with its emphasis on regulation, severity of judgment, and the mediation of state power—on human intimacy. In *Nature and Art* the trial of Hannah
for passing counterfeit bills, at which her former lover William sits in blind judgment, distills the social themes of the book into a theatrical scene mixing tragedy
and satire. The intersection, in a courtroom, of the two characters is reminiscent
of a similar encounter in Hogarth's *Industry and Idleness,* when Tom Idle, arrested
for theft on the word of a traitorous accomplice, is brought before his former fellow apprentice and now magistrate, Goodchild, but the moral (and social) valua-
tions placed on the scene are inverted. Hogarth's model success story becomes in
Inchbald a monster of sexual and social calculation, while the desperate, abject
criminal at the bar is constant in love, sincere, a victim of personal and institutional
betrayal.

The overall narrative structure of *Nature and Art,* in fact, resembles that of Hogarth's double, divergent, moral progress, except that Inchbald *redoubles* it in effect,
tracing the contrary paths of two pairs of allegorically polarized characters over
two generations—two brothers in the first; two cousins, their sons (of whom our
William is one), in the second—and greatly complicating that narrative structure
with the introduction of Hannah, whose strongly female-gendered experience of
poverty and displacement denaturalizes the simplistic opposition of virtue and vice
through an insistence on the social or material constraints within which courses of
action can be chosen.[11] The unprejudiced blindness of justice, held up as an ideal
within the discourse of the law, is personified in *Nature and Art* by the unseeing

William, whose failure to recognize Hannah represents both his moral blindness to his own private betrayals and the law's prejudicial blindness to the insupportable material conditions that lead to crime. William's legally constituted power to pronounce the death sentence against Hannah only authorizes him to repeat in the form of a public ritual his earlier abandonment of responsibility, an abandonment that condemns her to the shifts of prostitution and criminality.

The scene of trial that ends *Caleb Williams,* whose curious relegation to a postscript reflects Godwin's difficulty in working out how the story should end, is the last of several trials that govern the narrative's unfolding.[12] Haunted through all of Britain by the counterfeit history that proclaims him a criminal, blocked from leaving the kingdom by Gines—who, expelled from Raymond's gang of social bandits, has gone to work for Falkland, keeping Caleb under perpetual, harrowing surveillance—Caleb spends several years in a state of "solitude, separation, banishment," writing the memoirs that make up the text we are reading. Isolation "gradually gorged my heart with abhorrence of Mr. Falkland," Caleb writes (303), and he determines to fight against him by means of the only institutions of cultural power to which he has access, at least in theory: publication and the law.

Against the mercenary instruments Falkland has deployed, Caleb opposes a narrative whose truth, he supposes, is self-evident: "He has hunted me from city to city. He has drawn his lines of circumvallation round me that I may not escape. He has kept his scenters of human prey for ever at my heels. He may hunt me out of the world.—In vain! With this engine, this little pen I defeat all his machinations" (315). Yet, if writing seems to offer access to a truth exempt from the distorting effects of class privilege and inequalities of power, Caleb's experience suggests that such exemption is chimerical, for what counts is not writing in itself but, rather, the control of reading. Falkland can get his version of Caleb's life into general circulation and, more important, can secure its audience's implicit belief in its truth by virtue of his own unquestioned social privilege. Caleb imagines that his true story, if told with sincerity and all the circumstantial details of its authenticity, will compel belief, but of all those to whom he tells it only the outlaw Captain Raymond and the unjustly imprisoned Brightwel, both of them alienated from the discourses of law and received opinion, believe him on his word or care about his evidence. Caleb's bitterest recognition, in fact, is of the insignificance of evidence when divorced from a narrative *authorized* as true, and such authorization can only derive from the means of social power that Falkland, but not Caleb, possesses: property,

reputation, experience as a justice of the peace. These attributes give instant credibility to Falkland's testimony; without them Caleb's evidence cannot even be
heard.[13]

One of the ironies of the final trial scene of *Caleb Williams,* in which Falkland
is summoned to appear before a magistrate on Caleb's deposition charging him
with "repeated murders" (317), is that Caleb supplies no evidence he has not presented time and again before other judges, to negligible effect. This time, however,
Falkland countersigns Caleb's testimony, authorizing it by embracing his accuser.
Caleb's narrative is permitted to carry conviction not on its own account or because
of the transparency of truth but, rather, on Falkland's personal authority. The man
who, to preserve his own reputation, hounded his former servant Caleb throughout the realm to prevent the discovery of his own past crimes is won over by the
sincerity of Caleb's history of his own undeserved sufferings through the years of
confinement and flight.

Legal mechanisms fade into insignificance in this strangely subverted scene of
confrontation between accuser and accused. As soon as Falkland, near death, is
carried into the magistrate's chamber, Caleb bitterly repents being the "author of
this hateful scene," reliant on the compulsions of legal power to force a ravaged
man to attend him in public: "No penitence, no anguish can expiate the folly and
the cruelty of this last act I have perpetrated" in calling Falkland to the bar (320).
Even the extremity and injustice of his persecutions fail to justify this resort to the
oppression of law. "I am sure," Caleb asserts near the end of his testimony, that

if I had opened my heart to Mr. Falkland, if I had told him privately the tale that I have
now been telling, he could not have resisted my reasonable demand . . . Yes; in spite of the
catastrophe of Tyrrel [whom Falkland murdered], of the miserable end of the Hawkinses
[whom Falkland let hang for the crime], and of all that I have myself suffered, I affirm that
he has qualities of the most admirable kind. It is therefore impossible that he could have
resisted a frank and fervent expostulation, the frankness and the fervour in which the whole
soul was poured out. I despaired, while it was yet time to have made the just experiment;
but my despair was criminal, was treason against the sovereignty of truth. (323)

The passage is perhaps the most famous in *Caleb Williams* for its articulation of
Godwin's distinct brand of anarchism, which saw the idea of legality itself as oppressive, as a violence against the self-evidence of truth, because grounded in a logic
of compulsion and unequal power. "How great must be the difference between him
who answers me with a writ of summons or a challenge," Godwin had written in

the previous year's *Enquiry Concerning Political Justice,* "and him who employs the sword and the shield of truth alone?. . . [The latter] knows that a plain story, every word of which is marked with the emphasis of sincerity, will carry conviction to every hearer."[14] Caleb despairs, as he thinks, from learning this too late, after the machinery of the law has already been set in motion.

Yet there is something unsatisfying in Caleb's pained, impassioned call for "the just experiment" of a private confrontation between himself and Falkland as the solution to the struggle that has gone on between them for years and as a model for Godwin's revolutionary belief in the efficacy of truth—for they did have just such a meeting years earlier, before Caleb's flight to Wales. Caleb had refused, then, to sign a paper withdrawing his charges against Falkland, finding the ultimatum "repugnant to all reason, integrity and justice" (284), a symptom of the madness of Falkland's love of his own reputation. Wanting to justify his desperate statement before a Bow Street magistrate, Caleb opened his heart to his oppressor, told a plain story of his suffering, argued with feeling against "the prejudice of birth" which led Falkland to regard his servant's life as no more than a threat, or a sacrifice, to his own good name (283). Caleb, in other words, makes exactly "the just experiment" he calls for in the final scene of trial, pouring out his whole soul to Falkland. But, instead of responding to this "frankness and fervour" with the magnanimity Caleb seems to expect, Falkland, "gnashing his teeth, and stamping upon the ground," retorts: "You defy me! At least I have a power respecting you, and that power I will exercise; a power that shall grind you into atoms. I condescend to no more expostulation. I know what I am, and what I can be! I know what you are, and what fate is reserved for you!" (284). Inequalities of power sweep away truth, at least the kind of truth Caleb projects as an ideal.

Like Caleb with his call for the just experiment, Godwin in the *Enquiry* struggles to imagine a form of social life in which truth, conversely, could sweep away the inequalities of power the law exists to sustain. Of all those who wrote on criminality and the law in eighteenth-century England, either working within the traditional genres of criminal narrative or devising fictions that mixed, complicated, and undermined those genres, Godwin pursued with the greatest intensity the question of how truth is bound up with the legal and political means of its discovery and articulation. Criminal trial, for example, as a mechanism for reconstructing the truth of an event through memory and material traces, is disfigured in its very conception by the manifest, terrifying disparity of power between the individual on trial and the state and by the state's overriding interest in finding and punishing guilt. "A man tried for a crime," Godwin writes in the *Enquiry,* "is a poor deserted individual, with the whole force of the community conspiring his ruin" (657). As conspiracies of ruin, trials reduce "the vast train of actual and possible motives" behind every complex human action to a few simple patterns of guilt. Judgments upon the "inscrutable mystery" of intention rest in the hands of magistrates and juries "possessed of no previous knowledge, utter strangers to the person accused, and collecting their only materials from the information of two or three ignorant and prejudiced witnesses" (653).

So far, Godwin extends the suspension of certainty implicit in the unequally dialogical form of the trial only to a point of cautionary, reformist skepticism: we need to proceed carefully in the face of partial and uncertain evidence. But his critique really has a different emphasis, as his remarks on the disparity between the state and the accused in criminal trials suggest. The institutions of law are able, through their determination to know only so much of the truth as corresponds to their prohibitions, to compel the prisoner's agreement to a ready-made narrative of guilt—not (or not only) in the sense of Stalinist show trials, which fabricate crimes and confessions everyone knows are fake, but through the simplifying narratives of crime which circulate at every level of the culture. These narratives strip away the complexity of motivation or circumstances even from the self-representations of the accused: "Who will say that the judge, with his slender pittance of information, was more competent to decide upon the motives than the prisoner after the severest scrutiny of his own mind? How few are the trials which an humane and just man can read, terminating in a verdict of guilty, without feeling an uncontrollable repugnance against the verdict? If there be any sight more humiliating than all others, it is that of a miserable victim acknowledging the justice of a sentence against which every enlightened spectator exclaims with horror" (654). Instead of forcing acts of violence or transgression into the Procrustean bed of the law (*Enquiry* 688), true justice, for Godwin, would require a nuanced investigation into "all the circumstances of each individual case" (689), with no other standard than reason by which to determine the truth. Because of the infinite variation of individual motivations and circumstances, "no two crimes were ever alike; and therefore the reducing them, explicitly or implicitly, to general classes . . . is absurd" (649). A genuine commitment to discovering the truth of individual cases "would immediately lead," then, "to the abolition of all criminal law" (652).

Such a utopian *reductio* is remote from the oppressive atmosphere of the last trial in *Caleb Williams*. And perhaps, to return to the possibility D. A. Miller raises concerning the radical entanglement of novel and police, we should question whether, even if the "spontaneous justice" of Godwin's anarchism could somehow free us from the hegemony of criminal law (*Enquiry* 693), we would only be exchanging this for subjection to a still more oppressive regime of perpetual surveillance. James Thompson, for instance, has argued that, if "Godwin is primarily concerned with minimizing the encroachments of the state on the liberties of individual subjects," his method of writing *Caleb Williams*, like his ideal of an exhaustive, infinitely supple interrogation of individual circumstances and motives, only reinscribes the practice of the police. "The novelist's investigation into individual motivation," Thompson contends, "has the effect of legitimating surveillance."[15] Novelistic strategies for the representation of subjectivity have probably contributed to the elaboration of a psychological discourse that in turn can contribute to, and historically has facilitated, specific forms of political domination. But to infer that all "investigation into individual motivation" implicitly affirms the use of technologies of surveillance to enforce authoritarian power is facile. The realist strategies of circumstantial narration and the registering of individual voices, as the evidence from criminal trials, last dying speeches, and the fictions of Defoe and Fielding has shown, work against the imposition of unitary meanings and against the *resolution* of narrative contradictions. Counter-reading is implicit in the act of reading itself. *Caleb Williams* may well be the pessimistic verso to the optimistic, slightly unreal system of the *Enquiry*, but it is not complicitous in the apparatus of oppression it records: there is a powerful and material difference between the use of spying and imprisonment to thwart political opposition and the close registration of private experience and inward speech as a basis for protest against the misconstructions of the law.

In Godwin's two-part, discursively hybrid anatomy of the law, optimism of the will—the *Enquiry*'s hopeful contention that "law is merely relative to the exercise of political force, and must perish when the necessity for that force ceases, if the influence of truth do not still sooner extirpate it from the practice of mankind" (695)—is followed by pessimism of the intellect: Caleb's conviction that the "time to have made the just experiment" (323) and any corresponding hope for the vindication of uncorrupted reason are irrecuperable, for both himself and the society he is condemned to inhabit. "Political force" is no less tenacious than truth. If the criminal trial as a means for reconstructing that truth or settling disputes is inevitably corrupted by the effects of social hierarchy and political compulsion, the plain fact is that Caleb has no other recourse than the coercive power of law to get anyone, including Falkland, to listen to him. He can either inflict or submit to injustice; either way he suffers. The real tragedy of *Caleb*'s happy ending is that no other outcome would have saved him.

## Preface

1. William Godwin, *Caleb Williams,* ed. David McCracken (New York: Norton, 1977), 268. All references in the text are to this edition.

2. Daniel Defoe, *A Narrative of all the Robberies, Escapes, &c. of John Sheppard;* printed with *The Fortunate Mistress* (Oxford: Basil Blackwell for the Shakespeare Head Press, 1928), 2:225–26. All references in the text are to this edition.

## Introduction

1. This and the following excerpts from Godwin's discussion of the writing of *Caleb Williams* are included in an appendix to the McCracken edition of the novel.

2. At another point in the preface Godwin writes: "the thing in which my imagination revelled the most freely, was the analysis of the private and internal operations of the mind, employing my metaphysical dissecting knife in tracing and laying bare the involutions of motive, and recording the gradually accumulating impulses, which led the personages I had to describe primarily to adopt the particular way of proceeding in which they afterwards embarked" (339). Marilyn Butler explores the conflicts among readings of *Caleb Williams* in *Jane Austen and the War of Ideas* (Oxford: Clarendon Press, 1975), 57–75. As she explains there, the first part of Godwin's original title for the novel, *Things as They Are,* was dropped in 1831.

3. John Reynolds, *The Triumph of God's Revenge, against the Crying, and Execrable Sinne of Murther* (London, 1635), iv.

4. My partitioning of the field of criminal literature into genres is purely heuristic and is not meant to be exhaustive or rigid. Much scholarship has been published, especially in recent years, on various aspects of writing about crime in the seventeenth and eighteenth

centuries. Among the works that address the different forms criminal narrative could take, see: on the crime report, Lennard Davis, *Factual Fictions: The Origins of the English Novel* (New York: Columbia University Press, 1983); on criminal biography, John Richetti, *Popular Fiction before Richardson: Narrative Patterns, 1700–1739* (Oxford: Clarendon Press, 1969); Lincoln Faller, *Turned to Account: The Forms and Functions of Criminal Biography in Late Seventeenth- and Early Eighteenth-Century England* (Cambridge: Cambridge University Press, 1987); and *Crime and Defoe: A New Kind of Writing* (Cambridge: Cambridge University Press, 1993); and Philip Rawlings, *Drunks, Whores, and Idle Apprentices: Criminal Biographies of the Eighteenth Century* (London: Routledge, 1992); on criminal trials, John Langbein, "The Criminal Trial before the Lawyers," *University of Chicago Law Review* 45 (1978): 263–316; and "Shaping the Eighteenth-Century Criminal Trial: A View from the Ryder Sources," *University of Chicago Law Review* 50, no. 1 (Winter 1983): 1–136; Michael Harris, "Trials and Criminal Biographies: A Case Study in Distribution," in *Sale and Distribution of Books from 1700*, ed. Robin Myers and Michael Harris (Oxford: Oxford Polytechnic Press, 1982): 1–36; and Margaret Doody, "Voices of Record: Women as Witnesses and Defendants in the *Old Bailey Sessions Papers*," in *Representing Women: Law, Literature, and Feminism*, ed. Susan Sage Heinzelman and Zipporah Batshaw Wiseman (Durham, N.C.: Duke University Press, 1994): 287–308; on execution and gallows literature, V. A. C. Gatrell, *The Hanging Tree: Execution and the English People, 1770–1868* (Oxford: Oxford University Press, 1994); J. A. Sharpe, "Last Dying Speeches: Religion, Ideology and Public Execution in Seventeenth-Century England," *Past and Present* 107 (1985): 144–67; Peter Linebaugh, "The Ordinary of Newgate and His *Account*," in *Crime in England, 1550–1800*, ed. J. S. Cockburn (London: Methuen, 1977): 249–69; and Michael Mascuch, *Origins of the Individualist Self: Autobiography and Self-Identity in England, 1591–1791* (Stanford: Stanford University Press, 1996), 162–88. See also Frank Wadleigh Chandler, *The Literature of Roguery* (New York: Burt Franklin, 1958); Maximillian Novak, *Realism, Myth, and History in Defoe's Fiction* (Lincoln: University of Nebraska Press, 1983); and J. Paul Hunter, *Before Novels: The Cultural Contexts of Eighteenth-Century Fiction* (New York: Norton, 1990), 181–82 and 217–22.

On developments in printing and distribution, see Elizabeth Eisenstein, *The Printing Press as an Agent of Change: Communications and Cultural Transformations in Early-Modern Europe* (Cambridge: Cambridge University Press, 1979), esp. 43–159; and, for the eighteenth century, Alvin Kernan, *Printing Technology, Letters & Samuel Johnson* (Princeton: Princeton University Press, 1987).

5. Michael Mascuch, *Origins of the Individualist Self*, 52. Mascuch's use of the term *pathology* is never really explained but follows from his statement that "the modern individualist self is hypnotized by the illusion of individual personal authority"—that is, by the failure to recognize that what Mascuch calls "self-identity" is merely "a product of discursive relations" (52). The validity of that ontological claim lies outside the range of my argument here. Rather, the association of individualism with pathology seems most useful to me

as an anticipation of Mascuch's argument, later in the same work, that modern notions of the individual are first articulated in narratives of charismatic criminal deviance (162–88).

6. J. A. Sharpe, *Crime in Early Modern England, 1550–1750* (London: Longman, 1984), 145. See also Douglas Hay, "Property, Authority and the Criminal Law," in *Albion's Fatal Tree,* ed. Hay et al. (New York: Pantheon, 1975), 17–64, esp. 29–30; and E. P Thompson, *Whigs and Hunters: The Origin of the Black Act* (New York: Pantheon, 1975), 258–69. For a dissenting view, see Randall McGowen, "The Changing Face of God's Justice: The Debates over Divine and Human Punishment in Eighteenth-Century England," *Criminal Justice History: An International Annual* 9 (1988): 63–98.

7. Sharpe, "Last Dying Speeches," 159.

8. Cynthia Herrup, "Law and Morality in Seventeenth-Century England," *Past and Present* 106 (1985): 110 and 112.

9. Daniel Defoe, *Colonel Jack,* ed. Samuel Holt Monk (London: Oxford University Press, 1965), 309.

10. See Ian Watt, *The Rise of the Novel: Studies in Defoe, Richardson, and Fielding* (Berkeley: University of California Press, 1957), 74–85; G. A. Starr, *Defoe and Spiritual Autobiography* (Princeton: Princeton University Press, 1965), esp. 3–50; Michael McKeon, *The Origins of the English Novel, 1600–1740* (Baltimore: Johns Hopkins University Press, 1987), 90–100; and Mascuch, *Origins of the Individualist Self,* 55–131.

11. Henry Fielding, *The History of Tom Jones, a Foundling,* ed. Martin C. Battestin and Fredson Bowers (Middletown, Conn.: Wesleyan University Press, 1975), 118.

12. See Mascuch, *Origins,* for a discussion of the emergence of "an individual and self-determined rather than a collective and prescribed self-identity" (99).

13. Michel Foucault, *Discipline and Punish: The Birth of the Prison,* trans. Alan Sheridan (New York: Vintage, 1979), 192, 193.

14. Davis, *Factual Fictions,* 123.

15. Samuel Richardson, *Selected Letters,* ed. John Carroll (Oxford: Oxford University Press, 1963), 143, 127.

16. Mascuch, *Origins,* 163.

17. John Bender, *Imagining the Penitentiary: Fiction and the Architecture of Mind in Eighteenth-Century England* (Chicago: University of Chicago Press, 1987) 36; D. A. Miller, *The Novel and the Police* (Berkeley: University of California Press, 1988), 2.

18. Reynolds, *Triumph,* iv.

19. On the question of the "low" readership of some of the forms of criminal literature, see G. A. Starr, "Introduction" to Daniel Defoe, *Moll Flanders,* ed. G. A. Starr (Oxford: Oxford University Press, 1971), xvi–xvii; Foucault, *Discipline and Punish,* 67–69; and Faller, *Turned to Account,* 47–48 and 203–8.

20. Richetti, *Popular Fiction before Richardson,* 59.

21. McKeon, *Origins,* 98.

22. Defoe, *Colonel Jack,* 2.

23. John Zomchick, *Family and the Law in Eighteenth-Century Fiction: The Public Conscience in the Private Sphere* (Cambridge: Cambridge University Press, 1993), esp. 1–20. I have drawn the idea of symbolic centrality, especially as this is linked to social marginality and deviance, from Peter Stallybrass and Allon White, *The Politics and Poetics of Transgression* (Ithaca: Cornell University Press, 1986).

24. See P. N. Furbank and W. R. Owens, *The Canonisation of Daniel Defoe* (New Haven: Yale University Press, 1988); and *Defoe De-Attributions: A Critique of J. R. Moore's "Checklist"* (London: Hambledon, 1994).

25. Defoe, *Moll Flanders,* 1, 343.

26. Henry Fielding, *An Enquiry into the Causes of the Late Increase of Robbers and Related Writings,* ed. Malvin R. Zirker (Oxford: Clarendon Press, 1988), 77.

27. Fielding, *Enquiry,* 169.

28. Alexander Welsh, *Strong Representations: Narrative and Circumstantial Evidence in England* (Baltimore: Johns Hopkins University Press, 1992).

29. My thinking on the category of the perverse, and the cultural roles of the idea of deviance more generally, owes much to Jonathan Dollimore, *Sexual Dissidence: Augustine to Wilde, Freud to Foucault* (Oxford: Clarendon Press, 1991), esp. 103–4.

### ONE: Constructing the Underworld

1. *Select Trials, for Murders, Robberies, Rapes, Sodomy, Coining, Frauds, and other Offences: at the Sessions-House in the Old Bailey* (London, 1734–35), 2:193.

2. "The Woman-Hater's Lamentation," in *Secret Sexualities: A Sourcebook of 17th and 18th Century Writing,* ed. Ian McCormick (London: Routledge, 1997), 130–31.

3. Alan Bray, *Homosexuality in Renaissance England* (London: Gay Men's Press, 1988), 91.

4. *Select Trials,* 2:193.

5. For further examples, see Rictor Norton, *Mother Clap's Molly House: The Gay Subculture in England, 1700–1830* (London: Gay Men's Press, 1992), 92–105.

6. I am conscious of doing some violence to the idea of genre in calling the criminal anatomy one. Unlike such forms as the last dying speech or trial report, whose definitions are straightforward and which were recognizable *as* genres in the eighteenth century, the anatomy, as I use the term here, is a designedly open-ended aggregation—what Rodney Needham has called a polythetic class. These are "classes composed by sporadic or family resemblances"—as the phrasing suggests, Needham's formulation is indebted to Wittgenstein's concept of family resemblances in the *Philosophical Investigations*—and their pliancy is their point: "polythetic classes are likely to accommodate better than monothetic the variegation of social phenomena." See Rodney Needham, "Polythetic Classification: Conver-

gence and Consequences," *Against the Tranquility of Axioms* (Berkeley: University of California Press, 1983), 65 and 52. By beginning my discussion of criminal anatomies with excerpts from a series of trial reports, I mean to underline what I earlier called the purely heuristic function of my classification of criminal texts into overlapping and unstable—that is, familial—genres.

7. Quoted in McCormick, *Secret Sexualities*, 115.

8. *Select Trials*, 2:79, emphasis mine.

9. *A New Canting Dictionary* (London, 1725), unnumbered preface vi–vii.

10. Saunders Welch, *A Letter upon the Subject of Robberies* (London, 1758), 48. Peter Linebaugh discusses the disproportionate presence of Irish among those tried and convicted in eighteenth-century London in *The London Hanged: Crime and Civil Society in the Eighteenth Century* (London: Allen Lane, Penguin, 1991), chap. 9.

11. Captain Alexander Smith, *The History of the Lives of the Most Noted Highway-men* (London, 1714), 2:207–8.

12. Paul Salzman, *English Prose Fiction, 1558–1700: A Critical History* (Oxford: Clarendon Press, 1985), 205.

13. On the question of the authenticity of such accounts of cant language, see Peter Linebaugh, "The Ordinary of Newgate and His *Account*," 265–66. Clive Emsley, in *Crime and Society in England, 1750–1900* (London: Longman, 1987), raises doubts about the similar classification of criminal specialties in Mayhew's *London Labour and the London Poor* of 1861–62. Ian Bell argues that the canting dictionaries "provide the reticulated taxonomy of a constituent group within society, with its own subtly discriminated attitudes and labels for its own practices" (see his book *Literature and Crime in Augustan England* [London: Routledge, 1991], 63), but the question of how far those "attitudes and labels" were really the criminals' own remains open.

14. John Thurmond, *Harlequin Sheppard. A Night Scene in Grotesque Characters* (London, 1724), 22–23. The song also appears in the 1725 *New Canting Dictionary*. For the curious: *Famble* = ring, *Tattle* = watch, *Pop* = pistol, *Boman* = an eminent villain, *Diddle-shops* = gin shops.

15. *A Glimpse of Hell: or a Short Description of the Common Side of Newgate* (London, 1705), 3–4.

16. Smith, *History of the Most Noted Highway-men*, 198–99.

17. *The History of the Press-Yard* (London, 1717), 30–31.

18. For this reason I disagree with John Bender's contention in *Imagining the Penitentiary* that "the old prisons neither told stories nor assigned roles" (26). The stories may have been fragmented or partly incoherent, as the roles may have been overlapping or disguised, but all the early Newgate anatomies do attempt to find correspondences between personal histories and the public space of the prison.

19. But see also the 1707 *Memoirs of the Right Villainous John Hall*, reprinted in Philip

Pinkus, *Grub Street Stripped Bare* (London: Constable, 1968), 288–300, for a hybrid text comprising an almost equally detailed Newgate description, a canting dictionary, and a sort of autobiography.

20. Quoted in W. Eden Hooper, *History of Newgate and the Old Bailey* (London: Underwood, 1935), 36–37.

21. The author of *The History of the Press-Yard* accounts for his incarceration in this "Repository of Living Bodies" in narrowly political terms: "it being my Misfortune, amongst other Brethren of the Quill, to be caught Tripping, in Censuring the Conduct of my Superiors, and to fall under the Displeasure of the Government, for pretending to be displeas'd at their Proceedings" (4).

22. *History of the Press-Yard*, 8.

23. In an essay from the *Review* Defoe wrote of those put on trial for sodomy that "they are monuments of what human nature abandoned of divine grace may be left to do" (qtd. in McCormick, *Secret Sexualities*, 50). This substantiates Jeffrey Weeks's argument that in the eighteenth century "homosexuality was regarded not as a particular attribute of a certain type of person but as a potential in all sinful creatures" (*Coming Out: Homosexual Politics in Britain from the Nineteenth Century to the Present*, 2d rev. ed. [London: Quartet, 1990], 12). As my discussion here suggests, however, this is only half the story: for the essentializing discourse of deviance certainly also marks the sodomite, like the criminal, as another species.

24. *Select Trials*, 2:197.

25. *Select Trials*, 2:195.

26. *Select Trials*, 2:244.

27. *Select Trials*, 2:66. For an account of the relations between Hitchin and Wild in the early part of Wild's London career, and the background to their pamphlets, see Gerald Howson, *Thief-Taker General: The Rise and Fall of Jonathan Wild* (London: Hutchinson, 1970), esp. 100–111. Hitchin's pamphlet was published twice in 1718, first as *A True Discovery of the Conduct of Receivers and Thief-Takers*, then (in an edition to which a cant dictionary and lists of Wild's criminal associates had been added) as *The Regulator*.

The burden of Wild's response, *An Answer to a Late Insolent Libel*, is to show that Hitchin "is guilty of the same Crimes he pretends to fix upon others" (qtd. in the *Select Trials*, 2:68). He describes night rambles with Hitchin and his intimidation of publicans, pickpockets, and whores, whom he squeezes for information; he recounts negotiations involving a stolen watch and a "Bisket-Baker's" pocketbook, detailing Hitchin's criminal methods for profiting from thefts. Wild writes: "I need only mention the Cause of his being suspended; which was for his conniving at the Intrigues of the Pick-Pockets; taking the stolen Pocket-Books, and sending threatening Letters to the Persons that lost them" (*Select Trials*, 2:78). Wild ends by narrating Hitchin's "sodomitical adventures" in a molly house, where it's clear he is a regular customer. Spurned by the "young Sparks," or "He-Whores," with whom he's been dallying, the enraged Hitchin has them arrested, in the passage quoted here, wearing their "Female Habits" (2:79).

28. Charles Hitchin, *A True Discovery of the Conduct of Receivers and Thief-Takers in and about the City of London* (London, 1718), 6.

29. Charles Hitchin, *The Regulator: or, a Discovery of the Thieves, Thief-Takers, and Locks, alias Receivers of Stolen Goods in and about the City of London* (London, 1718), 20.

30. Foucault, *Discipline and Punish,* 47.

31. *Select Trials,* 2:211.

32. Smith, *Lives of the Highway-men,* preface to vol. 2 (unnumbered, iv).

33. Reynolds, *Triumph,* iv.

## T W O : Picaresque and Providential Fictions

1. See, for example, Robert Alter, *Rogue's Progress: Studies in the Picaresque Novel* (Cambridge: Harvard University Press, 1964), esp. 84. See also McKeon, *Origins,* 96–98, 176–78, and 292–94.

2. See Ernest Baker, *The History of the English Novel* (London: Witherby, 1924–39), 1:292–93 and 2:126–52.

3. See Baker, *History,* 2:18–44.

4. Thomas Nashe, *The Unfortunate Traveller and Other Works,* ed. J.B. Steane (London: Penguin, 1972), 254. All references in the text are to this edition.

5. See Chandler, *Literature of Roguery,* 2:144–45; and Watt, *Rise of the Novel* 94.

6. See J. Paul Hunter, *The Reluctant Pilgrim: Defoe's Emblematic Method and Quest for Form in Robinson Crusoe* (Baltimore: Johns Hopkins University Press, 1966), 56–57.

7. Reynolds, *Triumph of God's Revenge,* iii. Subsequent references will be given in the text.

8. Henry Fielding, *Examples of the Interposition of Providence in the Detection and Punishment of Murder,* included in Fielding, *An Enquiry into the Causes of the Late Increase of Robbers and Related Writings,* ed. Malvin R. Zirker (Oxford: Clarendon Press, 1988), 195–96. Subsequent references will be given in the text.

9. See William Nelson, *Fact and Fiction* (Cambridge: Harvard University Press, 1973). Lennard Davis discusses some of the implications of Nelson's discussion for a historical theory of genres in *Factual Fictions,* esp. 67–70.

## T H R E E : Crime Reports and Gallows Writing

1. These changes are described most extensively in Eisenstein, *The Printing Press as an Agent of Change,* esp. 43–159. Kernan discusses some of the effects of these developments in the later eighteenth century in *Printing Technology,* esp. 48–70.

2. Davis, *Factual Fictions,* 58, 48.

3. Mikhail Bakhtin, "Epic and Novel," in *The Dialogic Imagination,* ed. Michael Holquist, trans. Caryl Emerson and Michael Holquist (Austin: University of Texas Press, 1981), 7.

4. *Newes from the North: or a Relation of a Great Robberie which was committed nere Swanton in York-shire, July 12. 1641* (London, 1641), 5.

5. *News from Newgate: or, a True Relation of the Manner of Taking Seven Persons, Very Notorious for Highway-men, in the Strand* (London, 1677), 3–4.

6. Hunter writes in *Before Novels* that "by the 1670s individual accounts of murders appeared routinely almost every week, no doubt reflecting increased crime (especially in London) but also demonstrating heightened interest in a more individualized definition of current events" (181). The question of the relationship between levels of reported crime and levels of real crime is more complicated, however. Apart from uncertainty about the veracity of criminal reports from the seventeenth and early eighteenth centuries, there is the problem of why at certain times crimes are more widely and sensationally reported. There may be a connection to a real rise in the number of criminal acts, but, as Jennifer Davis has shown in her article on the garotting panic in Victorian England, such "moral panics" frequently have little to do with real danger. See "The London Garrotting Panic of 1862: A Moral Panic and the Creation of a Criminal Class in Mid-Victorian England," in *Crime and the Law: The Social History of Crime in Western Europe since 1500,* ed. V. A. C. Gatrell, Bruce Lenman, and Geoffrey Parker (London: Europa, 1980), 190–213. See also Ian Bell on the "Mohocks" panic, *Literature and Crime in Augustan England,* 53–54.

7. Davis, *Factual Fictions,* 73.

8. Bakhtin, *Dialogic Imagination,* 27.

9. See Beattie, *Crime and the Courts in England, 1660–1800* (Princeton: Princeton University Press, 1986), 362–76; and J. H. Baker, "Criminal Courts and Procedure at Common Law 1550–1800," in *Crime in England, 1550–1800,* ed. J. S. Cockburn (Princeton: Princeton University Press, 1977), 15–48, esp. 38–40.

10. See Hunter, *Before Novels,* 197–200; and, for a more wide-ranging discussion of "secularization and the epistemological crisis," Michael McKeon, *Origins,* 65–90.

11. Bakhtin, *Dialogic Imagination,* 30.

12. Bakhtin, *Dialogic Imagination,* 13–19.

13. Even of religious mysteries. If most journalistic reports of crimes resemble the anatomy, in laying open to view the activity of a criminal underworld, some use the temporal open-endedness of the news in order to extend the world of providential fictions into a materially observed and documented present. The 1651 pamphlet *Newes from the Dead* reports on events said to have transpired in Oxford in December and January just past. Anne Greene, a servant, was condemned to be hanged for the murder of her illegitimate child. On December 14, 1650, she was taken to the gallows and "turn'd off the Ladder, hanging by the neck

for the space of almost halfe an houre, some of her friends in the mean time thumping her on the breast, others hanging with all their weight upon her leggs; sometimes lifting her up, and then pulling her downe againe with a suddaine jerke, thereby the sooner to dispatch her out of her paine: insomuch that the Under-Sheriffe fearing lest thereby they should breake the rope, forbad them to doe so any longer" (2). Despite this charitable violence and further well-meaning blows when she was seen to breathe in her coffin, Anne Greene survived and was nursed back to full health over the next month. In the meantime the under-sheriff appealed to the judges for a reprieve: "Whereupon those worthy Gentlemen, considering what had happened, weighing all circumstances, they readily apprehended the hand of God in her preservation" (3). The reprieve was granted. At the time of the pamphlet's writing Anne Greene was "now perfectly recovered"; she had retired with friends into the country and was awaiting the result of her suit for pardon.

If the pamphlet exhibits the to-the-moment inconclusiveness of news reports, it interprets events as resonant with providential meanings—but the author presents these readings skeptically, provisionally. Whereas another writer might have taken Anne Greene's survival as a sufficient sign of her innocence, this author adduces further circumstantial evidence: the testimony of a midwife and of Anne Greene's fellow-servants; a close comparison of her testimony under different circumstances; a reconstruction of the alleged crime's chronology, pointing to apparent contradictions in the presumptions against her. The death, three days after her near-execution, of her accuser—Sir Thomas Read, who was also her master and the grandfather of Jeffery Read her seducer—is put forward as perhaps another providential sign, but tentatively, insinuatingly, not in the rapt or exhortatory voice of one seeing manifest signs of God's intervention.

14. Prisoners often made private agreements with publishers in advance, giving them the texts of their last words, but of course the broadsheets usually conclude with a description of the condemned's behavior at the gallows, and this part of the text is necessarily fanciful if the paper was sold on the day of execution. See Hogarth's *Industry and Idleness*, pl. 11, in which a poor woman hawks "The Last Dying Speech of Tom Idle" as Idle is conducted to the scaffold; see also Harris, "Trials and Criminal Biographies," esp. 19–20.

15. See Peter Linebaugh, "The Tyburn Riot against the Surgeons," in *Albion's Fatal Tree: Crime and Society in Eighteenth-Century England*, ed. Douglas Hay et al. (New York: Pantheon, 1975), 65–117, esp. 67; Gatrell, *Hanging Tree;* Frank McLynn, *Crime and Punishment in Eighteenth-Century England* (Oxford: Oxford University Press, 1989), 264–69; Sharpe, "Last Dying Speeches" 146–47, 161–62; and Christopher Hibbert, *The Road to Tyburn: The Story of Jack Sheppard and the Eighteenth-Century Underworld* (London: Longmans, Green, 1957), 136–46. The best (though polemically structured) eighteenth-century descriptions are in: Mandeville, *An Enquiry into the Causes of the Frequent Executions at Tyburn* (1725); Henry Fielding, *Enquiry*, 167–72, and *The Covent-Garden Journal*, ed. Bertrand A. Goldgar (Oxford: Clarendon Press, 1988), 416 (issue 25, March 28, 1752) and 447–48 (issue 55, July 18,

1752); and Samuel Richardson, *Familiar Letters* (London: Routledge, 1928), 217–20 (letter 160).

16. Quoted in Sharpe, "Last Dying Speeches," 158–59.

17. Sharpe, "Last Dying Speeches," 156. Pieter Spierenburg, in *The Spectacle of Suffering: Executions and the Evolution of Repression, from a Preindustrial Metropolis to the European Experience* (Cambridge: Cambridge University Press, 1984), cites a seventeenth-century Dutch traveler to England who noted "with surprise" the custom of the condemned speech: "The convict resembled a minister on the pulpit, Bekker wrote, were it not for the rope around his neck" (63).

18. *A Full and True Account of the Penitent Behaviour, Last Dying Words, and Execution of Mr. Edmund Allen, Gent.* (London, 1695).

19. Samuel Smith, *A True Account of the Behaviour, Confession, and Last Dying Speeches, of the Criminals that were Executed at Tyburn, on Friday the 12th of July, 1695* (London, 1695).

20. The Ordinary was widely reviled, most famously by Defoe in *Moll Flanders,* in which he is dismissed as a man "whose business it is to extort Confessions from Prisoners, for Private Ends, or for the farther detecting of other Offenders" (288). Paul Lorraine, who held the office from 1700 to 1719, was particularly criticized for what many perceived as the self-serving motivations of his efforts to extract confessions from the condemned. See Linebaugh, "The Ordinary of Newgate and His *Account,*" esp. 248–49 and 254–59; the 1717 *History of the Press-Yard* ("Mr. Ordinary has been very pressing with me to confess more Sins than I have been guilty of, but the badness of my Memory is a great Bar to such a Compliance"), 45–52; and Robert Singleton, "Defoe, Moll Flanders, and the Ordinary of Newgate," *Harvard Library Bulletin* 24, no. 4 (October 1976): 407–13.

21. Sharpe, "Last Dying Speeches," 150.

22. Samuel Smith, *A True Account of the Behaviour of Thomas Randal, who was Executed at Stone-Bridge, for Killing the Quaker, on Wednesday the 29th of this Instant January 1695/6* (London, 1695/6). See Linebaugh, "The Ordinary of Newgate and His *Account,*" for a description of the genre as it developed through the eighteenth century, especially under Paul Lorraine (1700–1719) and James Guthrie (1725–46). Describing the changes that took the *Account* from a folio broadsheet to a pamphlet of sixteen or twenty-eight quarto pages (and from a price of one penny to six pence), Linebaugh writes that these changes "reflected both its consolidation as a specific genre and its acceptance by the City officials" (247). The five-part structure of the later *Accounts* gave more emphasis to legal questions and the lives of the condemned and incorporated a wider range of materials, including letters and autobiographical narratives.

23. Sharpe, "Last Dying Speeches," 150.

24. Sharpe, "Last Dying Speeches," 155.

25. Sharpe, "Last Dying Speeches," 156.

26. Dependent as they were on oral testimony and the confrontation of accuser and accused, English common-law trials of the seventeenth and early eighteenth centuries were highly theatrical contests, as I discuss in the following chapter. Particularly in capital cases, a notion prevailed that the truth should, in effect, declare itself: according to J. H. Baker, Coke in his *Institutes* argued that "in capital cases the evidence against the prisoner should be so manifest that it could not be contradicted" (37). That in many instances the accused not only contradicted the evidence during the trial but continued to do so up to the moment of death must have made for a murkier and more disquieting picture of human justice.

See also Foucault's analysis of the ambiguous status of confession within the inquisitorial system of justice prevalent on the Continent (*Discipline and Punish*, 36–42). Confession, while never in itself sufficient to convict, "had priority over any other kind of evidence . . . an element in the calculation of truth, it was also the act by which the accused accepted the charge and recognized its truth" (38). Despite the differences between common-law and inquisitorial trials, confession serves in both as a ritual of validation and even of communal release from blood guilt.

27. Sharpe, "Last Dying Speeches," 164.

28. Sir John Johnson, *An Account of the Behaviour, Confession, and last Dying Speeche of Sir John Johnson, Executed at Tyburn on Tuesday the 23d day of December, Anno Dom. 1690 for stealing of Mrs. Mary Wharton* (London, 1690).

29. See Langbein, "Shaping the Eighteenth-Century Criminal Trial"; Beattie, *Crime and the Courts*, 356–76; J. H. Baker, "Criminal Courts," 36–40.

30. Sharpe, "Last Dying Speeches," 148.

31. Writing of the scaffold literature published in France during the same period, Hans-Jürgen Lusebrink writes that it "constitutes, in its virtual entirety, a direct appeal to the public" and suggests that through an analysis of the specific nature of this appeal we can begin to reconstruct a collective mentality, "a mental apparatus which is at once complex, evolving, and resistant." See "La letteratura del patibolo: Continuità e trasformazioni tra '600 e '800," *Quaderni Storici* 49 (April 1982): 287 (translation mine). In particular, "formal subversion through burlesque and masquerade points to nuclei of resistance which were certainly isolated and few in number, but indicative nonetheless of the persistence of popular mentalities dating back to ancient France" (293). See also Foucault, *Discipline and Punish*, 67–68; and Linebaugh, "Tyburn Riot against the Surgeons," 79–88, for an analysis of those sectors of the crowd expressing solidarity with the condemned.

32. In his analysis of the "disturbances around the scaffold" Foucault writes that "the people never felt closer to those who paid the penalty than in those rituals intended to show the horror of the crime and the invincibility of power; never did the people feel more threatened, like them, by a legal violence exercised without moderation or restraint" (*Discipline and Punish*, 63). Foucault's evidence for his discussion of the behavior of crowds around the

scaffold (in France) is anecdotal but compelling for the particular cases he describes; see 57–65 and, for his remarks on the genre of gallows speeches, 65–68. For a contemporary view of the effects of sympathy, see Henry Fielding, *Enquiry,* 167–69.

33. Sharpe, "Last Dying Speeches," 162.

34. Jonathan Swift, *The Last Speech and Dying Words of Ebenezor Elliston, who was Executed the Second Day of May, 1722,* in *Irish Tracts and Sermons* (vol. 9: *Prose Works*), ed. Herbert Davis (Oxford: Blackwell, 1948), 37–41. See also George Mayhew, "Jonathan Swift's Hoax of 1722 upon Ebenezor Elliston," in *Fair Liberty Was All His Cry: A Tercentenary Tribute to Jonathan Swift,* ed. A. Norman Jeffares (London: Macmillan, 1967), 290–310. esp. 298–304; and Ian Bell, *Literature and Crime,* 77–79.

FOUR: Criminal Trials

1. John Bunyan, *The Pilgrim's Progress from this World to That which is to Come,* 2d ed., ed. Roger Sharrock (Oxford: Clarendon Press, 1960), 91–92. All references in the text are to this edition.

2. The term is derived from Watt, *The Rise of the Novel.* Watt argues that what he calls "formal realism . . . is the narrative embodiment of a premise that Defoe and Richardson accepted very literally, but which is implicit in the novel form in general: the premise, or primary convention, that the novel is a full and authentic report of human experience." Formal realism is, "like the rules of evidence, only a convention" (32); as a mode of representation it has strict theoretical and historical limits. But the attempt to make the details of a text correspond to the features of the observable world with which readers, at first hand or through other texts, would already be familiar was a guiding authorial strategy during the period under examination here. See also Hunter, *Before Novels,* 199–200, for a discussion of the "circumstantiality" of the novel as the outcome of broader cultural habits of observation and recording.

3. John H. Langbein, "The Criminal Trial before the Lawyers"; J. M. Beattie, *Crime and the Courts in England,* 395–99.

4. See McKeon, *The Origins of the English Novel,* esp. 65–89. McKeon argues that "an optimistic faith in the power of empirical method to discover natural essences" was disturbed from the beginning by "a wary skepticism of the evidence of the senses" (68), an intimation that the truth they yielded could never be more than provisional.

5. *Majesty, justice,* and *mercy* are the key terms in Douglas Hay's discussion of "the criminal law as an ideological system" (26) in his introductory essay, "Property, Authority and the Criminal Law," to *Albion's Fatal Tree,* 26–56. Alexander Welsh, in *Strong Representations,* discusses the importance of circumstantial evidence in later eighteenth- and nineteenth-century narrative.

6. See Michael Harris, "Trials and Criminal Biographies." Very few copies of trials sur-

vive from the period before the mid-1680s. Harris cites a *Volume of Trials* in the Guildhall Library, London (shelf mark A.5.4. no. 34), which contains the earliest exemplar (1674) of what were soon to be regularized as the Old Bailey *Proceedings*.

7. Harris, "Trials and Criminal Biographies," 7.

8. Cited, respectively, in Langbein, "Criminal Trial," 268; and Harris, "Trials and Criminal Biographies," 7.

9. J. A. Sharpe has argued that by the later seventeenth century law "had come to replace religion as the main ideological cement of society" (*Crime in Early Modern England*, 145). See also Hay, *Albion's Fatal Tree*, 17–64; and Thompson, *Whigs and Hunters*, 258–69.

One instance of the increasing power of the law's ideological function can be read in the preface to a 1715–16 compilation of State Trials, *The History of the Most Remarkable Tryals in Great Britain and Ireland*. The editor writes that "to render the Work the more agreeable, he has made it as Historical as possible, and endeavour'd to shew the Causes which lead to such Tryals, and the Consequences that attended them, with the Variations which from time to time happened in the Constitution of our Government, to which no *Briton* ought wholly to be a Stranger; and by which it will very manifestly appear, how much 'tis mended, and that the Lives and Liberties of the People are now far better secured than they were in former Days" (1:iv). The idea that the history of the nation can be identified with the history of its laws, as these are embodied in the process of criminal trial, emphasizes the contingency of both law and nation and hinges on an openly secular notion of historical change.

10. Harris, "Trials and Criminal Biographies," 9–10.

11. Whether reports that are presented as verbatim transcripts are literally so is, of course, open to question, although the claim should not simply be dismissed. Langbein writes that "towards the end of the seventeenth century . . . major trials were transcribed in shorthand by professional scribes, promptly published in pamphlet editions represented to be accurate and complete, and scrutinized by contemporary audiences that included many of the official participants" ("Criminal Trial," 265). See also Harris, "Trials and Criminal Biographies," 12–13; and Langbein's "Shaping the Eighteenth-Century Criminal Trial," esp. 12–18. In the Lilburne case, which I will discuss later, a statement from the defendant was included opposite the title page, attesting to the accuracy of the "Pen-man's Discourse."

12. Langbein, "Criminal Trial," 266.

13. See *The Tryall of Lieut. Collonell John Lilburne* (Southwark, 1649). Lilburne brings a series of objections to the proceedings, of which these are representative:

And therefore Sir . . . seeing I am brought before you by a piece of parchment that truly I could not read, neither could he do it that shewed it me, (I mean the Lieutenant of the Tower) for admit that if I did well understand Latine, as indeed I do not, only some ordinary words, yet was it in such an unusual strange hand that I could not read it; and therefore being I am brought before you implicitly, and not as

I conceive an Englishman ought to be, who ought to see and read the Authority by vertue of which he is convened before any power . . . therefore being brought in an extraordinary manner to such an extraordinary place as this, which is no ordinary Assizes nor Sessions, no nor yet in mine own County, therefore I again humbly desire that you will be pleased to let me see and hear your extraordinary Commission, that so I may consider whether the extent or latitude of the Commission be consonant or no to the Petition of Right, and other the good old Laws of England. (15)

14. Langbein, "Criminal Trial," 270.

15. See Langbein, "Criminal Trial," 307–16.

16. Maximillian Novak quotes the editor of a 1720 compilation of *Tryals for High Treason*, who argues for summary over transcription: "I appeal to any Gentleman who has read a Tryal," he wrote, "if these Repetitions in Print do not create a Weariness and Disgust, and induce him to turn over many Pages unread, whereby perhaps he slips some things that might very well deserve his attention" (*Realism, Myth, and History*, 134). This was already on its way, however, to being a minority view. See also the introduction to the account of the trial of David Bathey for murder in 1723: "There is often so much obscurity in depositions, which are given in the third Person, that a Man must read them more than once to understand 'em, and tis well if he succeeds at last. The Trial before me is so remarkable an Instance of this, 'Tis so perplex'd with *him*'s and *he*'s, that (contrary to my usual method) I chuse to let it remain in its original dress" (*Select Trials*, 1:366). In fact, the editor's *usual method* was in crisis, and published trial reports increasingly comprised incongruous materials that readers had to work out for themselves.

17. Langbein, "Shaping," 15.

18. *The Proceedings at the Sessions at the Old-Baily, August the 27th and 28th, 1679. Containing the several Tryals of a great number of notorious Malefactors, and particularly of Peter du Val and Tho. Thompson, Condemned for Murder* (London, 1679).

19. Langbein, "Criminal Trial," 269.

20. Langbein writes that the sessions papers "throw light on all manner of legal and administrative topics, and they constitute a vast and fascinating repository of information about nonlegal subjects of every conceivable sort. They touch on countless facets of the social and economic life of the metropolis and give us sustained contact with the lives and language of the ordinary people of the time" ("Criminal Trial," 270–71). Although not the only source of such sociological or anthropological information to historians, trials were, I believe, their most significant source for contemporaries, at least until the emergence of the realist novel. See also Doody, "Voices of Record," 291.

21. Raymond Williams, *The Country and the City* (New York: Oxford University Press, 1973), 165–81. On the "eclipse of testimony" and the turn to a greater reliance on circum-

stantial evidence in both criminal trials and other kinds of narrative, see Welsh, *Strong Representations*, esp. 7–42; and Langbein, "Criminal Trial."

22. *Proceedings* for August 27 and 28, 1679.

23. Langbein, "Criminal Trials," 285.

24. Eighteenth-century trial reports are shot through with epistemological and social tensions and record both failed prosecutions and guilty verdicts proved wrong after the innocent accused had been killed; see, among many others, the trials of Charles Dean and Thomas Mars in *A Compleat Collection of Remarkable Tryals* (London, 1721), 31–38.

25. Their torment of Sarah Morduck was far more brutal than the term *scratch* suggests. According to her deposition, Richard Hathaway came up to her "as she was opening her Window, and being behind scratcht her face in a very cruel manner, and forced out one of her Teeth, and carried away her Cloaths." Later she was kidnaped from her house by six men in disguise, taken to the house of Hathaway's master, scratched again by Hathaway, "and afterwards *Elizabeth* wife to the said *Thomas Wellyn*, fell upon her and scratcht her in a most cruel manner, and tore her face, and tore off her head-cloaths and hair, and then the said *Thomas Wellyn* gave this Informant two or three kicks on her belly, and threw her on the ground and stampt upon her, and so much bruised her that she was forced to keep her bed for about a fortnight" (28). Two more incidents followed, forcing her to flee Southwark and take lodgings across the river, where she was still pursued by a mob (25). The unrelenting nature of Hathaway's persecution and the very suspect behavior of Elizabeth and Thomas Wellyn suggest some long-running local dispute, a tension of old standing in the community, but, apart from some vague remarks in the defense counsel's opening statement, nothing in the testimony or in any of the accompanying depositions and arguments sheds any further light on the origins of Hathaway's fraudulent enchantment (*The Tryal of Richard Hathaway* [London: Isaac Cleave, 1702]).

26. Erich Auerbach, *Mimesis: The Representation of Reality in Western Literature*, trans. Willard R. Trask (Princeton: Princeton University Press, 1953), 554.

27. See Langbein, "Criminal Trial," 282, 307–14; and "Shaping," 123–34; Beattie, *Crime and the Courts*, 352–64.

28. Surrey assizes may well, indeed must, have followed somewhat different rules than the Old Bailey for the Hathaway case to have been structured as it was, but even there Beattie first locates defense counsel in cases other than treason in the mid-1730s (*Crime and the Courts*, 356–59). Even in cases of high treason counsel for the defense was only allowed in 1696, or six years before the Hathaway trial.

29. Beattie, *Crime and the Courts*, 364.

30. In his opening statement one of the prosecution counsel argues that "the discovering and punishing such a Cheat as this, is highly necessary, and not only for the Vindicating the publick Justice of the Nation, but for the sake of Religion it self"—for "when Men

who are Sceptically inclined, find that the generality of Mankind run away with Stories of this Nature, and those Facts afterwards prove undeniably false; they carry their doubts on much too far, and are apt to conclude, that they cannot securely rely upon the Relation of others, and general Consent of Mankind, for the certainty of any Fact whatsoever" (*Tryal of Richard Hathaway,* 2–3). The case for fraud has to be made carefully because Hathaway's supporters insinuate that those who distrust his story must themselves be tainted with athe-ism, so the prosecution turns the charge against Hathaway, making his cynical manipula-tion of popular belief in witchcraft the real sign of a contagious unbelief. And the same infec-tious spirit of skepticism is represented as threatening the law: "Here was a Woman that underwent a solemn Tryal, and upon a full Hearing was acquitted; yet afterwards, notwith-standing the thorough Examination of the Fact, and such an Evidence given as convinced every unprejudiced Hearer of the innocence of the Defendant, and the malice and hypocrisie of the Accuser, such a Spirit did reign, that it was represented that the Defendant had hard measure; and not only the Jury, but the Court too, were reflected on" (3).

On law and religion see Hay, *Albion's Fatal Tree,* 29–30; and McGowen, "Changing Face of God's Justice." For a discussion of the background to witchcraft prosecutions in general, see Sharpe, *Crime in Early Modern England,* 78–79.

31. See Norbert Elias, *The History of Manners,* vol. 1: *The Civilizing Process* (New York: Pantheon, 1978), for a discussion of the "centralization and monopolization of the use of physical violence and its instruments" by the state (xv–xvi), the historical process by which punitive power, and the power of violence more generally, is wrested away from the indi-vidual and the crowd. "The pleasure of physical attack," he writes, "is now reserved to those few legitimized by the central authority (e.g., the police against the criminal), and to larger numbers only in exceptional times of war or revolution" (202).

32. See Hunter, *Before Novels,* 308–11, on the amassing of circumstantial details in diaries and in fiction, with particular reference to Sterne and Defoe.

33. *Select Trials* (London, 1734–35), 2:38.

34. After the early 1720s reports were increasingly liable to furnish readers the legal defi-nitions and precedents they would need in order to follow the lawyers' arguments and lo-cate specific cases within the broader history of the law the sessions papers implicitly com-posed. See Harris, "Trials and Criminal Biographies," 12; and Howson, *Thief-Taker General,* 199–200.

FIVE: Criminal Biographies

1. Thomas Dangerfield, *Dangerfield's Memoires, Digested into Adventures, Receits, and Ex-pences* (London, 1685), 23, 26–28, 30.

2. In the four months covered by the *Memoires* Dangerfield obtained twenty shillings from *Gentlemen* or *Gentlewomen* on a handful of occasions; his record was twenty-three

shillings from *a Farmer's Wife*. But, if Dangerfield's takes were rarely spectacular, ten shillings was a lot of money in 1685, especially for the farmers, millers, parsons, and housewives whom Dangerfield mostly robbed. In something under four months, working only about one day in three, he took an average of ten shillings each from 226 people, according to his own records. This enabled Dangerfield to live well: "For a Periwigg, 18s. 3 . . . Paid for Fringing a Pair of Gloves, 4s. 0" (35).

3. Jack Katz, *Seductions of Crime: Moral and Sensual Attractions in Doing Evil* (New York: Basic Books, 1988).

4. Dangerfield was chiefly notorious for his involvement in the trials and pamphlet wars that followed in the wake of the Popish and Mealtub Plots; the *Dictionary of National Biography*, in fact, lists his principal profession as "false witness."

5. See Mascuch, *Origins*, 144–46: "The emphasis on detail and authenticity," he writes, "possibly peaked at the height of absurdity with the publication of Thomas Dangerfield's *Memoires* in 1685" (144).

6. Spiritual autobiography presents a special case and in fact is radically different in kind from the biographies and autobiographies I am considering here. The form closest to spiritual autobiography in the criminal realm is the last dying speech or—in the third person—the Ordinary's *Account:* both of them are more concerned with constructing an exemplary narrative according to a preexisting pattern of fall and repentance than in conveying the vivid particularity of individual experience. It was inevitable, however, that the patterns of spiritual autobiography should make themselves felt in a variety of different genres, and, at a time when, as Cynthia Herrup has argued, criminality and sin were overlapping categories, criminal lives were certainly not immune to such patterning. But I think their influence was less pervasive than Michael McKeon suggests when he writes that the "accounting" in *Dangerfield's Memoires*, for example, is "suggestively reminiscent of the acts of 'spiritual bookkeeping' so common in spiritual autobiography" (*Origins*, 99). See Herrup, "Law and Morality," esp. 110–12; McKeon, *Origins*, 90–100; and, on spiritual autobiography, Starr, *Defoe and Spiritual Autobiography*, esp. 3–50.

7. Faller, *Turned to Account*, esp. 66–90, 146–73; Richetti, *Popular Fiction before Richardson*, esp. 35–59.

8. Richetti, *Popular Fiction*, 35.

9. Faller, *Turned to Account*, 4.

10. Richetti, *Popular Fiction*, 35.

11. Richetti, *Popular Fiction*, 59; Faller, *Turned to Account*, 4–5.

12. Faller, "Criminal Opportunities," 123.

13. *A Murderer Punished; and Pardoned. Or, A True Relation of the Wicked Life, and Shameful-happy Death of Thomas Savage*, 12 ed (London, 1679), 3–4.

14. Surprisingly, they offer no gloss on the last scene of his life. Cut down after hanging for "some considerable time" from the gallows,

he was conveyed by [his friends] into a house not far distant from the place of Execution, where being laid upon a Table, unto the astonishment of the beholders, he began to stir and breath, and rattle in his throat, and it was evident his life was whole in him; from the Table he was carried to a bed in the same House, where he breathed more strongly, and opened his eyes and his mouth (though his teeth were set before) and offered to speak, but could not recover the use of his Tongue; but his reviving being known within an hour the Officers came to the house where he was, and conveyed him to the place of Execution again, and hung him up again, until he was quite dead. (31)

Savage's luck was harder than that of most prisoners who were "resurrected" after being cut down from hanging; generally (such occurrences were very rare, of course), they were not taken back for a second try.

15. Richetti, *Popular Fiction,* 56.

16. See Faller, "Criminal Opportunities," 123 and *Turned to Account,* 101–3.

17. The story of Thomas Savage and Hannah Blay, and particularly the representation of the latter in *A Murderer Punished, and Pardoned,* was a key model for Lillo's treatment of the story of George Barnwell and his wicked mistress, Millwood, in *The London Merchant.* For studies of female criminality in the eighteenth century—in the context, for example, of domestic violence, "petty treason," and attitudes toward pregnancy—see Margaret Doody, "'Those Eyes Are Made So Killing': Eighteenth-Century Murderesses and the Law," in *Princeton University Library Chronicle* 46, no. 1 (Fall 1984): 49–80; Beattie, "The Criminality of Women in Eighteenth-Century England," in *Journal of Social History* 8 (1975): 80–116; and *Crime and the Courts,* esp. 113–24, 237–43; and McLynn, *Crime and Punishment,* 116–32. For crimes committed against women, see McLynn, 96–115; and Beattie, *Crime and the Courts,* esp. 124–32.

18. As Henry Fielding would later write in the *Enquiry,* "The Design of those who first appointed Executions to be public, was to add the Punishment of Shame to that of Death; in order to make the Example an Object of greater Terror" (168).

19. Richetti, *Popular Fiction,* 31.

20. *A True and Impartial Relation of the Birth and Education of Claudius du Val; Together with the manner of his Apprehending . . . And lastly, the manner of his Execution at Tyburn, on Fryday the 21. of this present January 1669* (London, 1669 [1670]), 2–3. Subsequent references are to this edition.

21. *The Memoires of Monsieur Du Vall: Containing the History of his Life and Death. Whereunto are Annexed His last Speech and Epitaph* (London, 1670), 1.

22. Linebaugh, "Tyburn Riot against the Surgeons," 113.

23. Defoe was a crucial figure in this fictional "invention" of biography—the lives of Jonathan Wild and John Sheppard were written by or in imitation of him after *Moll Flanders, Colonel Jack,* and *Roxana*—but two earlier books, hybrids of realistic fiction and chron-

icle or memoir, had elaborated a mixture of memory, testimony, and anecdote into narratives of the whole lives of their subjects: Francis Kirkman's *The Counterfeit Lady Unveiled* of 1673; and William Fuller's *The Whole Life of Mr. William Fuller* of 1703. See Ernest Bernbaum, *The Mary Carleton Narratives, 1663–1673: A Missing Chapter in the History of the English Novel* (Cambridge: Harvard University Press, 1914); and Robert Singleton, "English Criminal Biography, 1651–1722," *Harvard Library Bulletin* 18, no. 1 (January 1970): 63–83, esp. 69–71.

24. Ralph Wilson, *A Full and Impartial Account of All the Robberies Committed by John Hawkins, George Sympson, (Lately Executed for Robbing the Bristol Mails) and Their Companions . . . Written by Ralph Wilson, Late One of Their Confederates* (London, 1722), 7.

25. Singleton argues that Wilson's *Full and Impartial Account* was an important influence on Defoe's *Colonel Jack*. As the editor of *Applebee's Journal*, Defoe devoted three columns to Wilson's pamphlet, and there are a number of passages in the novel that correspond to episodes in Wilson. See Singleton, "English Criminal Biography," 72–75.

26. Thomas De Quincey, *On Murder Considered as One of the Fine Arts*, in *Selected Writings of Thomas De Quincey*, ed. Philip Van Doren Stern (New York: Random House, 1937), 983.

27. De Quincey, *On Murder*.

28. Quoted in Watt, *Rise of the Novel*, 53–54.

29. Kernan, *Printing Technology*, 74.

30. The fullest description of the closeness of authorship and criminality during the eighteenth century is in Pat Rogers's *Grub Street: Studies in a Subculture* (London: Methuen, 1972), esp. 18–93. See also Linebaugh, "The Ordinary of Newgate and His *Account*," 255–56 and 269.

31. Contrary to Furbank and Owens; see *Canonisation*, 72–74.

32. Hibbert, *Road to Tyburn*, 145.

33. See, in addition to Hibbert, the introductory note to the Shakespeare Head edition of Defoe's *Narrative* of the life of Sheppard (208).

34. Richardson, *Selected Letters*, 197.

PART II: Crime and Identity

1. See Furbank and Owens, *Canonisation;* and *Defoe De-Attributions*.

2. Daniel Defoe, *An Appeal to Honour and Justice, Tho' it be of His Worst Enemies* (London: J. Baker, 1715), 46.

3. Furbank and Owens, *Canonisation*, 148.

4. Paula R. Backscheider, *Daniel Defoe: His Life* (Baltimore: Johns Hopkins University Press, 1989), 58, 60, 119, and 322.

5. Backscheider, *Daniel Defoe*, 322–25.

6. Mascuch, *Origins*, 164.

7. Harris, "Trials and Criminal Biographies," 22. The writers in his employ were thus able to make use of Applebee's contacts in Newgate and at the Old Bailey and could count on a secure audience for whatever criminal texts they might produce. See also William Lee, *Daniel Defoe: His Life, and Recently Discovered Writings: Extending from 1716 to 1729,* 3 vols. (London: Hotten, 1869), 1:343–44.

8. See Howson, "The Fortunes of Moll Flanders," *Thief-Taker General,* 156–70.

9. Defoe, *Selected Writings from Applebee's Journal,* printed with *Moll Flanders,* vol. 2 (Oxford: Basil Blackwell for the Shakespeare Head Press, 1928), 179. All references in the text are to this edition.

10. On parallels between high- and low-life crimes, see Novak, *Realism, Myth, and History in Defoe's Fiction,* 130. He quotes a passage from *A General History of the Pyrates,* in which Defoe describes Captain England's crew "dividing the Spoil and Plunder of Nations among themselves": "I can't say, but that if they had known what was doing in *England,* at the same Time, by the *South-Sea* Directors, and their Directors, they would certainly have had this Reflection for their Consolation, *viz.* that whatever Robberies they had committed, they might be pretty sure they were not the greatest Villains then living in the World" (134).

11. See Homer O. Brown, "The Displaced Self in the Novels of Daniel Defoe," *Studies in Eighteenth-Century Culture* 4 (1975): 61–94, esp. 71–76. As Brown observes, the London of the *Plague Year* is just the most striking example of a recurring dread: "Any conversation, even the slightest human contact, carries the risk of death" (73).

12. See Howson, *Thief-Taker General,* 91–92.

13. Charles Gildon, *The Life and Strange Surprizing Adventures of Mr. D—— DeF——, of London, Hosier . . . in a Dialogue between Him, Robinson Crusoe, and his Man Friday,* 2d ed. (London, 1719), 33.

14. Maximillian Novak, "Defoe's Theory of Fiction," in *Studies in Philology* 61 (1964): 668.

15. John Beattie writes that "a great deal of concern was expressed through the 1720s in pamphlets and in the press and by the authorities about the extent of crime in the capital" (*Crime and the Courts,* 216), but it is impossible to know from the surviving court records how closely this concern reflected real shifts in the level of prosecution (which in turn never simply mirrors the incidence of crime) or to what degree it was a product of news reporting itself. "Even a small number of incidents reported in the press," as Beattie writes, "can create an impression of extreme danger" (218). Defoe and his contemporaries were aware of the potential for mischief in sensational reporting, as is evident in a (disputed) text first attributed to Defoe by James Crossley, *The Lives of the Six Notorious Street Robbers* of 1726. The author of that text complains that "on a sudden we found street-robberies became the common practice, conversation was full of the variety of them, the newspapers had them

every day, and sometimes more than were ever committed; and those that were committed were set off by the invention of the writers, with so many particulars, and so many more than were ever heard of by the persons robbed, that made the facts be matter of entertainment, and either pleasant or formidable, as the authors thought fit, and perhaps, sometimes, made formal robberies, *in nubibus,* to furnish out amusements for their readers" (*A Brief Historical Account of the Lives of Six Notorious Street Robbers,* in *Romances and Narratives by Daniel Defoe,* ed. George A. Aitken [London: Dent, 1895], 16:371).

16. See Faller, *Crime and Defoe,* for a consideration of Defoe's alterations to the generic conventions of criminal biography.

### SIX: Colonel Jack's Childhood

1. Defoe, *Colonel Jack,* 3, 7. Subsequent references will be given in the text.

2. Defoe, *Lives of the Six Notorious Street-Robbers,* 361. Samuel Johnson describes the glass houses as a harbor of impoverished authors as well as thieves and orphans in the 1744 *Life of Savage:* see Johnson, *Selected Writings,* ed. Patrick Crutwell (Harmondsworth: Penguin, 1968), 104.

3. See *Moll Flanders,* 212, for a similar episode of a pickpocket "delivered up to the Rage of the Street."

4. By various internal evidence this episode can be placed in the early 1680s, but, if the historical chronology underpinning Defoe's fictions is carefully controlled, the descriptive or more broadly sociological details generally refer to the time of composition rather than the ostensible historical period of the action. On the question of chronology, especially in relation to *Roxana,* see Rodney Baine, "The Evidence from Defoe's Title Pages," *Studies in Bibliography* 25 (1972): 189–91; and Samuel Holt Monk's introduction to *Colonel Jack,* xxii.

5. John Richetti writes that "*Colonel Jack* continues the exciting enumeration of the techniques of illicit survival, techniques which in their very exactness mitigate the blame we might attach to them"; see *Defoe's Narratives: Situations and Structures* (Oxford: Clarendon Press, 1975), 153. Richetti's analysis of Defoe's longer narratives centers on the problem of the construction of selfhood among the tangle of circumstances and "social and ideological realities" that both determine and imprison it (17). My concerns overlap with Richetti's, but his structuralist orientation (at least in this work), which leads him to seek the "mythic" structures and oppositions lying beneath the textual surface, is far from my interest in questions of verisimilitude, voice, and the appropriation of popular forms of representation—with what, in fact, lies *on* and *around* the textual surface.

6. Jack has earlier commented, with regard to pickpocketing, that "the Opportunities were so many, the Country People that come to *London,* so foolish, so gaping, and so engag'd in looking around them, that it was a Trade with no great hazard annex'd to it" (17).

7. Jack is fifteen when he first ventures out with Will, but both physically and as regards

his experience of the world he is much younger than his age—oddly, since he has been living for some years on the street, in poverty, in the company of beggars and pickpockets. When he and Will are dividing the spoils from this first robbery, he innocently asks, "*must we have it all? we have it!* says [Will], who should have it? Why says I, must the Man have none of it again that lost it"; which prompts this from Will: "He Laught at me, you are but a little Boy *says he,* that's true, but I thought you had not been such a Child neither" (21).

8.  A few pages after this episode, when Jack has successfully taken a pocketbook full of notes and bills from a gentleman's pocket, Will describes to him the gentleman's reaction to the loss: "why, the Gentleman is Raving and half Distracted: He Stamps and Crys, and Tears his very Cloths, *he says,* he is utterly undone, and ruin'd" (46). Unlike the passage of Colonel Jack at the tree, however, this glimpse of the gentleman's raving is comical precisely because we remain outside it, at the distance of secondhand report.

### SEVEN: Moll Flanders and Her Confederates

1.  Defoe, *Robinson Crusoe,* ed. Angus Ross (Harmondsworth: Penguin, 1965), 25.

2.  Defoe, *Moll Flanders,* 343. Subsequent references will be given in the text.

3.  See Defoe (attrib.), *Street-Robberies Consider'd* (London, 1728), 4–8. The text presents a number of interesting parallels to, and no less interesting divergences from, *Colonel Jack* and *Moll Flanders,* but the attribution to Defoe has been called into question, most notably by Clinton S. Bond, "*Street-Robberies Consider'd* and the Canon of Daniel Defoe," *Texas Studies in Literature and Language* 13 (1971): 431–45.

4.  On the first page of her narrative Moll lays the blame for her future "Course of Life" on the lack of provision, in the form of a "*House* of *Orphans,*" for the children of criminals, "where they are Bred up, Cloath'd, Fed, Taught, and when fit to go out, are plac'd out to Trades, or to Services, so as to be well able to provide for themselves by an honest industrious Behaviour . . . . Had this been the Custom in our Country, I had not been left a poor desolate Girl without Friends, without Cloaths, without Help or Helper in the World, as was my Fate . . . nor brought into a Course of Life, which was not only scandalous in itself, but which in its ordinary Course, tended to the swift Destruction both of Soul and Body" (8). Yet, given Moll's eminently respectable upbringing with a poor but "very sober pious Woman" in Colchester (10), and her terror and aversion at the prospect of having to "go to Service," her sociological protest has to be read with some skepticism, however earnestly Defoe proposed such a system of education for criminal orphans elsewhere. See, for example, Defoe's *Augusta Triumphans: or the Way to Make London the Most Flourishing City in the Universe . . . Concluding with an Effectual Method to Prevent Street Robberies* (London, 1728); and *Second Thoughts Are Best* (London, 1729 [for 1728]); also Michael Shinagel, *Daniel Defoe and Middle-Class Gentility* (Cambridge: Harvard University Press, 1968), 144–49.

5.  See Williams, *Country and the City,* 165–66.

6. *Imagining the Penitentiary,* 48.

7. Defoe, *Roxana: The Fortunate Mistress,* ed. Jane Jack (Oxford: Oxford University Press, 1964), 1. All references in the text are to this edition.

8. Defoe, *The Great Law of Subordination Consider'd; or, the Insolence and Unsufferable Behaviour of Servants in England Duly Enquir'd Into* (London, 1724), 210–11.

9. See Jürgen Habermas, *The Structural Transformation of the Public Sphere: An Inquiry into a Category of Bourgeois Society,* trans. Thomas Burger, with Frederick Lawrence (London: Polity Press, 1989), 20–26 and 31–43, for a discussion of the roles played by such institutions as the news and the coffeehouse in the construction of a public that set itself in opposition to many of the traditional institutions of ruling authority—only, of course, to replace them with more liberal forms of ideological hegemony.

10. Habermas, *Structural Transformation,* 36.

11. See Terry Eagleton, *The Function of Criticism: From "The Spectator" to Post-Structuralism* (London: Verso, 1984), 26–27.

12. Auerbach, *Mimesis,* 554.

13. Eagleton quotes—secondhand, from an unpublished manuscript by Timothy Foley—an observation attributed to Defoe on the social composition of the public sphere: "you'll find very few Coffee-houses in this opulent City, without an illiterate Mechanick, Commenting upon the most material Occurrences, and Judging the Actions of the greatest in *Europe,* and rarely a Victualing House but you meet with a *Tinker,* a *Cobbler,* or a *Porter,* Criticizing upon the Speeches of Majesty, or the writings of the most celebrated Men of the Age" (*Function of Criticism,* 14). Implausible as this sounds as a literal description, it points to a sense of social openness, a new discursive permeability: the coffeehouse as an instrument of cultural leveling.

14. Defoe, *The History of the Remarkable Life of John Sheppard,* printed with *The Fortunate Mistress* (1724; rpt., Oxford: Basil Blackwell for the Shakespeare Head Press, 1928), 2:161. All references in the text are to this edition.

15. On the profusion of Sheppard literature, see Howson, *Thief-Taker General,* 222–26 and 322–23; Faller, *Turned to Account;* and Rawlings, *Drunks,* 39–46.

16. Watt, *Rise of the Novel,* 134.

17. Watt, *Rise of the Novel,* 125. See more generally 124–130, for a discussion of the psychological character of the Puritanism Defoe inherited, its moralistic violence and "disengagement of economic matters from religious and moral sanctions" (127). What other critics have treated as ironies, Watt describes as "accidents produced by the random application of narrative authenticity to conflicts in Defoe's social and moral and religious world, accidents which unwittingly reveal to us the serious discrepancies in his system of values" (130).

18. Watt, *Rise of the Novel,* 134, 113, 114, 128.

19. Brown, "Displaced Self," 71, 80–86. Brown portrays Defoe as an existentially anguished allegorist, his anguish stemming from a sense of the slipperiness and vulnerability

of identity: "unable to give a true account of the self, he is doomed to speak the words of 'another-body' as if they were his own, putting on the disguise of one fictive self after another" (86).

20. Brown, "Displaced Self," 81.

21. Watt, *Rise of the Novel,* 128. In his notes to *Moll Flanders* G. A. Starr quotes passages from *Roxana, Captain Singleton,* and *Colonel Jack* which all turn on the same distinction between remorse for the crime and remorse out of fear of punishment—not a distinction of which Defoe can be said to be unaware.

22. Some hours after their first farewell—both have just discovered they were cheated in their expectations of a rich marriage—Moll falls "into a vehement Fit of crying, every now and then calling him by his Name, which was *James, O Jemy!* said I, *come back, come back,* I'll give you all I have" (153). He later tells her he heard her voice "very plain upon *Delamere Forest,* at a Place about 12 Miles off," and, when he also tells her the exact words she has earlier reported, "I then began to be amaz'd and surpriz'd," she writes, "and indeed frighted" (154).

23. Before the deployment of fingerprinting and the multiple instruments of naming—passports, identity cards, and the like—anonymity was easier to maintain, though both Defoe at the beginning and Caleb Williams at the end of the century were found out through the texts they had published. On fingerprints, see Carlo Ginzburg, "Clues: Morelli, Freud, and Sherlock Holmes," in *The Sign of Three: Dupin, Holmes, Peirce,* ed. Umberto Eco and Thomas A. Sebeok (Bloomington: Indiana University Press, 1983), 104–9.

EIGHT: Guilt and the Reader of *Roxana*

1. The idea of an "assumption of guilt" derives from Alexander Welsh's discussion in *Strong Representations* of what he calls the "modern construction of guilt," which he first finds articulated in Scott's *Waverley* and which he explicitly contrasts to traditional conceptions of guilt, innocence, and authority found in Fielding's *Tom Jones.* Defoe is in certain ways more "modern" than Fielding, despite the strong persistence in his work of an archaic religiosity, with its devils, portents, and prophetic dreaming. For all the traditional strains in his work, Defoe is closer than Fielding to a contractarian rather than patriarchal model of social relations; closer to a modern psychological understanding of memory and of identity as layered of memory; and, at least in *Roxana,* closer to a modern construction of guilt, in which its ineradicable surplus is displaced onto a double (89–99).

2. See Watt, *Rise of the Novel,* 74–85; G. A. Starr, *Defoe and Spiritual Autobiography.*

3. See Cynthia Herrup, "Law and Morality in Seventeenth-Century England," 110–12: if, in the later seventeenth century, "crimes were sins, yet sinning was universal" (110), this meant that "the threat of criminality was both internal and external; the criminal could not be defined simply as something alien and other" (112). Even with the shifts brought on by

secularization, the grounds for identification with transgressors remained strong. See also J. A. Sharpe, "Last Dying Speeches," 159.

4. Welsh, *Strong Representations,* 94.

5. See Bernbaum, *Mary Carleton Narratives,* esp. 31–32 and 84–87, for brief but suggestive discussions of the early history of realism as exemplified by the frequently mendacious and freely plagiarized texts of Kirkman and his late-seventeenth-century fellows.

6. See Defoe, *Roxana,* 204–5. The history of Roxana's daughter that I reconstruct here is spread out in fragments over more than a hundred pages; the reader is forced to piece it together, as young Susan herself pieces together the story of her origins and abandonment, from discontinuous episodes and strands of evidence.

7. Susan's powers of observation and recall are most worryingly displayed when she describes Roxana's Turkish dress to a company visiting near the ship which is to take Roxana out of England and away from her criminal past—for among the company is the Quaker woman, who has earlier seen Roxana show off the same dress to her Dutch husband. The *Turkish Habit,* under Susan's description, links the respectable merchant's wife (the Roxana the Quaker woman knows) to her past as a woman of scandal and glamour (the Roxana Susan worked for). Hoping to derail the girl's narrative, Roxana interrupts Susan to ask how she is able to remember so clearly her mistress's dancing before a crowd in her "fine Outlandish Dress" (288): "O Madam! *says she,* we that were Servants, stood by ourselves in a Corner, but so, as we cou'd see more than some Strangers; besides, *says she,* it was all our Conversation for several Days in the Family, and what one did not observe, another did" (289). The servants' unreciprocated gaze from the corner forms the basis of a collective epistemology, a socially marginal but potentially subversive custom of observation and judgment.

8. See, for example, Defoe, *Roxana,* 311, 315, and 328. This absence at the center of *Roxana,* the lack of any clear report of Amy's alleged crime against Susan, is in accord with Roxana's position and burden as narrator, her habit of pushing herself to the verge of an admission and then falling away into ominous, empty hints.

9. Shinagel, *Defoe and Middle-Class Gentility,* 170.

10. Defoe, *The True and Genuine Account of the Life and Actions of the Late Jonathan Wild,* printed with *Colonel Jack* (Oxford: Basil Blackwell for the Shakespeare Head Press, 1927), 2:236. All references in the text are to this edition.

11. See the picaresque-inflected *Life of Jonathan Wild, from His Birth to His Death . . . By H.D. late Clerk to Justice R——* (London, 1725); Defoe's authorship is unproved.

12. Like all of Defoe's protagonists, Roxana wants power, but her rejection of the merchant's and Sir Robert's views of marriage does not constitute, in any sense, a subjection of them to her will, whereas her acquiescence would entail her own subjection to theirs, even if in the event her subordinate position were not abused. Although Roxana frequently dis-

parages her own position, Defoe feels an apparently irresistible impulse to give us the debate in her voice, to allow her the stronger and more intensely felt arguments, and to contrast her use of reason to her opponents' dependence on uninterrogated custom.

13. A similar alignment with the outlaw is evident in the life of Captain Misson from the second volume of the *General History of the Pyrates,* published in 1728. The author of that text (the attribution to Defoe has been questioned) projects a communist utopia in order to articulate both the longing for an egalitarian commonwealth of free persons and the likely outcome of such longings in a world still governed by the laws of possessive individualism: criminality, that is, bleeds into the struggle for political and economic liberty. Misson's experiment collapses under the weight of dissension and the violence of the outside world, but *Libertalia's* demise does not lead the author to condemn the pirates' criminal appropriation of a freedom both dreamed and denied by their native cultures or Misson's outlaw desire for a community of equals unimaginable under the oppressive conditions of property and law in the old world. The aim is not necessarily to enlist our agreement with the pirates' anarchic critique but to strip the law of its ideological mystery, its pretensions to speak for a providentially sanctioned history or a natural human condition. See Defoe (attrib.), *A General History of the Pyrates,* ed. Manuel Schonhorn (London: Dent, 1972).

14. Foucault, *Discipline and Punish,* 194.

15. Auerbach, *Mimesis,* 554.

16. Auerbach, *Mimesis,* 463.

17. On social divisions among the audiences for the different criminal genres, see Linebaugh's "Ordinary of Newgate and His *Account,*" 246–47; and Starr's introduction to *Moll Flanders,* xvii. While contemporaries tacitly assumed that genre is an embodiment of class difference, they also betrayed an uneasy awareness that the distinctions were no longer so clear, that the tastes of "People of the better Sort" were suffering the contamination bred by contact with the pleasures of "the rabble" and, of course, vice versa.

18. McKeon, *Origins,* 98.

## PART III: The Judge and the Author

1. *An Apology for the Conduct of Mrs. Teresia Constantia Phillips* (London, 1748–49), quoted in Zirker, "General Introduction" to Henry Fielding, *Enquiry,* xxvi n. The passage is quoted in full as the epigraph to part 3 of the present book.

2. Martin Battestin, in Henry Fielding, *Amelia,* ed. Martin C. Battestin (Middletown, Conn.: Wesleyan University Press, 1983), 45 n. All references in the text are to this edition.

3. Henry Fielding, *Enquiry,* 77. Subsequent references will be given in the text.

4. Henry Fielding, *The Covent-Garden Journal* and *A Plan of the Universal Register Office,* ed. Bertrand A. Goldgar (Oxford: Clarendon Press, 1988), 59. All references in the text are to this edition.

5. Fielding, *A Charge Delivered to the Grand Jury*, in Zirker, *Enquiry*, 29.

6. Sarah Fielding, *Familiar Letters*, quoted in the "General Introduction" to *Covent-Garden Journal*, xxxiv.

7. Fielding, *Amelia*, 394. Subsequent references will be given in the text.

8. On the spate of anti-Pamela literature, see Alan Dugald McKillop, *Samuel Richardson, Printer and Novelist* (Chapel Hill: University of North Carolina Press, 1936), 73–86; and Bernard Kreissman, *Pamela-Shamela: A Study of the Criticisms, Burlesques, Parodies, and Adaptations of Richardson's "Pamela"* (N.p.: University of Nebraska Press, 1960), 23–53.

9. Henry Fielding, *Shamela*, published with *Joseph Andrews*, ed. Douglas Brooks (London: Oxford University Press, 1970), 345. All references in the text are to this edition.

10. The conflictual relationship between Richardson and Fielding is rehearsed in every discussion of either's work, as in every history of the emergence of the novel as a new genre. In *Natural Masques: Gender and Identity in Fielding's Plays and Novels* (Stanford: Stanford University Press, 1995) Jill Campbell elegantly distills the accumulated critical commentary on the Richardson/Fielding dyad as a point of origin for her reflections on the (often uninterrogated) gender dualisms that underlie it. On the conflict between first-person and omniscient modes of narration, see Bender, *Imagining the Penitentiary*, esp. 145–46.

11. Henry Fielding, *Joseph Andrews*, ed. Martin C. Battestin (Middletown, Conn.: Wesleyan University Press, 1967), 189.

12. Claude Rawson, *Henry Fielding and the Augustan Ideal under Stress* (London: Routledge and Kegan Paul, 1972), 61.

13. J. Paul Hunter, *Occasional Form: Henry Fielding and the Chains of Circumstance* (Baltimore: Johns Hopkins University Press, 1975), 192.

14. Fielding, *Amelia*, 66.

15. See Campbell, *Natural Masques*, 211; and Battestin's notes to pp. 27 and 66 of *Amelia*.

NINE: The Politics and Poetics of Crime and Punishment

1. *Parliamentary History*, May 8, 1780; quoted in Zirker, "General Introduction" to Fielding, *Enquiry*, xx.

2. Peter Linebaugh, *The London Hanged: Crime and Civil Society in the Eighteenth Century* (London: Allen Lane, the Penguin Press, 1991), 150.

3. See Linebaugh, *London Hanged*, xxi, 70, 98–100.

4. Beattie, *Crime and the Courts*, 226. Beattie gives the following estimates of the numbers of men discharged from the forces: "in 1698–99: 106,000; in 1713–14: 157,000; in 1749–50: 79,000; in 1764–65: 155,000; in 1784–85: 160,000" (226).

5. Smollett, *History of England* (1814 ed.), quoted in Beattie, *Crime and the Courts*, 227.

6. *Hanging, Not Punishment Enough, for Murtherers, High-way Men, and House-Breakers* (London, 1701), 2.

7. Walpole, *Correspondence with Sir Horace Mann*, 4:111, quoted in Beattie, *Crime and the Courts*, 219 and 226.

8. Beattie, *Crime and the Courts*, 229.

9. Fielding, *Charge to the Grand Jury*, 29.

10. The Constitution, as it was conceived in the political discourses of the eighteenth century, was not a document, a single foundational text, but rather an established, historically rooted political economy, as Fielding defines it in the preface to the *Enquiry:* "Now in this Word, *The Constitution*, are included the original and fundamental Law of the Kingdom, from whence all Powers are derived, and by which they are circumscribed; all legislative and executive Authority; all those municipal Provisions which are commonly called *The Laws;* and, *lastly*, the Customs, Manners, and Habits of the People. These, joined together, do, I apprehend, form the Political, as the several Members of the Body, the animal Oeconomy, with the Humours and Habit, compose that which is called the Natural Constitution" (65).

11. See, for example, issue 27 of the *Covent-Garden Journal*, April 4, 1752.

12. See the *Enquiry*, 80; and *Jonathan Wild*, ed. David Nokes (Harmondsworth: Penguin, 1982), 61. Fielding's loathsome Wild, interestingly, subscribes to the same view of the obligations of "the low, mean, useful part of mankind" which Fielding sets out in the *Enquiry*.

13. Malvin R. Zirker, *Fielding's Social Pamphlets: A Study of "An Enquiry into the Causes of the Late Increase of Robbers" and "A Proposal for Making an Effectual Provision for the Poor"* (Berkeley: University of California Press, 1966), 95.

14. See, in addition, Zirker, *Fielding's Social Pamphlets*, 109–12; and "General Introduction," lxii–lxiv.

15. *Hanging, Not Punishment Enough*, 2.

16. Welch elaborated on his observations in the 1753 *Letter upon the Subject of Robberies:* There have, within a few years, arisen in the out-skirts of this town, a kind of traffic in old ruinous buildings, which the occupiers fill up with straw and flock beds, which they nightly lett out at two-pence for a single person, or three-pence a couple; nor is the least regard paid to decency. Men and women are promiscuously entertained; and in my searches after villains, I have found two or three couple in one room, who were perfect strangers to each other before the preceding night, then in bed together. Indeed I have seen debauchery in these houses carried farther than this; for sometimes two women have been in bed with one man, and two men with one woman. Four or five beds are often in one room; and what with the nastiness of these wretches, and their numbers, such an inconceivable stench has arose from them, that I have been hardly able to bear it the little time my duty required my stay. (52)

17. Fielding, *Covent-Garden Journal*, 268.

18. See also the *Covent-Garden Journal*, 269–70; and, for critiques of modern appropriations of the "carnivalesque," Linebaugh, *London Hanged*, xvii–xviii; and E. P. Thompson,

*Customs in Common* (London: Merlin, 1992), 48–49. See also Natalie Zemon Davis, "The Reasons of Misrule," *Society and Culture in Early Modern France* (Stanford: Stanford University Press, 1975), 97–123.

19. Mandeville, *Enquiry,* 20.

20. Linebaugh elaborates on the criminalization of poverty and labor in *London Hanged,* esp. 70–73 and 101–11.

21. Linebaugh, "Tyburn Riot," 113.

22. The term *counter-theater* is taken from Thompson, *Customs in Common,* 48–49.

23. See Mandeville, *Enquiry,* 38–41; Fielding, *Proposal for Making an Effectual Provision for the Poor,* 268.

24. *Aristotle's Art of Poetry* (London, 1705), 234–35.

25. For a contemporary counterargument, see Samuel Johnson, *Rambler* 114 (2: 241–47).

26. Sir Joshua Reynolds, *Letters,* ed. Frederick Whiley Hilles (Cambridge: Cambridge University Press, 1929), 127. See also Burke's *Philosophical Enquiry into the Origin of Our Ideas of the Sublime and Beautiful,* ed. J. T. Boulton (London: Routledge and Kegan Paul, 1958), pt. 1, sec. 15; and Boswell, *The Hypochondriack,* 68: "the curiosity which impels people to be present at such affecting scenes, is certainly a proof of sensibility, not of callousness. For it is observed, that the greatest proportion of the spectators is composed of women" (qtd. in James Boswell, *Life of Johnson,* ed. George Birbeck Hill, rev. ed., ed. L. F. Powell [Oxford: Clarendon Press, 1934], 2:93).

## TEN: Fielding as Magistrate

1. Fielding, *A Clear State of the Case of Elizabeth Canning,* in Zirker, *Enquiry and Related Writings,* 297. All references in the text are to this edition.

2. See Judith Moore, *The Appearance of Truth: The Story of Elizabeth Canning and Eighteenth-Century Narrative* (Newark: University of Delaware Press, 1994), for a thorough presentation of the innumerable conflicting texts and oral accounts that proliferated around the Canning case. See also Zirker's "General Introduction," xciv–cxiv. The fullest compilation of evidence is in the *State Trials* 19 (1809–26): 283–692.

3. Zirker, "General Introduction," xcvii. Zirker reaches this conclusion from evidence that came out at a later trial, this time against Canning, for perjury.

4. Quoted in Zirker, "General Introduction," xcvii.

5. After presenting the principal objections to Canning's story, Fielding sets out the one point that he believes to be "incontestably true":

> That is, that the Girl, after the Absence of a Month, returned on the 29th of *January,* in the dreadful Condition above-described. This being an established Fact, a very fair Presumption follows, that she was confined some-where, and by some Person; that this Confinement was of equal Duration with her Absence; that she was

almost starved to Death; that she was confined in a Place, whence it was difficult to make her Escape; that, however, this Escape was possible; and that, at length, she actually made it: All these are Circumstances, which arise from the Nature of the Fact itself. They are what *Tully* calls *Evidentia Rei,* and are stronger than the positive Testimony of any Witnesses. (292)

Fielding's "presumptions" from the core "fact" of the case—Canning's absence and reappearance—are plausible but far from necessary inferences, even were the obvious possible complicating factors of lying and amnesia proved to be inapplicable. Fielding enlarges the field of *evidentia rei* to strengthen a case in which circumstantial evidence was sparse, while the "positive Testimony of Witnesses" and the array of theories were bewilderingly contradictory. On the question of circumstantial evidence and the presumptions it authorizes, see Welsh, *Strong Representations,* 10–18.

6. When, a month later, Hall recanted her testimony, she said that "when she was at Mr. *Fielding's* she at first spoke the truth, but that she was told that *that* was not the truth, and was *terrified and threatened to be sent to Newgate and prosecuted as a* felon, *unless she would speak the truth*" (Sir Crisp Gascoyne, *An Address to the Liverymen of the City of London* [1754], qtd. by Zirker in Fielding, *Clear State,* 301). Zirker also quotes an announcement from the *Public Advertiser* for February 10, 1753, which presents the Bow Street version of the interrogation: "On *Thursday* Evening a Girl who lived in the House, and who was apprehended by a Warrant from the Justice, was brought before him, and was under Examination from Six 'till Twelve at Night; when, after many hard Struggles and stout Denials of the *Truth,* she, at length, confessed the Whole" (qtd. in "General Introduction," c). But the "hard Struggles" and "stout Denials" could also be taken, and were taken by writers in the anti-Canning camp, as evidence of intimidation by Fielding.

7. Critics of the guilty verdicts handed down against Wells and Squires, and of Fielding's role in furnishing the crucial evidence for prosecution, zeroed in on the way Hall's affidavit had been obtained. "Can two persons who swear the same thing agree in all particulars, and yet that thing be false?" asked John Hill in his *Story of Elizabeth Canning Considered.* "Yes certainly, if one has heard the other's Story. As certainly if the same Hand drew up both the Informations, and both that swore are perjured." The following year, at the trial of Elizabeth Canning for perjury, for which Hall's recantation of her earlier affidavit was decisive, the prosecution observed that "it is very remarkable, that Virtue Hall's confession was not taken at first (for what reason I know not) *viva voce* before Justice Fielding. She was thrust out of the room to retire with her solicitor, who was also Canning's solicitor: her information was reduced into writing, and was two hours in preparing. After this, what mighty wonder is there, that when she came into the justice's presence again, she should repeat her lesson without the least hesitation?" (*State Trials* 19:317; both passages qtd. by Zirker in the *Clear State of the Case,* 308–9).

8. Welsh, *Strong Representations,* 48–49, 58.

9. See the *Clear State of the Case,* 285.

10. For a summary of the events in the case and a discussion of the political context, see Linebaugh, "The Tyburn Riot against the Surgeons," in *Albion's Fatal Tree,* 89–102; and Zirker, "General Introduction" to the *True State of the Case of Bosavern Penlez,* in Fielding, *Enquiry.* All references to the Penlez pamphlet in the text are to this edition.

11. Quoted in, respectively, Zirker, "General Introduction," xxxiv; and Linebaugh, "Tyburn Riot," 89.

12. Linebaugh, "Tyburn Riot," 92.

13. *The Case of the Unfortunate Bosavern Penlez* (London, 1749), 18.

14. *Case of the Unfortunate Bosavern Penlez,* 23.

15. Penlez's conflicting explanations (see 54–56) invite suspicion and the probability that the bundle of linen was stolen from Wood's house on the night of the riot by someone who broke into the house with the other rioters, combined with the fact that the bundle was found on Penlez, perhaps makes it appear obvious that he was involved in the rioting. No evidence in Fielding's text, however, places Penlez at the scene of the riot, and Fielding never attempts to make the inference from the testimony he has, so Penlez's guilt is, at least in the *True State of the Case,* purely speculative. Witnesses were produced at Penlez's trial to place him on the scene: Peter and Jane Wood, the owners of the house from which the linen was taken. But they were highly suspect witnesses: one of the defendants tried with Penlez was acquitted when it was proved, despite the Woods' sworn testimony, that he had only arrived at their house along with the soldiers sent to guard it. And a local tradesman testified during Penlez's trial that "for my part I would not hang a dog or cat upon their evidence, they keep such a bad house and other things" (*Old Bailey Sessions Papers,* September 6–14, 1749, 134).

16. "I hope I have said enough," Fielding writes near the end of his summation of the evidence, "to prove that this was a Riot as called for some Example, and that the Man who was made that Example, deserved his Fate" (59). Yet, even if we could agree to Fielding's reading of the bawdy-house demonstrations as a threat to the political order and could endorse capital punishment for crimes against property (or for any crimes), there is a discontinuity in the evidence Fielding assembles: Penlez "deserved his fate" for possession of stolen goods, not for pulling down houses. On the relative value of property and persons, see *True State of the Case,* 45.

ELEVEN: *Amelia*

1. Roland Barthes, *On Racine,* trans. Richard Howard (New York: Hill and Wang, 1981), 98. My thinking on the representation of space—especially the space of imprisonment—in *Amelia* has also been influenced by Gaston Bachelard, *The Poetics of Space,* trans. Maria Jolas (Boston: Beacon Press, 1969); and M. M. Bakhtin, "Forms of Time and Chronotope in the

Novel," in Bakhtin, *The Dialogic Imagination,* ed. Michael Holquist, trans. Caryl Emerson and Michael Holquist (Austin: University of Texas Press, 1981).

2. For the allegorical reading, see, for example, Thomas E. Maresca, *Epic to Novel* (Columbus: Ohio State University Press, 1974). The strongest presentation of the realist view is in Bender, *Imagining the Penitentiary.* Anthony J. Hassall, in "Fielding's *Amelia:* Dramatic and Authorial Narration," *Novel* (Spring 1972): 225–33, argues that Fielding found himself trapped by the conflicting demands of allegorical and realist modes. For a more complex variation of this last claim, see Terry Castle, *Masquerade and Civilization: The Carnivalesque in Eighteenth-Century English Culture and Fiction* (Stanford: Stanford University Press, 1986).

3. Ann Donnellan, quoted in Battestin, "Introduction," liii.

4. For the dialectical argument, see McKeon, *Origins of the English Novel,* esp. 1–22 and 410–21; for the convergence of the rival authors, see, for example, Peter Sabor, "*Amelia* and *Sir Charles Grandison:* The Convergence of Fielding and Richardson," *Wascana Review* 17, no. 2 (Fall 1982): 3–18. Also see Hunter, *Occasional Form,* 212–14. To Bender the movement toward realism represents a tightening rather than a loosening of authorial control.

5. In his "Advertisement" to the 1754 revision of *Jonathan Wild* Fielding himself raised the conflict between realist and allegorical readings of Newgate as the setting of his fiction: "The truth is, as a very corrupt state of morals is here represented, the scene seems very properly to be laid in Newgate; nor do I see any reason for introducing any allegory at all" (Fielding, *Jonathan Wild,* 34). Not only does Fielding's sentence cancel out its own meaning—for doesn't it say that Newgate was "properly" chosen as the site of a narrative of moral corruption precisely for its allegorical suitability?—but it continues with a proviso that mocks the denial of allegory. Fielding sees no "reason for introducing any allegory at all," that is, "unless we will agree that there are without those walls, some other bodies of men of worse morals than those within; and who have, consequently, a right to change places with its present inhabitants" (34). The story "seems very properly to be laid in Newgate" because the prison is so ideologically charged by ongoing struggles to control definitions of criminality and power that it can symbolically stand for a full range of social, political, and moral conflicts.

6. Roland Barthes, "The Reality Effect," in *The Rustle of Language,* trans. Richard Howard (New York: Hill and Wang, 1964), 146.

7. Barthes, of course, recognized that realist trivia are not *just* gratuitous, but it is the material excess, the naturalist residue, of such signifiers he means to account for. His explanation of the textual and ideological effects of realistic detail is useful, on its own terms, but the inescapable impurity of the descriptive sign argues against what Barthes calls in the same essay "the great mythic opposition of the *true-to-life* (the lifelike) and the *intelligible*" (146).

8. Quoted in David Bindman, *Hogarth* (New York: Thames and Hudson, 1985), 62.

9. Bender, *Imagining the Penitentiary*, 181.

10. This abstract quality of *Amelia*'s emblematic Newgate scenes is underlined by their isolation one from another: the only suggestion of temporal or spatial relationships among the inmates is provided in Fielding's stark transitions—"A little further they beheld . . . They now beheld . . . A great Noise now arose . . . his Attention was suddenly diverted by"— which frame the successive tableaux by noting a shift in Booth's attention. The scenes are linked rhetorically, generally by antithesis, rather than narratively. See also Castle, *Masquerade*, 199–202.

11. Peter LePage, "The Prison and the Dark Beauty of *Amelia*," *Criticism* 9 (1967): 341.

12. I owe the last term to Angus Fletcher, *Allegory: The Theory of a Symbolic Mode* (Ithaca: Cornell University Press, 1964), 23. For a discussion of Fielding's treatment of the private and public spheres in *Amelia* in terms of struggle over the enforcement of received categories of gender, see John P. Zomchick, "'A Penetration which Nothing Can Deceive': Gender and Juridical Discourse in Some Eighteenth-Century Narratives," *SEL: Studies in English Literature, 1500–1900* 29 (1989): 552–55.

13. Bachelard, *Poetics of Space*, xxxi; Castle, *Masquerade*, 204.

14. Miss Matthews's role in the presentation of Booth's story is much greater than most commentaries on *Amelia* suggest, and I think that neither her own nor Booth's narrative can be seen as straightforwardly first-person. During his recitation Miss Matthews offers a varied and subtly transformative commentary on the events he reports, by turns making light of Amelia's want of spirit, as she sees it, and responding to Booth's story as to a seduction. When Booth, for example, describing the early days of his marriage with a vividness of erotic recollection many readers seem not to have noticed, says, "I had not yet awakened from that delicious Dream of Bliss in which the Possession of *Amelia* had lulled me," Fielding reports that "here Miss *Mathews* sighed, and cast the tenderest of Looks on *Booth*, who thus continued his Story" (91). Several times she persuades Booth to recount in detail sexually charged episodes he intended to pass over in silence, and she flatteringly interprets his reports of Amelia's devotion as no more than what is due his prettiness. Her own interpolated memories—she had known Booth and, by reputation, Amelia's family several years before—trigger further explorations of *his* recollections of youth before marrying Amelia and so partially release him from the responsibilities his narrative assumes. Although Booth seems oblivious to Miss Matthews's sexual attentions to him, he responds more and more openly to her flirtations over the course of his story, and this leads him to give a greater emphasis to the implicit erotic theme than he seems to intend at the outset.

15. Zomchick argues that "the boundary between the public and the private spheres" in *Amelia* "is crossed and recrossed as the natives of one sphere attempt to infiltrate or are forced to remove into the other sphere" (552). But, in positing Amelia and Miss Matthews as the two "appropriate female types" for, respectively, the private and public spheres, he overstates, and even over-moralizes, the real contrast between them. Amelia becomes, in his

argument, a shrinking, proto-Victorian recluse, an asexual wraith, while Miss Matthews is described as the embodiment of "monstrous appetites."

16. Castle, *Masquerade*, 216.

17. Castle, *Masquerade*, 238–42.

18. On Fielding's elaboration of "an ideal of female heroism" in *Amelia* (2), see Campbell, *Natural Masques*, 203–41, esp. 206–12 and 233–41.

19. See Bakhtin, "Forms of Time and Chronotope in the Novel," *Dialogic Imagination*, 84–258. For a discussion of "liminal confinement"—the disorderly, borderline, promiscuous world of the old prison, before the elaboration of a technology of disciplined, isolating, reformative confinement in the new model penitentiary—as "the archetypal experience of contemporary life," see Bender, *Imagining the Penitentiary*, 185.

20. Martin C. Battestin, "The Problem of *Amelia*: Hume, Barrow, and the Conversion of Captain Booth," *English Literary History* 41 (1974): 630–31.

21. See also the discussion of "Liberty" between Booth and Bailiff Bondum (314): the contradictory entanglements of liberty with law, the constitution, and the "business" of a credit economy are captured with inadvertent precision in Bondum's self-consuming discourse. See also Fielding, *Enquiry*, 65–74.

22. John C. Stephens Jr., "The Verge of the Court and Arrest for Debt in Fielding's *Amelia*," *Modern Language Notes* 63 (1948): 106.

23. Fletcher, *Allegory*, 213.

24. Stephens, "Verge of the Court," 105. See also Foucault, *Discipline and Punish*, 49.

25. Castle, *Masquerade*, 204–5.

26. See chap. 1. Smith's Newgate, like Fielding's, is a tropological field of paradox and reversal, his description an accumulation of catchphrases for moral irregularity and social disorder. Compare, for example, the amassing of figures of inversion in Smith to the world-upside-down quality of Fielding's description. The rhetoric of inversion is clear from Booth's first impression of the yard: "Could his own Thoughts indeed have suffered him a Moment to forget where he was, the Dispositions of the other Prisoners might have induced him to believe that he had been in a happier Place: For much the greater part of his Fellow-Sufferers, instead of wailing and repining at their Condition, were laughing, singing and diverting themselves with various kinds of Sports and Gambols" (27). The pattern persists in the following chapter, "Disclosing further Secrets of the Prison-House," in which three fettered men awaiting execution "were enjoying themselves very merrily over a Bottle of Wine and a Pipe of Tobacco" (32), and "a very pretty Girl," whose beauty prompts Booth to declare that "he thought she had great Innocence in her Countenance," turns out, unsurprisingly now that we are used to the formula, to have been jailed "as an idle and disorderly Person, and a common Street-walker" (33). For an example of verbal echoes from the 1717 *History*, see *Amelia*, 152.

27. Bender, *Imagining*, 181.

28. Richardson, *Selected Letters,* 197; see also 199.

29. Henry Fielding, *Miscellanies,* vol. 1, ed. Henry K. Miller (Middletown, Conn.: Wesleyan University Press, 1972), 10.

30. Castle, *Masquerade,* 236; see also 198 and 203.

31. Bender, *Imagining,* 185; see also 147 and 186–93. On Harrison's role in *Amelia,* see also Eric Rothstein, *Systems of Order and Inquiry in Later Eighteenth-Century Fiction* (Berkeley: University of California Press, 1975), esp. 197–206; and Leo Braudy, *Narrative Form in History and Fiction: Hume, Fielding, and Gibbon* (Princeton: Princeton University Press, 1970), esp. 198–205. All three authors reach conclusions quite different from mine on the question of Harrison's epistemological reliability.

32. That the doctor's contempt for the idea of classical education for women may reflect Fielding's own attitudes does not seem to me to diminish what I am claiming is a distinct ambivalence in his characterization in *Amelia,* any more than Defoe's likely agreement with Sir Robert Clayton's views on women and marriage diminishes the force of Roxana's contrary argument. The significance of the ambivalence in both cases, of course, is that the authors are, like the culture their writing seeks to articulate, ideologically conflicted. It was Fielding's progressive accommodation to the circumstantial narrative strategies adopted also by Defoe which allowed this greater admission of ambivalence in *Amelia,* embodied here in Doctor Harrison's blustery and coarse provocations.

33. "Far from piecing out the truth from scattered fragments, Squire Allworthy has to be confronted with the declaration of a dying man before he arrives at an accurate judgment . . . the good-hearted Allworthy lacks the habits of mind and tools of inquiry necessary to unfold the complexities of concerted deception" (Bender, *Imagining,* 178–79). Bender sees Harrison as, epistemologically, a radical departure from the good but easily duped Allworthy, and Harrison does move more quickly than Allworthy to sort out the truth from the tangle of conflicting testimony. But he is identically imposed upon in his initial misjudgment and is equally dependent upon the confession of a dying man—Robinson in the sponging-house—for his final discovery of the crime, a fraudulent disinheritance, which sets the plot in motion.

34. The maid's mistaking of Harrison for an outlaw echoes two earlier scenes, in which Booth is mistaken, by the keeper of Newgate and his own sister, for a highwayman (see 79 and 95–97). In all these scenes the errors of interpretation seem also to hint at a destructive potentiality in even these good characters. See Campbell, *Natural Masques,* 217.

35. Bender, *Imagining,* 186.

36. Hunter, *Occasional Form,* 199–201.

37. Campbell writes, "The narrator of *Amelia* . . . frequently offers incompatible descriptions of characters or accounts of events in succession, seeming to hold himself responsible for local coherence but not for a sustained and total vision of the novelistic world he describes" (*Natural Masques,* 206; see also 226–28).

38. Fielding, *A Plan of the Universal Register Office*, published with *The Covent-Garden Journal*, ed. Goldgar, 6.

39. See Goldgar, "General Introduction" to the *Covent-Garden Journal*, xxx; also 381 n. 3.

40. Although he does not refer specifically to the Universal Register Office, Bender describes Fielding's general strategies of policing through the control of information and written resources (see esp 165–66). Linebaugh offers a critical view of the Fieldings' business enterprises as "police ventures" directed toward labor discipline (see *London Hanged*, 252). On the Universal Register Office more generally, see Goldgar, "General Introduction," xv–xxx; and Battestin, "General Introduction" to *Amelia*, xxxi–xxxii. For a discussion of John Fielding's extension of his brother's ideas on policing and criminal investigation—his creation of "a national system for collating and circulating information" (136) through handbills, newspapers, and "a central repository for criminal intelligence" (138)—see John Styles, "Sir John Fielding and the Problem of Criminal Investigation in Eighteenth-Century England," *Transactions of the Royal Historical Society*, 5th ser., 33 (1983): 127–49.

41. Fielding, *The Journal of a Voyage to Lisbon*, vol. 7 of *Works*, ed. Leslie Stephen (London, 1882), 187. All references are to this edition.

42. Criminal courts—from Fielding's examining rooms at Bow Street to the court at the Old Bailey—were, like prisons, incredibly unhealthy places. In 1750, in fact, as Gerald Howson notes in *Thief-Taker General*, "sixty people died, including several judges and aldermen, from gaol-fever (a form of typhus) in a single Sessions [at the Old Bailey]. Thereafter, the judges used nosegays, and the fumes from a neighbouring vinegar-distillery were piped in to counteract the stink of the prisoners" (316). Criminal environments were probably only a more concentrated version of the general unhealthiness of the habitations of urban poverty, but, because they were, by definition, entangled with the institutions of dominant culture (and peopled by the representatives of that culture), their unhealthiness was more threatening.

43. In his 1755 *Account of the Origins and Effects of a Police Set on Foot by His Grace the Duke of Newcastle in the Year 1753* John Fielding describes his brother's strategy of organizing a network for the rapid gathering and transmission of information, which could then be used to monitor and regulate the variously dangerous or illegal activities of the lower sort—and makes clear that it was only the lower sort whom law and the police were meant to control. Whereas "Religion, Education, and Good-breeding, preserve good Order and Decency among the superior Rank of Mankind, and prevent those Disturbances, Irregularities and Injuries to our Fellow-Creatures, that happen among the lower Order of the People" (viii), John Fielding writes, "in large and populous Cities, especially in the Metropolis of a flourishing Kingdom, Artificers, Servants and Labourers, compose the Bulk of the People, and keeping them in good Order is the Object of the Police" (vii).

44. Miller, *Novel and the Police*, 2.

45. Miller, *Novel and the Police*, 2.

46. Jeremy Bentham, *Panopticon: or, The Inspection-House* (Dublin, 1791), i–ii.

47. See, for example, Miller, *Novel and the Police*, 16–32; Bender, *Imagining*, 165–66, 197–98, and 201–13.

48. See Welsh, *Strong Representations*, 47–76.

## Epilogue

1. Godwin, *Caleb Williams*, 216. Subsequent references will be given in the text.

2. See Eric Hobsbawm, *Primitive Rebels* (New York: Norton, 1962), 13–28. Hobsbawm is highly critical of the limitations of banditry, which he describes as "a rather primitive form of social protest" (13), lacking any kind of real political analysis and unable to do more than "impose certain limits to traditional oppression in a traditional society, on pain of lawlessness, murder and extortion" (24). For this reason, Hobsbawm writes, "the romantic poets who idealized the bandit, like Schiller in *The Robbers*, were mistaken in believing them to be the real rebels" (27). Godwin perhaps invests Raymond's gang with some of the same glamour of political consciousness and rebellion, but he is acutely aware of the limitations of their revolt and, as the portrait of Gines shows, of the fact that many bandits, when the political battle lines are drawn explicitly, "cease to be champions of the poor and become mere criminals or retainers of landlords' and merchants' parties" (28).

3. Mary Wollstonecraft, *Maria, or The Wrongs of Woman* (New York: Norton, 1975), 23. All references in the text are to this edition.

4. See Mary Poovey, *The Proper Lady and the Woman Writer* (Chicago: University of Chicago Press, 1984), 97–112, for an analysis of one aspect of this contradiction in Wollstonecraft's writing: the conflict between her political project—to expose and condemn the infantilization and imprisonment of women through the institutions of law, the family, and education—and her adoption of the jargon and narrative structures of sentimentalism, which tend, ineluctably, to reinforce those institutions.

5. Michel Foucault, *Power/Knowledge: Selected Interviews and Other Writings, 1972–1977*, ed. Colin Gordon, trans. Colin Gordon, Leo Marshall, John Mepham, and Kate Soper (Brighton: Harvester, 1980), 153.

6. See Ronald Paulson, *Representations of Revolution (1789–1820)* (New Haven: Yale University Press, 1983), 217–25; also Butler, *Jane Austen and the War of Ideas*, 30–31.

7. See, for example, Caleb's outraged reflections during his own imprisonment: "Thank God, exclaims the Englishman, we have no Bastille! Thank God, with us no man can be punished without a crime! Unthinking wretch! Is that a country of liberty where thousands languish in dungeons and fetters? Go, go, ignorant fool! and visit the scenes of our prisons! witness their unwholesomeness, their filth, the tyranny of their governors, the misery of their inmates! After that show me the man shameless enough to triumph, and say, England has no Bastille!" (181). In *Maria* Wollstonecraft distills a complex analysis of the connec-

tions among gender, politics, and law into an angry, dashing epigram: "Marriage," Maria writes, "had bastilled me for life" (103).

8. Elizabeth Inchbald, *Nature and Art*, ed. Shawn L. Maurer (London: Pickering and Chatto, 1997), 112. All references in the text are to this edition. Maurer's text is based on the 1797 second edition of the novel; in later editions the character of "Hannah" was renamed "Agnes."

9. See Poovey, *Proper Lady*, 97–100.

10. See Beattie, *Crime and the Courts in England*, 421: "Equal treatment of prisoners was the ideology of the future, the cry of those inspired by the rationalism of the Enlightenment (and the evident failures of the existing system) who in the last third of the eighteenth century began to press for fundamental changes in the law and its administration." On the influence of Beccaria, see 555–58.

11. Not that the opposition of virtue and vice is simplistic in Hogarth: the obviousness of the plot and ideological message even of *Industry and Idleness*, apparently the most straightforwardly didactic of all Hogarth's series, is complicated or darkened by jarring presences at the margins of the engravings, from a legless beggar selling a ballad called "The Happy Pair" to Goodchild and his new wife, to the violence and disorder encircling Goodchild's progress to Guildhall after his election as Lord Mayor of London. Nevertheless, the predominant strain through the series as a whole is moralizing and monitory, positing worldly success as the outcome, and evidence, of inner virtue—which could not be more contrary to Inchbald's position.

12. See David McCracken, "Introduction" to *Caleb Williams*, xiv–xv; also David Punter, "Fictional Representations of the Law in the Eighteenth Century," *Eighteenth-Century Studies* 16, no. 1 (Fall 1982): 64–66. The original ending shows Falkland triumphant in court and Caleb confined in an asylum, turning out fragments of narrative as he goes insane. The political reflections of the published version and the paradox of Caleb's vindication and despairing self-recriminations are absent from the earlier ending, with its emphasis on the pathos of Caleb's persecution (see McCracken, "Introduction," xviii–xx).

13. See also Godwin, *Caleb Williams*, 276 and 299.

14. William Godwin, *Enquiry Concerning Political Justice, and Its Influence on Modern Morals and Happiness*, ed. Isaac Kramnick (Harmondsworth: Penguin, 1985), 602–3. All references in the text are to this edition.

15. James Thompson, "Surveillance in William Godwin's *Caleb Williams*," in *Gothic Fictions: Prohibition/Transgression*, ed. Kenneth W. Graham (New York: AMS Press, 1989), 187 and 191.

Alter, Robert. *Rogue's Progress: Studies in the Picaresque Novel.* Cambridge: Harvard University Press, 1964.

Aristotle. *Aristotle's Art of Poetry.* London: Dan. Browne & Will. Turner, 1705.

Armstrong, Nancy. *Desire and Domestic Fiction: A Political History of the Novel.* New York: Oxford University Press, 1987.

Auerbach, Erich. *Mimesis: The Representation of Reality in Western Literature.* Trans. Willard R. Trask. Princeton: Princeton University Press, 1953.

Bachelard, Gaston. *The Poetics of Space.* Trans. Maria Jolas. 1958. Reprint. Boston: Beacon, 1969.

Backscheider, Paula R. *Daniel Defoe: His Life.* Baltimore: Johns Hopkins University Press, 1989.

Baine, Rodney. "The Evidence from Defoe's Title Pages." *Studies in Bibliography* 25 (1972): 185–91.

Baker, Ernest A. *The History of the English Novel.* 8 vols. London: Witherby, 1924–39.

Baker, J. H. "Criminal Courts and Procedure at Common Law, 1550-1800." In *Crime in England, 1550–1800,* ed. J. S. Cockburn, 15–48. Princeton: Princeton University Press, 1977.

Bakhtin, M. M. *The Dialogic Imagination.* Ed. Michael Holquist and trans. Caryl Emerson and Michael Holquist. Austin: University of Texas Press, 1981.

Barthes, Roland. *On Racine.* Trans. Richard Howard. New York: Hill & Wang, 1964.

———. "The Reality Effect." *The Rustle of Language.* Trans. Richard Howard. New York: Hill & Wang, 1981.

Battestin, Martin C. "General Introduction." In *Amelia,* by Henry Fielding, ed. Battestin, xv–lxi. Middletown, Conn.: Wesleyan University Press, 1983.

———. "The Problem of *Amelia:* Hume, Barrow, and the Conversion of Captain Booth." *English Literary History* 41 (1974): 613–48.

Beattie, J. M. *Crime and the Courts in England, 1660–1800*. Princeton: Princeton University Press, 1986.

———. "The Criminality of Women in Eighteenth-Century England." *Journal of Social History* 8 (1975): 80–116.

Bell, Ian A. *Literature and Crime in Augustan England*. London: Routledge, 1991.

Bender, John. *Imagining the Penitentiary: Fiction and the Architecture of Mind in Eighteenth-Century England*. Chicago: University of Chicago Press, 1986.

Bentham, Jeremy. *Panopticon; or, The Inspection-House*. Dublin, 1791.

Bernbaum, Ernest. *The Mary Carleton Narratives, 1663–1673: A Missing Chapter in the History of the English Novel*. Cambridge: Harvard University Press, 1914.

Bindman, David. *Hogarth*. New York: Thames & Hudson, 1985.

Bond, Clinton S. "*Street-Robberies Consider'd* and the Canon of Daniel Defoe." *Texas Studies in Literature and Language* 13 (1971): 431–45.

Boswell, James. *Life of Johnson*. Ed. George Birbeck Hill, rev. and enlarged by L. F. Powell. 6 vols. Oxford: Clarendon Press, 1934.

Braudy, Leo. *Narrative Form in History and Fiction: Hume, Fielding, and Gibbon*. Princeton: Princeton University Press, 1970.

Bray, Alan. *Homosexuality in Renaissance England*. London: Gay Men's Press, 1982.

Brown, Homer Obed. "The Displaced Self in the Novels of Daniel Defoe." *Studies in Eighteenth-Century Culture* 4 (1975): 69–94.

Bunyan, John. *The Pilgrim's Progress from this World to That which is to Come*. Ed. James Blanton Wharey. 2d rev. ed. by Roger Sharrock. Oxford: Clarendon Press, 1960.

Burke, Edmund. *A Philosophical Enquiry into the Origin of our Ideas of the Sublime and Beautiful*. Ed. J. T. Boulton. London: Routledge and Kegan Paul, 1958.

Butler, Marilyn. *Jane Austen and the War of Ideas*. Oxford: Clarendon Press, 1975.

Campbell, Jill. *Natural Masques: Gender and Identity in Fielding's Plays and Novels*. Stanford: Stanford University Press, 1995.

*The Case of the Unfortunate Bosavern Penlez*. London, 1749.

Castle, Terry. *Masquerade and Civilization: The Carnivalesque in Eighteenth-Century English Culture and Fiction*. Stanford: Stanford University Press, 1986.

Chandler, Frank Wadleigh. *The Literature of Roguery*. New York: Burt Franklin, 1958.

*A Compleat Collection of Remarkable Tryals, of the most Notorious Malefactors, at the Sessions-House in the Old Bailey, from the Year 1706, to the last Sessions, 1720*. London: J. Brotherton, W. Meadows, F. Clay, J. Batley, 1721.

Cox, Joseph. *A Faithful Narrative of the Most Wicked and Inhuman Transactions of that Bloody-Minded Gang of Thief-Takers, alias Thief-Makers . . . .* London, 1756.

Dangerfield, Thomas. *Dangerfield's Memoires, Digested into Adventures, Receits, and Expences. By his Own Hand*. London: by J. Bennet, for Charles Brome, 1685.

Davis, Jennifer. "The London Garotting Panic of 1862: A Moral Panic and the Creation of a Criminal Class in Mid-Victorian England." In *Crime and the Law: The Social His-*

*tory of Crime in Western Europe since 1500,* ed. V. A. C. Gatrell, Bruce Lenman, and Geoffrey Parker, 190–213. London: Europa, 1980.

Davis, Lennard J. *Factual Fictions: The Origins of the English Novel.* New York: Columbia University Press, 1983.

Davis, Natalie Zemon. "The Reasons of Misrule." *Society and Culture in Early Modern France,* 97–123. Stanford: Stanford University Press, 1975.

Defoe, Daniel. *An Appeal to Honour and Justice, Tho' it be of His Worst Enemies.* London: J. Baker, 1715.

———. *Augusta Triumphans: or the Way to Make London the Most Flourishing City in the Universe . . . Concluding with an Effectual Method to Prevent Street Robberies.* London: J. Roberts, 1728.

———. *A Brief Historical Account of the Lives of Six Notorious Street Robbers.* Printed in *Romances and Narratives by Daniel Defoe.* 16 vols. Ed. George A. Aitken. Vol. 16. 1726. Reprint. London: Dent, 1895.

———. *Colonel Jack.* Ed. Samuel Holt Monk. London: Oxford University Press, 1965.

———. *A Continuation of Letters Written by a Turkish Spy at Paris . . . Written Originally in Arabick, Translated into Italian, and from Thence into English.* London: W. Taylor, 1718.

———. *A General History of the Pyrates.* Ed. Manuel Schonhorn. London: Dent, 1972.

———. *The Great Law of Subordination Consider'd; or, the Insolence and Unsufferable Behaviour of Servants in England Duly Enquir'd into . . . in Ten Familiar Letters.* London, 1724.

———. *The History of the Remarkable Life of John Sheppard.* Printed with *The Fortunate Mistress,* vol. 2. 1724. Reprint. Oxford: Basil Blackwell for the Shakespeare Head Press, 1928.

———. *The Life of Jonathan Wild, from His Birth to His Death . . . by H.D.* London: T. Warner, 1725.

———. *Moll Flanders.* Ed. G. A. Starr. Oxford: Oxford University Press, 1971.

———. *A Narrative of all the Robberies, Escapes, &c. of John Sheppard.* Printed with *The Fortunate Mistress,* vol. 2. 1724. Reprint. Oxford: Basil Blackwell for the Shakespeare Head Press, 1928.

———. *Robinson Crusoe.* Ed. Angus Ross. Harmondsworth: Penguin, 1965.

———. *Roxana. The Fortunate Mistress.* Ed. Jane Jack. Oxford: Oxford University Press, 1964.

———. *Second Thoughts Are Best: or a Further Improvement of a Late Scheme to Prevent Street Robberies . . . by Andrew Moreton, Esq..* London: W. Meadows, 1729 [for 1728].

———. *Selected Writings from Applebee's Journal.* Printed with *Moll Flanders,* vol. 2. Oxford: Basil Blackwell for the Shakespeare Head Press, 1928.

———. *Street-Robberies Consider'd: The Reason of Their Being so Frequent, with Probable Means to Prevent 'Em.* London: J. Roberts, 1728.

———. *The True and Genuine Account of the Life and Actions of the Late Jonathan Wild; Not*

*Made up of Fiction and Fable, but Taken from His Own Mouth.* London: Applebee, 1725.

De Quincey, Thomas. *On Murder Considered as One of the Fine Arts. Selected Writings of Thomas De Quincey.* Ed. Philip Van Doren Stern, 982–1089. New York: Random House, 1937.

Dollimore, Jonathan. *Sexual Dissidence: Augustine to Wilde, Freud to Foucault.* Oxford: Clarendon Press, 1991.

Doody, Margaret. "'Those Eyes Are Made So Killing': Eighteenth-Century Murderesses and the Law." *Princeton University Library Chronicle* 46, no. 1 (Fall 1984): 49–80.

———. "Voices of Record: Women as Witnesses and Defendants in the *Old Bailey Sessions Papers.*" In *Representing Women: Law, Literature, and Feminism,* ed. Susan Sage Heinzelman and Zipporah Batshaw Wiseman, 287–308. Durham, N.C.: Duke University Press, 1994.

Eagleton, Terry. *The Function of Criticism: From "The Spectator" to Post-Structuralism.* London: Verso, 1984.

Eisenstein, Elizabeth L. *The Printing Press as an Agent of Change: Communications and Cultural Transformations in Early-Modern Europe.* Cambridge: Cambridge University Press, 1979.

Elias, Norbert. *The History of Manners.* Vol. 1 of *The Civilizing Process.* Trans. Edmund Jephcott. New York: Pantheon, 1978.

Emsley, Clive. *Crime and Society in England, 1750–1900.* London: Longman, 1987.

Faller, Lincoln B. *Crime and Defoe: A New Kind of Writing.* Cambridge: Cambridge University Press, 1994.

———. "Criminal Opportunities in the Eighteenth Century: The 'Ready-Made' Contexts of the Popular Literature of Crime." *Comparative Literature Studies* 24 (1987): 120–45.

———. *Turned to Account: The Forms and Functions of Criminal Biography in Late Seventeenth-and Early Eighteenth-Century England.* Cambridge: Cambridge University Press, 1987.

Fielding, Henry. *Amelia.* Ed. Martin C. Battestin. Middletown, Conn.: Wesleyan University Press, 1983.

———. *The Covent-Garden Journal* and *A Plan of the Universal Register Office.* Ed. Bertrand A. Goldgar. Oxford: Clarendon Press, 1988.

———. *An Enquiry into the Causes of the Late Increase of Robbers and Related Writings* [*A Charge Delivered to the Grand Jury, A True State of the Case of Bosavern Penlez, Examples of the Interposition of Providence in the Detection and Punishment of Murder, A Proposal for Making an Effectual Provision for the Poor, A Clear State of the Case of Elizabeth Canning*]. Ed. Malvin R. Zirker. Oxford: Clarendon Press, 1988.

———. *The History of Tom Jones, a Foundling.* Ed. Martin C. Battestin and Fredson Bowers. Middletown, Conn.: Wesleyan University Press, 1975.

———. *Jonathan Wild*. Ed. David Nokes. Harmondsworth: Penguin, 1982.

———. *Joseph Andrews*. Ed. Martin C. Battestin. Middletown, Conn.: Wesleyan University Press, 1967.

———. *The Journal of a Voyage to Lisbon. Works*. Vol. 7. Ed. Leslie Stephen. London, 1882.

———. *Miscellanies, Volume 1*. Ed. Henry Knight Miller. Middletown, Conn.: Wesleyan University Press, 1972.

———. *Shamela*. Published with *Joseph Andrews*. Ed. Douglas Brooks. London: Oxford University Press, 1970.

Fielding, Sir John. *An Account of the Origin and Effects of a Police Set on Foot by His Grace the Duke of Newcastle in the Year 1753, upon a Plan presented to his Grace by the late Henry Fielding, Esq*. London, 1758.

———. *A Plan for Preventing Robberies within Twenty Miles of London. With An Account of the Rise and Establishment of the real Thieftakers*. London, 1755.

Fletcher, Angus. *Allegory: The Theory of a Symbolic Mode*. Ithaca: Cornell University Press, 1964.

Foucault, Michel. *Discipline and Punish: The Birth of the Prison*. Trans. Alan Sheridan. New York: Vintage, 1979.

———. *Power/Knowledge: Selected Interviews and Other Writings, 1972–1977*. Ed. Colin Gordon, trans. Colin Gordon, Leo Marshall, John Mepham, and Kate Soper. Brighton: Harvester, 1980.

*A Full and True Account of the Penitent Behaviour, Last Dying Words, and Execution of Mr. Edmund Allen, Gent. . . . On Friday, the 19th of this Instant July, 1695*. London: J. Williams, 1695.

Furbank, P. N., and W. R. Owens. *The Canonisation of Daniel Defoe*. New Haven: Yale University Press, 1988.

———. *Defoe De-Attributions: A Critique of J. R. Moore's "Checklist."* London: Hambledon, 1994.

Gatrell, V. A. C. *The Hanging Tree: Execution and the English People, 1770–1868*. Oxford: Oxford University Press, 1994.

Gildon, Charles. *The Life and Strange Surprizing Adventures of Mr. D—— DeF——, of London, Hosier . . . in a Dialogue between Him, Robinson Crusoe, and his Man Friday*. 2d ed. London: J. Roberts, 1719.

Ginzburg, Carlo. "Clues: Morelli, Freud, and Sherlock Holmes." *The Sign of Three: Dupin, Holmes, Peirce*. Ed. Umberto Eco and Thomas A. Sebeok, 81–118. Bloomington: Indiana University Press, 1983.

*A Glimpse of Hell: or a short Description of the Common Side of Newgate*. London, 1705.

Godwin, William. *Caleb Williams*. Ed. David McCracken. New York: Norton, 1977.

———. *Enquiry Concerning Political Justice, and Its Influence on Modern Morals and Happiness*. Ed. Isaac Kramnick. Harmondsworth: Penguin, 1985.

Habermas, Jürgen. *The Structural Transformation of the Public Sphere: An Inquiry into a Category of Bourgeois Society.* Trans. Thomas Burger, with Frederick Lawrence. London: Polity Press, 1989.

*Hanging, Not Punishment Enough, for Murtherers, High-way Men, and House-Breakers.* London: A. Baldwin, 1701.

Hanway, Jonas. *The Defects of Police the Cause of Immorality.* London, 1775.

Harris, Michael. "Trials and Criminal Biographies: A Case Study in Distribution." *Sale and Distribution of Books from 1700.* Ed. Robin Myers and Michael Harris, 1–36. Oxford: Oxford Polytechnic Press, 1982.

Hassall, Anthony J. "Fielding's *Amelia:* Dramatic and Authorial Narration." *Novel* (Spring 1972): 225–33.

Hay, Douglas. "Property, Authority and the Criminal Law." In *Albion's Fatal Tree,* ed. Douglas Hay et al., 17–64. New York: Pantheon, 1975.

Head, Richard. *The Canting Academy; or Villanies Discovered.* 2d ed. London, 1674.

Herrup, Cynthia B. "Law and Morality in Seventeenth-Century England." *Past and Present* 106 (1985): 102–23.

Hibbert, Christopher. *The Road to Tyburn. The Story of Jack Sheppard and the Eighteenth Century Underworld.* London: Longmans, Green, 1957.

*The History of the Most Remarkable Tryals in Great Britain and Ireland, in Capital Cases.* London: A. Bell, J. Pemberton, J. Brown, 1715 (vol. 1) and 1716 (vol. 2).

*The History of the Press-Yard: Or, a Brief Account of the Customs and Occurrences that are Put in Practice, and to be Met with, in that Antient Repository of Living Bodies, Called, His Majesty's Gaol of Newgate in London. . . .* London, 1717.

Hitchin, Charles. *The Regulator: or, a Discovery of the Thieves, Thief-Takers, and Locks, alias Receivers of Stolen Goods in and about the City of London.* London, 1718.

———. *A True Discovery of the Conduct of Receivers and Thief-Takers in and about the City of London.* London: Printed for the Author and Given Away Gratis, 1718.

Hobsbawm, E. J. *Primitive Rebels.* New York: Norton, 1962.

Hooper, W. Eden. *History of Newgate and the Old Bailey.* London: Underwood, 1935.

Howson, Gerald. *Thief-Taker General: The Rise and Fall of Jonathan Wild.* London: Hutchinson & Co., 1970.

Hunter, J. Paul. *Before Novels: The Cultural Contexts of Eighteenth-Century English Fiction.* New York: Norton, 1990.

———. *Occasional Form: Henry Fielding and the Chains of Circumstance.* Baltimore: Johns Hopkins University Press, 1975.

———. *The Reluctant Pilgrim: Defoe's Emblematic Method and Quest for Form in Robinson Crusoe.* Baltimore: Johns Hopkins University Press, 1966.

Inchbald, Elizabeth. *Nature and Art.* Ed. Shawn L. Maurer. London: Pickering and Chatto, 1997.

Johnson, Sir John. *An Account of the Behaviour, Confession, and last Dying Speeche of Sir John*

*Johnson, [who was] Executed at Tyburn on Tuesday the 23d. day of December, Anno Dom. 1690 for stealing of Mrs. Mary Wharton.* London: Langley Curtiss, 1690.

Johnson, Samuel. *An Account of the Life of Mr. Richard Savage.* In *Selected Writings,* ed. Patrick Crutwell. Harmondsworth: Penguin, 1968.

———. *The Rambler.* Ed. W. J. Bate and Albrecht B. Strauss. 3 vols. New Haven: Yale University Press, 1969.

Katz, Jack. *Seductions of Crime: Moral and Sensual Attractions in Doing Evil.* New York: Basic Books, 1988.

Kernan, Alvin. *Printing Technology, Letters & Samuel Johnson.* Princeton: Princeton University Press, 1987.

Kreissman, Bernard. *Pamela-Shamela: A Study of the Criticisms, Burlesques, Parodies, and Adaptations of Richardson's "Pamela."* N.p.: University of Nebraska Press, 1960.

Langbein, John H. "The Criminal Trial before the Lawyers." *University of Chicago Law Review* 45 (1978): 263–316.

———. "Shaping the Eighteenth-Century Criminal Trial: A View from the Ryder Sources." *University of Chicago Law Review* 50, no. 1 (Winter 1983): 1–136.

Lee, William. *Daniel Defoe: His Life, and Recently Discovered Writings: Extending from 1716 to 1729.* 3 vols. London: Hotten, 1869.

LePage, Peter. "The Prison and the Dark Beauty of *Amelia*." *Criticism* 9 (1967): 337–54.

Linebaugh, Peter. *The London Hanged: Crime and Civil Society in the Eighteenth Century.* London: Allen Lane, Penguin Press, 1991.

———. "The Ordinary of Newgate and His *Account.*" In *Crime in England, 1550–1800.* Ed. J. S. Cockburn, 246–69. London: Methuen, 1977.

———. "The Tyburn Riot against the Surgeons." In *Albion's Fatal Tree,* ed. Douglas Hay, Peter Linebaugh, and E. P. Thompson, 65–117. New York: Pantheon, 1975.

Lusebrink, Hans-Jürgen. "La letteratura del patibolo. Continuità e trasformazioni tra '600 e '800." *Quaderni storici* 49 (April 1982): 285–301.

———, ed. *Histoires curieuses et veritables de Cartouche et de Mandrin.* Paris: Montalba, 1984.

McCormick, Ian, ed. *Secret Sexualities: A Sourcebook of 17th and 18th Century Writing.* London: Routledge, 1997.

McGowen, Randall. "The Changing Face of God's Justice: The Debates over Divine and Human Punishment in Eighteenth-Century England." *Criminal Justice History: An International Annual* 9 (1988): 63–98.

McKeon, Michael. *The Origins of the English Novel, 1600–1740.* Baltimore: Johns Hopkins University Press, 1987.

McKillop, Alan Dugald. *Samuel Richardson: Printer and Novelist.* Chapel Hill: University of North Carolina Press, 1936.

McLynn, Frank. *Crime and Punishment in Eighteenth-Century England.* Oxford: Oxford University Press, 1989.

Mandeville, Bernard. *An Enquiry into the Causes of the Frequent Executions at Tyburn: and a*

*Proposal for Some Regulations Concerning Felons in Prison, and the Good Effects to be Expected from Them.* London: J. Roberts, 1725.

Maresca, Thomas E. *Epic to Novel.* Columbus: Ohio State University Press, 1974.

Mascuch, Michael. *Origins of the Individualist Self: Autobiography and Self-Identity in England, 1591–1791.* Stanford: Stanford University Press, 1996.

Mayhew, George P. "Jonathan Swift's Hoax of 1722 upon Ebenezor Elliston." In *Fair Liberty Was All His Cry: A Tercentenary Tribute to Jonathan Swift,* ed. A. Norman Jeffares, 290–310. London: Macmillan, 1967.

*The Memoires of Monsieur Du Vall: Containing the History of his Life and Death. Whereunto are Annexed His last Speech and Epitaph.* Attributed to Dr. Walter Pope. London: Henry Brome, 1670.

Miller, D. A. *The Novel and the Police.* Berkeley: University of California Press, 1988.

Moore, Judith. *The Appearance of Truth: The Story of Elizabeth Canning and Eighteenth-Century Narrative.* Newark: University of Delaware Press, 1994.

*A Murderer Punished; and Pardoned. Or, A True Relation of the Wicked Life, and Shameful-happy Death of Thomas Savage.* 12th ed. 1668. Reprint. London, 1679.

Nashe, Thomas. *The Unfortunate Traveller and Other Works.* Ed. J. B. Steane. London: Penguin, 1972.

Needham, Rodney. "Polythetic Classification: Convergence and Consequences." *Against the Tranquility of Axioms,* 36–65. Berkeley: University of California Press, 1983.

Nelson, William. *Fact or Fiction: The Dilemma of the Renaissance Storyteller.* Cambridge: Harvard University Press, 1973.

*A New Canting Dictionary: Comprehending All the Terms, Antient and Modern, Used in the Several Tribes of Gypsies, Beggars, Shoplifters, Highwaymen, Foot-Pads, and all other Clans of Cheats and Villains.* London, 1725.

*Newes from the Dead. Or a True and Exact Narration of the miraculous deliverance of Anne Greene, who being Executed at Oxford Decemb. 14. 1650. afterwards revived; and by the care of certain [P]hysitians there, is now perfectly recovered.* 2d impression with additions. Oxford: Leonard Lichfield, 1651.

*Newes from the North: or a Relation of a Great Robberie which was committed nere Swanton in York-shire, July 12. 1641.* . . . London, 1641.

*News from Newgate: or, a True Relation of the Manner of Taking Seven Persons, Very Notorious for Highway-men, in the Strand.* . . . London, 1677.

Norton, Rictor. *Mother Clap's Molly House: The Gay Subculture in England, 1700–1830.* London: Gay Men's Press, 1992.

Novak, Maximillian E. "Defoe's Theory of Fiction." *Studies in Philology* 61 (1964): 650–68.

———. *Realism, Myth, and History in Defoe's Fiction.* Lincoln: University of Nebraska Press, 1983.

Paulson, Ronald. *Representations of Revolution (1789–1820).* New Haven: Yale University Press, 1983.

Pinkus, Philip. *Grub Steet Stripped Bare.* London: Constable, 1968.

Poovey, Mary. *The Proper Lady and the Woman Writer.* Chicago: University of Chicago Press, 1984.

Poulter, John. *The Discoveries of John Poulter.* London, 1754.

*The Proceedings at the Sessions at the Old-Baily, August the 27th and 28th, 1679. Containing the several Tryals of a great number of notorious Malefactors, and particularly of Peter du Val and Tho. Thompson, Condemned for Murder. . . .* London, 1679.

*The Proceedings on the King's Commissions of the Peace, Oyer and Terminer, and Gaol Delivery for the City of London . . .* [Also referred to as the *Old Bailey Sessions Papers*]. No. 7, for September 6–14, 1749.

Punter, David. "Fictional Representation of the Law in the Eighteenth Century." *Eighteenth-Century Studies* 16, no. 1 (Fall 1982): 47–74.

Rawlings, Philip. *Drunks, Whores, and Idle Apprentices: Criminal Biographies of the Eighteenth Century.* London: Routledge, 1992.

Rawson, Claude. *Henry Fielding and the Augustan Ideal under Stress.* London: Routledge and Kegan Paul, 1972.

Reynolds, John. *The Triumph of God's Revenge, against the Crying, and Execrable Sinne of Murther. . . .* 6 vols. 1621–. Reprint. London: William Lee, 1635.

Reynolds, Sir Joshua. *Letters.* Ed. Frederick Whiley Hilles. Cambridge: Cambridge University Press, 1929.

Richardson, Samuel. *Clarissa: or The History of a Young Lady.* Ed. Angus Ross. Harmondsworth: Penguin, 1985.

———. *Familiar Letters on Important Occasions.* London, Routledge, 1928.

———. *Selected Letters.* Ed. John Carroll. Oxford: Oxford University Press, 1963.

Richetti, John J. *Defoe's Narratives: Situations and Structures.* Oxford: Clarendon Press, 1975.

———. *Popular Fiction before Richardson: Narrative Patterns, 1700–1739.* Oxford: Clarendon Press, 1969.

Rogers, Pat. *Grub Street: Studies in a Subculture.* London: Methuen, 1972.

Rothstein, Eric. *Systems of Order and Inquiry in Later Eighteenth-Century Fiction.* Berkeley: University of California Press, 1975.

Sabor, Peter. "*Amelia* and *Sir Charles Grandison:* The Convergence of Fielding and Richardson." *Wascana Review* 17, no. 2 (Fall 1982): 3–18.

Salzman, Paul. *English Prose Fiction, 1558–1700: A Critical History.* Oxford: Clarendon Press, 1985.

*Select Trials, for Murders, Robberies, Rapes, Sodomy, Coining, Frauds, and other Offences: at the Sessions-House in the Old Bailey. To which are Added, Genuine Accounts of the Lives, Behaviour, Confessions and Dying-Speeches of the most Eminent Convicts.* 2 vols. London: J. Wilford, 1734 and 1735.

Sharpe, J. A. *Crime in Early Modern England, 1550–1750.* London: Longman, 1984.

———. "'Last Dying Speeches': Religion, Ideology and Public Execution in Seventeenth-Century England." *Past and Present* 107 (1985): 144–67.

Sheehan, W. J. "Finding Solace in Eighteenth-Century Newgate." In *Crime in England, 1550–1800,* ed. J. S. Cockburn, 229–45. London: Methuen, 1977.

Shinagel, Michael. *Daniel Defoe and Middle-Class Gentility.* Cambridge: Harvard University Press, 1968.

Singleton, Robert R. "Defoe, Moll Flanders, and the Ordinary of Newgate." *Harvard Library Bulletin* 24, no. 4 (October 1976): 407–13.

———. "English Criminal Biography, 1651–1722." *Harvard Library Bulletin* 18, no. 1 (January 1970): 63–83.

Smith, Captain Alexander. *The History of the Lives of the Most Noted Highway-men, Footpads, House-breakers, Shop-lifts, and Cheats, of Both Sexes, in and about London, and other Places of Great-Britain, for above Fifty Years Last Past.* 2 vols. London, 1714.

Smith, Samuel (Ordinary of Newgate). *A True Account of the Behaviour, Confession, and Last Dying Speeches, of the Criminals that were Executed at Tyburn, on Friday the 12th of July, 1695.* London: E. Mallet, 1695.

———. *A True Account of the Behaviour of Thomas Randal, who was Executed at Stone-Bridge, for Killing the Quaker, on Wednesday the 29th of this Instant January 1695/6.* London: E. Mallet, 1696.

Spacks, Patricia Meyer. *Imagining a Self: Autobiography and Novel in Eighteenth-Century England.* Cambridge: Harvard University Press, 1976.

Spierenburg, Pieter. *The Spectacle of Suffering. Executions and the Evolution of Repression: from a Preindustrial Metropolis to the European Experience.* Cambridge: Cambridge University Press, 1984.

Stallybrass, Peter, and Allon White. *The Politics and Poetics of Transgression.* Ithaca: Cornell University Press, 1986.

Starr, G. A. *Defoe and Spiritual Autobiography.* Princeton: Princeton University Press, 1965.

Stephens, John C., Jr. "The Verge of the Court and Arrest for Debt in Fielding's *Amelia.*" *Modern Language Notes* 63 (1948): 104–9.

Styles, John. "Sir John Fielding and the Problem of Criminal Investigation in Eighteenth-Century England." *Transactions of the Royal Historical Society,* 5th ser., 33 (1983): 127–49.

Swift, Jonathan. *The Last Speech and Dying Words of Ebenezor Elliston, who was Executed the Second Day of May, 1722.* In *Irish Tracts and Sermons.* Vol. 9 of *Prose Works,* ed. Herbert Davis, 37–41. Oxford: Blackwell, 1948.

Thompson, E. P. *Customs in Common.* London: Merlin, 1992.

———. *Whigs and Hunters: The Origin of the Black Act.* New York: Pantheon, 1975.

Thompson, James. "Surveillance in William Godwin's *Caleb Williams.*" In *Gothic Fictions: Prohibition/Transgression,* ed. Kenneth W. Graham, 173–98. New York: AMS Press, 1989.

Thurmond, John. *Harlequin Sheppard. A Night Scene in Grotesque Characters.* London, 1724.

*A True and Impartial Relation of the Birth and Education of Claudius du Val; Together with the manner of his Apprehending . . . And lastly, the manner of his Execution at Tyburn.* London: T. Ratcliff and T. Daniel, 1669 [1670].

*The True Briton,* no. 10 (Wednesday, March 6, 1751).

*The Tryal of Richard Hathaway, upon an Information for being a Cheat and Impostor, for endeavouring to take away the Life of Sarah Morduck, for being a Witch, at Surry Assizes.* London: Isaac Cleave, 1702.

*The Tryall of Lieut. Collonell John Lilburne, by an extraordinary or special Commission, of Oyear and Terminer at the Guild-Hall of London, the 24, 25, 26 of Octob. 1649.* Southwark: Theodorus Varax, 1649.

Uffenbach, Zacharias Conrad von. *London in 1710.* Ed. and trans. W. H. Quarrel and Margaret Mare. London: Faber and Faber, 1934.

Watt, Ian. *The Rise of the Novel: Studies in Defoe, Richardson, and Fielding.* Berkeley: University of California Press, 1957.

Weeks, Jeffrey. *Coming Out: Homosexual Politics in Britain from the Nineteenth Century to the Present.* 2d rev. ed. London: Quartet, 1990.

Welch, Saunders. *A Letter upon the Subject of Robberies* [1753]. Published as an appendix to *A Proposal to Render Effectual a Plan, to Remove the Nuisance of Common Prostitutes from the Streets of this Metropolis.* London, 1758.

Welsh, Alexander. *Strong Representations: Narrative and Circumstantial Evidence in England.* Baltimore: Johns Hopkins University Press, 1992.

Williams, Raymond. *The Country and the City.* New York: Oxford University Press, 1973.

Wilson, Ralph. *Full and Impartial Account of all the Robberies Committed by John Hawkins, George Sympson (lately Executed for Robbing the Bristol Mails) and their Companions . . . Written by Ralph Wilson, late One of their Confederates.* London: J. Peele, 1722.

Wollstonecraft, Mary. *Maria, or The Wrongs of Woman.* New York: Norton, 1975.

Zirker, Malvin R., Jr. *Fielding's Social Pamphlets: A Study of "An Enquiry into the Causes of the Late Increase of Robbers" and "A Proposal for Making an Effectual Provision for the Poor."* Berkeley: University of California Press, 1966.

———. "General Introduction." In *An Enquiry into the Causes of the Late Increase of Robbers and Related Writings,* by Henry Fielding, ed. Zirker, xvii–cxiv. Middletown, Conn.: Wesleyan University Press, 1988.

Zomchick, John P. *Family and the Law in Eighteenth-Century Fiction: The Public Conscience in the Private Sphere.* Cambridge: Cambridge University Press, 1993.

———. "'A Penetration Which Nothing Can Deceive': Gender and Juridical Discourse in Some Eighteenth-Century Narratives." *Studies in English Literature, 1500–1900* 29 (1989): 535–61.

*Account of the Behaviour, Confession, and Last Dying Speeche of Sir John Johnson*, 55–57
*Accurate Description of Newgate*, 28, 198
Aleman, Mateo, 34
Allen, Edmund (executed for murder), 51–52, 53
Alloway, John (accused of rape and robbery), 70
anonymity: in Defoe, 95–97, 127–30, 134–35; possibility of maintaining, 248n. 23
anti-sodomite texts, 21–23, 29–30, 230n. 23
*Apology for the Conduct of Mrs. Teresia Constantia Phillips*, 151, 153
Applebee, John (publisher), 89–90, 91, 95, 97, 98, 244n. 7
*Applebee's Journal*, 89, 97, 98–100
Aristotle, 170, 171
Auerbach, Erich, 68, 121, 148–49
authenticity, claims of: in canting dictionaries, 229n. 3; in criminal biographies, 72–76, 86; in criminal trials, 62–63, 237n. 11; in Defoe, 13, 100–101, 113–19, 121–23
authorship and criminality, 88–92, 95–97, 113–15, 121–22, 154–55, 245n. 2

B. L. of Twickenham, 28
Bachelard, Gaston, 192, 255n. 1
Backscheider, Paula, 96
Baine, Rodney, 245n. 4

Baker, J. H., 235n. 26
Bakhtin, M. M., 45, 48, 49; chronotope of the threshold, 195; incorporation of other genres in novel, 216
banditry, as form of social protest or rebellion, 210, 261n. 2
*Barnaby Rudge* (Dickens), 79, 138
Barthes, Roland, 187; "reality effect," 190, 256n. 7
Battestin, Martin C., 195
Beattie, J. M., 59, 68, 159–61, 217, 239n. 28, 244n. 15, 251n. 4, 262n. 10
Beccaria, Cesare, 217, 262n. 10
*Beggar's Opera* (John Gay), 86, 99
Bell, Ian, 229n. 13
Bender, John, 8, 116, 191, 197–98, 200, 203, 207, 229n. 18, 256nn. 2, 4, 258n. 19, 259n. 33, 260n. 40
Bentham, Jeremy, 207
Bernbaum, Ernest, 242n. 23, 249n. 5
Billings, Thomas (tried for murder), 48
biography, defined as genre, 75–76, 86
Blay, Hannah (accessory to murder), 78–82
Bond, Clinton S., 246n. 3
Boswell, James, on executions, 253n. 26
Bow Street Runners, 206
Braudy, Leo, 259n. 31
Bray, Alan, 22
Brinden, Matthias (tried for murder), 71

Brogden, Joshua (H. Fielding's clerk), 206
Brown, Homer O., 124, 244n. 11, 247n. 19
Brown, William (arrested for sodomy), 31–32
Bunyan, John, 27, 58–59
Burke, Edmund, 159
Butler, Marilyn, 225n. 2
Butler, Richard (hanged for housebreaking), 54

*Caleb Williams* (Godwin), ix–xi, 1–4, 8, 41, 90–91, 209–11, 214–16, 219–24
Campbell, Jill, 251n. 10, 258n. 18, 259nn. 34, 37
Canning, Elizabeth (kidnapping victim or false witness), 174–81
*Canting Academy* (Richard Head), 24
canting dictionaries, 23–24, 25–26
Carleton, Mary (the "German Princess"), 134
*Case of the Unfortunate Penlez*, 182–83
Castle, Terry, 190, 192, 193, 197, 199, 256n. 2
*Clarissa* (Richardson), 188–89, 191, 194
class antagonism and emulation, as underlying causes of crime, 144–45, 159–62, 165–67, 211, 213–14
*Compleat Collection of Remarkable Tryals*, 239n. 24
confession, as part of legal procedures, 235n. 26
conversion, as turning point in Defoe's narratives, 123–26, 131, 133–34
crime, levels of, 101, 159–61, 232n. 6, 244n. 15
crime, theories on the causes of: in Fielding, 159–66; in Inchbald, 212–13
crime reports, 11, 45–49
criminal anatomies, 11, 21–32; defined, 22–23, 228n. 6
criminal biographies, 9–10, 12, 72–88
Curtiss, Langley (publisher), 55

Dangerfield, Thomas (highwayman), 72–77, 240n. 2
Davis, Jennifer, 232n. 6
Davis, Lennard J., 7, 45, 231n. 9

Davis, Natalie Zemon, 253n. 18
Defoe, Daniel, 12–14, 24, 67, 89–90; ambivalence toward gender roles, 145–47, 249n. 12, 259n. 32; anonymity and pseudonymity, 95–97, 127–30, 134–35; attribution of criminal texts to, 95–98; connection to publisher John Applebee, 95, 97; debts to older narrative forms, 104, 106, 137–38, 149; identification with narrators' voices, 116; periods in prison, 96; political ambivalence, 119–20, 144–48; verisimilitude, 100–101, 102–12. Works (including contested attributions): *Appeal to Honour and Justice*, 95–96; contributions to *Applebee's Journal*, 97–101; *Augusta Triumphans*, 147, 246n. 4; *Colonel Jack*, 6, 10, 13, 102–12, 117, 131, 149, 245nn. 5, 6, 7, 246n.8; *Continuation of Letters Written by a Turkish Spy*, 93; *General History of the Pyrates*, 211, 244n. 10, 250n. 13; *Great Law of Subordination Consider'd*, 119, 211; *History of the Life of John Sheppard*, 90, 121–22; *Lives of the Six Notorious Street Robbers*, 102, 244n. 15; *Moll Flanders*, 13–14, 96, 113–17, 123–30, 131–32, 137, 246n. 4; *Narrative of all the Robberies, Escapes, &c. of John Sheppard*, x–xi, 89–91, 121; *Robinson Crusoe*, 7, 96, 98, 113; *Roxana*, 14, 96, 117–19, 131–47, 248n. 1, 249nn. 6, 7, 8, 249n. 12; *Second Thoughts Are Best*, 147, 246n. 4; *Shortest Way with Dissenters*, 95; *Street-Robberies Consider'd*, 115, 119, 246n. 3; *True and Genuine Account of the Life and Actions of the Late Jonathan Wild*, 144–45
DeQuincey, Thomas, 88
deviance: racialized notions of, 11, 14, 23–25, 161, 164, 230n. 23; relation to individualism, 5–10, 11, 97, 148
Dickens, Charles, 79, 111, 135
Dollimore, Jonathan, 228n. 29
domestic sphere. *See* prison
Donnellan, Ann (friend of Richardson), 91, 188, 198

*Dunciad* (Pope), 27
DuVal, Peter (tried for murder), 63–65
DuVall, Claude (highwayman), 82–86

Eagleton, Terry, 247n. 13
Elias, Norbert, 240n. 31
Elliston, Ebenezer (Irish horse thief), 57
Emsley, Clive, 229n. 13
*English Rogue* (Richard Head), 34
*Enquiry Concerning Political Justice* (God-
   win), 2, 210, 220–23
*Enquiry into the Causes of the Frequent Execu-
   tions at Tyburn* (Mandeville), 167–70
executions, public, 14–15, 50–51, 166–73;
   Fielding's argument against, 166–67,
   169–72; reports of, 45–46. *See also* last
   dying speeches; Ordinary of Newgate's
   *Accounts*

Faller, Lincoln, 9, 76–77, 78, 245n. 16
Fielding, Henry, xii, 14–16, 111; antirealist
   model of narrative, 15, 156–57, 171–72; on
   class conflict and mobility, 161–66; disenchantment and epistemological anxiety,
   16, 153–54, 158, 179–81, 185–86, 188–89, 199–
   204, 207–8; as magistrate, 153–54, 159, 174–
   86, 205–6; as moral/literary censor, 153–58,
   161; physical deterioration due to police
   work, 159, 205–6, 207–8; relationship to
   Richardson, 155–57, 188–89, 251n. 10; role in
   the history of the police, 204–8, 260nn.
   40, 43. Works: *Amelia*, 15–16, 91, 154, 157–
   58, 187–208, 257nn. 14, 15; *Charge to the
   Grand Jury*, 153, 154, 161; *Clear State of the
   Case of Elizabeth Canning*, 15, 174–81, 253n.
   5, 254nn.6, 7; *Covent-Garden Journal*, 154–
   58, 165–67, 170, 172, 198; *Enquiry into the
   Causes of the Late Increase of Robbers*, 14,
   161–67, 169–73, 186, 205, 252n. 10; *Examples
   of the Interposition of Providence*, 39–40, 42;
   *Jonathan Wild*, 99, 163, 187, 252n. 12, 256n.
   5; *Joseph Andrews*, 14, 156–57; *Journal of a

*Voyage to Lisbon*, 159, 205–6, 208; *Miscella-
   nies*, 198; *Plan for the Universal Register
   Office*, 204–5, 206; *Shamela*, 156–57; *Tom
   Jones*, 6, 7, 14, 179–80, 203, 208; *True State
   of the Case of Bosavern Penlez*, 15, 166,
   181–86, 255nn. 15, 16
Fielding, John, 204, 206, 260nn. 40, 43
Fielding, Sarah, 154
Fletcher, Angus, 196, 257n. 12
Foley, Timothy, 247n. 13
Foucault, Michel, 7, 31, 56, 148, 207, 212, 235n.
   26, 235n. 32
*Full and Impartial Account of all the Robberies
   Committed by John Hawkins*, 86–88
Furbank, P. N., 95, 97–98

Garrick, David (as Macbeth), 171
Gascoyne, Sir Crisp, 254n. 6
Gay, John, 86, 99
gender and sexual transgression: in Defoe,
   138–40, 145–47, 249n. 12; in Fielding, 157–
   58, 192–95, 198–99, 257nn. 14, 15, 259n. 32;
   in Inchbald, 218–19; in sodomy trials,
   21–23, 29–30; in Wollstonecraft, 213–14,
   216–18
genres of criminal narrative, x–xii, 3–5, 9–12,
   225n. 4, 228n. 6, 250n. 17
*Gentleman's Magazine*, 23, 29
Gerald, Joseph (tried for sedition), 3
Gildon, Charles, 101, 113, 114
Ginzburg, Carlo, 248n. 23
*Glimpse of Hell*, 26
*God's Revenge Against Murder*. See *Triumph of
   God's Revenge Against Murder* (Reynolds)
Godwin, William, ix–xi, 1–4, 8, 41, 90–91,
   209–11, 214–16, 219–24
Goldgar, Bertrand, 205
Goldsmith, Oliver, 89
Gothic romance, 16, 211–12
Greene, Anne (hanged for child murder and
   resurrected), 232n. 13
Greene, Robert, 34

guilt, cultural attitudes toward, 14, 131–33, 248n. 1
Guthrie, James (Ordinary of Newgate), 98
*Guzman de Alfarache* (Aleman), 34

Habermas, Jürgen, 120, 247n. 9
*Hanging, Not Punishment Enough*, 160, 164
*Harlequin Sheppard* (Thurmond), 25
*Harlot's Progress* (Hogarth), 190
Harris, Michael, 60, 98, 236n. 6
Harrison, Henry (tried for murder), 66
Hassall, Anthony, 256n. 2
Hathaway, Richard (tried for fraud), 67–69, 239n. 25
Hawkins, John (gang leader), 86–87
Hay, Douglas, 236n. 5, 237n. 9
Hays, Catherine (tried for murder), 48
Head, Richard, 24, 34
Herrup, Cynthia, 6, 241n. 6, 248n. 3
Hibbert, Christopher, 89–90
Hill, John, 254n. 7
*History of Mlle. De St. Phale*, 3
*History of the Criminal Law of England* (Stephen), 62
*History of the Most Remarkable Tryals*, 237n. 9
*History of the Press Yard*, 27–28, 197, 230n. 21
Hitchin, Charles (corrupt City Marshal), 24, 25, 30–31, 230n. 27
Hobsbawm, Eric, 210, 261n. 2
Hogarth, William, 190, 218, 262n. 11
Howson, Gerald, 98, 230n. 27, 260n. 42
Hunter, J. Paul, 157, 203, 232n. 6, 236n. 2, 240n. 32

Inchbald, Elizabeth, xii, 8, 16–17, 212–15, 216, 218–19
individualism, anxieties and conflicts within, 5–10, 33–34, 97, 144–49
*Industry and Idleness* (Hogarth), 218, 262n. 11
Irish, as criminal by nature, 24, 165

James, Mervyn, 51
Johnson, Samuel, 245n. 2
Johnson, Sir John (hanged for kidnapping), 55–57
judgment, problems of: in *Amelia*, 199–204, 259nn. 33, 34; in criminal trials, 12, 69–71; in Elizabeth Canning case, 176–81

Katz, Jack (quoted), 74
Kernan, Alvin, 89
King, Moll (pickpocket and shoplift), 97, 98–101
Kirkman, Francis, 134, 242n. 23, 249n. 5
Knight, Valentine (executed for murder), 54

Langbein, John, 59, 61, 64, 66, 68, 237n. 11, 238n. 20
last dying speeches, 9, 50–51, 54–57, 121, 132
law, ideological centrality of, 5, 9, 47, 51, 60, 61–63, 77, 132, 216, 218, 236n. 5, 237n. 9
law, in Bunyan, 58–59; in criminal trials, 61–63, 65–66, 237n. 13; in Fielding, 185–86, 191; in Godwin, 209–11, 219–24; ideological critiques of, xii, 8, 55–56, 122, 250n. 13; in Inchbald, 213, 218–19; in Wollstonecraft, 213–14, 216–18
*Lazarillo de Tormes*, 34
Lee, William, 97–98
LePage, Peter, 192
*Life and Strange Surprizing Adventures of Mr. D—— DeF——* (Gildon), 101
Lilburne, John (tried for treason), 61–63, 218, 237n. 13
Linebaugh, Peter, 56, 159, 168, 234n. 22, 252n. 18, 253n. 20, 255n. 10, 260n. 40
*Lives of the Highway-men* (Smith), 19, 24, 26–27, 29, 32, 35, 197, 258n. 26
*Lives of the Pirates*, x, 2. *See also* Defoe, *General History of the Pyrates*
*London Merchant* (Lillo), 242n. 17

Lorraine, Paul (Ordinary of Newgate), 234n. 20

Lusebrink, Hans-Jürgen, 235n. 31

Mabbe, James, 34

Macheath, Captain (*Beggar's Opera*), 86

Madan, Martin, 161, 174

Mallet, David, 60

Mandeville, Bernard, 167–70

Maresca, Thomas, 256n. 2

*Maria, or The Wrongs of Woman* (Wollstonecraft), xii, 8, 211–18

Mascuch, Michael, 5, 7, 97, 226n. 5

McCracken, David, 262n. 12

McKeon, Michael, 9, 149, 236n. 4, 241n. 6, 256n. 4

*Memoires of Monsieur Du Vall* (attrib. Walter Pope), 84–86

*Memoires of the Right Villainous John Hall*, 229n. 19

military demobilization, as cause of crime increase, 160–61

Miller, D. A., 8, 206–7, 223

Mist, Nathaniel (publisher), 98, 99

Moore, John (executed for treason), 54

Moore, Judith, 253n. 2

Morduck, Sarah (accused of witchcraft), 67–69, 239n. 25

Moreton, Andrew (pseudonym of Defoe), 119, 153

Muns, Sarah (witness in rape trial), 70

*Murder Considered as One of the Fine Arts* (DeQuincey), 88

*Murderer Punished; and Pardoned*, 78–82, 241n. 14

myth, criminal biography as, 9–10, 76–82

name, as marker of identity in Defoe, 95–97, 98, 127–30

Nashe, Thomas, 34–38, 149

*Nature and Art* (Inchbald), xii, 8, 212–15, 216, 218–19

Needham, Rodney, 228n. 6

*New Canting Dictionary*, 24

*Newes from the Dead*, 232n. 13

*Newes from the North*, 46–47

*Newgate Calendar*, x, 2, 4

Newgate descriptions, 26–29, 31, 258n. 26; in Fielding's *Amelia*, 187–88, 190–91, 197–98, 257n. 10; in Fielding's *Jonathan Wild*, 256n. 5. *See also* prison

*News from Newgate*, 47–48

*News from the Sessions House in the Old Bailey*, 60

news reports. *See* crime reports

Novak, Maximillian, 101 (quoted), 238n. 16, 244nn. 10, 14

novel: emergence as genre, 6–7, 97; relation to criminal genres, xi-xii, 8, 71, 148–49

Old Bailey Sessions House, 59–60, 63, 66, 68

*Old Bailey Sessions Papers*, 60, 66, 255n. 15

*Oliver Twist* (Dickens), 138

openendedess and epistemological uncertainty: in crime reports, 45–49; in criminal trials, 12, 69–71; in Fielding, 15, 176–77, 179–81, 184–85; in realist fiction, 223

Ordinary of Newgate's *Accounts*, 9, 50, 52–54, 77, 82, 89, 98, 234nn. 20, 22

Owens, W. R., 95, 97–98

*Pamela* (Richardson), 7; Fielding's critique of, 155–57

*Panopticon* (Bentham), 207

Paulson, Ronald, 212

Penlez, Bosavern (accused of riot), 166, 181–86, 255nn. 15, 16

picaresque fictions, 11, 33–38

*Pilgrim's Progress* (Bunyan), 27, 58–59

*Poetics* (Aristotle), 171

Poovey, Mary, 215–16, 26n. 4

Pope, Walter, 84–86

Poulter, John (highwayman), 25

poverty, culture of, in London: in *Amelia*,

poverty (*continued*)
198; antagonistic relationship to law,
159–60, 165–68, 235nn. 31, 32; in *Colonel
Jack*, 102, 108–9, 111–12; Fielding on, 161,
163–67; Mandeville on, 167–69; in *Moll
Flanders*, 115–16; Welch on, 252n. 16
print, impact of new technologies, 45, 47, 89
prison: radical critiques of, 261n. 7; relation
to private or domestic sphere in *Amelia*,
16, 187–88, 189–96. *See also* Newgate
descriptions
private sphere. *See* prison
providential fictions, 11, 33–34, 38–44
public sphere, emergence of, 120–21, 247nn. 9, 13
Punter, David, 262n. 12

racializing of otherness. *See* deviance
Radcliffe, Ann, 212
Randal, Thomas (hanged for murder), 52–54
Rawson, Claude, 157
reader identification with criminal subjects,
6–10, 11, 13–14, 16, 29–30, 33–34, 43–44, 101,
130, 131–32, 147–48, 170, 248n. 3
readers, perversity of, 16, 31–32, 116–17, 132
realism, narrative, 12, 58–59, 65, 69–71, 223,
236n. 2, 256n. 7; in Defoe, 106–7, 117, 142,
148–49; Fielding's arguments against, 155–
57, 171–72; in Fielding, 15, 176, 185–86, 188,
189–91, 197–98; in Wollstonecraft, et al.,
213–14, 215. *See also* verisimilitude
*Regulator* (Charles Hitchin), 24, 25, 30–31
Reynolds, John, 1–2, 4, 8–9, 11, 16, 32, 38–41,
91, 137
Reynolds, Sir Joshua, 172–73
Richardson, Samuel, 7, 155–57, 169, 188–89,
194; on *Amelia*, 91, 198
Richetti, John, 9, 76–77, 78–79, 245n. 5
Rogers, Pat, 243n. 30
Rothstein, Eric, 259n. 31

Sabor, Peter, 256n. 4
Sade, Marquis de, 37, 140

Salzman, Paul, 25, 26
Savage, Thomas (hanged for murder), 78–82,
241n. 14
*Select Trials*, 22, 30, 48–49, 70–71, 238n. 16
Sharp, Tom (murderer and housebreaker), 27
Sharpe, J. A., 5, 51, 52, 54–55, 56, 237n. 9
Sheppard, John/Jack (housebreaker and
escape artist), x-xi, 89–91, 121–23, 144
Shinagel, Michael, 144, 246n. 14
Singleton, Robert, 242n. 23, 243n. 25
Smith, Capt. Alexander, 19, 24, 26–27, 29, 32,
35, 197, 258n. 26
Smith, Samuel (Ordinary of Newgate), 52–54
Smollett, Tobias, 160
Spierenburg, Pieter, 234n. 17
spiritual autobiography: compared to crimi-
nal, 97, 241n. 6; incorporated in Defoe's
fiction, 132, 137
Stallybrass, Peter, 228n. 23
Starr, G. A., 248n. 21
State Trials, 61, 63, 66, 67, 68, 218, 237n. 9,
254n. 7
Stephen, Leslie, 62
Stephens, John, 196
Sterne, Laurence, 69
Styles, John, 260n. 40
Swift, Jonathan, 57
Swinney, Edward (tried for murder), 66
sympathy, as effect of public executions, 56,
80, 166–67, 170, 235nn. 31, 32

testimony, 60–61, 62–63, 69–71; and circumstantial evidence, 65, 238n. 21; and *evidentia rei* (Fielding), 177, 253n. 5; in Fielding's
legal narratives, 176–81, 183–86
Thompson, E. P., 237n. 9, 252n. 18, 253n. 22
Thompson, James, 223
Thompson, Thomas (tried for murder), 63–65
Thurmond, John, 25
trial reports, 12, 21–23, 59–71, 185; accuracy of
verbatim transcripts, 237n. 11; as documentary sources on everyday life, 65, 66–67,

238n. 20; incorporated in fiction of Woll-
stonecraft, Inchbald, and Godwin, 216–24;
mock trial of *Amelia*, 154–55, 157–58
*Tristram Shandy* (Sterne), 69
*Triumph of God's Revenge Against Murder*
(Reynolds), x, 1–2, 4, 8–9, 11, 16, 32, 38–41,
91, 137
*True and Impartial Relation of the Birth and
Education of Claudius du Val*, 82–84
*Truest News from Tyburn*, 60

*Unfortunate Traveller* (Nashe), 34–38, 149
Universal Register Office (Henry & John
Fielding), 204–5, 206, 207
urbanization and social dislocation, 159–61,
164–66

Verge of the Court, 196–97
verisimilitude: in criminal biographies,72–77,
82, 84, 86–88; in Defoe, 13, 100–101, 102–12;
relation to authenticity of narrative voice,
13–14, 113–19, 121–23. *See also* realism

Walpole, Horace, 161, 212
Watt, Ian, 7, 110, 123–25, 247n. 17; on formal
realism, 236n. 2
Weeks, Jeffrey, 230n. 23
Welch, Saunders (constable), 24, 165, 181–82,
183–84, 252n. 16
Welsh, Alexander, 132–33, 179–80, 238n. 21,
248n. 1, 254n. 5
White, Allon, 228n. 23
Wild, Jonathan (thief taker and crime boss),
30–31, 91, 98, 100, 119, 144–45, 230n. 27
Williams, Raymond, 65, 116
Wilson, Ralph (gang member), 86–88
Wollstonecraft, Mary, xii, 8, 16–17, 211–18
*Woman-Hater's Lamentation*, 21–22
Wood, Thomas (tried for murder), 48

*Zelig* (Woody Allen), 120
Zirker, Malvin R., 164, 176 (quoted), 253n. 3,
254nn. 6, 7, 255n. 10
Zomchick, John P., 11, 193, 257n. 12, 257n. 15